NOTE

Oxford Historical Monographs will consist of books which would formerly have been published in the Oxford Historical Series. As with the previous series, they will be carefully selected studies which have been submitted, or are based upon theses submitted, for higher degrees in this University.

THE LIBERAL IMPERIALISTS

*The ideas and politics of
a post-Gladstonian élite*

BY

H. C. G. MATTHEW

OXFORD UNIVERSITY PRESS

1973

Oxford University Press, Ely House, London W. 1

GLASGOW NEW YORK TORONTO MELBOURNE WELLINGTON
CAPE TOWN IBADAN NAIROBI DAR ES SALAAM LUSAKA ADDIS ABABA
DELHI BOMBAY CALCUTTA MADRAS KARACHI LAHORE DACCA
KUALA LUMPUR SINGAPORE HONG KONG TOKYO

Printed in Great Britain
at the University Press, Oxford
by Vivian Ridler
Printer to the University

TO MY PARENTS

PREFACE

JOHN MORLEY described the generation of Liberals after
1860 as 'a happy generation'. The same cannot be said
of the next Liberal generation, in the years after 1886.
The unhappiness and disintegration of the Liberal party, and
the consequent Unionist dominance, characterized British
party politics after 1886. *Pari passu* with Liberal weakness
went ideological confusion.

W. E. Gladstone, for so long the unifier and inspirer of
the Liberal party, felt himself by 1896 'a dead man, one
fundamentally a Peel–Cobden man'.[1] But if mid-century
laissez-faire was dying as the main article of liberalism's
intellectual creed, it was neither clear what was to take its
place, nor how the party could be effectively reconstructed
politically and ideologically. It was the function of the generation of Liberals after 1886 to solve these problems.

'What is the position, what is to be the future of the
Liberal party?' asked H. H. Asquith pertinently at the
height of the party crisis during the Boer War.[2] This was
the question which confronted all Liberals, and which conditioned all the disputes of the post-Gladstonian period. It
was this question that the Liberal Imperialists tried to
answer.

Some—perhaps most—Liberals believed that in the end
right would triumph, and that little more could be done than
to stress party unity, hold fast to the old maxims, and await
the collapse of the enemy. In the end, the events of 1903–6
seemed to prove this view correct; though the pendulum
might swing slowly, swing it did.

Others, mostly the younger men in the party, called for
a more positive approach. But the discussions amongst them
over the form that this more positive approach should take
were vitiated by lack of agreement about what liberalism
should become. Could a theory of state intervention be

---

[1] Gladstone to Bryce, 5 Dec. 1896, BP 10, f. 167.
[2] Asquith in London, 19 July 1901, Liberal Publication Dept.

successfully grafted on to the individualism of traditional liberalism? If it could, what balance between the two should be struck, and what criteria should be used to weigh this balance? Was imperialism progressive or reactionary? Were free trade and Home Rule necessary articles of the Liberal creed? To what extent was the party to be 'democratized', that is, what was the responsibility, if any, of the leadership to the various federations and associations in the making of policy?

These were important questions for Liberal politicians to answer, and, being members of the party of progress, they involved themselves in their ideological disputes with the bitterness characteristic of the disputes of that party. For almost all Liberals took the view that they must be seen and believed to be right, and that ideology was an important factor in the mind of the electorate. They believed that ideas could win votes, and that voters did not necessarily vote according to class or interest. Thus most of the controversy amongst M.P.s about the future success of the party centred on arguments for and against policies, rather than on discussions about the almost complete absence of efficient party organization.

This book is a study of the political and ideological development of some of the most prominent activists in these arguments: the group of politicians most conveniently described as the Liberal Imperialists, as they became known after 1898. It is not primarily an attempt to describe an abstract concept, 'Liberal Imperialism', and it is not an attempt to deal with every person who was at some time described as a Liberal Imperialist. Such an amorphous group would include men as disconnected as Cecil Rhodes, Sir Wilfrid Laurier, Sir Charles Dilke, and Benjamin Kidd. Rather, I have taken as my point of identification the existence of a closely knit group of British politicians, of whom the chief were, in the Commons, Haldane, Asquith, and Grey, and, in the Lords, Rosebery. Connected with this group were a number of otherwise quite dissimilar groups: imperialistically minded methodists, the Webbs and other Fabians, Unionists seeking to rejoin the Liberals, young Liberals ardent for social reform, old Liberals wanting

moderate and respectable liberalism. This book is mainly
a description and analysis of the actions and opinions of the
central group of Haldane, Asquith, Grey, and Rosebery, but
it also shows their relationship to the wider and less co-
ordinated body of Liberal Imperialists in British politics.

The members of this central group were, with the partial
exception of Rosebery, practising politicians to whom political power was as important as ideology. They therefore
differed from theorists like Benjamin Kidd, Sidney Webb,
and Halford Mackinder, all of whom joined the Liberal
Imperialist organization, the Liberal League, in that they
themselves would be responsible for executing, through
legislation and administration, their ideas about policy.
These ideas were therefore developed in the context of
British party politics, and in the context of the group's potential membership of a Liberal government.

The group believed that to restore the Liberals as the
naturally predominant party in British politics required a
shift in the balance of power within the party, accompanied
by nothing less than a complete reappraisal of the nature of
liberalism as a political creed. The success of each of these
aims was dependent on the success of the other. Political
power and electoral success could not, the group thought,
be achieved without a fundamental overhaul of Liberal
policy, and were anyway pointless unless relevant policies
had been developed to be put into practice. Ideological reform could not be effectively worked out unless the group
had achieved a dominant position within the party, and was
of little value unless its means of execution were at hand.

These were daring aims, and required for their success a
capacity for resolute organization and detailed planning, and
a consistency of approach to policy based on mutual trust.
But these qualities occurred only spasmodically amongst the
Liberal Imperialists, a fact which went far to frustrate their
grand design.

Because politics were as time-consuming and as important
to these men as the development of ideas, and because their
ideas were continually affected by the changing political
situation, the book is divided into two parts. The first deals
with the formation, development, and changing interests and

relationships of the group and with its attempt, and for the most part its failure, to gain power within the Liberal party. The second part analyses, in the light of the group's political development, its attempt to reform liberal thinking on domestic, Irish, imperial, foreign, and defence policy. The group worked together most effectively during the opposition years 1895–1905, and I have therefore laid my main stress on that period. To follow into the cabinet of 1905 the plans of policy drawn up in these opposition years might be desirable, but would require another volume, and I have not tried to do more than indicate briefly the fate of policies developed in opposition.

Moreover, the Liberal Imperialist group as it existed before 1905 did not survive into government. Its leader, Rosebery, virtually retired from politics; its organization, the Liberal League, no longer had prominence or importance. Its most effective policy-maker, R. B. Haldane, was concerned almost entirely with the huge task of army reform. Only in foreign and defence policy was there anything which, after 1905, could be called Liberal Imperialist collusion, but the details of foreign policy, though important, were only a minor aspect of the Liberal Imperialists' attempt, in their heyday, at a wholesale reconstruction of liberalism.

The book deals with what was undoubtedly an important period in the development of liberalism, but it is also, I hope, interesting as an examination of two aspects of a continuing argument within the British party of progress, whether Liberal or Labour: first, should that party be orientated towards the capture of the 'centre', or should it move to the 'left'; second, what part should the idea of the 'national interest' play in progressive ideology?

For kind permission to quote from private papers, I must thank the following: Mr. M. Bonham Carter, Mrs. E. Clay, Sir William Gladstone, Lady Graves, Dr. A. R. B. Haldane, Mr. T. G. N. Haldane, Viscount Harcourt, Mr. A. B. L. Munro-Ferguson, Sir Malcolm Perks, Professor Keith Robbins, the Hon. Margaret Sinclair, the Beaverbrook foundation and Mr. A. J. P. Taylor, the Passfield Trust, the Warden and Fellows of New College, Oxford, the National Library of Scotland, and the Trustees of the British Museum.

I am also grateful to those who gave me permission to read their unpublished theses. The Librarians of the British Museum, Mr. Dennis Porter of the Bodleian Library, Mr. Alan Bell of the National Library of Scotland, and Dr. John Mason of Christ Church, Oxford and their Staffs have been long-suffering and indulgent, thus greatly facilitating my research.

I take this opportunity of thanking Mr. Charles Stuart and the late Dean and Governing Body of Christ Church for arranging and supplying financial assistance. Many people have generously given their time and advice in discussing the topics covered by this book. The following are particularly to be thanked for reading and commenting on all or some of my various drafts: Lord Blake and Professor Jack Gallagher who examined this work in an earlier form as a thesis, Mrs. Ann Braham, Mr. Michael Freeden, Dr. Ross McKibbin, Dr. Kenneth Morgan, Dr. Deryck Schreuder, Mr. Maurice Shock, for a time a temporary supervisor, and Herr Felix Thiede. Mr. A. F. Thompson has, first as a supervisor and then as an editor of the series, given most helpful advice as to both the form and the details of this book, and my thanks are due to him for his comments, encouragement, and patience. Of course, none of the above bears any responsibility for this book's defects.

An author's debt to his wife is incalculable, and a preface is not the place to try to express it; my family—Sue, David, and Lucy—have, however, kept me in mind of Haldane's favourite quotation:

> Grau, teurer Freund, ist alle Theorie,
> Und grün des Lebens goldner Baum.

COLIN MATTHEW

Christ Church, Oxford
July 1971

CONTENTS

ABBREVIATIONS

1. Abbreviations used for collections of private papers

AP	Asquith Papers
Bal P	A. J. Balfour Papers
BP	Bryce Papers
CBP	Campbell-Bannerman Papers
DP	Dilke Papers
EHD	Edward Hamilton's Diary
EHP	Edward Hamilton Papers
FP	Ferguson Papers
GP	W. E. Gladstone Papers
Hal P	Haldane Papers
HGP	Herbert Gladstone Papers
HP	Harcourt Papers
JC	Joseph Chamberlain Papers
LGP	Lloyd George Papers
MP	Milner Papers
Rip P	Ripon Papers
RP	Rosebery Papers
SP	J. A. Spender Papers

2. Abbreviations used for printed works

3 H	Hansard's Parliamentary Debates, 3rd series.
4 H	Hansard's Parliamentary Debates, 4th series.
Bannerman	*The Life of the Right Hon. Sir Henry Campbell-Bannerman, G.C.B.* (n.d. [1923]), by J. A. Spender.
Butler	*The Liberal Party and the Jameson Raid* (Oxford, 1968), by Jeffrey Butler.
Crewe	*Lord Rosebery* (1931), by the Marquess of Crewe.
E.H.R.	*English Historical Review.*
Grey	*Twenty Five Years 1892–1916* (1925), by Viscount Grey of Fallodon.
Haldane	*An Autobiography* (1929), by Richard Burdon Haldane.

Headlam	*The Milner Papers* (1931–3), ed. by C. Headlam.
James	*Rosebery* (1963), by Robert Rhodes James.
Jenkins	*Asquith* (1964), by Roy Jenkins.
LLP	Liberal League Publications.
Spender and Asquith	*Life of Herbert Henry, Lord Oxford and Asquith* (1932), by J. A. Spender and Cyril Asquith.
Stansky	*Ambitions and Strategies* (Oxford, 1964), by Peter Stansky.

PART I

BABIES IN INTRIGUE

I

THE FORMATION AND
CONSOLIDATION OF THE LIBERAL
IMPERIALIST GROUP
1886–1899

Glad confident morning

THE opposition years of 1886 to 1892 were the years,
R. B. Haldane recalled, when 'the foundation of the
so-called Liberal Imperialist Party ... was really laid'.[1]
This was true in the sense that the personal relationships of
the later Liberal Imperialists were established during those
years. It was false in the implication that imperialism played
a significant part in the formation of the group.

In the early years of the 1886 Salisbury parliament, a
small group of Liberal M.P.s came together. Its essential
members were Richard Haldane, Henry Asquith, Sir
Edward Grey, Arthur Acland, and Ronald Munro-
Ferguson. Moving on the periphery of the group in the
1880s were Tom Ellis and Sydney Buxton. Merely to mention these names is to indicate the intellectual ability and
political significance of the group.[2]

Richard Haldane was a member of an old Scottish family,
landed and well-connected, but not wealthy. He was a shy
and gentle man, and he himself was the first to admit that
he entirely lacked the qualities required of a British party
political leader. A period of studying philosophy under Lotze
in Göttingen had a most important intellectual influence
upon him. He visited Germany annually before 1906, and
German ideas, methods, and achievements pervaded his
thinking about British politics. His willingness to use German analogies, expressed in a complex and often tortuous

[1] Haldane, p. 79.
[2] Earl of Oxford and Asquith, *Memories and Reflections* (1928), i. 114; Lord
Morley, *Recollections* (1917), i. 323.

style of public speaking, made him easy game for ridicule, and even his close friends, while willing to adopt many of his ideas, seem to have had little understanding of his Idealist philosophy of life. Haldane was a man of great physical and intellectual stamina, and succeeded throughout the years between 1886 and 1905 in combining full-time work at the Bar with an almost equal amount of political work.

After studying at the Edinburgh Academy, and Edinburgh, Göttingen, and Dresden universities, Haldane came, with only a small reserve of funds, to practise at the English Bar. His distinguished academic record was no guarantee of legal success, and at first he had few briefs, despite his relationship to Farrer Herschell, later Liberal Lord Chancellor.[1] Haldane's background, and his view of life as a social and personal journey along a pathway towards progress, led him naturally to the Liberal party; his future was taken 'thoroughly in hand' in 1878 by Lord Camperdown, a Whig Perthshire neighbour, and as a result he was 'committed to Whig politics somewhat prematurely . . . but this would have been so at any rate'.[2] Thus introduced to politics, Haldane became involved with Albert Grey's 'Whig Committee' and was made its Honorary Secretary when it became the Eighty Club in March 1881.[3]

Through his Eighty Club work in the early 1880s Haldane met Herbert Henry Asquith, like himself a young lawyer with few briefs.[4] They made a formidable couple. Asquith complemented Haldane's virtues and compensated for his shortcomings. Asquith was a very effective public speaker, trenchant, incisive, practical, hard-headed, with a gift for stating a case unrivalled by British politicians of his day, or since. But such a gift had its dangers, not least being the knowledge that a good case for a policy could always be made, regardless of the amount of thought given to its conception. Asquith made little pretence to intellectual originality, but he was by no means closed to new ideas, and recognized in Haldane a man who could supply him with the sort

---

[1] See Haldane, ch. 1.

[2] Haldane to Mother, n.d. [16 Apr. 1878], Hal P 5928, f. 185. Haldane wrote almost daily to his mother until her death, aged a hundred, in 1925.

[3] Haldane to Mother, 23 Jan. 1880, Hal P 5930, f. 3.

[4] Oxford and Asquith, op. cit. i. 83.

of moderate development of liberalism he wished to support. Unlike his friends, Asquith had a sure sense of the realities of politics, though he tended to allow considerations of party unity excessively to counterbalance the excitement of new ideas and their consequent disruptive effect within the party.

Asquith was the second son of the owner of a small York-shire wool mill, but, following his father's early death, lived with relatives in London, attending, from the age of eleven, the City of London School. He won a scholarship to Balliol, Oxford, where he had a distinguished academic record, and was also President of the Oxford Union in 1874. But this auspicious start was not followed up. Asquith married a woman with no social or political ambition, though she brought with her a small private income, the only financial reserve on which he could draw. From 1875 to 1885 he lived obscurely in Hampstead, fathering children, tutoring, examining, writing anonymously for the *Spectator* and *The Economist*, making little money at the Bar. Asquith's career in these years had little of the aura of remorseless success which later surrounded it. He made little attempt to use his Oxford con-tacts to advance himself politically; his oratorical powers lay fallow. Asquith revealed his difficulties subsequently in an uncharacteristically personal speech supporting the payment of M.P.s:

Take the case of a young man . . . the bent of whose mind and abilities is in the direction of politics. He has equipped himself at all points for the work of public life, but he does not possess that modicum of fortune necessary . . . to become a candidate . . . What is this young man to do? He may be driven to the Bar. And what is the result? After his best powers, perhaps the best years of his life have been absorbed in other pursuits . . . he comes and offers to the service of the State the fag-end of his time, the dregs of his abilities.[1]

Haldane was elected for East Lothian in 1885, followed Gladstone in 1886, and persuaded a hesitant Asquith to stand for East Fife in 1886, the crucial moment of Asquith's career. Had he not stood in 1886, he could have had no chance of the cabinet in 1892. In 1886 Haldane was thirty and Asquith thirty-four. As young members for Scottish

---

[1] 3 H, cccxxxiv. 1183 (29 Mar. 1889).

seats they worked together on Scottish legislation, concerned mainly with land ownership and conveyancing.[1] Interest in Scottish land legislation led naturally to Irish land legislation, and thence to John Morley, who was already acquainted with Haldane, who had spoken for him in the 1880 election. By 1887 Haldane was 'advising John Morley on the Constitutional aspects of the Home Rule question'.[2] Friendship with Morley brought contact with the 'Gladstonian Court', personal acquaintance with Gladstone, and a request from Gladstone to Asquith and Haldane 'to get up and study the Crimes and Land Bills in order to assist him'.[3]

Having become M.P.s, Asquith and Haldane thus had little difficulty in quickly establishing themselves socially and politically with the Liberal leadership. At the same time they were making contacts with their young contemporaries. By 1888 Haldane had become very friendly with Sir Edward Grey, since 1885 M.P. for Berwick-upon-Tweed. From this time on Haldane, previously the constant dining and holiday companion of Asquith, divided his time and affections between Asquith and Grey, and acted as a link between them.[4]

Unlike Asquith and Haldane, Grey was in no sense self-made. His totally undistinguished academic career at Winchester and Balliol was no barrier to his immediate entry to the political hierarchy as private secretary to Sir Evelyn Baring and then to H. C. E. Childers in 1884, when he was twenty-two. His Whig ancestry pushed him into the Commons as a Liberal in the election of November 1885 and, under Morley's influence, he did not become a Unionist.[5] Even as a young man, Grey assumed the air of imminent departure from politics for which he became renowned. But despite his continual complaints—'doomed to be immolated on the altar of office', he remarked in 1892[6]—Grey never

---

[1] Haldane to Mother, 4 Nov. 1886, Hal P 5938, f. 208.

[2] Haldane to Mother, 8 Feb. 1887, Hal P 5939, f. 42.

[3] Haldane to Mother, 18 Apr. 1887, Hal P 5939, f. 77. 'Gladstonian Court' is the apt phrase used in Stansky, p. xi.

[4] The trio of Asquith, Grey, and Haldane was described by the last as 'the Asquith committee'; I have used this phrase, for brevity's sake, throughout this book (Haldane to Mother, 6 Aug. 1901, Hal P 5966, f. 33).

[5] Grey, i, p. xxviii.

[6] Grey to his wife, Aug. 1892, in G. M. Trevelyan, *Grey of Fallodon* (1937), p. 34.

left public life from the year after being sent down from Balliol until his resignation from the Foreign Office in 1916. As he observed in 1923, 'the tendency is, in the long run, for a man's view of public life to be decided not by the interest of the country but by the desire for personal success'.[1]

Grey's key to parliamentary and personal popularity was his directness and his apparent integrity. Whereas Haldane's friendship for Asquith was based on a common interest in politics and the Bar, his affection for Grey stemmed from admiration of his character. Haldane admired men in whom 'there unfolds itself a higher view of things', for 'the highest . . . lies in the Here and Now, in just this world comprehended at a loftier plane'.[2] In Haldane's view, Grey achieved this plane. Staying at Fallodon, Haldane wrote: 'He is the same as ever—they have a good life here—at a very high level and with no pretence of any kind.'[3] Although Grey had this air of simplicity of character and outlook, it was complicated by a tendency to impetuousness, even wilfulness, which sometimes led him, particularly during the Boer War, into absurd political positions. He had little understanding of politics, but this did not prevent him from speaking his mind, and contemporaries of both parties assumed that his blunt public utterances masked at least some degree of private intellectual sophistication.

Haldane and Grey were soon co-operating politically, and in 1888 voted with the Unionists on the Land Purchase (Ireland) Bill. This was a considered vote, given after discussion, and despite pressure from Morley. Haldane told his mother, 'Sir E. Grey and Munro-Ferguson go too. Asquith we cannot persuade.'[4] 'The Whips and Mr. G. were vexed' by this vote, and the incident indicates a readiness to vote independently of the party which later became a dominant feature of their political behaviour. Asquith's private involvement but public separation also pointed to a future trend.

[1] Viscount Grey, *Earl Grey Memorial Lecture* (1923), p. 16.
[2] Haldane, *The Pathway to Reality* (1905), i. 91, 98.
[3] Haldane to Mother, 12 Aug. 1897, Hal P 5958, f. 91.
[4] Haldane to Mother, 17 Nov. 1888, Hal P 5958, f. 91.

Ronald Munro-Ferguson was a Scottish neighbour of Haldane, and a laird in Asquith's constituency. He was married to Lord Dufferin's daughter, and Haldane was briefly engaged to his wayward sister Valerie in 1890.[1] Unlike his friends, Ferguson had a military rather than a university education, and, after Sandhurst, had served in the Grenadier Guards from 1879 to 1884. He became M.P. for Ross and Cromarty in 1884, was defeated by a crofter candidate in 1885, and was defeated in Dumbartonshire in 1886 when he was twenty-four. However, on the intervention of Rosebery, he became M.P. for Leith Burghs, which Gladstone won in 1886 as well as Midlothian.[2] In 1886 and 1892 Ferguson was Rosebery's private secretary. He was interested in land and forestry legislation, and his interest in imperial and military affairs helped to widen the horizons of his friends.

Wider horizons of a different kind were offered by Arthur Acland, M.P. for Rotherham after 1885, an older man who was regarded by Asquith as 'our corporate conscience'.[3] Acland was the third son of Sir Thomas Acland, one of Gladstone's oldest friends, and had been an Anglican deacon, bursar of Balliol, and steward of Christ Church. He had become interested in labour questions and deserved, as Morley quaintly put it, 'special credit for keeping in touch with the labour people and their mind'.[4] He was also very interested in education, particularly at the elementary level.[5] Acland was much more profoundly critical of British society than the other members of the group, and, had his health allowed, his influence might have worked with that of Haldane to alter the rather conservative thinking behind the Liberal Imperialist approach to social reform. He was never

[1] See D. Sommer, *Haldane of Cloan* (1960), p. 82. She subsequently lampooned Haldane in 'V' [V. Munro-Ferguson], *Betsy* (1892), *Music Hath Charms* (1894), *Life Again, Love Again* (1897), and died insane in 1897.

[2] Rosebery to W. E. Gladstone, 10 July 1886, GP 44289, f. 54.

[3] Oxford and Asquith, op. cit. i. 157. Acland was thirty-nine in 1886.

[4] Morley, *Recollections*, i. 324. See A. H. D. Acland and B. Jones, *Working Men Cooperators: What They have Done and What They are Doing* (1884).

[5] For a character-sketch of Acland, otherwise an ill-documented and rather shadowy figure, see Oxford and Asquith, op. cit. i. 156–60; see also Gillian Sutherland, 'Some Aspects of the Making of Policy in Elementary Education in England and Wales 1870–1895' (Oxford D.Phil. thesis, 1970), pt. III, sect. 9.

wholly fit. He told Haldane in 1898: 'I knocked up my brain early in life and have overstrained it ever since and ought to be thankful that I got past fifty.'[1] Acland's influence was therefore spasmodic, and after 1898 he retired from politics. Socially, Acland, through his father's connections, was another useful link with the 'Gladstonian Court'.

Less important members of the group were Tom Ellis and Sydney Buxton. Ellis was a leading Welsh politician who had been to New College, Oxford. He became associated with the group mainly through Acland's interest in education and Welsh affairs. Clearly a man of great sweetness of character—even the gruff Ferguson described him as 'a saint'[2]—Ellis was markedly less effective in politics after becoming first a junior whip in 1892, and then chief whip in 1894. His relationship with Haldane, Asquith, and Grey seems to have deteriorated after 1895. Like Acland he was often ill, and he died in 1899, aged forty, following his honeymoon. Sydney Buxton, though not himself a Friend, was a scion of the distinguished Quaker family. He became an M.P. earlier than his friends (in 1883) and was well known in the 1880s as a writer on financial and social questions. Though he maintained social ties with the group, and especially, as a fisherman, with Grey, he became less associated with them after 1895, and played no part in any of the various leagues after 1898. Though his career in the cabinet between 1905 and 1914, and subsequently in South Africa, was by no means undistinguished, he did not live up to his promising start in the early 1880s, which suggested that he might become a politician of the first rank.

This group of young M.P.s was almost exclusively interested in domestic questions in the 1880s. In the Commons, with the exception of Ferguson, they did not speak at all on defence or on foreign or imperial questions. They took little interest in attacking the government, and devoted their energies to amending government bills constructively and to proposing their own. Typical of such activity was Haldane's amendment to the Irish Land Law Bill of 1887 and Asquith's attempted amendment to the Local Government

[1] Acland to Haldane, 2 July 1898, Hal P 5904, f. 139.
[2] See T. I. Ellis, *Thomas Edward Ellis Cofiant* (1948), p. 299.

Act in 1888.[1] Original bills sponsored by all or some mem-
bers of the group included the Land Charges Registration
and Searches Bill of 1888, the Limited Owners (Scotland)
Bill of 1888, the Copyhold Amendment Bill of 1889, the
Women's Disabilities Removal Bill of 1892, the Small Hold-
ings (Scotland) Bill of 1892, the Watermen and Lightermen
(Thames) Bill of 1890, and the Local Authorities (Land
Purchase) Bill of 1891 and 1892.

The last of these was their most radical, most substantial,
and best organized attempt at legislation; the Bill gave
councils powers for compulsory acquisition of land and
powers to deal with unearned increment. It was sponsored
by Haldane, Grey, Acland, Ferguson, and Buxton. Characteristically, Asquith gave support to the Bill in the Commons, but his name was not on it. The Bill was unsuccessful,
and was denounced by Sir Harry Lawson, a Liberal M.P.,
as coming

from a well-known body of 'Possibilists' or Progressive Socialists, the
Fabian Society, of which I think [Haldane] is one of the chief priests
[Mr. Haldane: No]. I only know that this Bill is adopted by them.[2]

Despite Haldane's denial, Sidney Webb had helped
Haldane with drafting the Bill, and the Bill reflected an
important Fabian influence upon the group. Haldane had
become friendly with the Webbs before their marriage, and
involved a number of the group in Fabian meetings before
1892. Haldane's letters to his mother show that Asquith
and Grey were quite regular attenders. Haldane hoped to
attach the Fabians firmly to the Liberal party, and to this end
'Ed Grey and I have been having a great deal of discussion
and negotiation with some of the better socialists (Webb,
Wallas and others) . . . important results have been arrived
at.'[3] Haldane hoped that such attachment would prevent the
Liberals from becoming too much of a purely Home Rule
party.[4]

---

[1] Haldane, 3 H, cccxvii. 1665 (21 July 1887), and Asquith, 3 H, cccxxvi. 1594
(8 June 1888).
[2] 4 H, iv. 97 (4 May 1892).
[3] Haldane to his sister Elizabeth, 30 Jan. 1891, Hal P 6010, f. 83.
[4] See Haldane, 'The Liberal Party and its Prospects', *Contemporary Review* (Jan.
1888).

Concern for the future of the party, allied with interest in their own future promotion, encouraged the young group in the Commons to make contact with Archibald Primrose, fifth Earl of Rosebery, marked out by Gladstone in 1886 as 'the man of the future'.[1] Rosebery seemed enigmatic to his contemporaries and has remained so in history. Moody, vain, and hypersensitive he certainly was, but there is no doubt that after Gladstone's death only Chamberlain rivalled him as a public orator. Rosebery used his rhetoric to popularize imperialism and national efficiency—the slogans of the *fin de siècle* Britain of which he was so typical an ornament. It is doubtful whether Rosebery ever intended these slogans to be much more than rhetorical. Certainly he did little to assist their development into practical policies. But his ability to create and to echo the public mood and his flair for publicity seemed major assets for the Liberals.[2] Rosebery's ability to balance Chamberlain rhetorically, and his appearance, if not his reality, as an effective political leader, maintained his stock in Liberal circles long after the point at which his inconsistent and perverse behaviour would have ruined a lesser man. In 1886 Rosebery was only thirty-nine, but was already Foreign Secretary. During the Gladstone Ministry of 1880–5 he had emerged as a possible future contender for the Liberal leadership. Reginald Brett told him in 1885: 'Morley (and Chamberlain) consider *you* a possible and dangerous competitor in the Race for Power with the Democracy.'[3] Rosebery's position was greatly enhanced by the exodus of Whig peers from the Liberal party in 1886; as one of the small number of remaining Liberal peers, he was transformed from a rather junior, but promising, Liberal into a vital asset of the party. Rosebery was concerned at the lack of progressive thought in the party, and saw the need to bring forward new talent. Through Ferguson, he met Haldane, who soon became a frequent dining companion, and Ferguson organized for Rosebery a series of dinners for promising young Liberals in 1887 to which

[1] See James, p. 194, and *passim* for the best attempt to explain Rosebery's behaviour.

[2] His appearances at Professional Cup Finals, long before those of other public figures, typified this flair.

[3] R. Brett to Rosebery, 20 Jan. 1885, RP, box 6.

Haldane, Asquith, and Acland were invited.[1] These dinners
continued, and in 1889 were put on a more formal basis,
becoming the Articles Club, with thirty-nine members.
Haldane described its formation:

> Last night we formed a new club of 31 persons—to be increased to
> 39—being members of the House of C and Lords. Ld. Rosebery,
> Spencer, Aberdeen and Wolverton represented the Lords, and John
> Morley, Sir E. Grey, Asquith, Munro-Ferguson, myself and others
> the Commons. We are to dine at the National Liberal Club together
> once a week . . . It is to be a select and secret organisation.[2]

Apart from Harcourt, Campbell-Bannerman, and Lloyd
George, the club contained all those prominent in shaping
political liberalism after Gladstone's retirement.

The Articles Club's function was mainly social, and was
useful in enabling young M.P.s to meet the party leadership. Politically, it was 'a pleasant but rather useless institution'.[3] Haldane hoped to turn these social contacts into an
effective political force in 1889 by 'the formation of a *group*
bound together by a common point of view', to put forward
'constructive propositions' and 'to criticise . . . the people
with whose names we [the Liberals] were at present being
labelled, i.e. Labouchere and Company'.[4] In November
1889, with the support of Morley, Asquith, Buxton, Grey,
and Ferguson, Haldane put the idea to Rosebery and Fowler,
who approved of it,[5] and a dinner was held at Grey's
house which 'settled many important matters'.[6] That the
project was not merely an example of the secret political
planning to which Haldane tended to give exaggerated importance is shown by a letter from Asquith to Buxton which
summarizes the aims and methods of the group before
1892:

[1] Ferguson to Rosebery, 26 Mar. 1887, RP, box 14.
[2] Haldane to Mother, 1 Mar. 1889, Hal P 5942, f. 70; Acland was the secretary.
See A. E. Pease, *Elections and Recollections* (1932), pp. 258–90 for a membership
list and accounts of its dinners. Other members included A. Birrell, J. A. Bryce,
S. Buxton, Lord Carrington, H. Gladstone, E. Marjoribanks, J. M. Paulton.
Eleven of the 1905 cabinet were members in the 1880s.
[3] Haldane to Mother, 8 Mar. 1889, Hal P 5942, f. 82.
[4] Haldane to Ferguson, 4 Nov. 1889, Hal P 5903, f. 139; printed, with serious
errors of transcription, in Sommer, op. cit., pp. 76–7.   [5] Ibid.
[6] Haldane to Mother, 14 Nov. 1889, Hal P 5943, f. 113.

We [Haldane, Asquith, Morley] have been talking, and shall probably talk more on Wednesday, of the practicability of independent action from behind the front bench, which may put an end to the assumption that the Jacobyn [*sic*] tail is the only vital part of the party dog.

There is, so far as I know, no idea of starting a new party organisation, but there are many of us who feel (1) that the better kind of Radicalism is not articulate enough and is unduly backward in putting out constructive proposals, (2) that, to remedy this, we need concerted action and distribution of labour, and (3) that in everything that is done it is well to be in touch with the worthier elements in the front bench.[1]

The plan was to be kept secret, 'Harcourt being the *bête noire* of the whole gathering'.[2] Little seems to have come of this organizationally, but the plan illustrates the working of the group: Haldane was the co-ordinator, Morley the immediate mentor,[3] Rosebery the man to associate with, Harcourt and Labouchere the men to be excluded; radicalism was to be strong enough to impress the party and the electorate, but not so strong as to estrange the front bench.[4]

In the period of opposition from 1886 to 1892, the future programme of the Liberal party was being planned not by small, secret dining groups, but by the National Liberal Federation, an institution with which only Acland had much contact. Asquith, Grey, Haldane, and Ferguson moved into national politics with virtually no experience of local politics or local government.[5] They distrusted the N.L.F. and deplored the idea that it should draw up programmes for the parliamentary party to execute.[6] However, at the famous 1891 Newcastle meeting, when Gladstone promulgated the Newcastle programme, Acland, Grey, and Buxton were present, probably at the instigation of Morley who was drumming up support 'to hold up the hands of our veteran'.[7]

[1] Asquith to Buxton, 10 Nov. 1889, Buxton Papers.

[2] Haldane to Ferguson, 4 Nov. 1889, Hal P 5903, f. 139.

[3] Haldane to Mother, 25 Oct. 1889, Hal P 5943, f. 79.

[4] Rosebery had his own fruitless scheme to reform policy and deal with Harcourt: see Crewe, i. 339–41, and James, p. 203.

[5] Of the subsequent Liberal Imperialist M.P.s only Fowler was clearly identified with regional politics.   [6] See below, pp. 125–7.

[7] Morley to Asquith, 13 Aug. 1891, AP 9, f. 1. Asquith was not at Newcastle; his first wife died in Sept. 1891.

Grey moved the Irish Home Rule motion, and Henry Fowler, later one of the foremost denouncers of programmes, seconded the 'Omnibus Resolution'.[1] Though they might subsequently deplore the influence of the Newcastle programme, the Commons group was associated with its inception.

By 1892 the group had established itself by parliamentary activity and by social infiltration. The kernel of the Commons Liberal Imperialist group in the 1890s—Haldane, Grey, Ferguson, and Asquith—had been formed, and was well positioned for subsequent influence on the Liberal leadership.

Its aim was to obtain influence by reserved, often secret, political activity—not to storm the leadership from without from a regional base, as Chamberlain had done, and Lloyd George was to do. Imperialism had played little part in establishing these relationships. It was, if anything, a divisive factor. Haldane, for example, voted against funds for the 1887 Jubilee, and, when trying to construct the 'group' of 1889, disagreed with Rosebery over Imperial Federation, a compromise being worked out that 'the programme is to be defined to consist for the present of Colonial Conferences to which even a Morleyite like myself can wish "God speed"!'[2]

The group looked to Morley for intellectual encouragement and to Rosebery for political leadership. It was 'not the John Morley of the H. of Commons—but the old John Morley of Compromise' who was admired.[3] It was not the Rosebery of the Imperial Federation League, but the Rosebery of the London County Council who was expected to give the lead. In the years ahead both these relationships changed; Morley's intellectual influence declined, Rosebery showed the way to a wider conception of liberalism which was to embrace world-wide as well as local problems.

---

[1] National Liberal Federation *Report*, 1891. H. H. Fowler was becoming increasingly linked with the group politically but not socially.

[2] Haldane to Ferguson, 4 Nov. 1889, Hal P 5903, f. 139, misquoted in Sommer, op. cit., p. 77.

[3] Haldane to his sister, 30 Oct. 1890, Hal P 6010, f. 77; quoted in D. Hamer *John Morley* (1968), p. 246.

In office: allegiance to Rosebery increases

In the rush for places in the Liberal government of 1892, 'the claims of the "young men" were . . . fully and even generously acknowledged'.[1] The group had planned its tactics, and a primitive version of the 1905 'Relugas compact' was attempted, Haldane strongly promoting Acland for the cabinet, and Grey refusing office unless 'some such arrangement were made'.[2] Asquith also made conditions about 'a strong infusion of new blood', and would only accept political, not legal, office.[3] Haldane, who acted as 'a sort of referee' during the ministry's formation, was the only one of the group not to achieve some office.[4] The group had established a claim to an important role in liberalism when the old guard moved off.[5]

Office widened the group's horizons, and transferred its members' primary focus of activity to their respective departments. Grey, whose appointment at the Foreign Office 'decided the destiny of his life',[6] and Ferguson became very closely associated with Rosebery. Grey was 'personally devoted to Lord Rosebery . . . and was particularly in agreement with him on Imperial matters'.[7] Rosebery believed that Grey fully supported his foreign policy and told Kimberley after the 1895 'Grey declaration' on the Sudan:

> It is true that E. Grey made his statement without consulting me; but that was unnecessary as he knows the views I hold and the policy I maintain . . . Harcourt knows them too; but the difference between them is that Grey shares them and Harcourt does not.[8]

---

[1] Earl of Oxford and Asquith, *Fifty Years of Parliament* (1926), i. 202.

[2] H. G. Hutchinson (ed.), *Private Diaries of Rt. Hon. Sir A. West* (1922), p. 39 (6 Aug. 1892).

[3] Oxford and Asquith, *Fifty Years*, i. 202.

[4] Haldane to Mother, 6 Aug. 1892, Hal P 5948, f. 57. In the cabinet were Asquith (Home Secretary), Acland (Education). Outside it were Grey (Under Secretary F.O.), Buxton (Under Secretary C.O.), Ferguson (private secretary to Rosebery). Haldane was diffident about office, Ferguson had hoped for better; see Haldane to Mother, 2 Aug. 1892, Hal P 5948, f. 49, and Ferguson to his wife, 17 Aug. 1892, FP.

[5] In 1892 eight of the cabinet were over sixty-two; all were over fifty-four, except Rosebery (45), Acland (45), and Asquith (40). In 1892, Buxton was 39, Haldane 36, Ferguson 32, and Grey 30.

[6] G. M. Trevelyan, *Grey of Fallodon* (1937), p. 35.   [7] Grey, i. 32.

[8] Rosebery to Kimberley (copy), 6 Apr. 1895, RP, box 54.

Grey and Ferguson were therefore ardent supporters of Rosebery in the struggle for the leadership.[1]

The position of Asquith was more complex. Asquith differed sharply from Rosebery's support for the annexation of Uganda, and tried to prevent it, working with Harcourt and encouraging W. E. Gladstone to this end.[2] Ferguson told Rosebery that Asquith was 'so much in with Mr. G. in this matter that I would trust him with nothing . . . He is the leading counsel against you.'[3] As the arguments of the Uganda question widened into a general dispute, Asquith moderated his position, informed Rosebery of a meeting of himself, Harcourt, and Morley about Uganda, and, by implication, cast himself in the role of honest broker and general conciliator, a gambit he was to employ often in the future.[4] Asquith remained hostile to Rosebery's policy, in particular to Rosebery's anti-French views, but he avoided a major quarrel with Rosebery.[5] None the less, his behaviour seemed dubious, and Eddy Hamilton, a close friend of Rosebery, commented on Asquith: 'Is he playing his own game? And is he running quite straight with Rosebery . . . ? I sometimes have doubts which are shared by others who know him better than I do.'[6]

Asquith's difference on foreign affairs was balanced by a fellow feeling with Rosebery on Ireland, and by Asquith's antipathy to Harcourt as a possible leader to follow Gladstone.[7] Loulou Harcourt, Sir William's secretary and son, found Asquith, on this issue, an 'out and out Roseberian'.[8] Asquith was not, however, as unqualified a 'Rosebery man' as was Grey, at any rate in public. When Loulou Harcourt asked Morley if Asquith 'was *very* Roseberian', Morley 'said that he did not know; that Asquith was very thick with

---

[1] This struggle is well analysed in Stansky, pp. 1–96.

[2] See Asquith to Harcourt, 21 Oct. 1892, HP 9; Asquith to W. E. Gladstone, 22 Oct. 1892, GP 44516, f. 53.

[3] Ferguson to Rosebery, 7 Oct. 1892, RP, box 15.

[4] Asquith to Rosebery, 6 Nov. 1892, RP, box 1.

[5] See Harcourt to Kimberley, 12 June 1894, RP, box 95 for a report of Asquith's views.

[6] EHD, 25 May 1895.

[7] Asquith to Rosebery, 10 Feb. 1893, quoted in Stansky, p. 16, and L. V. Harcourt's Journal, 3 Mar. 1894, HP.

[8] L. V. Harcourt's Journal, 3 Mar. 1894, HP.

Rosebery . . . but that he was very discreet . . . He was a young man with a future, and wise to hold his tongue.'[1]

Haldane agreed with Asquith on Uganda, despite Grey's efforts to persuade him otherwise.[2] But Haldane was only mildly interested in foreign and imperial policy at this time. His main aim was to promote Rosebery as the future leader of a party committed to domestic reform. He therefore organized a number of meetings on domestic reform, at which Rosebery was the main speaker,[3] and campaigned strongly for him for the leadership on the ground that only Rosebery could unite the party on domestic questions.[4] At first Rosebery seemed to give this lead. Haldane wrote of one of Rosebery's speeches: 'The idealism of its peroration, the sympathy with the aims and ends we believe in and aspire after most, has gone to our heads.'[5] Rosebery's reluctance, having become Prime Minister in March 1894, to act decisively on domestic questions led soon to disillusion, and in August 1894 Haldane, after discussing the situation with Asquith, felt: 'I have no confidence in Lord R. He is so anxious to please everybody that he ends up by doing things which please nobody. We none of us have the least idea of what he is at just now.'[6] Despite this Haldane continued to encourage Rosebery to give a lead, since 'there is latent in the electors an energy which would sweep these difficulties from your [Rosebery's] path' if it could be released.[7] Haldane remained personally and politically friendly with Rosebery even after Rosebery had clearly let him down by making first Robert Reid, and then Frank Lockwood, rather than Haldane, Solicitor-General in 1894.[8]

Haldane was also unsuccessful in his other chief interest, the continued adhesion to the Liberals of the Fabians. At

---

[1] L. V. Harcourt's Journal, 21 Feb. 1894, HP.

[2] See Trevelyan, op. cit., p. 60.

[3] Haldane to Mother, 16 Dec. 1892, Hal P 5948, f. 172.

[4] Haldane to Mother, 1 Mar. 1894, Hal P 5951, f. 96.

[5] Haldane to Rosebery, 23 Mar. 1894, RP, box 24.

[6] Haldane to Mother, 10 Aug. 1894, Hal P 5952, f. 95.

[7] Haldane to Rosebery, 6 June 1894, Hal P 5904, f. 23; quoted in Sir F. Maurice, *Haldane* (1937-9), i. 71.

[8] Haldane to Rosebery, 15 Oct. 1894, RP, box 24. Grey and Asquith had both urged Haldane's claim (Grey to Haldane, 14 Oct. 1894, Hal P 5904, f. 10; Asquith to Rosebery, 15 June and 17 Oct. 1894, RP, box 1).

first, all went well, and Haldane was 'acting as a go-between from Sidney Webb to Asquith with great success'.[1] From this co-operation came an 'able and useful' memorandum from the Webbs which formed the basis of some of Asquith's Home Office factory reforms.[2] In November 1893, however, the Fabians, exasperated by the Liberals' failure to pass social reforms, withdrew their support from the Liberal party. To Haldane this was

a heavy blow . . . We younger men were striving to bring those with whom we were immediately in contact into relation with you. We were making an impression. The Liberal machine was in course of modification.[3]

Despite further efforts by Haldane, he was not able to persuade the Webbs to co-operate again with the Liberal party until the Boer War.[4]

The cohesion that existed in the 1880s between the 'matchless band of young men'[5] and John Morley broke down during the 1892–5 government. Illustrative of Morley's estrangement from the group is the fact that in 1893 Asquith, Haldane, Acland, Grey, and Morley dined together to celebrate the anniversary of the government, but in 1894 the dinner was attended by Asquith, Haldane, Acland, Grey, and Rosebery.[6] Morley was, he told Haldane, 'tired of politics'.[7] Frustrated in his Irish policy and in his hopes for the Foreign Office in 1894, Morley supported Rosebery for the premiership *faute de mieux*, and after the crisis of 1894 a gap widened between them, partly because of policy disputes and partly, Rosebery believed, because of personal antipathy on the part of Morley.[8] Morley and Rosebery could no longer be regarded as working together

[1] Grey to his wife, Oct. 1892, in Trevelyan, op. cit., p. 60.
[2] Asquith to H. Gladstone, 3 Oct. 1892, HGP 45989, f. 3.
[3] Haldane to Mrs. Webb, 2 Nov. 1893, in B. Webb, *Our Partnership* (1948), p. 114, quoted in Stansky, pp. 17–18.
[4] See below, pp. 68–9. Haldane continued to address Fabian meetings: Haldane to Mother, 2 Nov. 1894, Hal P 5952, f. 164.
[5] Morley to Asquith, 13 Aug. 1891, AP 9, f. 1.
[6] Haldane to Mother, 16 Aug. 1893, Hal P 5950, f. 78.
[7] Haldane to Mother, 7 Aug. 1894, Hal P 5952, f. 89.
[8] See EHD, 4 Jan. 1896; for Morley's attitude, see Stansky, chs. iii–v, Hamer, op. cit., ch. 19, and, less clearly, S. E. Koss, 'Morley in the Middle', *E.H.R.* lxxxii, July 1967.

for the new liberalism; the group had therefore to make a choice. All chose Rosebery. From the view-point of power and office, Rosebery seemed the man of the future. From the view-point of policy, Rosebery also seemed preferable. It was not yet his imperialism that appealed, but rather his style, his antipathy to programmes, his general demand for a new start for liberalism. Morley increasingly played the part of the guardian of the Gladstonian tradition, a tradition which was beginning to seem an irrelevance and a liability.[1]

Back in opposition: Rosebery resigns as party leader

The years of opposition after 1895 were, for the Liberals, dominated by two main, partially connected, features—the resignations of Rosebery and Harcourt, and the growing dispute within the party about the future of liberalism. These years also saw the development of the Commons group into Liberal Imperialists. Haldane, Grey, Ferguson, and Asquith continued to meet socially and to co-operate politically, though they no longer attempted to promote legislation as they had done between 1886 and 1892.[2] Their attention focused increasingly on foreign and imperial affairs, partly because these dominated the political scene, and partly because the development of a 'patriotic' Liberal approach to imperial affairs was seen by the group as a *sine qua non* of a Liberal revival.[3] The Articles Club was revived by Rosebery to provide a regular meeting-point, as 'a sort of Rosebery society'.[4]

The resignation of the Rosebery government in June 1895 removed the restraints of office on public quarrelling about personalities and policies within the Liberal party. Rosebery, and with less publicity Haldane, attacked the Newcastle programme and called for a new approach to liberalism, based on pragmatism and 'national efficiency'. At the personal level, Rosebery believed 'the first essential step

[1] See Hamer, op. cit., ch. 20, esp. pp. 306–10.

[2] For typical meetings to discuss policy, see Haldane to Mother, 12 and 13 May 1896, Hal P 5955, ff. 166–8.

[3] See below, Ch. IV *passim*.

[4] Ferguson to his wife, n.d. [1897], FP; see also Rosebery to Ferguson, 6 Feb. 1896, RP, Letter Book 89.

was to formalize the divorce from Harcourt'.[1] The dispute between the Roseberians and Harcourt, Haldane's *bête noire* in 1889, was a matter both of personalities and of policies. The bitter struggle for the leadership in 1894, Harcourt's grea: disappointment, and Rosebery's unsympathetic diffidence had led to a virtually complete lack of communication between the Prime Minister and the leader of the Commons.[2]

Most of Rosebery's supporters agreed that there should be a clear break with Harcourt. Ferguson, since 1894 Liberal Scottish whip, told Rosebery: 'What made me restless was not our position as regards the Tories but as regards Harcourt, for if we couldn't jump on him before we should be able to now.'[3] Rosebery discussed with Asquith, Haldane, and Ferguson the idea of a formal break with Harcourt. Haldane and Ferguson supported the idea; Asquith urged caution.[4] With the help of Haldane and Ferguson, Wemyss Reid compiled a favourable report of expected constituency reaction.[5] Ferguson consulted the other whips, finding McArthur 'most violent against Jumbo' [Harcourt], and reporting that 'in the Whips' room we are all of one mind'.[6] Rosebery associated Asquith with the break by writing to him that 'the contingency which we foresaw has arrived', and by threatening resignation, 'if that be judged best for the Party'.[7] Fortified by at least the support of his close political colleagues, Rosebery wrote to Spencer on 12 August 1895 stating that 'any mutual responsibility between Harcourt and myself has ceased'.[8] Though the letter was private, its substance was soon known to most politicians.[9] Ferguson tried to encourage the Commons men also to 'divorce' Harcourt, but got little support,[10]

[1] See James, p. 386.
[2] Stansky, p. 142.
[3] Ferguson to Rosebery, 9 Aug. 1895, RP, box 15. Harcourt was defeated at Derby in the election.
[4] Ferguson to his wife, n.d. [early Aug. 1895], FP.
[5] Rosebery to Wemyss Reid, 10 Aug. 1895, RP, Letter Book 89, and Ferguson to his wife, 15 Aug. 1895, FP.
[6] Ferguson to Rosebery, 12 Aug. 1895, RP, box 15.
[7] Rosebery to Asquith, 12 Aug. 1895, RP, Letter Book 89.
[8] See Stansky, p. 186.
[9] Ibid., pp. 186–93.
[10] Ferguson to Rosebery, 17 Aug. 1895, RP, box 15.

and by October 1895 Ferguson thought that 'any immediate and open rupture' in the Commons was inadvisable.[1]

Rosebery's letter, and Harcourt's intransigence, produced a stalemate. Asquith tried, fruitlessly, to act as a broker at the end of 1895, and Rosebery in the first part of 1896 was isolated from his colleagues.[2] Rosebery was not, however, oratorically inactive. *The Times* commented that 'Mr. Gladstone in his palmy days was hardly more frequently on the stump'.[3] Rosebery's position was, nevertheless, being eroded. His attitude to the Jameson Raid inquiry in 1896 isolated him from most of his colleagues.[4] Harcourt's credit was restored by his success in the debates on the 1896 Education Bill, and Gladstone re-emerged over the Armenian question in the summer of 1896, an obvious challenge to Rosebery's leadership on his own subject of foreign affairs. After discussion with Ripon, Rosebery resigned as party leader on 6 October 1896.[5]

Rosebery's resignation transformed the position of his supporters who wished to see him as the next Liberal Prime Minister. Before October 1896 all the Roseberians needed, wrote Haldane, was 'time and patience' for the Unionists to become unpopular and for Harcourt to retire, die, or accept Rosebery's terms.[6] Now the Harcourtians were no longer the men of faction; if Rosebery was to return as leader, men would have to stand and be counted, and perhaps engineer a coup. Rosebery's complaint in his resignation letter that he received little 'explicit support' made this point.[7] If Rosebery returned, it would be on his own terms, with 'explicit support'.

Rosebery's manner of resignation certainly suggested that he intended to return. He had already invited Asquith, Haldane, West, Fowler, Harold Tennant, Arnold Morley, and Bryce to Dalmeny for his speech to be made in Edinburgh on 9 October 1896. In this dramatic speech, made

---

[1] Ferguson to Rosebery, 3 Oct. 1895, RP, box 15.
[2] See Stansky, ch. 4, section III.
[3] *The Times*, leader, 13 Mar. 1896.   [4] See Butler, pp. 89-101.
[5] See Rosebery to Ripon, 16 Aug. and 13 Oct. 1896, Rip P 43516, ff. 233-42; see also Stansky, pp. 203-23.
[6] Haldane to Rosebery, 4 Apr. 1896, RP, box 24.
[7] Printed in Crewe, ii. 523-4.

three days after his resignation, Rosebery drew attention to his supporters, and praised their allegiance to him.[1] Rosebery was careful to associate Asquith with himself, publicly in his speech, as a loyal colleague and a future Liberal leader, and privately by informing him in advance of his resignation.[2] Asquith was thus more closely identified with Rosebery's cause than his policies or inclinations warranted. Rosebery saw, as Haldane had seen in the 1880s and Campbell-Bannerman saw in the Boer War, that Asquith was a man who moved on the periphery of groups, thus making himself, with his undoubted oratorical and administrative powers, a vital man to catch.

Rosebery's house-party in October 1896 also gained the impression that he intended future action. Haldane wrote to his mother: 'Asquith, Henry Fowler, and I are the party and the whole time is spent in consultations and talks—nothing but politics—Rosebery in grand spirits.'[3] Haldane expected 'a revolution in our party'.[4] Rosebery also contemplated 'a complete reshuffling of parties', though Chamberlain 'might constitute a stumbling block'.[5]

Given that Rosebery intended to return, Grey and Haldane did not regret his resignation, since, as 'there is at present no Liberal party worth leading', Rosebery's resignation meant 'we are all free as air'.[6] Asquith took a more strictly party view, and criticized Rosebery for acting 'selfishly: he had no doubt improved his personal position for the moment, but in doing so he had sacrificed the interests of his colleagues and friends'.[7]

A considerable number of Liberals revealed themselves as 'Rosebery men' following his resignation. R. W. Perks, M.P. for Louth and a leading methodist, Alexander Ure, M.P. for Linlithgowshire, J. Fletcher Moulton, after 1898 M.P. for Launceston, and other important back-benchers identified themselves to Rosebery as his political friends. E. T. Cook, editor of the *Daily News*, wrote privately that

---

[1] The presence of Bryce, a hostile critic of Rosebery on Armenia, was an ironic accident. For Rosebery's speech, see *The Times*, 10 Oct. 1896.
[2] Rosebery to Asquith, 6 Oct. 1896, RP, box 1.
[3] Haldane to Mother, ? 11 Oct. 1896, Hal P 5956, f. 89; some in Stansky, p. 217.
[4] Ibid.   [5] EHD, 27 Oct. 1896.
[6] Grey to Rosebery, 13 Oct. 1896, RP, box 23.   [7] EHD, 3 Nov. 1896.

'journalistically, it is a great blow for those of us who have had the privilege of agreeing with you'.[1] But in his paper he asked for support or opposition to the Edinburgh resolution praising Rosebery—in effect an invitation publicly to support or oppose Rosebery. Twenty-eight M.P.s wrote to support Rosebery, and fifteen to oppose him.[2] Cook commented: 'The rally to Lord Rosebery . . . is unmistakably setting in . . . This feeling of confidence is much deeper and more widespread than his enemies imagined and perhaps than he himself knew.'[3] Tom Gibson-Carmichael, the Roseberian chairman of the Scottish Liberal Association, reported that apart from Dundee and Arbroath he did 'not believe there is any part of Scotland where there is not a large majority in the Liberal party who are anxious to be led by you'.[4] Ferguson made a similar report.

Rosebery undoubtedly had a good deal of support on the back benches and in the constituencies, but this was in itself useless unless it could be mobilized. How to do this, and when to strike, was to be a major problem for the Roseberian 'wire-pullers' in the coming years.

With his resignation Rosebery claimed to have retired from public life. He regarded a brief appearance in December 1896 in the City Liberal Club as 'my last public engagement in the world'.[5] This statement was absurd. He continued to speak frequently in public, sometimes on non-political subjects, but usually on quasi-political topics such as municipal socialism, the Manchester Chamber of Commerce centenary, and the Jubilee celebrations.[6] Rosebery was only forty-nine in 1896, was still interested in politics, and had put himself in an embarrassing, almost ridiculous position.

Rosebery was adept at the in-fighting required in government interdepartmental disputes, and he was skilful at making contact with the electorate.[7] He had, however, little

[1] Cook to Rosebery, 7 Oct. 1896, RP, box 73.
[2] For their names, see *Daily News*, 10, 12, and 13 Oct. 1896.
[3] Ibid., 13 Oct. 1896.
[4] Carmichael to Rosebery, 22 Oct. 1896, RP.
[5] Crewe, ii. 535.   [6] See Crewe, ii. 540-6.
[7] See R. Robinson and J. Gallagher, *Africa and the Victorians* (1961), ch. XI and A. Low, 'Public Opinion and the Uganda Question, October–December 1892', *Uganda Journal*, xviii, Sept. 1954.

facility for, or interest in, sustained political management. But it was this quality which the Liberal party needed for reconstruction. Rosebery correctly recognized that 'the Liberal party needs very tender handling just now', but that was exactly what he never gave it.[1] His speeches were like the monologues of the Victorian music-hall, melodramatic and popular, but the opposite of the persuasive soliloquies carefully integrated into the structure of the play which the situation required.

The gradual emergence of imperialism as a major issue

As Rosebery began to plough his furrow alone, changes were taking place, independently of him, but to a large extent influenced by his views, in the attitude of the Commons group. Imperialism had been a potent source of disagreement within the Liberal party at least since the 1880–5 government. Hitherto, however, it had not been the main divisive factor within the party. '"The confusion of conflicts within the Liberal party", as Dilke observes in his "Memoir" for 1881, "made it difficult to act with anybody for long without being attacked by some other section with which it was necessary to act at other times." '[2] In this situation, the authority of Gladstone's personality, the ambiguity of his speeches, and his combination as prophet and statesman had prevented polarization and disintegration within the party, except on Ireland in 1886. Even those who disagreed with Gladstone felt his influence: 'We realise how great Mr. Gladstone's hold on us had been', wrote Haldane on Gladstone's death.[3] During the long opposition period from 1886 to 1892, the lack of great drama in imperial affairs and the common commitment to Home Rule forced disagreements on imperialism into the background. In the period of opposition after 1895 this changed. Gladstone no longer unified, Home Rule as an 'umbrella' policy was unworkable, imperial dramas were in the forefront, and there was little

---

[1] Rosebery's memorandum, 25 Aug. 1896, in Crewe, ii. 522.

[2] Dilke, 'Memoir' in S. Gwynn and G. M. Tuckwell, *The Life of Sir Charle Dilke* (1917), i. 364, quoted in *The Cambridge History of the British Empire* (1959), iii. 133.

[3] Haldane to Mother, 18 May 1898, quoted in Maurice, op. cit. i. 80.

domestic legislation as an alternative focus of attention. Arguments about imperialism were an important disruptive factor in the 1892–5 government, but open dissention was, to some extent, prevented by the need to maintain the Liberal majority.[1] After 1895 the way was clear for a freer expression of opinion.

Events up to 1898 failed to produce any clear definition of thinking on imperial matters within the Liberal party. The Near Eastern crisis of 1896 produced some nostalgic yearnings for 1878, but though these were the apparent cause of Rosebery's resignation, they did not spark off any major ideological row. The Near Eastern crisis did, however, produce some hardening of attitude within the party. Though the leadership expressed a surprising degree of unanimity in this crisis,[2] rank and file action caused divisions. H. W. Massingham, since 1895 editor of the *Daily Chronicle* which supported unilateral action over Armenia and fighting for Greece in the 1897 Greek–Turkish war, disagreed with E. T. Cook of the *Daily News*, the other London Liberal morning paper. The two papers became engaged in a slanging-match, in which the Near Eastern crisis and Rosebery's leadership and opinions became intertwined. The *Chronicle* attacked Rosebery's advocacy of 'the dogma of "British interests" as against the interests of humanity', and declined 'to see the Liberal-Radical party dragged back into a sham Palmerstonian revival'.[3] The *Daily News* complained that 'those who without the most searching consideration are shouting to Athens to defy Europe and to declare war are incurring the most grievous responsibility'.[4] One result of this duel was the formation of the Liberal Forwards, originally designed as 'a British volunteer force to fight for Greece', but which quickly became a general anti-imperialist organization.[5] The Forwards soon achieved size and publicity by their attacks on the government and on Rosebery;

---

[1] See Robinson and Gallagher, op. cit., p. 322.
[2] See Stansky, pp. 205–18.
[3] *Daily Chronicle*, 11 Oct. 1896 and 6 Oct. 1896.
[4] *Daily News*, 27 Feb. 1897; see also 19 Sept. 1896.
[5] H. W. Nevinson, *Changes and Chances* (1923), p. 143. The Forwards were by no means pacifists (ibid., p. 130, and H. N. Brailsford, *The Broom of the War God* (1898), *passim*).

respectability was achieved by the attendance of Sir Robert
Reid at their anniversary dinner.[1] The other anti-imperialist
organization was the Radical Committee founded in March
1896 to attack Rosebery, and dominated by Labouchere.
The Radical Committee hoped to gain control of the N.L.F.
by separating its headquarters from the whips office, and to
make it a platform for anti-imperial views.[2]

The initiative of forming sectional organizations was thus
taken by anti-imperialist groups, who formed their organizations during the Near Eastern crisis of 1896. This crisis was
only indirectly about British imperialism, but the organizations were maintained for subsequent use on specifically
imperial issues.[3] The Roseberians disapproved of the actual
policies of such organizations, but they were even more
hostile to the existence of such institutionalized dissent. In
their view, groups like the Forwards, by dissenting from
the idea of continuity in imperial policy, harmed the
Liberals by making them seem unpatriotic to the electorate.[4]

The Roseberians were, however, slow to organize themselves. There was still no major issue which clearly divided
them both from the Forwards and from the non-Roseberian
members of the ex-cabinet. The committee of inquiry on
the Jameson Raid did not raise issues of policy in any very
obvious form in the Commons. Attention centred round the
personal dramas of Chamberlain's possible complicity and
Harcourt's ineffectual leadership. Debates in the Commons
concentrated for the most part on the activities of the committee, and only indirectly on the imperial issues involved.
In the Commons divisions on the Raid inquiry in July 1897
the thirty-eight Liberals who rejected Harcourt's leadership
did so as a protest against his failure to expose fully the evils
of Chartered Company government. The thirty-eight were
in fact 'Labby & Co.', the Little England core, including
Labouchere, Lawson, Lloyd George, and Robert Reid. But

---

[1] *Daily News*, 12 Nov. 1897.

[2] Ibid., 30 Mar. 1896. At a local level, attempts were being made to purge
the Scottish Liberal Association of Ferguson, Carmichael, and other Roseberians
(Ferguson to Rosebery, 6 Feb. 1898, RP, box 15).

[3] See the Forwards' pro-French resolution during the Fashoda crisis, *Daily
Chronicle*, 27 Oct. 1898.

[4] See below, pp. 132 ff.

those who followed Harcourt's lead into the lobby included men of very varied imperial opinions—from Morley to McArthur; they were voting as party men, not as 'pro-' or 'anti-imperialists'.[1]

It was not South Africa, but the question of the Nile Valley, the main point of intra-cabinet dispute on imperial policy in the 1892–5 government, which split 'official' liberalism after 1895. Even here, the fissures took time to open. When the government announced its tentative advance into the Sudan in 1896, Liberal reaction was cautious and largely hostile; there was no rush of imperialists to praise the government. The *Daily News* argued that 'the case against it is obvious . . . partly sentimental and partly practical'.[2] The best that could be said was that the move was 'really defensive and therefore defensible', but, the *News* concluded, 'the Government have not made out a case'.[3] Rosebery privately denounced 'this futile, feeble, unreasonable and unexplained expedition in the Sudan'. While making the observation that 'I hold strong and un-Gladstonian (I fear) views about the Sudan', he still thought that 'this expedition seems . . . to have nothing at all to recommend it'.[4] Such objections were more of timing than of principle, but they were sufficient for the Liberal leadership to work together in the Sudan debates in 1896.[5]

By 1897 the situation had changed. On the Motion for Grant in Aid for expenditure on the Sudan expedition in February 1897, forty-six Liberals, including Harcourt, Morley, and Ellis, voted to deny funds, 133 abstained, were absent, or were paired, and two Liberal whips, Ferguson and McArthur, voted with the government.[6] In 1898, on the

---

[1] See Butler, pp. 203–4 and Appendix C. Butler's conclusion (p. 204) that 'this division was of considerable importance in the history of the debate within the Liberal Party on South Africa and imperial issues and, indeed, in the history of the leadership' seems questionable. The leadership, with the exception of Reid, was united; 'Labby & Co.' had been notorious Little Englanders for years.

[2] *Daily News*, 14 Mar. 1896.   [3] Ibid., 16 and 18 Mar. 1896.

[4] Rosebery to Spencer, 21 Mar. 1896, RP, Letter Book 89.

[5] On the first vote, Labouchere's motion for adjournment, 4 H, xxxviii. 1027–60 (16 Mar. 1896), Harcourt, Asquith, Bryce, and Ellis, amongst others, abstained (*The Times*, political notes, 18 Mar. 1896). On the second vote, Morley's amendment to the Vote on Account, 4 H, xxxviii. 1478 ff. (20 Mar. 1896), voting followed normal party lines, only McArthur abstaining.

[6] Div. List 19, 4 H, xlv. 1519 (5 Feb. 1897).

remission of the Egyptian loan, sixty Liberals, including Harcourt, Morley, and Campbell-Bannerman, opposed remission, and the remainder abstained, were absent, or paired, including Asquith, Grey, Haldane, Ferguson, and McArthur.[1] Thus even before the Fashoda crisis of autumn 1898, a number of prominent Liberals had broken on the Sudan question with the party leadership as represented by Harcourt and Morley, who were after 1896 the two most prominent active remaining members of the ex-cabinet, Harcourt being party leader in the Commons.

The Fashoda crisis of 1898 brought together various developing elements within the Liberal party—the growing split in the Commons, the support for Rosebery's restoration, the increasing discontent of Harcourt and Morley with their own position in the party. Since the start of 1898 growing pressure had been put on Rosebery to make a move. After a talk with Haldane, Hamilton told Rosebery that Haldane

believed that you [Rosebery] occupied a better and stronger position than you ever had before. It was not a question of there being, in the event of unforeseen circumstances, substitutes, the present front Opposition Bench for the Government Bench; but the alternative to the present Ministry was you by yourself.[2]

Rosebery seemed to respond to such pleas by playing a prominent role in the County Council elections in March 1898, the results of which were, according to Haldane, 'a triumph for Lord R.'[3] Following this, R. W. Perks began to prepare the ground for a complete return by bringing

Lord Rosebery into touch with members of the party with whom he was personally unacquainted, and they [Perks and others] have carried on a diligent, though, as far as possible, secret canvass in his interest.[4]

This preparation, and Rosebery's prominence as orator and pall-bearer after Gladstone's death in May 1898,[5] ensured that Rosebery's intervention in the Fashoda crisis did not

[1] Div. List 169, 4 H, lx. 285 (27 June 1898).

[2] Hamilton to Rosebery, ? 5 Feb. 1898, RP, box 25; see also EHD, 28 Jan. 1898.

[3] Haldane to Mother, 4 Mar. 1898, Hal P 5959, f. 51.

[4] London Letter, *The Scotsman*, 4 Apr. 1898. For similar canvassing, see Williams Benn to Rosebery, 31 July 1898, RP, box 75.

[5] *Daily News*, 28 May 1898, the day of Gladstone's funeral, called for Rosebery's return.

occur in a political vacuum, but in a carefully developed situation.

The Fashoda crisis started on 19 September 1898. Rosebery made his first speech on 12 October 1898; he was, therefore, speaking after the press had formed public opinion. At first, the Liberal press showed considerable agreement. 'You observe', Morley wrote to Harcourt, 'the violent jingoism of the Daily News, Westmr. Gazette, Speaker, and Chronicle.'[1] This 'jingoism' took different forms. The *Chronicle*, while admitting the justice of the British case, called for the government to be reasonable, and thought that the situation was not 'too grave . . . we think that it is a question of "seeming" only'.[2] The *News*, however, called for a tough line: 'The chief element of danger . . . is to be found in the widespread belief prevailing on the Continent that Lord Salisbury's squeezability is unlimited.'[3]

Rosebery also felt this, and his speech at Epsom on 12 October was clearly designed both to strengthen the government's hand and to make it difficult for the government to withdraw.[4] Rosebery told Hamilton:

He was amused at the haste with which the Blue Book had been got out. It was evidently . . . necessary for the Government to expose its cards: otherwise it would never be believed, after what had happened in the Far East, that they really 'meant business'.[5]

The speech met with much approval, even the *Chronicle* finding it a 'proper and necessary' intervention.[6] The Roseberians were delighted. 'Just what we wanted', commented Ferguson, and Haldane wrote, 'we are proud of our chief today.'[7] Their pleasure was as much at Rosebery's return to politics as at the specific content of the speech.

---

[1] Morley to Harcourt, 9 Oct. 1898, HP 10.
[2] *Daily Chronicle*, 10 Oct. 1898.
[3] *Daily News*, 27 Sept. 1898.
[4] Rosebery in Epsom, *The Times*, 13 Oct. 1898.
[5] EHD, 13 Oct. 1898.
[6] *Daily Chronicle*, 13 Oct. 1898.
[7] Ferguson to Rosebery, 17 Oct. 1898, RP, box 15; Haldane to Rosebery, 13 Oct. 1898, RP, box 24. The unsubstantiated claim of Sommer, *Haldane of Cloan*, p. 105 (repeated by Stansky, p. 259), that Haldane drafted Rosebery's speech is prima facie most improbable. Haldane was in Ireland after 9 Oct. (Haldane to Mother, 9 Oct. 1898, Hal P 5960, f. 62); though he and Rosebery had met a week earlier (Haldane to Mother, 2 Oct. 1898, Hal P 5960, f. 58).

Asquith, for example, was pleased at Rosebery's return and 'spoke highly of R's speeches',[1] but 'objected to [Rosebery's] laying so much stress on the unfriendly act'.[2] Ferguson told Asquith that 'that was the point, which is what our people too often evade'.[3]

In his speeches, Rosebery emphasized his responsibility, 'ministerially and personally', for the 'Grey declaration' of March 1895.[4] This was in reply to Labouchere's charge in *Truth* that Grey's statement 'was made . . . on his own initiative'.[5] Labouchere's statement was in fact more accurate than Rosebery's; Grey had not consulted Rosebery about his 'declaration'.[6] The importance of Rosebery's remarks was, however, that it linked him clearly with the Asquith, Haldane, and Grey group on an issue of imperial policy.[7] Hitherto, their support for Rosebery, except in Grey's case, had been on general party grounds; foreign and imperial policy had been a divisive rather than a unifying factor. Now, however, on the leading imperial issue of the day they stood unanimous, and in clear opposition to the tone of the speeches of Harcourt and Morley.[8] Up to this point, they had been Roseberians; they were now becoming identifiable also as Liberal Imperialists.

Sir William Harcourt's resignation as leader of the Liberal M.P.s in December 1898 followed what seemed to be a concerted Liberal Imperialist attack on his leadership. Rosebery's repeated oratorical appearances, his upstaging of Harcourt at the Mansion House dinner on 4 November,[9] the resolutions of the Nottingham Liberal Association hostile to Harcourt's leadership, and the 'leadership competition' run by the *Daily Mail* seemed like a co-ordinated attack.[10] This impression was false; there was certainly general discontent with Harcourt, but no organized plot, though

---

[1] EHD, 24 Oct. 1898; Asquith also told Hamilton that Rosebery's 'craze' against Harcourt was 'evidence of an improperly balanced mind'.

[2] Ferguson to Rosebery, 17 Oct. 1898, RP, box 15.

[3] Ibid. See below, pp. 203 ff., for the place of Fashoda in foreign policy developments.

[4] Rosebery in Epsom and in Perth, *The Times*, 13 and 24 Oct. 1898.

[5] Quoted in *Daily News*, 13 Oct. 1898.   [6] See above, p. 15.

[7] See *The Times*: Asquith, 14 Oct. 1898; Grey, 14 Nov. and 3 Dec. 1898.

[8] See Stansky, pp. 252–75 for Harcourt's and Morley's views.

[9] EHD, 5 Nov. 1898.   [10] *Daily Mail*, 8 Dec. 1898.

Rosebery had had recent contacts with Harmsworth of the *Daily Mail*.[1]

Harcourt was, however, right in feeling that imperial policy was being developed without his acquiescence. Centred on Grey, an anti-Harcourt 'Cave' had been developing since 1897. Ferguson described its stage-management:

E. Grey will have to appear in the debate on Friday—which will turn on the reduction of S's salary. I have been busy ever since you [Ferguson's wife] left. Found T. Ellis . . . and tried to do a deal with him viz. that E. Grey sd. stay away if there was no regular party divn. in the F.O. vote. Ellis wants E. Grey to cont. [*sic*] I was rather for him staying away on terms, for if E. Grey were to chuck (as he may) it wd. be the end of all things for a while. But as terms are not likely to be made E. Grey will have to come on Thursday. I will see Aj [Rosebery] and R.B.H. abt it today.[2]

Planning of this type continued. In 1898 Haldane reported: 'I have decided not to speak tonight [foreign affairs debate] —Edward Grey is going to speak for us all we want. Harcourt and Balfour have spoken and neither of them well.'[3] Asquith must have been aware both of this planning and of Ferguson's and McArthur's votes for the government on the Sudan, but he told Hamilton there was 'no political issue, no intrigue'[4] to justify Harcourt's resignation, which, Asquith concluded, 'was stamped . . . by cowardice and egotism and undignified by even the faintest tincture of a sense of public duty'.[5]

Asquith's verdict, revealing a harshness and toughness of judgement usually hidden by a bland exterior, was that of a man who had party unity as his priority. Most of his colleagues reacted differently, welcoming Harcourt's resignation as a vital step towards the return of Rosebery. Grey told Ferguson that the resignation would be beneficial, for if Harcourt took a 'strong independent line . . . we shall all do it'. Grey thought: 'These struggles help to clear the air, and

[1] EHD, 17 Dec. 1898.

[2] Ferguson to his wife, n.d. [summer of 1897], FP.

[3] Haldane to Mother, 29 Apr. 1898, Hal P 5959, f. 74. Balfour drew public attention to the Grey/Harcourt split in 4 H, lxiv. 821 (10 Aug. 1898).

[4] EHD, 19 Dec. 1898.

[5] Asquith's memorandum of Dec. 1898, quoted in Spender and Asquith, i. 119-22.

the more things are knocked about, the more things will
tend to a more normal balance of parties, and in the Liberal
party towards the ascendancy of Rosebery.'[1] Grey and
Haldane thought that, to achieve 'the ascendancy of
Rosebery', the 'best thing for us, far and away the best thing,
would be for Asquith to . . . take the lead in the House'.[2]
Haldane tried to mobilize support for Asquith as a locum
tenens in the Commons until Rosebery returned to the over-
all party leadership.[3] Haldane was 'as certain as he can that
A (whom he has seen) will be perfectly loyal to you [Rosebery]
. . . looking to you eventually to come back as the real head
when the moment is opportune'.[4] Despite this pressure,
Asquith decided against leaving the Bar, and Sir Henry
Campbell-Bannerman gradually emerged in January 1899
as Harcourt's successor.[5] Campbell-Bannerman had been in
the Commons since 1868, but he was still something of
a dark horse. His bluff appearance and his pawky Scots
humour concealed both an agile skill for political manœuvring and a stern determination to preserve Liberal unity.
Few who crossed him politically or personally got the better
of him in the long run, though they often thought they had
in the short.

C-B as leader: an open split on an imperial question

The Roseberians were not alarmed by Campbell-
Bannerman's emergence as leader of the Liberals in the
Commons. They found him personally and politically
acceptable. Personally, he was regarded as unambitious and
as a locum tenens for Rosebery, less close than Asquith, but
in no way hostile. Politically, Campbell-Bannerman was also
thought of as a good candidate. The Roseberians were
anxious about the result of the developing quarrel on im-

---

[1] Grey to Ferguson, 16 Dec. 1898, RP, box 23.

[2] Grey to Haldane, 16 Dec. 1898, Hal P 5904, f. 174.

[3] Haldane to Mother, 16 Dec. 1898, Hal P 5960, f. 170.

[4] Hamilton to Rosebery, 13 Dec. 1898, RP, box 24.

[5] See Stansky, pp. 275–92. Ferguson distrusted Asquith and supported Bannerman from the first (Stansky, pp. 281–2; Ferguson to Rosebery, 16 Dec. 1898, RP,
box 15; Ferguson to his wife, n.d., FP). Ferguson, with his military background,
disliked Asquith's air of intellectual superiority and regarded him as an ungrateful
carpet-bagger in East Fife.

perialism; Ferguson thought 'McArthur is right about a split in the party, our opponents being partly radicals and partly . . . the remains of Manchesterthianism.'[1] But in recommending the former Secretary for War, Ferguson was sure that 'if it comes to trouble in the House, within the party, on Foreign Affairs, it could not come better for us'.[2] Henry Fowler was similarly optimistic, and hoped under Campbell-Bannerman the party would be 'more loyal and more united'. '*But*', Fowler noted, 'there is a "below the gangway"' which Campbell-Bannerman would have to disavow to achieve unity;[3] he told Campbell-Bannerman he was 'satisfied that no support will be given to the Little England Policy'.[4] Haldane made the same point to Campbell-Bannerman, telling him: 'What is of vital importance is that the gentlemen who sit on the front bench below the gangway should be reduced to their proper dimensions.'[5] Rosebery's followers' support for Campbell-Bannerman was therefore solid enough, but was conditional in the sense that it depended on Campbell-Bannerman following a Roseberian line in policy and in denouncing 'Labby & Co.'[6]

Campbell-Bannerman confirmed his position as something of a Rosebery man by writing to Rosebery in January 1899.[7] He did not correspond with Harcourt. He received an encouraging reply, Rosebery hoping that 'the four leaders' would be 'absolutely united, cordial and loyal'.[8] Since Rosebery already knew from Fowler that Fowler's support for the new leader was conditional on an attack on the 'men below the gangway', there was in Rosebery's encouragement an implied threat.[9] But Rosebery, like his

---

[1] Ferguson to Rosebery, 16 Dec. 1898, RP, box 15.
[2] Ibid.
[3] Fowler to Rosebery, 30 Dec. 1898, RP, box 75.
[4] Fowler to Bannerman, 22 Dec. 1898, CBP 41214, f. 219.
[5] Haldane to Bannerman, 30 Dec. 1898, CBP 41218, f. 145.
[6] Rosebery's followers were agreed that Rosebery should lie doggo (Ferguson to Rosebery, 16 Dec. 1898, RP, box 23, and EHD, 3 Jan. 1899). Rosebery deliberately did so, though not in 'definite political quarantine' (Rosebery to Spender, 15 Jan. 1899, SP 46387, f. 23).
[7] Bannerman to Rosebery, 6 Jan. 1899, RP, box 2.
[8] Rosebery to Bannerman, 8 Jan. 1899, copy, RP, box 2.
[9] Fowler to Rosebery, 30 Dec. 1898, RP, box 75.

friends, assumed that Campbell-Bannerman would be strongly hostile to the Little Englanders.

This faith in Campbell-Bannerman was soon to be shattered. Following the resignation crisis of December 1898 there was, as W. T. Stead predicted, 'a slight slump in Imperialism'.[1] Morley thought his action in resigning from the ex-cabinet had 'effectively checked the Jingo craze in our camp'.[2] Certainly, the *Daily Chronicle* considerably modified its attitude to the Sudan question. In January 1899 it criticized Morley's Brechin speech in which he attacked jingoism, but by February it was supporting him and attacking Grey's views on the Sudan.[3] Campbell-Bannerman did not take this dispute about imperialism very seriously, and thought 'this Jingo and anti-Jingo business is purely factitious'.[4] After an inconclusive speech on Morley's motion to reduce the Vote on 24 February 1899, Campbell-Bannerman voted for Morley's amendment with thirty-eight other Liberals. Grey had already spoken in support of the government, and, with twelve other Liberals, voted with the government.[5]

Morley thought Campbell-Bannerman's action 'one of the most dramatic things I have ever seen'.[6] The vote was important from the view-point of both sides. It rescued Morley from isolation, and even suggested that the main stream of liberalism might be flowing in a Little England direction.[7] To have gained the support, and thus the recognition, of the new leader in his first major crisis was a tactical triumph for the Little England group. It also exposed the lack of organization amongst the Imperialists. Asquith and Fowler both knew that Campbell-Bannerman did not intend to vote with Grey, and that he intended either to abstain or to vote with Morley.[8] They both deliberately stayed away

[1] EHD, 15 Jan. 1899.

[2] Morley to A. Carnegie, 27 Jan. 1899, Bodleian MS, film 569.

[3] *Daily Chronicle*, 18 Jan. and 25 Feb. 1899.

[4] See Stansky, p. 285.

[5] Grey in 4 H, lxvii. 489 ff. (24 Feb. 1899), and ibid., Div. List 17, col. 523.

[6] Morley to Harcourt, 24 Feb. 1899, HP.

[7] Morley told Harcourt, 25 Feb. 1899, HP: 'if he had taken another line I should have been politically dead.'

[8] Morley to Harcourt, 27 Feb. 1899, HP: Bannerman 'took counsel with Asquith and Fowler, the question being between voting with me and abstaining'.

from the Commons, but they did not inform their colleagues of their knowledge.[1] Haldane and Ferguson were both unintentionally absent;[2] Grey had clearly failed to organize support. The thirteen Imperialists contrasted poorly with the thirty-nine Morleyites. As Harcourt remarked: 'The fact that E. Grey could only take 12 men into the lobby (incl. one of our whips) was a tremendous slap in the face to the expansionists.'[3]

The Roseberians in the Commons reacted bitterly to what they saw as Campbell-Bannerman's apostasy. Ferguson, 'thoroughly disgusted', thought Campbell-Bannerman had 'dropped into Harcourt's rut'.[4] Haldane told Rosebery that 'the events of tonight have formed an odd commentary on your hopeful view of CB.'[5] Rosebery himself was not so gloomy. Campbell-Bannerman was careful to call on him before making his vote, and to write to him afterwards,[6] and Rosebery told him that 'as regards a parliamentary situation you are incomparably a better judge than I am', though Rosebery stressed that he agreed with Grey on the matter of policy.[7] It was characteristic of Rosebery to misunderstand, or to ignore, the difficulties of his followers in the day-to-day *mêlée* of the Commons, a characteristic which subsequently became even more pronounced. Rosebery's tendency was recognized by Haldane, who pointed out to him that the blow which Campbell-Bannerman's 'action has dealt to his authority is more serious than anyone who is not of his followers in this House can realise'.[8]

Campbell-Bannerman's vote meant that in the months leading up to the Boer War he was distrusted by the Imperialists, and accepted by the Little Englanders, perhaps

---

[1] Labouchere told Harcourt, 28 Feb. 1899, HP 8, that 'Asquith and Fowler had "headaches" '.

[2] Ferguson to Rosebery, 25 Feb. 1899, RP, box 15.

[3] As Harcourt told Morley, 1 Mar. 1899, HP, the division list was 'very curious'. The 'expansionists' included F. S. Stevenson, a well-known Liberal Forward! The others were: Buxton, W. O. Clough, Ld. E. Fitzmaurice, Grey, H. E. Kearley, Sir J. F. Leese, McArthur, T. W. Nussey, J. M. Paulton, R. Wallace, J. L. Walton, Joseph Walton.

[4] Ferguson to Rosebery, 25 Feb. 1899, RP, box 15.

[5] Haldane to Rosebery, 24 Feb. 1899, RP, box 24.

[6] Bannerman to Rosebery, 24 Feb. 1899, RP, box 2.

[7] Rosebery to Bannerman, 25 Feb. 1899, CBP 41226, f. 245.

[8] Haldane to Rosebery, 24 Feb. 1899, RP, box 24.

more than his true position warranted. Haldane's view was
that the vote 'of course . . . will be forgotten. But it will not
less certainly find his authority in the House less.'[1]

The events of December 1898 to February 1899 found
the Commons group of the 1880s still intact, and still be-
having in much the same way, though with some significant
differences. They were still promoting Rosebery for the
leadership, but their political association with Morley had
changed to political hostility. Harcourt was still their *bête
noire*, 'Labby & Co.' still the group to be defeated. They had
one new recruit, Henry Fowler, a much older man; Acland
had retired from political life in 1898, but maintained a fitful
correspondence. Tom Ellis, never wholly connected with
the group, was to die in April 1899.[2] Asquith remained a
somewhat enigmatic figure, hovering on the periphery. No
longer, however, were they the carefree young radicals of
the 1880s. They had, through default and death, been
catapulted to the summit of the party at a speed inconceivable
in Gladstone's day. Their primary point of identification in
the public mind was becoming empire, not radicalism and
land reform as it had been in the 1880s. In status and in
attitude, therefore, the group had changed considerably; in
its personal relationships it remained remarkably constant.

[1] Haldane to Rosebery, 24 Feb. 1899, RP, box. 24.
[2] At the time Ellis's death seemed a great blow. 'Lockwood, Ellis, Herschell . . . it
would be difficult to name three more irreplaceable men', wrote Asquith, with a
strange lack of perspective, to Bannerman, 9 Apr. 1899, CBP 41210, f. 165. In
fact Ellis had lost contact with his Welsh base, and had proved an ineffective chief
whip, leaving the whips' office ripe for H. Gladstone's reforms.

II

PARTY POLITICS, 1899–1901:
DISSENTERS OR THE ORTHODOX
CHURCH?

1899: preparations for war

DURING the spring and summer of 1899 an uneasy peace lay over the Liberal party. Imperialism was not allowed to become a divisive factor. Morley, busy with Gladstone's biography, thought 'the anti-Jingo business has gone far enough at present & votes for peace & reunion on finance'.[1] The Imperialists on their side, when Thomas Ellis died in April 1899, made no issue of the appointment of Herbert Gladstone as Chief Whip, a vital appointment for Campbell-Bannerman's future control of the party. On the basis of promotion from the existing whips, William McArthur would have had seniority. For Rosebery's supporters to have canvassed for McArthur, a well-known Imperialist, would have been provocative, and they made no move. The other side, however, made sure that McArthur was excluded. Harcourt, Morley, Massingham, Gladstone, and Lloyd George dined together, and Ferguson understood as a result of their meeting that 'they would not hear of Willie as Whip'.[2]

Rosebery's position continued to distress his neglected friends. 'He fairly puzzles me,' complained Hamilton, 'does he intend to return to active politics? If so, he might at any rate be frank about it with his intimate friends.'[3] Asquith found Rosebery 'almost impossible to get hold of'.[4] Rosebery was not merely being awkward. His position was difficult. Even if he wanted to make a move, little had been done to prepare the ground. His supporters seemed to think that

---

[1] Spender to Rosebery, 6 Mar. 1899, RP, box 75.
[2] Ferguson to Rosebery, 14 Apr. 1899, RP, box 15.
[3] EHD, 25 Apr. 1899, quoted in James, p. 409.   [4] EHD, 5 May 1899.

Rosebery must make the first move, but Rosebery had always made it clear that there must be 'explicit support' for him to return. He was not prepared to initiate the political manœuvres to achieve such support. There was therefore a deadlock. The Commons men wanted Rosebery back without a major upheaval in the party. Rosebery saw that his return must involve such an upheaval. He hoped to modify his party's policy, and to widen the basis of its electoral support by a return to the situation before 1886. He made this clear in an important speech in May 1899 to the City Liberal Club, which had many Liberal Unionist members. Rosebery called for a modification of Liberal policy on Ireland, and for a recognition by the Liberals of the value of the 'new Imperial spirit' which was stimulating the nation to a 'larger patriotism'.[1] Given this view, and the existing tensions within the party, Rosebery's opinion that his return would 'not bring peace, but a sword' was quite correct.[2]

Rosebery's friends did not realize this. Their reactions to his challenging speech were varied, but mainly hostile. Asquith was, according to his wife, 'much exercised' by the speech, and wrote a long, unsent letter to Rosebery, displaying antipathy to Rosebery's hopes of 'patriotising' the Liberal party.[3] Eddy Hamilton and Wemyss Reid were also upset by the speech, and Reid wrote to Gladstone to tone down its effect, and to Rosebery asking him to modify his attitude.[4] Haldane was more favourable, appreciating Rosebery's attempts to make the party think about its future policy and organization. Haldane did 'not think Lord R is so far wrong' and saw the speech 'simply as aiming at a great reorganisation of the party'. After visiting Rosebery, Haldane found that 'much more will be heard of this business & I am not sorry'.[5]

As the South African question became dominant, during

---

[1] Rosebery to the City Liberals, *The Times*, 6 May 1899.

[2] Memorandum, ? 26 July 1899, in Crewe, ii. 560.

[3] For Margot Asquith's opinion, see EHD, 9 May 1899; for Asquith's letter, see Jenkins, pp. 111–12. But soon Asquith was propagating most of these views.

[4] Reid to Gladstone, 9 May 1899, HGP 46041, f. 141. Rosebery told Hamilton he 'had said nothing which precluded his return to power ... But he could not and would not make a bid for himself' (EHD, 8 May 1899).

[5] Haldane to Mother, 10 and 12 May 1899, Hal P 5961, ff. 108–12.

the summer of 1899, Liberals began to make provisions for future troubles. After the publication of Milner's notorious dispatch of June 1899, which compared the Uitlanders to 'helots', it became clear that, as the *Daily News* said, 'public opinion is being formed both at home and in South Africa'.[1] E. T. Cook, a strong Roseberian, consistently supported the Uitlanders' claims after his appointment as editor of the *Daily News* in January 1896. He went so far as to argue that 'if, in the end, Great Britain fails to obtain justice and fair play for the Outlanders, the German Emperor will one day try his hand. In such an event, who could blame him?'[2] Cook's call for organized Liberal support for the Uitlanders went unheeded and Cook found himself isolated, writing to Milner: 'I doubt if 20 Liberals would support it [Milner's policy] . . . even a South African Liberal, like Hawksley, is very uneasy and thinks I have gone too far in supporting you.'[3] The Little Englanders, however, mobilized opinion on behalf of their view-point, the Liberal Forwards publishing a letter deprecating any 'forward' movement in South Africa,[4] and in July 1899, a 'Protest Committee' was formed to oppose warlike moves.[5]

Liberal Imperialists made little attempt to counter these moves. Few of them expected that war would occur. 'I still believe that Chamberlain will not be allowed to go to war', wrote Hamilton, who, as deputy head of the Treasury, was well placed to know.[6] In June, Haldane was 'pretty sure the Govt. do not wish to fight in the Transvaal', and thought that 'Chamberlain's speech is bluff, & nothing more'.[7] Two months later, Asquith still privately believed that 'everything at present points to a pacific arrangement on the basis of give and take'.[8]

As the South African situation deteriorated, there was some perfunctory political contingency planning centred on Rosebery. Asquith arranged to visit Rosebery at the end of July, possibly to try to keep Rosebery within the line agreed

[1] *Daily News*, 17 June 1899.   [2] Ibid., 22 June 1899.
[3] Cook to Milner, 16 June 1899, MP, box 32, n.f.
[4] *Daily News*, 19 June 1899.   [5] *Daily Chronicle*, 14 July 1899.
[6] Hamilton to Rosebery, 4 July 1899, RP, box 25.
[7] Haldane to Mother, 26 June 1899, Hal P 5961, f. 188.
[8] Asquith to Harcourt, 4 Aug. 1899, HP 9.

by the ex-cabinet, for there was apprehension that Rosebery would disrupt the moderate line taken at Ilford by Campbell-Bannerman on 17 June.[1] Morley reported Spender, 'a great friend of R', as saying 'if he [Rosebery] does repeat Fashoda . . . that *will* be the last straw.'[2] Haldane was careful to get Rosebery to dine with the Asquiths, 'as he has not been for a long time',[3] and even Campbell-Bannerman arranged a meeting with Rosebery 'to "report progress" generally'.[4] Following his own successful meeting, Campbell-Bannerman sent Gladstone to visit Rosebery, just before his speech of 28 July 1899, for a general review of policy. Gladstone encouraged Rosebery to return to politics and 'pointed out that the basis of his resignation in the 1896 speech was temporary'.[5] Rosebery did not deny this and said 'that after a rough and tumble with H. Fowler he had reread his Edinburgh speech [of 1896] & must admit that it was not as final as he cd. wish'. Gladstone came away heartened:

> The impression on my mind is that he is *fighting* to keep out for the present, but contemplates coming back to politics, either in the event of a national crisis, or in the event of the party going wrong about F[oreign] P[olicy] or when H[arcourt] finally disappears.[6]

Rosebery's potentially disruptive speech of 28 July 1899 proved to be uncontroversial, and avoided South Africa. Hamilton found him 'very sphinx-like over the Transvaal question'.[7] Rosebery's modest and cautious attitude was that 'he was incompetent to make answers to questions & it was safest to make none [about the Uitlanders]'.[8]

Planning thus centred, unnecessarily, on keeping Rosebery moderate on South Africa. It was difficult for the Imperialists to organize support in the Commons, for, whereas the Forwards could argue that their organizations were peaceful in intention, any Imperialist organization would be accused of 'warmongering'. Until war actually

[1] Asquith to Rosebery, 26 July 1899, RP, box 1.
[2] Morley to Harcourt, 27 July 1899, HP.
[3] Haldane to Mother, 29 July 1899, Hal P 5962, f. 49.
[4] Bannerman to Rosebery, 8 July 1899, RP, box 2; he added: 'the progress is satisfactory.'
[5] H. Gladstone, Memorandum, 26–27 July 1899, HGP 45986, f. 39.
[6] Ibid.   [7] EHD, 30 Aug. 1899.
[8] H. Gladstone, Memorandum, 26–27 July 1899, HGP 45986, f. 39.

broke out nothing could be done without the accusation of provocative action. Thus, though Sydney Buxton found Campbell-Bannerman's speech 'a trifle too "peaceful"', he agreed with the other front benchers that 'nothing further should be said from our Front Bench', and so remained silent.[1]

Contact between Liberal politicians was difficult after the dissolution of parliament at the end of July 1899 because of the annual dispersal to grouse moors, golfing centres, and spas. Campbell-Bannerman used the holiday season to his advantage by removing himself to Marienbad until 3 October, thus avoiding political contacts until the last possible moment.[2] Haldane met Rosebery at Tweedmouth's seat, Guisachan, but apart from this, there was little contact between the Roseberians. Grey was at his house, Fallodon, Asquith golfing with Herbert Gladstone and A. J. Balfour at St. Andrews. Haldane's speech of 29 August in East Lothian, and Asquith's of 2 September at Leven, Fife, were made without consultation with other Roseberians, and were 'very guarded'.[3] Grey gave no public lead throughout the summer. On 11 July and in mid September he received letters from Milner, which he forwarded to Rosebery and Asquith, but mentioned their existence to nobody else.[4]

Liberal Imperialists did not contradict Morley's great anti-war speech at Manchester on 15 September, and no firm base, either public or private, was established for Liberal Imperialists before the war started. Only Ferguson made a move to gain support in the Commons, telling Rosebery there were two things to be done: 'The first is to strengthen the House of Commons, upon which we have to depend . . . The other is to keep a clear space for you & E. Grey.' As a whip, Ferguson was trying to get Imperialists adopted as by-election candidates, and thought 'we are getting some good men forward'.[5]

---

[1] Buxton to Ripon, 28 July 1899, Rip P 43555, f. 132.
[2] See *Bannerman*, i. 243–4.
[3] Haldane to Mother, 30 Aug. 1899, Hal P 5962, f. 71. See Haldane, *The Scotsman*, 29 Aug. 1899, and Asquith, *The Times*, 4 Sept. 1899.
[4] Grey to Milner, 4 Oct. 1899, MP 17, f. 594A. His secrecy was unnecessary; Milner had sent a copy of his first letter to Cook to show around (Cook to Milner 20 July 1899, in Headlam, i. 355).
[5] Ferguson to Rosebery, 27 Aug. 1899, RP, box 15.

This lack of private co-operation and planning would work if the Imperialists expected to be able to follow the party line in the event of war—if party unity was to be their criterion of action. But they already knew that this was unlikely. The Little England group was well organized, and Campbell-Bannerman's position was suspect since his Sudan vote in February 1899. The Imperialists could count on a majority in the Commons 'ex-cabinet': Grey and Buxton (added to it for the October 1899 meetings), Fowler, and probably Asquith against Bryce, Campbell-Bannerman, and probably Gladstone. But this would mean little if Campbell-Bannerman differed from them. Those Liberals intending to support a war on South Africa must expect open conflict with many of their party.

The ex-cabinet meeting of 4 October achieved unanimity by stressing the opposition's role as 'peace makers'.[1] This unanimity was conditional on war being avoided for, hearing a rumour that the Boers had invaded Natal, Fowler at once wrote that 'the situation is altered & that the line agreed to yesterday is to a great extent superseded'.[2]

The start of the war: a defeat for the Imperialists

The tension was broken by the Boer ultimatum of 9 October 1899 and the start of the war on 11 October. Hitherto, Liberal Imperialists had felt that, for reasons of party unity and national interest, they must be careful to say nothing inflammatory. This obligation was now removed. 'Isn't the news good', wrote Ferguson, 'it is like the breaking of a spell.'[3] The dramatic emergency created by the invasion of British territory allowed the Liberal Imperialists to express themselves in black and white terms. 'It was', claimed Haldane, 'a situation in which people stood at the parting of the ways ... There was no possibility of pursuing both ways, or of following a middle course.'[4] Haldane's statement was

[1] Gladstone's Memorandum, 4 Oct. 1899, HGP 45987, f. 21. As Gladstone noted, the ex-cabinet had little information to go on; none of the South African experts—Kimberley, Ripon, Buxton, Bryce—seems to have explained the historical development of the situation in depth.

[2] Fowler to Bannerman, 5 Oct. 1899, CBP 41214, f. 239.

[3] Ferguson to his wife, n.d. [? 12 Oct. 1899], FP.

[4] Haldane in East Linton, *The Scotsman*, 11 Oct. 1899.

a deliberate counter-attack to what he regarded as the 'pro Boer' position taken by Morley and Harcourt in their recent speeches. He wrote the next day to Milner to reassure him: 'do not think that because of Harcourt's & Morley's speeches it is to be taken that Liberals as a whole have mis-understood your policy.' Haldane was 'satisfied that four fifths of our people really follow and assent to it'.[1]

It was, however, important that these four-fifths should be seen to support Milner's policy in the special parlia-mentary session called for 17 October 1899. Rosebery set the tone by his letter of 11 October in which, though criticizing the government's diplomacy, he called for the nation to 'close its ranks and relegate party controversy to a more convenient season'.[2] Asquith, isolated in his consti-tuency, also called for an 'unbroken front', but indicated his ambivalent position by explicitly disavowing annexation, a remark which later caused him embarrassment.[3] M.P.s returning to Westminster prepared their various approaches to the war. Haldane reported that 'there is lots of foolish talk & there will be still more foolish amendments'.[4] Ferguson took the initiative in trying to prevent the capture of the party by the Little Englanders. By the evening of 17 October, the lines of schism were clear; Ferguson accurately predicted 'on the vote . . . which is to be moved by P. Stanhope, that (1) CB will walk out (2) Bryce (perhaps) and others will vote for Ht & Morley (3) Fowler, E. Grey & Co. voting with Govt.'[5] In this situation Ferguson thought he had sufficiently organized back-bench opinion so that 'we have settled to vote agst. all the amendments at least that is the united view of 46'.[6]

Ferguson was dismally wrong in his numerical calculation of support in the lobbies for the Liberal Imperialists' posi-tion. On the Irish Nationalists' amendment to the address

---

[1] Haldane to Milner, 11 Oct. 1899, MP 17, f. 602A.
[2] Rosebery to a correspondent, *The Times*, 12 Oct. 1899.
[3] Asquith in E. Fife, *The Times*, 12 and 13 Oct. 1899. He also praised the 'highly satisfactory condition' of the army, 'a thoroughly equipped and most efficient military force'.
[4] Haldane to Mother, 17 Oct. 1899, Hal P 5962, f. 99.
[5] Ferguson to his wife, 'Tuesday evening', n.d. [17 Oct. 1899], FP.
[6] Ibid.

thirty-nine Liberals voted with the government. But Philip
Stanhope's pro-Boer amendment, moved from within the
Liberal party, was the vital vote, and on it only fif-
teen Liberals voted with the government, while ninety-four
Liberals voted for the amendment, and forty-two abstained.[1]
Many of the forty-six whose support Ferguson had expected
on the Stanhope vote abstained or were absent.[2] This was
an incompetent beginning. Grey, Asquith, Fowler, and
Haldane had organized a speaking rota between themselves,[3]
but little had been done to organize back-bench support.
Asquith, moreover, when it came to the division, followed
Campbell-Bannerman, not Grey. The Liberal Imperialists
were clearly out-manœuvred. Grey was embarrassed, and
wrote to Rosebery: 'I don't think that the division of
Thursday represented the feeling of the party: people did
not realise how much the division that evening must govern
the line & tone of subsequent speeches.'[4] Grey's remarks
were true only of his own side; Stanhope's men had fully
realized the importance of staking out an early claim to be
the 'majority' opinion within the party.

Some attempts at propaganda and organization

Grey had made no public move before the meeting of parliament. He had not publicly disclosed the 'very stormy'
differences which existed between many of the ex-cabinet
and himself.[5] Following the Stanhope division, however,
Grey was determined to cut loose. He told Rosebery: 'After
the Fashoda division I minimised it [the party schism on
imperialism], but this time I shall do nothing of the kind.'
Grey intended to make 'the difference in the party . . . un-
mistakable'.[6] Haldane agreed with this course of action. He

[1] The 'Fifteen' were: Beaumont, Carmichael, Douglas, Evershed, Ferguson,
Fowler, Grey, Haldane, Holden, Johnson-Ferguson, Kearley, Mendl, Paulton,
C. E. Shaw, Sir W. Wills.

[2] Among the abstainers were: Asquith, McArthur, Tennant, Ure, R. Wallace.
Among those absent were: Buxton, Perks, W. S. Robson, Joseph Walton, J.
Lawson Walton; see whips' voting analysis, HGP 46105, f. 11.

[3] Haldane to Mother, 20 Oct. 1899, Hal P 5962, f. 103.

[4] Grey to Rosebery, 22 Oct. 1899, RP, box 23; in James, pp. 413–14.

[5] Ibid.   [6] Ibid.

spoke on the Stanhope amendment 'on behalf of Sir H. Fowler, Asquith & Grey', knowing that his speech would mean 'a breach to some extent'.[1] He and Grey were excited, and Haldane told Rosebery: 'Our minority is depressed tonight. Fowler talks of retiring, Asquith is silent. But it is not so with E. Grey & myself. We are going to Glasgow to have a little sport.'[2]

Haldane's and Grey's aim was to spread the message of Liberal Imperialism in public speeches, rather than to establish a base for it in the Commons. They spoke to the students in Glasgow on 28 October, greatly aided by Rosebery's speech at Bath on 26 October.[3] Rosebery was interested in the war from two view-points: first, its effect on Britain's world position, and its exposure of the inadequacies of British government, and secondly, its effect on the debate about the role of imperialism within the Liberal party. Thus in his Bath speech Rosebery gave only passing notice to the detailed arguments about the situation in South Africa, and concentrated on the dangers to Britain—'so lonely in these northern seas'—and on his claim that 'the party of Liberal Imperialism is destined to control the destinies of this country'.[4] The aim was to force Liberals to take sides on imperialism, and the term 'Liberal Imperialism' was deliberately provocative. Rosebery thought 'the name itself will purge the Liberal Party of the ranker elements which have done it so much harm'.[5]

Rosebery's hoped for 'purge' was one of two lines of action open to the Liberal Imperialists. The alternative was to permeate the party with Liberal Imperialist ideas. It was

[1] Haldane to Mother, 19 and 20 Oct. 1899, Hal P 5962, ff. 101–3.
[2] Haldane to Rosebery, 23 Oct. 1899, RP, box 24. The Glasgow meeting was to support Rosebery's candidature as Rector of Glasgow University.
[3] Haldane was mobbed by friendly students at the station on his way to Glasgow. Cultivation of student enthusiasm was a shrewd move; see H. Pelling, *Popular Politics and Society in Late Victorian Britain* (1968), pp. 90–1; and E. H. Shepard, *Drawn from Life* (1961), pp. 150–2 for recollections of art students' jingoism, including a drawing of Shepard as 'Oom Paul'.
[4] Rosebery in Bath, *The Times*, 28 Oct. 1899. In his speech Rosebery revived the term 'Liberal Imperialists' previously used in the 1880s. Similar sobriquets were used in the 1890s; see R. B. Marston, *War, Famine and Our Food Supply* (1897), p. 178 for W. Allan's self-description as a 'Radical Imperialist'; Allan was Liberal M.P. for Gateshead.
[5] Rosebery to Haldane, 4 Nov. 1899, Hal P 5904, f. 208.

characteristic of Rosebery's dislike of long-term 'wire-pulling' that he should opt for the quick result. For the men in the Commons, the situation was more complex. When Rosebery pointed out to Grey that his 'speech at Glasgow went beyond the line he takes', Grey told Haldane that

> it was so, but that though his speech at Bath struck a full and fine note, it was hardly possible for us, who have several speeches to make & to wrestle with constituents, to keep within the same limits: we had to argue and to say whether we were in the right in this war with the Boers, it was impossible for us to avoid discussing the merits of the war.[1]

In addition to this, the Liberal Imperialists, who had been able to raise only fifteen votes on an important division, were hardly in a position to 'purge' their opponents. Haldane thought that 'our split marks the beginning of a new development of Liberalism'.[2] So it might be, but it was a small beginning.

The necessity for patriotic liberalism was as much stressed in Liberal Imperialist speeches as detailed arguments about the war. Haldane put the point to a meeting of Liberal Forwards. He angered them by arguing that the lack of Liberal Imperialist spirit in the party accounted for the 'alienation of a large section of voters . . . the silent voters'.[3] Haldane followed this sally into the enemy camp with an attempt at Christmas 1899 to organize the 'growing body of Liberalism which the official organizations wholly fail to represent'.[4] Attempts to get Roseberian candidates selected in Scotland infuriated Campbell-Bannerman, who complained that 'all their candidates are of the militant Imperialist type'.[5] Haldane, he told Herbert Gladstone, 'was busy laying pipes & pulling wires . . . all the time he was down here at Xmas'.[6] One clear success for the Imperialists was the capture of the pro-Boer *Daily Chronicle* and the resignation of Massingham as editor. Until January 1901

---

[1] Grey to Haldane, 10 Nov. 1899, Hal P 5904, f. 210.
[2] Haldane to Mother, 25 Oct. 1899, Hal P 5962, f. 111.
[3] *Daily News* and *Daily Chronicle*, 29 Nov. 1899.
[4] Haldane to Rosebery, 29 Dec. 1899, RP, box 24.
[5] Bannerman to Gladstone, 21 Jan. 1900, HGP 45987, f. 78.   [6] Ibid.

both London Liberal morning papers now supported the Liberal Imperialists.

During the Christmas recess, Haldane also organized Rosebery's resignation as president of the Eighty Club and the Scottish Liberal Association, Rosebery's remaining official positions.[1] Occupation of these posts might be valuable in a crisis, and it is curious that Haldane should encourage Rosebery's resignations. The explanation is probably that Haldane, believing 'a resignation of the Government though not likely, is just possible', was preparing a non-party position for Rosebery as a coalition Prime Minister. A coalition was generally expected, and Milner was thought a likely Chancellor in a Rosebery ministry.[2]

Rosebery's formula of unspecific patriotic speeches could only work in the short term. He was 'in much excitement' about the 'ineptness' of the Government,[3] and was calling for a campaign of 'scientific methods' to 'put your Empire on a business footing'.[4] But such a campaign would require sustained action from Rosebery, and he was not yet ready for this. Thus in January 1900 Haldane found him 'a good deal perplexed as to how to steer . . . I do not think he sees his future as clearly as other people see it.'[5]

While Haldane and Ferguson worked the constituencies, and Rosebery brooded, Grey was 'a man at a distance' who had 'no political talk with anybody'.[6] Grey was 'very inclined just now to splash about & not make the sacrifice of being careful'. Since he was 'not at all sure that it matters much',[7] he had little interest in party developments, and made no attempt to assist his colleagues.

Asquith's main concern was to preserve contact between Campbell-Bannerman and the Liberal Imperialists, who

---

[1] See Haldane to Rosebery, 6 and 17 Jan. 1900, RP, box 24, and Rosebery to Haldane, 2, 8, and 11 Jan. 1900, Hal P 5905, ff. 1–12.

[2] Haldane to Mother, 30 Jan. 1900, Hal P 5963, f. 37, and T. A. Brassey to Milner, 28 Nov. 1899, MP 17, f. 627A.

[3] Gladstone to Bannerman, 18 Dec. 1899, CBP 41215, f. 184.

[4] Rosebery in Chatham, *The Times*, 24 Jan. 1900.

[5] Haldane to Mother, 13 Jan. 1900, Hal P 5963, f. 11.

[6] Grey to Haldane, 4 Dec. 1899, Hal P 5904, f. 212.

[7] Grey to Rosebery, 9 Jan. 1900, RP, box 23.

regarded Asquith as part of 'our minority',[1] though he had
not voted with them. Hence he announced in advance to
Campbell-Bannerman his intention of dropping 'a shell or
two . . . into the camp of the Chronicle and its friends'.[2]
Asquith consistently stressed the need for party unity, and
claimed that 'I have kept as silent as I could, and when I
had to speak . . . I pitched it in as low a key as I could'.[3]

Campbell-Bannerman appreciated Asquith's unifying
efforts and was 'very glad to hear of Asquith being so reasonable'.[4] Campbell-Bannerman regarded some Liberals as ex-
pendable and agreed with Gladstone that 'we can afford
surely to stand the defection of Grey & Fowler', but he
recognized that Asquith was the man to catch and concurred
that 'it is very desirable to secure Asquith & Ld Kimberley'.[5]

Continued disorganization at Westminster:
Perks's remedial attempts

Asquith hoped to achieve party unity by an amendment in
February acceptable to all, and worked on such an amendment with Gladstone by 'informal talks before the full
ex-Cabinet conference'.[6] The moderate Fitzmaurice amendment of 6 February 1900 was a victory for the conciliatory
line of Asquith, Gladstone, and Campbell-Bannerman.[7] But
an amendment for which both Grey and Labouchere could
vote was necessarily vague, a gesture to party unity. It was,
however, something of a defeat for the Liberal Imperialists,
some of whom had wanted a much more pro-Government
amendment,[8] and the vote again displayed their total lack
of organization. Two Liberal back-benchers voted with the
government, and twenty-two abstained, almost all of them
Imperialists, but their protest was ineffectual, since their

[1] See above, p. 45.
[2] Asquith to Bannerman, 23 Nov. 1899, CBP 41210, f. 177.
[3] Asquith to Bannerman, 20 Dec. 1899, CBP 41210, f. 179.
[4] Bannerman to Gladstone, 21 Jan. 1900, HGP 45987, f. 78.
[5] Gladstone to Bannerman, 4 Jan. 1900, and Bannerman to Gladstone (copy),
5 Jan. 1900, CBP 41215, ff. 194–6. Kimberley, a man with great experience of
South African problems, seems to have had no contact with the Liberal Imperialists
at this time.
[6] Gladstone to Bannerman, 16 Jan. 1900, CBP 41215, f. 205.
[7] For the amendment and the debate, see Bannerman, i. 268–75.
[8] Gladstone to Bannerman, 24 Jan. 1900, CBP 41215, f. 222.

leaders, including Grey, Haldane, and Fowler, voted with Campbell-Bannerman for the amendment.[1]

The Imperialists were therefore still disorganized and short in numbers. Haldane hoped that after a few Rosebery speeches 'the country would as to 3/4 of it say "we are all Liberal Imperialists"', but this was certainly not happening in the Commons.[2] Asquith's position, in particular, was dissociated from that of the others; he was not yet publicly committed to the Grey group, though privately Rosebery and Haldane helped to draft his speech on the Fitzmaurice amendment.[3]

The initiative to break the deadlock of disorganization came, not from the better-known Imperialists, but from Robert Perks, M.P. for Louth since 1892. Perks was a methodist solicitor who had at one time been Henry Fowler's partner; he had subsequently made a fortune out of railway finance, speculation, and construction, especially on the Continent and in Latin America. Like many methodists— for example, Fowler, Hugh Price Hughes, and Reginald Campbell—Perks was a very keen Imperialist and a scourge of the Little Englanders. But he was also fiercely anti-anglican, and thus anti-Tory, on the traditional aspects of political nonconformity, especially education. In 1898 he had founded with Lloyd George the Nonconformist Parliamentary Council, which soon became an effective lobby, particularly on educational matters. Perks's aim was to make nonconformity a powerful and active political, as well as religious, force. He believed there was no available effective nonconformist leader, and he therefore, rather improbably after his horse-racing troubles in 1894 and 1895, cast Rosebery in this role.[4] During 1896 he built up a friendship with Rosebery in which he was quite prepared to play servant to Rosebery's master in order to achieve his ends. Perks had no ambition for office, and was the only leading Liberal Imperialist who could be described as primarily a business man, though even he was originally a solicitor. His

---

[1] See the whips' list, HGP 46105, f. 97.
[2] Haldane to Rosebery, 2 Dec. 1899, RP, box 24.
[3] Haldane to Mother, 5 Feb. 1900, Hal P 5963; 4 H, lxxviii. 731 ff. (6 Feb. 1900).
[4] Rosebery's Derby wins when Prime Minister (Ladas II, 1894; Sir Visto, 1895) were strongly criticized by some nonconformists.

public ability was proved by his success with the Nonconformist Council and by his fund-raising for the 'Methodist
Million Fund', and he intended to use the 'council' method,
which had consolidated nonconformist M.P.s, to build up
Liberal Imperialist strength in the Commons.[1]

Perks invited Haldane, W. S. Robson, Lawson Walton,
and others 'to talk things over'.[2] Simultaneously, Heber
Leonidas Hart, a young barrister, once a member of the
Liberal Forwards,[3] but now a strong Imperialist, was organ-
izing 'a number of Junior Liberals who want to form an
active organization'.[4] By April 1900, Hart had assembled
a hundred members, 'including nearly 40 candidates, the
flower of young Liberalism', and Perks presided at the
inaugural meeting of the Imperial Liberal Council.[5] The title
was deliberately provocative, adopted as a symbol of 'the
Liberal revolt against the Little England policy'.[6]

Preparations for the 1900 election: a successful vote and a possible purge

By March 1900 the British had regained the initiative in
South Africa after the disasters of the 'Black Week' in
December 1899, and it seemed that the war would shortly
end. For the Liberals, the immediate problem was the likeli-
hood of a post-war election fought on Chamberlain's terms.
The already small body of Liberal M.P.s faced the probabi-
lity of a disastrous election. Whereas before the war the
Liberals were showing some signs of electoral recovery, the

---

[1] For this and Perks's life (1849–1934) see Sir Robert Perks Bt., *Notes for an Autobiography*, privately printed, 1936; D. Crane, *The Life-story of Sir Robert W. Perks, Baronet, M.P.*, 1909, and M. S. Edwards, 'S. E. Keeble and Nonconformist Social Thinking, 1880–1939' (unpublished Bristol M.Litt. thesis, 1969).

[2] Perks to Rosebery, 17 Feb. 1900, RP, box 39. Others invited were: Leese, Moulton, Whitely, Oldroyd, C. P. Trevelyan, E. T. Cook, Runciman, Mendl, R. Wallace, Raphael. George Whitely was a converted Tory.

[3] *Daily News*, 4 Feb. 1898.

[4] Perks to Rosebery, 17 Feb. 1900, RP, box 39. Hart was Liberal candidate for Islington, but did not stand in 1900.

[5] Perks to Rosebery, 6 Apr. 1900, RP, box 39. For this meeting, see J. Saxon Mills, *Sir Edward Cook, K.B.E.* (1921), p. 182.

[6] Perks to Rosebery, 10 Apr. 1900, RP, box 39; Perks was Vice-President; it was hoped Rosebery would become President.

best they could hope for now was to avoid losing any further seats.[1]

The aim of the Imperial Liberal Council was to prevent the Little Englanders appearing to represent the party at the polls. By May 1900 the I.L.C. had 220 members and held its first dinner. Liberal front-benchers refused to co-operate. Grey was asked to preside at the dinner, but refused, sending a 'friendly reply'. Asquith was then asked, and refused, sending 'a rude message', so Perks had to preside.[2] The I.L.C. avoided publishing 'any declaration of policy' until it had '3 or 4 hundred' members, since any policy statement would be controversial and might exclude possible members.[3]

The front-bench Imperialists were in the difficult situation that, though they might sympathize with the I.L.C.'s aims, they could hardly overtly support it without logically also condoning the Little England organizations, which they had already proscribed as 'directed not merely or mainly against political opponents, but against fellow Liberals'.[4] The early summer of 1900 was, therefore, a period of relative inactivity for the front-benchers.

The arrival of Lord Roberts in Johannesburg on 31 May made an imminent election even more likely, and, as Morley wrote, 'the panic in the H of C is terrific.'[5] The election, predicted Harcourt in June, 'will be a case of *sauve qui peut*'.[6] Campbell-Bannerman recognized that the vague central position of the leadership on the war was inadequate, for 'there is no longer room for vague philosophising such as we thought would suffice . . . It is either aye or no.'[7] He therefore came out 'aye' on 7 June for annexation with unspecific provisos for 'the conciliation and harmonious cooperation of the two European races'.[8] The Liberal Imperialist front-benchers still gave no lead. The I.L.C. remedied this by

[1] See J. P. D. Dunbabin, 'Parliamentary Elections in Great Britain, 1868–1900', *E.H.R.* lxxxi. 1966.

[2] Perks to Rosebery, 28 May 1900, RP, box 39.

[3] Perks to Rosebery, 12 Apr. 1900, RP, box 39.

[4] Asquith at the Oxford Eighty Club, *Daily News*, 26 Feb. 1900.

[5] Morley to Harcourt, 3 June 1900, HP.

[6] Harcourt to Morley, 6 June 1900, HP.

[7] Bannerman to Gladstone, 1 June 1900, in *Bannerman*, i. 279.

[8] *Bannerman*, i. 281–3.

publishing a long 'statement of policy' on 9 July 1900. This
mentioned South Africa only to support annexation, and
devoted its main attention to the general theme of national
reform to 'put the Empire on a business footing'. It called
for the reformation of the Liberal party, and for a new
Liberal approach to Ireland.[1] The declaration put heart into
the Imperialists, for there was a 'fear which Fowler &
Haldane have expressed that our cause is not making the
headway . . . which it was a few months ago'.[2] The front-
bench remedy for this decline was that Rosebery should make
more speeches. Perks disagreed and recommended that 'I
should not advise you [Rosebery] at *this* juncture to do what
some of your friends so eagerly desire—viz. make a series of
political speeches.' Rosebery followed Perks's advice to avoid
'getting aboard a sinking ship'.[3]

The work of the I.L.C. produced good results in the
parliamentary crisis of 25 July 1900. The party split over
Sir Wilfred Lawson's Colonial Office List amendment:
thirty-eight Liberals voted with the government, forty-two
abstained, and only thirty voted with Lawson.[4] On 'an
urgent demand from Haldane, Perks & a lot of other
people', Grey spoke against Lawson's amendment, knowing
from Asquith that the consequences of his speech 'would be
CB's withdrawal'.[5] Grey and Haldane hoped that Campbell-
Bannerman would resign, for 'if he goes, the fiction of a
united Liberal party can no longer be kept up'.[6] The way
would then be clear for Rosebery's return 'with Asquith
and Grey as lieutenants in the House', the Little Englanders
leaving the party to 'form some sort of organisation like the
Radical Committee' which would 'steadily dwindle'.[7] The
division, with almost 'the entire cohort of Imperial Perks'
present, was, Labouchere ruefully told Harcourt, 'a *coup
ménagé*', and a clear tactical victory.[8] Fowler thought it was
'the best thing that could have happened for the special

[1] *Daily News*, 9 July 1900.
[2] Perks to Rosebery, 9 July 1900, RP, box 39.   [3] Ibid.
[4] Whips' list, 25 July 1900, HGP 46105, f. 101.
[5] Grey to Rosebery, 26 July 1900, RP, box 23.
[6] Ibid.
[7] Haldane to Rosebery, 25 July 1900, RP, box 24, part in James, pp. 416–17.
[8] Labouchere to Harcourt, 26 July 1900, HP.

section that he and I [Perks] belong to'.[1] For the first time, the Imperialists had outmanœuvred the Little Englanders.

But, granted Campbell-Bannerman's resignation as a result of the vote, the far-reaching results expected by Haldane and Grey were based on two assumptions. The first was that the Liberal Imperialists could get control of the party organization. It would only 'be a good chance for the purgation of the party'[2] if they could be sure that it was not they themselves who were purged. Haldane was confident: 'we have the machinery and the Whips & the future & this means that we grow and become the party.'[3] This was improbable. Rosebery had recently resigned from all his official positions, and McArthur offered his resignation as whip after voting with the government on Lawson's amendment.[4] The second assumption was that Asquith, 'the only man who could hold his own as leader in the H of Commons', would be 'ready to act as chief of our group should CB not go on'.[5] This was also unlikely. Asquith had abstained with Campbell-Bannerman in the Lawson division. Haldane thought Asquith 'was with us but did not vote', but Asquith had given no indication that he would be privy to a purge, and his general attitude suggests that, had he become leader, he would have followed much the same line as Campbell-Bannerman as regards party management.[6]

It was, in fact, a false crisis, for Campbell-Bannerman had, early in the war, 'written off resignation', and did not resign.[7] The incident was nevertheless important, for it gave the Liberal Imperialists greater political confidence, and, in particular, persuaded Grey to play a more active political role. From this point onwards, during the war, Grey became more involved in the details of political management, and seems to have become, briefly, genuinely interested in politics.[8]

---

[1] Perks to Rosebery, 26 July 1900, RP, box 39.
[2] Haldane to Rosebery, 25 July 1900, RP, box 24.
[3] Ibid.
[4] McArthur to Gladstone, 25 July 1900, HGP 46023, f. 45.
[5] Haldane to Rosebery, 25 July 1900, RP, box 24.
[6] Ibid.
[7] *Bannerman*, i. 287.
[8] Ferguson told Gladstone (2 Sept. 1900, HGP 46058, f. 36), he had found Grey at Fallodon 'full of politics'.

The 1900 general election

The 1900 'khaki' election was, Haldane thought, 'a strange election'.[1] For the first time since 1868 the pendulum was not expected to swing, and many Liberals downed tools in the face of inevitable defeat. Gladstone complained: 'I have had some disgusting rebuffs in my appeals for money . . . A disgusting number of candidates have skied off.'[2] The only answer the Liberals had to Chamberlain's raucous oratory was Rosebery, and it was the hope of Campbell-Bannerman, Gladstone, and Asquith that he would lead the Liberals into the election. After conferring with the party leaders, Asquith went to Mentmore, Rosebery's Buckinghamshire seat, and 'spoke out in very strong terms, urging R, notwithstanding the difficulties of the situation, to "take the bull by the horns"'.[3] Grey, Haldane, and Perks did not advocate any bold action by Rosebery, but they did recognize the need for some gesture, 'in order to keep our group in good fighting form, & united'.[4] Perks suggested a letter to one of the candidates, which would give Imperialists something to refer to in election speeches, and would not 'allow Chamberlain to say he had spiked your guns', but which would not involve Rosebery too deeply in the anticipated Liberal disaster.[5] Rosebery accordingly wrote his public letter to Hedworth Lambton, hero of the siege of Ladysmith, brother of the Earl of Durham, and Liberal candidate for Newcastle,[6] Perks had a million copies printed and distributed by Liberal Imperialists, of whom Perks was appointing 'a trusted representative in every constituency'.[7]

Rosebery's half-hearted intervention could only have marginal influence, and Perks supplemented it by getting Lord Brassey to become President of the I.L.C.[8] and to

[1] Haldane to Mother, 28 Sept. 1900, Hal P 5964, f. 95.
[2] Gladstone to Bannerman, 16 Sept. 1900, CBP 41216, f. 7. Excluding Ireland, 156 out of 567 seats, or 20·8%, were uncontested by Liberals.
[3] EHD, 20 Aug. 1900; see also Asquith to Gladstone, 31 Aug. 1900, HGP 45989, f. 36.   [4] Perks to Rosebery, 14 Sept. 1900, RP, box 39.
[5] Perks to Rosebery, 19 Sept. 1900, RP, box 39.
[6] Rosebery's letter, *The Times*, 24 Sept. 1900, stresses 'National Efficiency' and hardly mentions South Africa.
[7] Perks to Rosebery, 17 Aug. 1900, RP, box 39.
[8] Harcourt blamed Grey and Fowler (Harcourt to Morley, 23 Nov. 1900, HP).

address its first public meeting on 22 September. Brassey surveyed the world scene in 'a long and cautious' speech, but also said that Liberal Imperialists might have to 'invite support from an independent party'.[1] Perks thought this remark was 'the only real slip'; Perks's aim had 'always been to secure sufficient power to capture control of the old [party]'.[2] 'Proscription *versus* permeation' was soon to be the focus of post-election controversy.

The I.L.C. also issued a list of 142 candidates which it judged 'to be in general agreement with the policy of the council'.[3] This list and its approbation were made without the approval or consent of the candidates concerned; some declared their allegiance by joining the Council, but these were many fewer than the 142 candidates claimed by Hart and the 109 pre-election M.P.s claimed by Perks.[4] The only M.P.s to join the Council before the election were Perks, Hudson Kearley, and Andrew Provand. The vast majority of M.P.s refused to participate in the I.L.C., though many welcomed its speakers for their election campaigns.[5]

Grey, who, like Fowler, was unopposed, intended 'to speak for all the Liberal Imperialists I can', and did so.[6] Haldane, Ferguson, and Asquith all had tough fights and spoke mainly in their constituencies. Ferguson, who was opposed in Leith by E. T. Salvesen, a member of a distinguished Edinburgh–Scandinavian shipping firm, paid back Chamberlain's tactics in his own coin. Outside the Leith polling booths were lines of yellow posters, saying 'Up with the British ensign and down with the foreign flag.'[7]

It is hard to estimate the extent to which Chamberlain was successful in making the war the dominant issue of the election. The result of the election was a Unionist net gain of four seats, but though this was not as many as had been

[1] Perks to Rosebery, 22 Sept. 1900, RP, box 39; *Daily News*, 24 Sept. 1900.

[2] Perks to Rosebery, 22 Sept. 1900, RP, box 39.

[3] See *The Times*, 25 and 29 Sept. and 2 Oct. 1900, for their names; this total is often wrongly given as 56.

[4] *Daily News*, 24 Sept. 1900.

[5] Hart in *Daily News*, 26 Sept. 1900. For the I.L.C. committee at this time, see Saxon Mills, op. cit., p. 182. Council members elected were: Perks, Kearley, J. Fuller, Sir W. D. Pearson, Freeman-Thomas, J. Barker.

[6] Grey to Rosebery, 23 Sept. 1900, RP, box 23.

[7] *The Scotsman*, 13 Oct. 1900. Salvesen stood as a Tory.

expected, it still left a very large government majority of 134.
Liberal candidates dealt with the war as the primary issue in
their speeches, but they did not see it as the deciding issue.
In Scotland, where the Liberals had a minority of seats for
the first time since 1832, Ferguson, the Scottish whip, was
'shocked'. In particular, 'the Tories swept the West where I
[Ferguson] did not expect to lose more than a couple of seats
on the balance.' Ferguson thought 'the Catholic Vote & the
Register did for us in the West'.[1] In England the static
nature of the Liberal vote impressed contemporaries. E. T.
Cook, who 'occupied the undisputed position of first electoral
statistician',[2] pointed to 'the enormous Tory vote in the
English boroughs'. Showing that the poll had increased by
the same amount as the increased number of possible
borough voters, Cook thought that 'nearly the whole of this
increase has been secured by the Tories'. To regain ascendancy, liberalism must 'attract the rising generation in the
great centres of population'.[3] Liberal Imperialism, Cook
argued, would regain for liberalism 'its former appeal to the
national imagination'.[4]

In Wales, an area in which the Liberal Imperialist leaders
had little influence and less interest, the Imperial Liberal
Council made little effort or impact.[5] The Liberal Imperialist
Pritchard Morgan was dramatically defeated by Keir
Hardie, but this was not because of his imperialism,[6] and Sir
Edward Reed, who gained Cardiff from a Tory, had little
contact with the front-bench group.[7]

The I.L.C. policy was to get Imperialists selected by the
associations, but to avoid any proscription of official candidates once selected, whatever their views on the war. There
was, therefore, no real test case between a Liberal Little

---

[1] Ferguson to Gladstone, 22 Oct. 1900, HGP 40658, f. 145; Bannerman agreed
(*Bannerman*, i. 297). In Leith, the United Irish League (500 members) voted
Unionist; Ferguson's majority fell by about 500 votes (*The Scotsman*, 11 Oct. 1900).

[2] W. T. Stead, *Review of Reviews*, Nov. 1900, p. 421.

[3] *Daily News*, 13 Oct. 1900.

[4] *Daily News*, 19 Oct. 1900.

[5] Two of the five I.L.C.-endorsed candidates, Horniman and Reed, were elected.

[6] See K. O. Fox, 'Labour and Merthyr's Khaki Election of 1900', *Welsh History
Review*, 2 (1964).

[7] For Wales and this election, see K. O. Morgan, 'Wales and the Boer War—a
Reply', *Welsh History Review*, 4 (1969).

Englander and a Liberal Imperialist.[1] The nearest to a test case was in Newcastle, a double-barrelled constituency, where Hedworth Lambton and Sam Storey, a Little Englander, were the Liberal candidates. Despite Rosebery's letter of support, Lambton came bottom of the poll, 33 votes behind Storey and 4,299 behind the second Tory, a very poor result, a thousand fewer votes than Morley when he lost the seat in 1895. The Liberal Imperialists were much embarrassed by this result, which got wide press coverage. They argued that Storey's pro-Boer views were responsible, J. M. Paulton writing to Rosebery that 'the explanation is only too simple—Hedworth and Storey were utterly incompatible. If the former had fought single-handed he would certainly have got in.'[2]

The Lambton result confirmed all Rosebery's worst fears about politics, and he wrote angrily to Fowler, who had yet again requested his return:

. . . if they want me back they should have taken steps to make their wishes known . . . the only interference in party politics of which I have been guilty in the past four years was my letter to Lambton. Its general effect (i.e., that on the country) was nil . . . Lambton was at the bottom of the poll. Talk about commanding influence! Few letters have accomplished more [sic].[3]

The Imperial Liberal Council makes the running

The I.L.C. thought they had done well in the election. Perks told Rosebery that 'the new Liberal party will be much more loyal to your views than the old was', and calculated that 'out of the 29 seats *won* by our men . . . no less than 26 were won by your avowed supporters'.[4] Feeling

---

[1] L. Harmsworth beat three other candidates, including the pro-Boer G. B. Clark, in Caithness, but this was hardly a typical constituency; see H. Pelling, *Social Geography of British Elections 1885–1910* (1967), pp. 382–3.

[2] Paulton to Rosebery, 7 Oct. 1900, RP, box 76. Saxon Mills made the same point in an acrimonious correspondence with Massingham in *The Times*, 5, 6, and 19 Oct. 1900.

[3] Rosebery to Fowler, 14 Oct. 1900, RP, box 76; typically, Lambton's chances of winning had not been calculated.

[4] Perks to Rosebery, 7 and 14 Oct. 1900, RP, box 39. Fifty-two of the 142 I.L.C.-endorsed candidates were elected: 36 sitting members kept their seats, 5 new members kept Liberal-held seats, 11 gained a seat; 12 sitting members were defeated, 2 new

that they were in a strong post-electoral position, the rank-and-file Imperialists decided to try to gain the initiative within the party, and on 20 October published three resolutions of the I.L.C. committee. These stressed 'the large measure of success' of I.L.C. candidates, blamed the Liberals' poor showing 'on the narrow and insular views on Imperial questions advocated by an extreme but diminishing section of the party', and claimed that 'it is necessary to clearly and permanently distinguish Liberals in whose policy with regard to Imperial questions, patriotic voters may justly repose confidence'.[1]

Whereas Grey and Haldane had hoped in July 1900 that a split would occur without positive action on their part, by the Little England group somehow removing itself from the party, the I.L.C. resolution called for active proscription by the Imperialists. Perks opposed this at the committee, thinking it unwise 'to accentuate past differences by aggressively pushing first now the Lib. Imp. Council'. Perks thought Imperialists would

be wiser to concentrate all our forces upon the reorganisation of existing Liberal institutions which we can easily control, using the Lib. Imp. Council merely as a medium of friendly consultation.[2]

Perks was overruled by the youthful committee members, and the resolutions were passed and published, sparking off a formidable row. Even the *Daily News* argued that 'permeation is better than proscription'.[3] Campbell-Bannerman publicly denounced the 'proscription' as 'intolerable',[4] but privately he welcomed the I.L.C. manifesto as 'a happy incident as showing quiet Liberals . . . something of the spirit of the men we have to deal with'.[5] Campbell-Bannerman publicly attacked the I.L.C. at Dundee, in the speech where he made his famous slip of the tongue, referring to 'the

candidates lost Liberal-held seats, 76 lost in Unionist-held seats. The I.L.C. selections were arbitrary, especially in Scotland where they omitted Ferguson, R. Wallace, Ure, and Asquith, *pace* Jenkins, p. 121, though Asquith's omission was perhaps deliberate.

1 *Daily News*, 20 Oct. 1900, which observed 'they are determined on splitting—even their infinitives'.
2 Perks to Rosebery, 14 Oct. 1900, RP, box 39.
3 *Daily News*, 20 Oct. 1900.   4 *Daily News*, 23 Oct. 1900.
5 *Bannerman*, i. 297.

Liberal Unionist Council—I mean the Liberal Imperialist Council—there is not much difference perhaps . . .'[1]

It is clear that, in all this, the senior Liberal Imperialists had lost control of the movement; the initiative had passed, through default and inertia, to younger, largely unknown men. The senior men's reactions to the resolutions were variable. Ferguson, who had further reduced contact between the Imperialists and the party organization by resigning as Scottish whip during the election, declared: 'I would have nothing to do with the Imperial Council . . . I hate all these sectional organisations.'[2] McArthur, still a whip, had 'always been against it [the I.L.C.]'.[3] Asquith was very hostile to the I.L.C. and told Harcourt that 'it has no title to speak for anybody whose opinion is of real weight', and that it should be ignored.[4] Asquith still hoped to unite the party under the joint leadership of Rosebery and Campbell-Bannerman, and encouraged the latter to appeal to Rosebery to return, as Campbell-Bannerman himself did in his Dundee speech.[5]

Grey and Haldane were more sympathetic to the I.L.C. Haldane disliked the 'aggression' of the I.L.C., but this was not because of its schismatic effect, but because 'we ought to be . . . defendants and not plaintiffs in any [? ejectment]'.[6] Grey agreed and wrote to Campbell-Bannerman to complain about the latter's Dundee speech. Despite appeals, Grey refused to preside at the I.L.C. dinner on 13 November 1900, but he warned Campbell-Bannerman:

I do agree with the general views of those who call themselves Liberal Imperialists, & both their name and action are the natural result of the claim of men like Labouchere . . . to be the only true Liberals . . . it will be intolerable to go on as the party has been doing, ever since Mr. Gladstone resigned.[7]

[1] Bannerman in Dundee, *The Times*, 16 Nov. 1900.
[2] Ferguson to Gladstone, 22 and 24 Oct. 1900, HGP 46058, ff. 145–6. Sinclair, C-B's private secretary, succeeded Ferguson as Scottish whip.
[3] McArthur to Gladstone, n.d. [22 Oct. 1900], HGP 46023, f. 64.
[4] Asquith to Harcourt, 27 Oct. 1900, HP 9.
[5] Asquith to Bannerman, 13 Nov. 1900, CBP 41210, f. 192.
[6] Haldane to Rosebery, 30 Oct. 1900, RP, box 24.
[7] Grey to Bannerman, 17 Nov. 1900, CBP 41218, f. 8, written after consultation with Haldane and Asquith; see Haldane to Mother, 16 Nov. 1900, Hal P 5964, f. 147.

Rosebery's Glasgow Rectorial speech, on 16 November 1900, and his more prosaic but more pointed speech made during the borough elections on 26 October, considerably reinforced the Liberal Imperialist position. 'It gives us', wrote Haldane, 'what we need to work upon, the foundation of a constitutional peace policy.'[1] The success of the Glasgow speech showed that Rosebery was still a very potent force, despite the Lambton letter fiasco. Rosebery was in close contact about the I.L.C. with Perks, Wemyss Reid, and others, but made no public move towards it.[2] He did, however, make a semi-political move by placing his name first on the list of the 'Committee of Vigilance for considering and promoting administrative reform', organized by James Knowles of the *Nineteenth Century*.[3]

The short December 1900 session was unexpectedly harmonious. After protests from Grey, Asquith, and Haldane, the amendment criticizing Milner's appointment as administrator of the annexed territories was not moved, and many of the Liberal Imperialists voted for Lloyd George's amendment on ministers and public contracts, in effect an attack on Chamberlain's character. Ferguson thought that if Asquith had proposed the amendment, as originally was intended, even more would have voted.[4] This illustrated the advantage of their allegiance to Milner. By making it clear that it was Milner's policy that they were defending, they felt themselves free to denounce Chamberlain, without prejudicing their support for a 'national policy'.

Perks's varied success in developing the I.L.C.'s role

The absence of a major row in December 1900 encouraged party unity, and in January 1901 the I.L.C. virtually withdrew its proscribing resolutions of the previous autumn.[5] The I.L.C. was not less active, but it had been persuaded to

1 Haldane to Rosebery, 17 Nov. 1900, RP, box 24, quoted in James, p. 420.

2 Rosebery to Wemyss Reid, 18 Nov. 1900, RP, Letter Book, and to Sir E. Reed, 22 Nov. 1900, RP, Letter Book.

3 *Nineteenth Century and After*, no. 48, July 1900, p. 1; later Grey, Haldane, Fowler, Perks, and E. T. Cook joined; see also below, p. 257.

4 Ferguson to Gladstone, 17 Dec. 1900, HGP 46058, f. 164.

5 See *The Times* and *Daily News*, 17 Jan. 1901.

try to permeate the party, rather than proscribe its opponents. The object of this permeation was first to get more efficient Liberal Imperialist co-operation in the Commons, and secondly to establish a base in the national organizations. Perks hoped to bring the front-bench men into the I.L.C., and asked Rosebery to persuade Grey to speak at the I.L.C., 'as we find it very difficult at present to secure any patronage at all from prominent men, & some of the committee seem quite depressed at their isolation!'[1] For the time being, nothing came of this, but Perks succeeded in getting general agreement for action in the Commons. He told Rosebery in February 1901: 'We have decided . . . to take a trial of strength on Lloyd George's amendment. We are quietly rallying up all our forces. We propose not to abstain but to speak and *vote* against Lloyd George.'[2] Fowler and Grey were to be the main speakers, but Perks rightly thought that 'our cause would be much strengthened if Asquith would speak', and asked Rosebery's help in this.[3] The planned repeat of the staged coup of July 1900 was abortive, for Lloyd George decided during the debate not to move his amendment, perhaps having heard of Perks's preparations. Lloyd George had already foiled the Imperialists early in 1901 by helping to organize the purchase by seven Little Englanders of the *Daily News*, thus robbing the Imperialists of their main propaganda organ, and E. T. Cook of an effective outlet for his views.[4]

Having been forestalled in his attempt to achieve a victory in the Commons, Perks hoped, instead, to capture the National Liberal Federation. This plan had been developed by Perks as an alternative to parliamentary action in November 1900, when it was to coincide with a major initiative by Rosebery, coupled with support from the Harmsworths' *Daily Mail*.[5] At the N.L.F. meeting in February 1901, Perks was disappointed. The meetings were, he reported, 'unsatisfactory . . . *our* attempt to carry Baring, Mendl, E. Tennant, Benson & L. Holland also failed'. The

[1] Perks to Rosebery, 15 Dec. 1900, RP, box 39.
[2] Perks to Rosebery, 15 Feb. 1901, RP, box 39.   [3] Ibid.
[4] For a good account of this see W. T. Stead, *Review of Reviews*, xxiii. The Liberal Imperialist *Leeds Mercury* was also in financial difficulties, but was saved by the Harmsworths.   [5] Perks to Rosebery, 3 Nov. 1900, RP, box 39.

consolation was that the N.L.F. elections 'have not resulted in a triumph for the . . . Lloyd George people', for many of these, including Loulou Harcourt and Philip Stanhope, were not elected.[1] The Liberal Imperialists had, however, over-estimated their strength in the local associations.

The opening months of 1901 thus showed little success either in Parliament or elsewhere. Perks had, however, one triumph for which he had been working since the start of the war. On 25 March 1901, Grey, Haldane, and other Liberal Imperialist M.P.s attended a dinner of the I.L.C. Grey praised the Council's activities, and, posing the question 'was it necessary to have a separate organisation to express the views which the Council held in these times of con-troversy?' answered: 'he thought it was inevitable.'[2] Thus, over a year after its foundation, the I.L.C. received public recognition from the front-bench Imperialists. They did this partly to control its youthful exuberance and partly to secure a political base for themselves, for Rosebery, to whom they looked for political security, seemed less likely than ever to return to politics.[3]

'Methods of barbarism': the crisis of June-July 1901

Campbell-Bannerman did not attack this increase in the status of the I.L.C., and, apart from some uneasy moments in the Commons in March, violent squabbles were avoided until June 1901. The I.L.C. had never taken much interest in the details of the war; South Africa occurred almost incidentally in its declarations. The Council's main aim was to reapportion the balance of power within the party, using the war as a catalyst, and support for it as a criterion for

---

[1] Perks to Rosebery, 27 Feb. 1901, RP, box 39. For the elections, for which 'the attendance of delegates was the largest on record', see the N.L.F. *Report* for 1901.

[2] Grey at Hotel Cecil, *The Times*, 26 Mar. 1901. Other M.P.s present were: A. Brand, L. Harmsworth, Elibank, Lawson Walton, J. Walton, Ure, R. Wallace, Freeman-Thomas, J. Fuller, H. Tennant.

[3] Rosebery refused the Liberal leadership of the Lords when Kimberley wanted to retire; Hamilton, with Asquith's consent, tried to get the King to persuade Rosebery to return, EHD, 24 Feb. 1901 and 8 Mar. 1901. Rosebery explained to Hamilton that he anticipated 'a sort of coalition government formed of the best men of both parties, who might perhaps unite under him, because he had taken no side decidedly' (EHD, 17 Mar. 1901).

'patriotism'. In the spring of 1901, however, the details of
the war, which had been to some extent out of the headlines
since October 1900, again became prominent, with the controversy over the new methods introduced to pacify the
Transvaal, where the Boer commandos continued to demon-
strate their resilience. These methods were condemned by
the N.L.F. resolutions of 27 February 1901.[1] Emily
Hobhouse's disclosures about the concentration camps[2] and
the subsequent campaign against the camps soon led to the
most famous phrase of the war, 'methods of barbarism',
delivered by Campbell-Bannerman on 14 June 1901 at a
dinner of the National Reform Union, chaired by Stanhope
and attended by Morley and Harcourt.

The context of this famous speech was important. The
general acclaim for Milner on his arrival in England on 24
May 1901 had been answered by strong attacks on Milner's
position by, amongst others, Morley on 4 June and Bryce
on 12 June. Milner had made, by his general competence
and clarity of exposition, a deep impression on Asquith,
Grey, and Haldane after dinner on 12 June, Haldane
writing: 'it is a pleasure always to see any one with a large
grasp of events.'[3] Though they might have reservations
about some of his policies, they were confirmed in their
respect for Milner's character and in their belief that Milner
was an exception to the general inefficiency of the government.[4] Campbell-Bannerman's speech thus came at a
moment when the Imperialists were particularly impatient
with Little Englander opinions.

Campbell-Bannerman's speech confirmed the worst fears
of most Liberal Imperialists. Rosebery regarded the dinner
at which it was given as 'a sinister event', for 'there was
nothing unforeseen and unexpected about it'.[5] Their hostile
reactions to the speech followed a well-established pattern.
The new factor was the attitude of Asquith. In every previous crisis Asquith had seemed to sympathize with Grey,
Haldane, and Fowler, but had consistently followed

[1] S. Maccoby, *English Radicalism, 1886–1914* (1953), p. 309.
[2] E. Hobhouse, *Report on a Visit to the Camps* (1901).
[3] Haldane to Mother, 14 June 1901, Hal P. 5965, f. 215.
[4] See Grey to Haldane, 28 May 1901, Hal P. 5905, f. 65.
[5] Rosebery to Spender, 20 June 1901, SP 46387, f. 45.

Campbell-Bannerman in the division lobby. Asquith's long personal association with Grey and Haldane had perhaps made him seem more of a Liberal Imperialist than he was. His views on the war had been varied, but his political position had been clear: unity of the party was his priority. He had avoided flirtation with the I.L.C. The *Daily News* commented that 'the great controversy of the war has found Mr. Asquith in an attitude of cautious neutrality'.[1] Asquith had been very self-contained. His son records that as Prime Minister he would let 'his feelings flow forth in a roaring spate of unmeasured language . . . almost always extreme'.[2] If he indulged himself thus at this time, no record of it remains.

Asquith at first thought that Campbell-Bannerman had made an error, only unintentionally allowing himself to seem allied with the pro-Boers. He accordingly wrote to his leader, without protest, recognizing 'a regrettable incident', and putting the main blame on Morley, saying 'I shall do all I can to discourage reprisals.'[3] But it was soon clear that Campbell-Bannerman had meant just what he said. Unlike Rosebery in similarly tricky circumstances, he did not try to explain away his challenging words, but reaffirmed them in the Commons.[4] For Asquith this was an entirely new situation. If Campbell-Bannerman abandoned the centre, Asquith would be left alone, and the Liberal Imperialists would be likely to carry out the long-expected schism. There is no reason to suppose that Asquith abandoned his priority of unity; he had no intention of provoking a split, and wrote to Spence Watson, the president of the N.L.F.:

It may be, as you say, that it will not be found possible to keep the party together. But God forbid! I am at least ready to sacrifice everything, short of my honest convictions and the right to state and act upon them, to avert such a catastrophe.[5]

But to hold the party together, Asquith would need a new tactic. Preservation of unity by supporting Campbell-Bannerman in the centre was now no longer possible.

---

[1] *Daily News*, 20 Feb. 1901.   [2] Spender and Asquith, i. 216.
[3] Asquith to Bannerman, 15 June 1901, in Jenkins, p. 124.
[4] 4 H, xcv. 599 (17 June 1901).
[5] Asquith to Watson, 5 July 1901, in P. Corder, *The Life of Robert Spence Watson* (1914), p. 285.

Asquith, therefore, had to take the lead of the Imperialist section in order to control it and keep it within the party.[1] Though in the debate it was Haldane who 'by the desire of Asquith and Grey . . . made the speech for our section', Asquith for the first time in the war did not follow Campbell-Bannerman in the lobby, and abstained with about fifty other Liberals.[2] On 20 June, Asquith replied to Campbell-Bannerman and Morley in a speech which Haldane regarded as 'more than backing me up'.[3]

Campbell-Bannerman's original speech was intended to expose the specific evil of the concentration camps. It was not a general indictment of the aims of the war, nor of the British army. The Liberal Imperialists, however, treated it in very general terms. Haldane took his stand because 'the party must be rescued from getting wholly & uselessly out of relation to the national sense'.[4] Asquith's speech of 20 June dealt with the war generally. Fowler, praising it, stressed that what was tactically vital was that 'we must not allow the idea to spread that we are the authors of a new departure'; Liberal Imperialists must appear 'not Dissenters but the Orthodox Church'.[5]

The main dispute with Campbell-Bannerman was thus about the condition of the party, not primarily about the concentration camps, though Liberal Imperialists certainly defended these as a military necessity.[6] The crisis which the 'methods of barbarism' speech occasioned, and which lasted, with various fits and starts, for almost a year, was only

[1] As Grey wrote later to Rosebery (20 July 1901, RP, box 23) 'If he [Asquith] had not stood by us there would have been a secession of myself & a few, but *very few*, others from the Liberal party.'

[2] Haldane to Mother, 18 June 1901, Hal P 5965, f. 221; for the abstentions see *The Scotsman*, 19 June 1901; Austin and Mellor voted with the government.

[3] Haldane to Mother, 21 June 1901, Hal P 5965, f. 227; Asquith, *The Times*, 21 June 1901. Haldane characteristically attempted to alleviate the camp atrocities by using his personal influence at the War Office (Haldane to Mother, 19 June 1901, Hal P 5965, f. 223).

[4] Haldane to Mother, 20 June 1901, Hal P 5965, f. 225.

[5] Fowler to Asquith, 23 June n.d. [1901], AP 10, f. 3. Though the most uncompromising of the Liberal Imperialists, Fowler played no part in the tactical discussions. He hated 'weekends' and 'always spent his Sundays at home', thus excluding himself from the main time for Edwardian political planning (E. H. Fowler, *The Life of H. H. Fowler* (1912), p. 630).

[6] See Grey at Peterborough, *The Times*, 18 July 1901.

incidentally about imperialism. It demonstrated a fundamental difference within the party about its style and objectives. 'Methods of barbarism' was an echo of the Midlothian campaign. It directly challenged the strategy which the Liberal Imperialists believed essential for the restoration of the party's fortunes.[1]

Asquith and Haldane spent the week-end together in Somerset and Haldane thought 'a large step is likely to result from it'.[2] Meeting in conclave 'at Asquith's on 26 June', the Liberal Imperialists decided 'to give Asquith a dinner on July 19th', then the normal way of showing respect and support for a public figure.[3] Haldane and Grey were very keen. To Grey, 'politics have suddenly become very interesting . . . because I think I may be in the beginning of new things.'[4] Haldane was all for 'going forward without looking to right or left', and complained that 'it is no time for weakkneed people and there are plenty of them', though Grey was 'splendidly cool and efficient'.[5]

Asquith had taken the lead of the Imperialist group and asked Perks to 'arrange as privately as may be—for a meeting of those who are in general sympathy with us', so as to 'organise a counteracting policy', since it was clear 'that the so-called National Reform Union mean business'.[6] To the party officials, however, Asquith gave a quite different impression, telling Gladstone: 'The dinner, as you may imagine was no idea of mine, but it was put up to me in such a way that I did not feel able to decline.'[7] When forty Liberal M.P.s wrote to complain about the dinner, Asquith explained conciliatorily that its object was to dispel the idea that the Liberal Imperialists were 'in the early stage of a process of political evolution'.[8]

[1] For this strategy, see below, Ch. IV.

[2] Haldane to Mother, 24 June 1901, Hal P 5965, f. 231.

[3] Haldane to Mother, 26 June 1901, Hal P 5965, f. 235.

[4] Grey to Louise Creighton, 7 July 1901, Bodleian MS. Eng. Letts. e. 73, f. 1.

[5] Haldane to Mother, 28 June 1901, Hal P 5965, f. 239.

[6] Asquith to Perks, 19 June 1901, Perks Papers, courtesy of Professor Keith Robbins; the National Reform Union was operating as a pro-Boer organization.

[7] Asquith to Gladstone, 27 June 1901, HGP 45989, f. 49. Gladstone thought Asquith was 'misled' by 'Haldane, Ferguson, Dr. C. Douglas, Grey & C. P. Trevelyan', Memorandum, 30 July 1901, HGP 46105, f. 210.

[8] Asquith to the forty Liberals, 29 June 1901, AP 10, f. 9. Both letters appeared in the press.

It was true that the Liberal Imperialists were not intending to form a new party at this time. The circumstances were unpropitious, for, despite the work of the I.L.C., they remained in a weak position. Indeed, it was thought at first that 'the promoters of the dinner . . . will find themselves compelled through lack of Parliamentary support to abandon the gathering'.[1] Haldane was greatly agitated about the 'great timidity and wavering',[2] and told Beatrice Webb that 'we are fighting for our lives . . . the whole movement may be a failure.'[3] The Liberal Imperialists did not consider joining the Unionists. Their aim was still to be 'the Orthodox Church' within the Liberal party if a split came. Haldane thought Milner 'was right in thinking that there is a danger —we may not be able to carry the bulk of our people. But I do think that we can carry enough of them to paralyse the energies of the rest for mischief.'[4]

The dinner preparations were interrupted by the party meeting on 9 July, Campbell-Bannerman's ultimate weapon, short of a threat of resignation. On 3 July, the Liberal Imperialists had 'a meeting of our party & decided our line for the general meeting on Tuesday'.[5] This 'line' was to demand 'full and unfettered liberty . . . to express and to act upon our honestly entertained convictions, without any imputation of party disloyalty'.[6] This meant in effect that the unity of the Liberal party was to be maintained, in return for agreement that there was no official Liberal policy. At the party meeting the unanimous vote of confidence in Campbell-Bannerman as Commons leader was supported by the presence of all the Liberal Imperialists. In one of those curiously baseless political judgements to which Liberal Imperialists were prone, Haldane thought that as a result of the meeting 'ours is the winning side to all appearances'.[7]

Heavy official pressure was put on Asquith to abandon

---

[1] Political notes, *The Times*, 29 June 1901.
[2] Haldane to Mother, 5 July 1901, Hal P 5966, f. 9.
[3] B. Webb, *Our Partnership* (1948), p. 217 (9 July 1901).
[4] Haldane to Milner, 6 July 1901, MP 39, f. 166.
[5] Haldane to Mother, 4 July 1901, Hal P 5966, f. 7. Asquith knew of C-B's intentions in advance and promised to 'do all I can to keep the peace' (Asquith to Gladstone, 5 July 1901, HGP 45989, f. 51).
[6] Asquith at the party meeting, *The Times*, 10 July 1901.
[7] Haldane to Mother, 10 July 1901, Hal P 5966, f. 17.

the dinner, before the party meeting by Gladstone, after it by Campbell-Bannerman.[1] Asquith seems to have resented Campbell-Bannerman's suggestion that he was involved in 'sectional' activities, and that he, Asquith, should publicly withdraw while Campbell-Bannerman remained unrepentant about his original move towards the Little Englanders in his 'methods of barbarism' speech.[2]

The Asquith dinner was to be a general display of Liberal Imperialist strength, and was at first intended to point the way to a possible restoration of the 'pre-1886' Liberal party, by inviting Liberal Unionists. Prominent pro-Boers were to be excluded. It became clear, however, that on these terms very few would attend; the Unionists' invitations were withdrawn, and all Liberals were invited.[3] The hope was that Rosebery would preside.

Haldane intended the dinner to show the wide range of Liberal Imperialist interests, particularly in domestic questions. For some time he had been trying to revive the co-operation of the late 1880s between his group and the Webbs. During the war Haldane had arranged a number of dinners at which Rosebery met the Webbs. At first these were unsuccessful, but as the cry of 'efficiency' grew louder, the value of Rosebery as a spokesman became clear to the Webbs, and was proved by Rosebery's assistance in fund-raising for the L.S.E.[4] Haldane thought 'we have to see what we are to do as a Progressive party.'[5] After spending the week-end of 7 July 1901 with the Webbs, he found that 'they have formed a movement . . . we are going to elaborate, if we can, a real programme of social reforms. He is to be at the dinner. This is important.'[6] As a result of his meeting with Webb, Haldane saw 'clearly, very clearly'.[7] Sidney

---

[1] Gladstone's Memorandum, 30 July 1901, HGP 46105, f. 210, and Bannerman to Asquith, 10 July 1901, AP 10, f. 19. Gladstone expected the dinner to be a failure, and wanted 'to save Asquith from his friends' (Gladstone to Bannerman, 12 July 1901, CBP 41216, f. 122).

[2] See Jenkins, p. 126.

[3] See Gladstone's Memorandum, op. cit.

[4] See B. Webb, *Our Partnership*, pp. 197, 200-1, 211.

[5] Haldane to Mother, 2 July 1901, Hal P 5966, f. 3.

[6] Haldane to his sister Elizabeth (a friend of Beatrice), 8 July 1901, Hal P 6010, f. 184.

[7] Ibid.

Webb had 'paid little or no attention' to the war, but attended the dinner because of its importance for Liberal domestic policy.[1] The object of the Asquith dinner was thus to reassert the need for what had been the Imperialists' central aim since the 1880s: a new Liberal ideology based on a constructive policy of social reforms.

Rosebery's intervention in the crisis

Abroad until 5 July, Rosebery misinterpreted the crisis. He 'did not see . . . how a schism can be avoided',[2] and thought 'that the long-suffering L.I.'s have at last lost patience'.[3] Rosebery's extreme view of the crisis seems to have been confirmed by a letter from Grey, to which Rosebery replied: 'I have learned of recent events with the greatest pleasure— the first political pleasure indeed that I have known for some years.' Rosebery rejoiced that 'you have a leader and an authoritative voice'.[4] Rosebery was pleased he was abroad, as this foiled 'the old cry of Rosebery intrigue'.[5]

Rosebery intended, as in previous crises, to avoid all contact with his friends, since 'the whole movement should be Asquithian'.[6] However, he saw Grey on Friday, 12 July, and they discussed 'the sort of letter he [Rosebery] is thinking of writing to the papers'.[7] Rosebery did not want to embarrass Asquith 'by saying anything which might put the fat in the fire before the dinner', but Grey told him 'making the fat frizzle couldn't hurt us', though Asquith should not be involved with the letter.[8] This was clear encouragement from Grey to Rosebery to cut loose. Rosebery asked for a conference with 'the committee' on Monday, 15 July, but at the last moment did not attend.[9] The conference was held without Rosebery, but was 'inconclusive', since Asquith

[1] B. Webb, *Our Partnership*, p. 219.
[2] Rosebery to Spender, 20 June 1901, SP 46387, f. 45.
[3] Rosebery to Ferguson, 25 June 1901, RP, box 16.
[4] Rosebery to Grey, 28 June 1901, RP, Letter Book.
[5] Rosebery to Ferguson, 28 June 1901, RP, box 16.
[6] Rosebery to Grey, 29 June 1901, RP, Letter Book.
[7] Grey to Asquith, 12 July 1901, AP 10, f. 3, some in Jenkins, pp. 126–7.
[8] Ibid.
[9] Haldane to Rosebery, 11 Nov. 1901, RP, box 24; the letter surveys the July crisis.

refused 'to pledge himself to a definite line in circumstances which we can none of us forecast'.[1] Rosebery did not attend the conference because he realized that, while he held to his original view that the time had come for a party split, the other Liberal Imperialists did not hold this view. Rosebery said his reason for non-attendance was the old one, that the 'committee' should not be compromised on the details of the public letter he was about to write.[2]

Though Haldane said he had 'not any idea what he [Rosebery] means to do', the Commons men knew of Rosebery's general attitude from his interview with Grey, and knew that Rosebery intended to write a letter. The letter appeared in *The Times* on 17 July 1901. Rosebery argued that 'statesmen who dissociate themselves from the nation in a great national question, such as a war . . . dissociate themselves for much longer than they think', and quoted the Foxites as an example. Other Liberal Imperialists agreed with this, but Rosebery went further and attacked the view that the party could or should keep a unity of form devoid of any agreed content, for 'a party cannot be conducted on the principles of Issachar', and could not contain an 'irreconcilable division of opinions on a group of questions of the first importance'.[3]

The Commons men ignored Rosebery's views on the party and his call for a split, but attacked his personal position, for Rosebery had written that he would 'never voluntarily re-enter the arena of party politics', and would plough his own 'furrow'. Grey told Rosebery publicly that he was in danger of becoming 'like some astral body outside the planetary system of party politics' and that there 'is no such thing as a political conscript'.[4] This was the old deadlock: Rosebery demanded 'explicit support' as a prerequisite of his return; the Commons men expected Rosebery to take the initiative. Grey's public attack was, however, the first public airing of this disagreement.

Asquith's dinner was in the evening of 19 July, and on

[1] Haldane to Rosebery, 11 Nov. 1901, RP, box 24.
[2] Rosebery to Haldane, 17 July 1901, Hal P 5905, f. 91.
[3] Rosebery to the City Liberals, *The Times*, 17 July 1901.
[4] Grey in Peterborough, *The Times*, 18 July 1901.

that afternoon Rosebery spoke to 300 City Liberal Club members. The only Liberal M.P.s present were Ferguson, Perks, McArthur, and two others. Rosebery denounced the Reform Club compact made at the party meeting as 'an organised hypocrisy', and argued that the division in the party dated from the 1880–5 government, though Gladstone had in its early years 'veiled these discrepancies . . . from the public'. Rosebery called for Liberal Unionists to rejoin a Liberal party 'with a clean slate . . . disembarrassed from some entangling alliances'; if the Liberal party would not clean its slate, 'some party will create itself'.[1]

This was the most outspoken speech Rosebery had made on the condition of the Liberal party. He must have known that its clearly provocative tone would contrast with Asquith's speech that evening. Rosebery was annoyed with his friends. He had always argued 'that the Liberal party must work out its own salvation' and that 'intervention from without would do more harm than good'.[2] In Gastein Rosebery had thought that the Imperialists were working out their own salvation: Asquith, he thought, had at last taken the lead and would lead the Imperialist group to a new development in British politics. He returned to find the usual unwillingness to plunge. In such circumstances, it was natural that he should, as *The Times* put it, have 'thought his friends so badly in want of a shaking that nothing but a couple of surprises would serve the turn.'[3]

Asquith's speech at the dinner on 19 July was a firm antidote in tone, if not in content, to Rosebery's. Asquith played down the specific arguments about South Africa. He devoted the bulk of his speech to the question: 'What is to be the future of the Liberal party?' Asquith denied that the time had come for a schism. He pointed out: 'I have never called myself a Liberal Imperialist. The name of Liberal is good enough for me.' However, he followed Rosebery's line, in moderate words, on the need for the party to be 'a national party to which you can safely entrust the fortunes of the Empire', and he preached the need for domestic reform 'not

---

[1] Rosebery to the City Liberals, *The Times*, 20 July 1901.
[2] Rosebery to Grey, 29 June 1901, RP, Letter Book.
[3] Leader, *The Times*, 22 July 1901.

as a moral question . . . but as a question of social and Imperial efficiency'.[1]

Rosebery's speech certainly stole Asquith's thunder, but the Commons men were glad to see him back in action, almost on any terms. Haldane regarded Rosebery's speech as 'all to the good. It means new Life.'[2] Grey apologized to Rosebery for his public attack on him, and found Rosebery's speech 'that of a man stripped for combat—and when you are stripped (if I may say so without irreverence) you make a very fine appearance'.[3] Even Asquith sent protestations of friendship, in reply to a rather nervous letter from Rosebery, and hoped that their two furrows would soon converge.[4]

After the crisis: the autumn campaign and preparations for Chesterfield

After spending the week-end with Asquith and Milner, Haldane saw Rosebery on 22 July 1901 and reported to Asquith and Grey that 'Lord R. is working with us from the outside and I think things will go smoothly'.[5] 'In high spirits', Haldane also saw the Webbs to arrange for the furtherance of their 'efficiency' plans.[6] July to October 1901 were months of detailed co-operation between the members of what Haldane called 'the Asquith committee'.[7] A meeting was held in Asquith's house to settle 'the lines of the speeches in October when we begin to work'.[8] 'The autumn plans of campaign' were to include a general drive for

[1] Asquith, *The Times*, 20 July 1901. Fowler disturbed the atmosphere of moderation by praising Rosebery's speech and stressing party differences. Thirty-nine M.P.s attended the dinner.

[2] Haldane to Mother, 20 July 1901, Hal P 5966, f. 35.

[3] Grey to Rosebery, 20 July 1901, RP, box 23.

[4] Asquith to Rosebery, 22 July 1901, RP, box 1; and Rosebery to Asquith, 20 July 1901, in Jenkins, pp. 128-9.

[5] Haldane to Mother, 23 July 1901, Hal P 5966, f. 39. Though Rosebery also saw Milner at this time he evidently did not tell Milner of his secret attempts at a negotiated peace in South Africa (James, pp. 427-9, and MP 264, 30 July 1901).

[6] Beatrice Webb, *Our Partnership*, p. 220.

[7] Haldane to Mother, 6 Aug. 1901, Hal P 5966, f. 63.

[8] Ibid. Perks's absence was regretted by Asquith, who told him on 10 Aug. 1901: 'I am most anxious that we should not dissipate our forces or lose (thro' inactivity, or unorganized movement) any of the real & solid ground which we have gained during the last two months' (Perks Papers, courtesy of Professor Keith Robbins).

'efficiency', and particular proposals for Liberal Irish policy.[1] Asquith, Grey, and Haldane even missed some of the holiday season to develop these plans in London, which were finalized at various Scottish shooting-lodges in September by Asquith, Grey, Haldane, and Ferguson.

Meanwhile, unknown to the Asquith committee, Rosebery was drawing much closer to the I.L.C. which had played little part in the July crisis. Rosebery thought the I.L.C. must be improved in form and in management. On his suggestion the name was changed to the clumsy 'Liberal (Imperialist) League'. Rosebery also suggested a fund of £10,000 to sponsor candidates, and he and Perks subscribed £1,000 each.[2] Perks was a good deal closer to Rosebery in the recess than he was to the Asquith committee, who felt neglected. He even took the initiative in acting as a link between Rosebery and the 'committee', and in trying to start a policy meeting.[3]

Independently of the committee, Rosebery was also already contemplating a speech at Chesterfield. In August, A. B. Markham, an I.L.C. member and Rosebery's agent in the July peace initiative, invited Rosebery to speak at Chesterfield. Rosebery refused, but said that in certain circumstances he might have to speak. He told Markham:

> My view is that if Asquith can succeed in his endeavour to influence the party from within, that is the best course, and I can stand aside. If, however, that does not succeed (and I have my doubts) it may be necessary for me to speak on my own account.[4]

The committee was thus on trial. The Webbs also regarded it, and Rosebery, with suspicion, for they had 'no illusions about the Lib. Imps. We think neither Rosebery nor Asquith mean to declare themselves in favour of our measure of collectivism.'[5] To force the Liberals' hand, Webb wrote his famous article 'Lord Rosebery's Escape from

---

[1] Perks to Rosebery, 8 Aug. 1901, RP, box 39. For this campaign see below, pp. 273–5.

[2] Perks to Rosebery, 7 and 23 Aug. 1901, RP, box 39. Perks thought the money would be better spent on agents.

[3] Perks to Rosebery, 20 Sept. 1901, RP, box 39. Haldane in particular felt estranged; see EHD, 1 Nov. 1901, and B. Webb, op. cit., p. 225 (1 Nov. 1901).

[4] Rosebery to Markham, 22 Aug. 1901, RP, Letter Book.

[5] B. Webb, op. cit., p. 224 (1 Oct. 1901).

Houndsditch' in which he exposed the differences in political view-point amongst the Liberal Imperialists, and urged them to the exorcism of 'Gladstonian ghosts', concluding:

... if even one half of the study and conviction, money and capacity, were put into such a campaign for the next five years, that Cobden and Bright put into the Anti-Corn-Law League the country could be won for a policy of 'National Efficiency'.[1]

Thus fortified, the committee men made their speeches at the end of September and beginning of October. They dealt first with Ireland, and then outlined a general policy of efficiency at home, defence reform, and measures to improve the imperial race. The South African situation was hardly mentioned.[2]

Liberal Imperialism proscribed?
Haldane and Grey join the I.L.C.

The timing of the Asquith committee's autumn campaign was excellent, for it immediately followed the North-East Lanark by-election of 25 September 1901, and enabled the campaigners to emphasize the legitimacy of their position as party members. The candidate of the local Liberal association for this by-election, the result of the death of the Liberal incumbent, J. Colville, was C. B. Harmsworth, a well-known Liberal Imperialist, strongly supported by the *Daily Mail*. The main interest in the election was the contest between Harmsworth and Robert Smillie, the I.L.P. candidate. Campbell-Bannerman withdrew the support of the national organizations from Harmsworth and regretted that 'we cannot openly support him [Smillie] against the local Liberal Association.'[3] A number of Liberals did, however, openly support and speak for Smillie, and he had letters of endorsement from Sir Wilfrid Lawson, the Master of Elibank, and other Liberal M.P.s. In reply to this C. M. Douglas spoke, and Haldane spoke twice, for Harmsworth,

---

[1] S. Webb, 'Lord Rosebery's Escape from Houndsditch', *Nineteenth Century*, Sept. 1901.
[2] Asquith in *The Times*, 30 Sept. and 17 Oct. 1901; Haldane in *The Scotsman*, 4, 5, and 9 Oct. 1901; Grey in *The Times*, 12 Oct. 1901.
[3] Bannerman to Harcourt, 19 Sept. 1901, HP 9.

and Colville's brothers supported the Unionist candidate. The stated intention of the Little England Liberals was that 'they do not expect to win the seat, but they do hope to keep Mr. Harmsworth out.'[1]

As a result of the split Liberal vote, the Unionists gained the seat.[2] The Little Englanders had done what the I.L.C. had always avoided doing: having lost the selection battle in the association, they had openly worked against the official Liberal candidate.[3]

The North-East Lanark election confirmed the Liberal Imperialists in their view that they were being hounded from the party, and convinced the senior Imperialists that they must at last join a sectional organization to protect their own position. In October 1901 they had extensive negotiations with the Liberal (Imperialist) League. As a result of these discussions the name was yet again changed, to the Liberal Imperialist League, and Grey became President instead of Lord Brassey. Haldane was to help Perks with organization, and William Allard, a top Liberal agent and secretary of Harcourt's Home Counties Liberal Federation, was to be secretary.[4]

Haldane thought 'we have burned our boats', and he therefore devoted much energy to setting the L.I.L. on its feet.[5] Despite the work of Perks and his keen but inexperienced young men, the organization was in poor shape. Gladstone thought that 'in point of activity & organising power up to the present time the "League of Liberals" has been far ahead of the Imperial Liberals. While the latter have been talking the League has been acting.'[6] A chief difficulty was the lack of an effective proselytizer. Neither Brassey, the first President, nor his successor, Sir Edward Grey, was a major national figure, and they had little influence in the

[1] *Daily Chronicle*, 25 Sept. 1901.

[2] The result was Rattigan, 5,673; Harmsworth, 4,769; Smillie, 2,900.

[3] Bannerman was unrepentant, writing to D. Crawford: 'I am thoroughly delighted this Harmsworth man is not in: I abhor hoc genus omne: rather Smillie, smell he never so highly' (1 Oct. 1901, CBP 52517, n.f.).

[4] Perks to Rosebery, 3 Nov. 1901, RP, box 39. Under angry pressure from Gladstone, Allard withdrew until Feb. 1902.

[5] Haldane to Rosebery, 6 Nov. 1901, RP, box 24.

[6] Gladstone to Rosebery, copy, 13 Dec. 1901, HGP 45986, f. 44; the 'League of Liberals' was the Little England organization.

constituencies. Asquith, though not yet a member of the L.I.L., but since the July 1901 dinner the apparent leader of the Imperialist M.P.s, was at his best in the Commons. Haldane recognized that 'it is a hard fact that H.H.A. does not magnetise the public. It is one of our chief difficulties . . .' Asquith's ability lay in what Haldane called 'the work of clear explanation'; he never attempted the emotional heights of Chamberlain and Rosebery.[1] When Chamberlain died, Asquith said of him that he was 'not only a combination of unusual gifts, but what is rarer still, a new type of personality . . . the pioneer of a new generation'.[2] On the political stage Asquith never tried to mirror this personality; it was certainly not his own.

Progressive isolation and dependence on Rosebery

As all Liberal Imperialists knew, Rosebery was the only man who could get their movement off the ground. The possibility, slight though it seemed, that Rosebery would return to party politics was sufficient to maintain the loyalty of his supporters, despite all his peculiarities. During August and September 1901, he had drifted away from the Asquith committee.[3] In September and October his insomnia returned, itself a sign of his perplexity. For Rosebery, all the old difficulties about his position remained. However, there were some new factors; Rosebery's attempts to end the war by a compromise peace in July 1901 were not generally known, and neither was the thinking behind them.[4] During the Asquith committee's October campaign, which Rosebery had said would decide his position, the details of 'efficiency' had been expounded with clarity, but no major impact had been made on the party or the nation.[5] Rosebery therefore announced on 6 November 1901 his intention to speak to the Chesterfield Liberal Association. Liberal Imperialists

[1] Haldane to Mother, 22 Nov. 1901, Hal P 5966, f. 149.

[2] 5 H, lxiv. 847 (6 July 1914).

[3] See Haldane's complaint to Rosebery, 11 Nov. 1901, RP, box 24, that he was getting 'all personal news through Winston Churchill & McCrae'.

[4] See James, pp. 427–9.

[5] See Rosebery to C. B. Harmsworth, 7 Oct. 1901, RP, Letter Book. Rosebery considered another public letter, calling for a coalition government, but Spender recommended a speech (Spender to Rosebery, 8 Oct. 1901, RP, box 76).

were delighted, though a little apprehensive. Rosebery speeches were unpredictable, and it was vital that the speech should be a success, and should support their general position. A failure or a repudiation could make their political position absurd.

Rosebery's announcement encouraged the L.I.L. organizers to renewed effort in what Morley called their 'desperate push to the front'.[1] The members of the L.I.L. were in a tight corner. The General Council of the Scottish Liberal Association gave 'strenuous and unreserved support' to Campbell-Bannerman's leadership, an exuberance of terminology which Gibson-Carmichael, the Roseberian President, was unable to moderate.[2] Much worse, the N.L.F. Derby meeting early in December 1901 passed resolutions on the concentration camps which the *Chronicle* regarded as a call for 'another Majuba settlement'.[3] During the summer of 1901 the stalemate position at the February 1901 N.L.F. elections had been clearly resolved against the Liberal Imperialists. The effect of the Derby resolution, Harcourt thought, was that 'CB is finally fixed in the motor machine of the Party and Perks & Co will find it impossible to displace him.'[4] The best that the Imperialists could hope for was to consolidate the L.I.L. as a haven in the event of a split.[5] The initiative had been lost to the pro-Boers and the L.I.L. returned to its original function as a defensive organization.

Haldane tried, too late, to whip up support for the L.I.L. Grey, who was nominally its President, contributed nothing to it but his name; indeed, Herbert Gladstone thought Haldane had gained such intellectual dominance over Grey that Grey had become 'his "chela" [disciple]'.[6] The L.I.L. was too weak and had too murky a past to attract many M.P.s, but there was one major success. Asquith and Fowler

---

[1] Morley to Harcourt, 3 Oct. 1901, HP.
[2] S.L.A. Minute Book, 25 Oct. 1901, Edinburgh University Library.
[3] *Daily Chronicle*, 5 Dec. 1901.
[4] Harcourt to Morley, 8 Dec. 1901, HP.
[5] The other side was also aware of the plaintiff/defendant ploy; Harcourt told Morley: 'The great thing is so to manœuvre that if the split is to come it shall be made by them and not by us' (26 Nov. 1901, HP).
[6] Gladstone to Bannerman, 6 Dec. 1901, CBP 41216, f. 164.

became honorary members on 25 November 1901, Asquith hoping to continue his hitherto successful policy of leading the Imperialists to keep them within the Liberal party.[1]

Thus in November 1901, Grey, Haldane, Asquith, and Fowler stood at the head of a sectional organization which had some money, some views, but few followers. They had trapped themselves in a corner. In the early days of the war they had adopted an individualistic pose, separate from their party, but disorganized. When they tried to co-operate during the various crises in 1900 and 1901, their haphazard planning and lack of co-ordination mocked their claim that Liberal Imperialism was the predominant partner within the party. They had, through their own lack of resolution and by the unexpected prolongation of the war, lost the initiative to a body of youthful enthusiasts with even less political judgement than their own. Amongst the senior men only Perks had shown consistency and control in his political actions. But Perks was of insufficient stature to achieve substantial results.

Asquith, Grey, and Haldane found themselves, therefore, in charge of an organization which had already failed in most of its initiatives, yet in a situation in which this already partially discredited organization might prove to be their only political hope. Their standing in the party was low; they had little to offer to the Unionists or to a coalition, should there be a schism within the Liberal party. In this gloomy situation they relied upon Rosebery to bail them out. Rosebery had so often disappointed them, and 'what Lord R may say we do not know.'[2] Whatever he said was vital for them, for 'it is a very serious time in public affairs, & much turns upon Chesterfield.'[3]

---

[1] Asquith remained in contact with Bannerman, without commenting on his apostasy (Asquith to Bannerman, 4 Dec. 1901, CBP 41210, f. 211).

[2] Haldane to Mother, 12 Dec. 1901, Hal P 5966, f. 183.

[3] Haldane to Mother, 14 Dec. 1901, Hal P 5966, f. 187.

III

THE RISE AND FALL OF THE LIBERAL LEAGUE

Chesterfield and the formation of the Liberal League

'SIX weeks of fuss and of genuine enjoyment: never did any one get so much out of the penny-a-liners before', wrote Campbell-Bannerman, sardonically awaiting the '4th or 5th Advent of a new Messiah'.[1] Public discussion of the probable content of the speech to be delivered on 16 December 1901 was equalled by interest in the physical preparations, such as the special train organized by Perks to transport reporters and M.P.s from London. There was no doubt that Rosebery remained unsurpassed—though perhaps equalled by Chamberlain—as a political entertainer. But many Liberals feared, and some hoped, that the speech would not match the excitement of the occasion.

Rosebery received advice on what to say from 'the whole human race, headed by Canon MacColl',[2] but the only advice he solicited was that of Perks. Perks urged him not to 'shake the authority' of Milner, as Asquith, Grey, Fowler, and Haldane were 'very anxious on this point', and suggested Lincoln's second Inaugural as an appropriate text.[3]

Rosebery ignored both Perks's suggestions, and in the first part of the speech repeated the demand for a reform of the Liberal party which had been the central theme of his speeches since becoming Prime Minister in 1894. He discussed the condition of the Liberal party, the need for the 'clean slate' and for Liberal association with 'the new sentiment of Empire which occupies the nation'.[4] Rosebery

---

[1] Bannerman to Crawford, 16 Dec. 1901, CBP 52517, n.f.
[2] Rosebery to Spender, 13 Nov. 1901, SP 46387, f. 47.
[3] Perks to Rosebery, 6 and 10 Dec. 1901, RP, box 39.
[4] Rosebery, *National Policy* (1901), the approved version, preface dated 25 Dec. 1901; most press reports omit the passage on 'methods of barbarism'.

denounced 'Tory Liberals', and sketched the development of liberalism along the lines of 'efficiency', with special reference to defence, commerce, and industry, and the 'physical degeneracy of our race'. He attacked the general incompetence of the government, declaring that 'the nation that cannot produce an alternative to the present government is more fit to control allotments than an Empire'.

The concluding part of the speech dealt with the war. Rosebery gave various reasons for the need for a swift end to the war, of which the situation within South Africa was the least important.[1] He condemned the phrase 'methods of barbarism', but accepted the N.L.F. resolution on the camps. He required the retention of both Chamberlain and Milner, but thought 'the Boers can make peace with Lord Kitchener.' To make peace, he was ready to recognize the Transvaal government-in-exile in Holland, though the Boers had to make the first move. Rosebery explicitly sided with Kitchener rather than Milner on the subject of amnesty. In conclusion, he appealed to 'the tribunal of public opinion and common sense'.

This formidable utterance was at first generally welcomed by all Liberals. On the war, in particular, Rosebery's appeal to 'common sense', and his obvious flexibility, seemed to straddle the muddied ruts into which most Liberals had fallen. It was not at first noticed that the main bulk of the speech dealt with topics like the 'clean slate' which, when previously discussed, had aroused a chorus of Liberal indignation.

For the Liberal Imperialists, the speech saved the situation. Haldane felt 'like those at Kimberley when General French with his 10,000 of cavalry suddenly appeared on the horizon and swept to the relief of the besieged'. Chesterfield 'transformed the situation by simply inverting it' in the Imperialists' favour,[2] in the sense that within the Liberal party 'the presumption is now with us, not against us.'[3] This was an exaggeration, but it was certainly true that Rosebery could appeal at this time to a wider spectrum of Liberal

1 See below, p. 185, for these reasons.
2 Haldane to Rosebery, 16 Dec. 1901, RP, box 24.
3 Haldane to Mother, 19 Dec. 1901, Hal P 5966, f. 195.

opinion than Asquith or Grey, and that at Chesterfield he seemed to have made a successful appeal for unity which regained the initiative for the Liberal Imperialist group.

The Liberal Imperialists in the Commons had no option but to abandon aspects of their detailed position on the war. Though they had moved away from Milner's policy of 'unconditional surrender', there was an obvious difference in tone between the Chesterfield speech and the much less flexible public position of Grey and Haldane. On the platform at Chesterfield and at subsequent meetings they strenuously denied suggestions that Rosebery's views differed substantially from their own.[1] They pointed out that there might be points of 'minor importance' which conflicted with comments 'in the innumerable speeches' which they as 'working politicians' had to make, but claimed 'to be prepared to sacrifice that which is unimportant to that which is fundamental' on the war issue.[2] They laid stress on the first part of the Chesterfield speech, dealing with the party, as 'the most important part of his speech', and drew attention to the similarity of Rosebery's views on 'efficiency' with those of their own campaign of October 1901.[3]

In private, the committee reacted very variously. Grey recognized the weakness of his position:

To the other side we are the trimmers, to our own side we are hated; and there remains for us now nothing, but to cling to the faint hope that the genius of Rosebery may succeed in redeeming a party which seems past redemption.[4]

Though in this weak position, Grey wrote long, extremely intemperate letters to Campbell-Bannerman and Gladstone, demanding that Campbell-Bannerman should 'for the sake of union take the Rosebery point of view'; if he did not, the Reform Club compact of July 1901 would be abolished and 'with it on my part the recognition of C-B's leadership'.[5] To

[1] Grey told Spender that suggestions of a discrepancy between his and Rosebery's position were 'the most damnable misconstruction' (21 Dec. 1901, SP 46389, f. 1).
[2] Asquith in Hanley, The Times, 15 Jan. 1902.
[3] Ibid. See also Asquith in Wolverhampton, The Times, 20 Dec. 1901; Grey in Newcastle, The Times, 8 Jan. 1902.
[4] Grey to Spender, 21 Dec. 1901, SP 46389, f. 1.
[5] Grey to Gladstone, 24 Dec. 1901, HGP 45992, f. 81.

his nominal leader, Grey made the unqualified statement that 'if . . . you and he [Rosebery] decide that you cannot cooperate, I must say this also, and that I go with him.'[1] Grey stated this position without reference to his position as President of the Liberal Imperialist League, and, as he told Gladstone and Campbell-Bannerman, without consulting Rosebery, whom he had not seen for a political talk for some time.

Haldane's reaction was, as usual, organizational. He accepted that there were differences on policy, and wrote to Milner, explaining these away by arguing that 'it was part of his [Rosebery's] art that by being critical he has detached the centre Liberals from CB . . . and made continuity of policy an assured thing.'[2] To capitalize quickly on this new political strength, Haldane visited Mentmore to urge Rosebery to action. He found Rosebery, as always, 'not easy & I had my work cut out & am not sure that I did much good.'[3] Despite this disappointment, Haldane and Ferguson went to Glasgow in January 1902 to begin a new organization, the 'Scottish National Liberals', which was to be unconnected with the rather discredited L.I.L. It was to be organized in suitably receptive localities, its policy being based on the Chesterfield speech and on opposition to the Home Rule Bills of 1886 and 1893.[4]

As usual, there was a struggle for Asquith's support. Rosebery ensured his attendance at Chesterfield by explicitly asking him to come.[5] At Chesterfield and on 18 December, Asquith generally endorsed Rosebery's views.[6] But though an honorary member of the L.I.L., Asquith had joined the sectional organization at the last moment, and his active participation in a new Roseberian organization could not be guaranteed.

Campbell-Bannerman was ready enough to accept Grey's

---

[1] Grey to Bannerman, 2 Jan. 1902, AP 10, f. 43. C-B thought this 'd—d egotism and impertinence' (to Harcourt, 2 Jan. 1902, HP 9).

[2] Haldane to Milner, 22 Dec. 1901, MP 39, f. 164.

[3] Haldane to Mother, 24 Dec. 1901, Hal P 5966, f. 203.

[4] Haldane to Rosebery, 3 Jan. 1902, RP, box 24; this later became the Glasgow and West of Scotland Liberal League branch.

[5] See Asquith to Rosebery, 4 Dec. 1901, RP, box 1.

[6] Asquith in Wolverhampton, The Times, 20 Dec. 1901.

defection from the Liberal party, but felt rightly that 'Asquith is the man of real importance', and asked Gladstone to find out Asquith's position.[1] Gladstone already had satisfactory communications with Asquith; each worked on his respective chief to moderate his attitude. But Asquith, though he sympathized with Gladstone 'in these accumulated & unmerited "ructions"', spoke clearly as a member of the Rosebery group. He refused an invitation to appear publicly with Campbell-Bannerman, and he strongly condemned Campbell-Bannerman's 'fatal blunder in tactics' in not immediately endorsing Rosebery's peace policy.[2] Rosebery arranged a meeting with Asquith in early January 1902 to plan political development, but in public Asquith continued to stress that he was a 'party man'.[3] He made no hints about 'new movements', and declared: 'I was brought up in the Liberal party, and in the Liberal party I intend to remain.'[4] Rosebery's return—if such it was—meant that Asquith's policy of leading in order to control was much more difficult, for he was no longer the leader.

Campbell-Bannerman visited Rosebery on 23 December 1901. He claimed to have asked Rosebery to 'cooperate and consult', and to have had his overtures rebuffed;[5] Rosebery mentions no actual proposals.[6] It is clear from both accounts of the interview that it was Ireland, and not South Africa, which formed the main point of policy disagreement.[7] The effect of the visit was to spoil the post-Chesterfield unity which had been felt throughout the party. The dispute about Ireland meant that Liberal Imperialism would not end with the war. As news of the conversation spread, the taking of sides again seemed necessary.

Haldane's impression that Rosebery would not move was false. For once, Rosebery was intent on action. In the preface to *National Policy* he declared that 'public opinion, to be effective, must be organized', and called for 'spadework on

---

[1] Bannerman to Gladstone, 6 Jan. 1902, HGP 45988, f. 6.
[2] Asquith to Gladstone, 28 Dec. 1901 and 5 Jan. 1902, HGP 45989, ff. 53–7.
[3] Rosebery to Haldane, 6 Jan. 1902, Hal P 5905, f. 156.
[4] Asquith, *The Times*, 20 Dec. 1901.
[5] See *Bannerman*, ii. 16–18.
[6] Rosebery memorandum, 23 Dec. 1901, in Crewe, ii. 573–4.
[7] See below, p. 276.

behalf of this policy'.[1] He encouraged young Liberals to activity,[2] and agreed to address a meeting in the Albert Hall in February 1902 when 'the Lib. Imperial League should change its name etc.'[3] In mid January, Asquith, Grey, Haldane, and Perks had a series of meetings, and on 14 January 1902 Rosebery met Grey, Haldane, and Perks, and with them drew up the main lines of the 'Liberal League', and decided upon its name. Rosebery was 'leading with his coat off'.[4]

The Liberal Imperialists hoped to maintain their strengthened position within the party by action both at Westminster and in the constituencies. In the Commons, it was decided in January 1902 to agree to a unity amendment, similar to the moderate Fitzmaurice amendment of February 1900. Asquith, in consultation with Rosebery and his friends, negotiated the amendment with Campbell-Bannerman.[5] The Cawley amendment conciliated the Imperialists in its preamble which supported the prosecution of the war, and the rest of the party in its resolution which called for a swift peace.[6] But at the last moment, following a moderate speech by Chamberlain, the Imperialists decided 'not to vote tonight—Lord R takes this view—but also not to speak'.[7] Thus, on the vote on Cawley's amendment, Campbell-Bannerman carried 123 Liberals with him, including Fowler. Most senior Imperialists abstained with a few Little Englanders, but the junior men and Fowler went with the party leader.[8] This was political manœuvring at its most inept. By silently abstaining on an important amendment to which they had agreed a few days previously, they appeared deceitful in their loyalty and absurd in their judgement, for,

---

[1] Preface, 25 Dec. 1901, to *National Policy*. Bannerman regarded the preface as 'a declaration of war' (to Harcourt, 2 Jan. 1902, HP).

[2] Rosebery to C. P. Trevelyan, 25 Dec. 1901, RP, Letter Book.

[3] Haldane to Asquith, 5 Jan. 1902, AP 10, f. 49.

[4] Haldane to Mother, 15 Jan. 1902, Hal P 5967, f. 9; Perks to Rosebery, 13 Jan. 1902, RP, box 40.

[5] Asquith to Bannerman, 16 Jan. 1902, CBP 41210, f. 219.

[6] 4 H, ci. 335 (20 Jan. 1902).

[7] Haldane to Mother, 21 Jan. 1902, Hal P 5967, f. 19.

[8] The *Daily Chronicle* noted only Grey, Asquith, Haldane, Perks, J. L. Walton, Douglas, Freeman-Thomas, L. Harmsworth, and Emmott as abstaining Imperialists (22 Jan. 1902).

far from having swung the 'presumption' within the party in their favour, they seemed to be left with a tiny number of supporters. Campbell-Bannerman had retained the initiative despite Chesterfield, and, at least numerically, had improved his position. As Morley had predicted in December, 'they are such babies in intrigue that they may be on the rocks before they know it, and without intending it'.[1]

Constituency activity began with Rosebery's speech at Liverpool in February. The committee awaited the speech with some apprehension, Haldane telling Milner: 'I rather quake over what he may say as to things outside the war— He is too fond of surprising his friends!'[2] The speech was to deal with domestic topics, and the committee doubtless hoped for an endorsement of the 'step-by-step' Irish policy they had outlined in October 1901. In his speech, Rosebery went much further than this on Ireland, and made it clear that the application of the 'clean slate' to Liberal domestic policy was his main task for the future.[3]

Campbell-Bannerman had already told Rosebery to define his position as regards the party, and on 19 February he denounced Rosebery's 'clean slate' both as a philosophical concept and as a practical possibility.[4] Rosebery responded rapidly by announcing his 'definite separation' in a letter to *The Times*, declaring himself 'outside his [C-B's] tabernacle, but not, I think, in solitude'.[5] As usual, Rosebery had plumped for the dramatic gesture, and this one was hardly likely to win the support of the party centre for which the committee hoped. Rosebery's letter was sent without any consultation with his friends. Some, however, welcomed it. For Grey, it was 'a great relief to see the "status quo" broken up', the end of 'a nightmare of futility'. Two younger M.P.s, J. Fuller and R. Vaile, saw the letter as a hopeful move towards a new party.[6] Haldane, however, now inured

---

[1] Morley to Harcourt, 12 Dec. 1901, HP.

[2] Haldane to Milner, 26 Jan. 1902, MP 40, f. 121.

[3] Rosebery in Liverpool, 14 Feb. 1902, LLP 3.

[4] Bannerman in London, *The Times*, 14 Jan. 1902, and in Leicester, 19 Feb. 1902 (*Bannerman*, ii. 27–9).

[5] Rosebery to the Editor, *The Times*, 21 Feb. 1902.

[6] Grey to Rosebery, 22 Feb. 1902, RP, box 23; J. Fuller and R. Vaile to Rosebery, 20 and 22 Feb. 1902, RP, box 106.

to Rosebery's unreliability, feared some further violent proclamation, and nervously advised that 'it will be best to leave the centre men in the H of C to make up their own minds.'[1]

Despite Rosebery's uncertain political position, Asquith, Grey, and Haldane immediately joined him in launching the already projected Liberal League. The League was founded at a meeting in Rosebery's London house on 24 February 1902.[2] At the meeting Rosebery warned M.P.s present that there were 'one or two prominent careers . . . which might be gravely affected by the course they took', since 'he stood on a very thin edge and that in fact there was little to separate him from the Liberal Unionists, more especially if they pursued a Liberal domestic policy'. Rosebery made no clear statement of the function of the League, apart from its duty to promulgate the Chesterfield policy. Asquith, who followed Rosebery, denied that there was a personal problem, and said

he was of opinion that the MPs who agreed with Lord R should not allow themselves to be drummed out of the Liberal party by Sir H. C. B., but should remain in the House of Commons without forming a separate organisation, though acting in connection on important questions.

Asquith was thus trying to preserve the *status quo*, 'without . . . a separate organisation'. 'In fact,' he said, 'he would not disturb the existing situation.' Rosebery replied by drawing attention to 'that floating opinion which decides elections', and said that unless some organization was founded, his supporters in the constituencies would be disappointed. Following this, the start of the League was 'cordially and unanimously' agreed to. Rosebery was President, with Asquith, Grey, and Fowler Vice-Presidents, joined by Haldane in 1905. Freeman-Thomas and J. M. Paulton were joint Secretaries, and Perks was Treasurer.

[1] Haldane to Rosebery, 21 Feb. 1902, RP, box 24.
[2] See minutes kept by Waterfield, Rosebery's secretary, in RP, box 106, from which quotations in this paragraph are taken. Present were: Rosebery, Lord Durham (brother of H. Lambton and a lapsed Unionist), Grey, Asquith, Perks, J. L. Walton, C. M. Douglas, Ferguson, E. T. Cook, and Haldane (who came in at the end of the meeting). Fowler was not present but was reliable, despite his vote on the Cawley amendment (Fowler to Rosebery, 23 Feb. 1902, RP, box 106).

The vagueness about the function of the League, apparent at its inaugural meeting, soon led to public controversy in the Liberal Imperialist League, whose members were expected to form the bulk of the Liberal League membership.[1] A committee meeting of the L.I.L. was held on 25 February 1902. According to Heber Hart, Grey, as President, made a statement at this meeting suggesting that the Liberal League was in some sense the formation of a new party, and that it might run its own candidates.[2] In reply, Hart read a letter from W. S. Robson, M.P., L.I.L. Vice-President, which attacked 'Rosebery's impetuous letter of definite separation . . . which shows an astounding want of appreciation of the conditions of modern party organisation'.[3] Hart said he agreed with every word of Robson's angry letter, and he resigned as Chairman of the L.I.L. Hart's position was repudiated by 'Raphael, Grieg, Waterfield & several others', and the committee adjourned.[4]

The inauguration of the League was made public on 26 February. Its start gave the appearance of haste, confusion, and a general lack of panache. *The Times* did not even think it worthy of an immediate leader. The *Chronicle* welcomed the brief announcement 'with equal relief and satisfaction', but had no story to catch the public interest.[5] A few days later the League called upon defunct constituency organizations to revive themselves on the lines of Chesterfield, and 'to identify themselves with the Liberal League'.[6] This seemed to suggest a campaign to capture the local organizations.

The function of the League remained unclear, and the extent of the identification of its members with Rosebery's 'definite separation' was also unknown. Asquith countered his defeat of 24 February (when he had tried to persuade the meeting at Rosebery's house not to start the League at

[1] As Perks told Rosebery: 'We must be careful how we deal with the Lib. Imps . . . we must not alienate them' (24 Feb. 1902, RP, box 40).

[2] See H. L. Hart, *Reminiscences and Reflections* (1939), pp. 225–30 for Hart's account, confirmed by Perks to Rosebery, 25 Feb. 1902, RP, box 40.

[3] Robson to Hart, n.d., Hart, op. cit., p. 228; M.P.s present were Grey, Haldane, Ferguson, Perks, Freeman-Thomas, A. Brand, Fuller.

[4] Perks to Rosebery, 25 Feb. 1902, RP, box 40.

[5] *Daily Chronicle*, 27 Feb. 1902.

[6] Ibid., 3 Mar. 1902.

all) by writing to his constituency chairman and narrowing the scope of the League to that of a propaganda organization. The League was formed, Asquith wrote, 'not for the purpose of developing and inflaming differences, but to press forward Liberal work in the country upon the lines and in the spirit of Chesterfield'.[1] This was a clear antidote to 'definite separation' from the party organization. On questions of policy, however, Asquith followed Rosebery. In the doctrine of 'the clean slate' Asquith recognized 'the same doctrine which I have preached to you for years past in less picturesque language, the doctrine of selection and concentration'; he went further than he had before on Ireland, and repeated the need for 'efficiency'.[2] Asquith's letter was a formidable blow to Campbell-Bannerman's personal authority, but, given that Asquith had decided to join the League, it was as conciliatory as the circumstances allowed, and made it clear that the League members were not in 'definite separation'.

On 3 March, the L.I.L. committee reconvened, and following a letter of invitation by Rosebery to join the League, read out by Grey, the committee recommended self-dissolution and subsequent joining of the Liberal League, a recommendation confirmed at the last L.I.L. meeting on 10 March.[3] Despite Heber Hart's efforts, most L.I.L. members joined the League.

The founding of the Liberal League did not produce any immediate improvement in the Imperialists' position in the Commons. Hamilton saw 'no great flocking of persons to the Rosebery standard',[4] and Campbell-Bannerman was undismayed, finding that 'the League is laughed at in the H of Commons, very few joining . . . R seems universally condemned.'[5] In the constituencies, however, prospects were brighter. Robertson Nicoll, editor of the influential, nonconformist *British Weekly*, was confident that 'both in England and Scotland, Nonconformists are very largely

[1] Asquith to Scott, *The Times*, 3 Mar. 1902.
[2] Ibid. See below, pp. 274, 278–9, for Asquith's Irish views.
[3] Rosebery to Grey, 28 Feb. 1902, RP, Letter Book; *Daily Chronicle*, 4 and 11 Mar. 1902.
[4] EHD, 3 Mar. 1902.
[5] Bannerman to J. B. Smith, 1 Mar. 1902, CBP 46388, f. 46.

with you [Rosebery].' Harold Harmsworth, Rosebery's
London neighbour, promised the support of his provincial
papers, especially that of the *Leeds Mercury* and the *Glasgow
Herald*, and proposed starting a League paper in
Edinburgh.[1]

After Chesterfield, Haldane was careful to keep the
Webbs informed of developments, and Beatrice noted in
February that 'we are at present very thick with the
"Limps".' The Webbs were still cautious about this relationship, feeling that Haldane 'has to some extent manipu-
lated us into this position', and their identification with the
League should not be overstressed.[2] They were, however,
keen about Chesterfield, intrigued by Rosebery's character,
and Sidney joined the literature committee of the League.[3]
The League seemed to offer the best chance for permeating
the Liberal party with collectivist thinking.

The vagueness about the League's purpose and policy
was in some respects a source of strength, for it allowed
Fabians, nonconformists, and the *Daily Mail* to rally under
one banner. Its nebulous early position was well defined in
the *New Liberal Review*, a Liberal Imperialist magazine
edited by Cecil and Leicester Harmsworth: 'It is more than
a rift but less than a fission . . . The slate has not broken; it
has laminated. Lord Rosebery is outside the tabernacle but
inside Liberalism.'[4]

Rosebery attempted to bring together these diffuse
elements in his speech in Glasgow on 10 March 1902. He
made it clear that the League appealed to the 'many . . . who
have not touched politics for many years', and offered to
these 'a new departure'. The new departure was partly
negative—opposition to Home Rule—but largely positive:
'not measures of emancipation, but measures of construction', of which the greatest was to be 'efficiency, because it
combines them all'.[5] Rosebery thus laid stress on the fresh,

[1] R. Nicoll and H. Harmsworth to Rosebery, 5 Mar. and 22 Feb. 1902, RP, box 106.
[2] B. Webb, *Our Partnership*, pp. 226–8 (28 Feb. 1902).
[3] See B. Webb to Haldane, 17 Dec. 1901, RP, box 24: 'It [Chesterfield] changes
the situation from one of gloom to one of great hopefulness . . . the speech seemed
to me almost perfect.'
[4] 'The Liberal League', by 'M.P.' in *New Liberal Review*, Apr. 1902.
[5] Rosebery in Glasgow, 10 Mar. 1902, LLP 3.

ideological, 'efficiency' approach to liberalism; he barely
mentioned the organization aspects of the League. The
latter were to some extent clarified by Asquith who, having
said that he had been 'slow and reluctant' to join the League,
defined its organizational function as 'machinery for inter-
communication, for counsel, and, if need be, for concerted
action' on behalf of the 'efficiency' programme.[1]

The organization and manifesto of the Liberal League

The summer of 1902 saw the Liberal League off to a
reasonably satisfactory start. Allard, the Home Counties secretary, was eventually recruited and planned the organization
with Haldane and Perks. Although the object of the League
was to attract popularity for the policy of 'efficiency', it was
not intended to be a popular movement. At first £1,000 per
annum was the basic subscription, and in 1902, £9,916.
3s. 10d. was raised, there being only eight or nine subscribers.[2] Of this, some £2,500 per annum was spent on
permanent staff, and some £2,300 on propaganda and by-
elections, the remainder going into a general fund. Allard
ran the London office in Victoria Street. There were three
permanent regional agents, Stores in Lancashire, Skinner in
Yorkshire, and Bass in the southern counties. In addition to
these there were twenty Liberal association agents in various
districts who were paid ten guineas per annum to act as
'correspondents'.[3] These agents were either to start local
branches of the League, or to keep the League's views
prominent in their associations without founding separate
branches.

The most effective of the local branches was the Glasgow
and West of Scotland Liberal League branch. The League
there found a ready response to its views, and Maclay, of the
Glasgow branch, told Rosebery: 'there are comparatively
few Liberals who do not appear to agree with the League's
aims.'[4] Glasgow, with its empire-orientated economy, was

---

[1] Asquith in St. Leonards, *The Times*, 15 Mar. 1902.
[2] Perks to Rosebery, 21 May 1903, RP, box 40. Most members were non-
subscribers.
[3] Perks to Rosebery, 16 May 1903, RP, box 40.
[4] Maclay to Rosebery, 19 June 1902, RP, box 106.

well known for its imperialism.[1] Grey and Haldane went there to raise support for their cause in October 1899, and Haldane went to Glasgow immediately after Chesterfield to start his 'Scottish National Liberals' scheme. As Hector Macpherson, scourge of the League in Edinburgh, noted, the Imperialists 'astutely sought an alliance between trade and Imperialism' in the west.[2]

Liberals in Edinburgh and the east generally were much more hostile to imperialism.[3] Macpherson, editor of the Edinburgh *Evening News*, and the Young Scots group consistently attacked imperialist ideas, and there was considerable doubt as to whether an Edinburgh branch could be successfully launched.[4] After much discussion, a small branch was started in July 1902, as it was felt that the League could not go completely unrepresented on Rosebery's home ground. Rosebery devoted more time and thought to this branch than to any other aspect of League organization.

The Scottish branches were the main independent local organizations; the League had no organization in Wales, and in England local meetings were mostly organized through local Liberal associations. Rosebery specifically warned Liberals not to leave their associations, but to stay on and permeate them.[5]

The other main League organization was the London branch, which M.P.s and political celebrities were encouraged to join. The council, the League's executive body, was appointed, not elected. Its membership reflected the wide range of Liberal opinion to which the League hoped to appeal, and an analysis of those attending its first meeting, in October 1902, indicates both the potential and the weaknesses of the League membership.[6] Rosebery, Grey,

[1] H. Pelling, *Popular Politics*, p. 86.
[2] H. Macpherson, 'Scottish Liberalism, Past and Present', *The Speaker*, 6 June 1903.
[3] Most of the 'pro-Boer' resolutions in the S.L.A. came from eastern associations (S.L.A. Minute Book, *passim*, Edinburgh University Library).
[4] Carmichael to Rosebery, 28 June 1902, RP, box 106.
[5] Rosebery in Glasgow, 10 Mar. 1902, LLP 3.
[6] *The Times*, 25 Oct. 1902; the Council's representative nature can be seen from the attendance at the first League dinner, on 31 July 1902, with sixteen M.P.s and twenty candidates; see LLP 20.

Asquith, Haldane, and Sidney Webb represented the
collectivist wing of the Liberal party. They were supported
on the council by a number of Fabian-minded young M.P.s
and candidates: Paulton, Freeman-Thomas, Lawson Walton,
Rufus Isaacs, and Emmott, and by William Allard, the best
Liberal agent of his day. The second group comprised
wealthy landowning and more traditionally minded Liberals:
Lords Brassey and Arran, Sir Thomas Glen-Coats, and,
though not Council members, Sir Charles Tennant and later
the Duke of Sutherland. Though men like these supported
the League for its 'patriotism', they showed little enthusiasm
for its collectivism. The third group were the nonconformists: Fowler, Perks, and the Revd. Reginald Campbell, all
methodists, and the Revd. J. Guinness Rogers, a well-known
congregationalist. These agreed on imperialism, but were
split on collectivism. Campbell, Rogers and, less enthusi-
astically, Fowler represented the 'forward movement' which
linked nonconformity with social reform and even considerable class realignment. Perks, on the other hand, while he
wanted nonconformity to be politically strong, wished it to
be so to safeguard traditional nonconformity as anti-
anglican, self-reliant, and, on the whole, hostile to state
intervention.

The fourth group were the journalists: Wemyss Reid,
E. T. Cook, and Leicester and Cecil Harmsworth, though
the last did not attend the council meeting. Cook, Reid,
Cecil Harmsworth, Sidney Webb, and F. W. Maude made
up the literature committee of the League, which produced
some two hundred pamphlets by 1906.

These four groups were characteristic of the support the
council got from rank-and-file Leaguers.[1] The League
leaders had effectively used the subject of 'sane imperialism'
to unite in one body otherwise very disparate Liberals.
Whether its membership could be sufficiently reconciled to
work together for 'efficiency' would depend very much on
the quality of leadership and consistency of purpose shown
by Rosebery. He certainly had a good supply of wealth,
intelligence, and influence on which to draw.

During 1902 the League thus became organizationally

[1] See Appendix II.

quite well established, with a basis for future development laid both at Westminster and in the constituencies. The question of the League's policy presented more difficulties. A good deal of trouble was taken over the League's manifesto, and a number of memoranda were submitted.[1] The manifesto produced by Rosebery in May 1902 was, however, a disappointing document.[2] It omitted most of the specific suggestions contained in the preliminary drafts, and merely repeated the main points of the Chesterfield speech, on non-South African matters, without developing them. The manifesto dealt almost entirely with domestic questions, and made it clear that the League took 'efficiency' as its criterion for action.

The League's lack of detailed proposals reflected the general Liberal difficulty at this time of agreeing about specific policies—but it was exactly this lack of unity in the Liberal party which its founders wished the League to eliminate. Instead of solving the Liberals' policy problems—'politicians in search of a cry', as Chamberlain called them[3]—the League mirrored within itself Liberal disunity and lack of purpose.

The main reason for this nebulous policy was the failure of Rosebery to give a clear and positive lead to his supporters. It was certainly very difficult to produce a detailed policy which wealthy, landowning members, Fabians and young Fabian-minded M.P.s, and nonconformists would accept. As Beatrice Webb observed, 'as for the rank and file, they are a most heterogeneous lot, bound together by their *dislikes*, and not by their positive convictions.'[4] The application of 'efficiency', which the League leaders undoubtedly wished to develop, which implied an expansion of the power of the state, was particularly unpopular with the landowners who paid the League's subscriptions, such as Sutherland and

[1] For Asquith's memorandum (n.d., RP, box 106), see Appendix III.

[2] Liberal League Manifesto, May 1902, LLP; for Rosebery's drafts see RP box 106.

[3] See Butler, p. 288.

[4] B. Webb, *Our Partnership*, p. 231 (19 Mar. 1902). The Webbs soon became impatient at the League leaders' failure to cajole their followers into a more positive declaration of 'efficiency', finding Asquith 'wooden' and 'slack', Grey 'slight' and a 'mere dilettante', Perks 'an unclean beast', and Rosebery 'an enigma'; ibid., pp. 226–31. Webb, however, remained on the council and on the literature committee.

Sir Charles Tennant, who joined the League because of its anti-Home Rule stance. But it was for the reconciliation of such disparate views that the League, with Rosebery as its President, had been founded.

Rosebery always appeared above the throng; it was the assumption of his followers that, being above it, he was also superior to it in potential leadership. Rosebery had always used the absence of formal political support as his reason for inactivity; he now had this support in the form of the League. It was now up to him to prove that Haldane had been wrong in 1895 to say Rosebery 'wanted to be a Pitt, but ended in being a Goderich'.[1] His first moves as President of the League had not been auspicious.

Education: a suitable case for 'efficiency'?

The Education Bill of 1902 was the first major challenge to the League in its attempt to educate the Liberal party towards using the criterion of 'efficiency' in its judgement of policies.[2] Liberal Imperialists claimed to regard educational reform as a top priority in their campaign to restore Britain's economic strength, and, though they had voted with the rest of the party against the abortive 1896 Education Bill, Campbell-Bannerman thought the League might support the Bill of 1902.[3] His opinion was sensible enough. If the Liberal Imperialists applied their declared criterion of 'efficiency' and the suspension of individual rights in the face of national needs, they could hardly do other than support the Bill. Haldane and the Webbs took this view of the Bill and were determined to 'put education first . . . and other interests second'.[4] At first Rosebery also took this view and told the councillors of Colchester that 'if to what you do already you add the task of education you will be advancing by leaps and bounds', thus endorsing the major change made by the Bill, the creation of the county council education

[1] In H. G. Hutchinson (ed.), *Private Diaries of . . . Sir A. West* (1922), p. 303.

[2] For the place of education in their social reform thinking, see below, pp. 228 ff.

[3] Bannerman to Gladstone, n.d. [? 4 May 1902], HGP 45988, f. 13.

[4] Haldane to a correspondent, *The Scotsman*, 30 June 1902; to avoid party disunity, Haldane spoke little in the Commons on the Bill (Haldane to Mother, 22 July 1902, Hal P 5968, f. 29).

committee as the 'single authority' for secondary and primary education.[1]

But like the rest of the Liberal leadership, the 'efficiency' men of the League had greatly underestimated nonconformist grass-roots opposition to the Bill. Most Liberal M.P.s would have agreed with Campbell-Bannerman that the apparently interminable debates on the Bill, requiring a special autumn session, were 'monotonous, dull and uninspiring'.[2] Campbell-Bannerman seemed surprised to find that 'evidently the Noncons are working up to a heat they have never been in before',[3] and Herbert Gladstone had to send out a special whip to Liberal M.P.s because their attendance had 'not been so full and regular as the importance of the subject and the intense interest taken in it by our supporters in the country would seem to demand'.[4] During the summer of 1902 nonconformists declared their intention, which many carried out, of refusing to pay rates if the Bill became law.

How were League members to deal with this situation? They knew not merely that the bulk of their own party was bitterly hostile to the Bill, but also that the Unionists were deeply divided, and that the Bill might be withdrawn because of Unionist hostility, as had happened in 1896. They also believed that the government might resign on the education issue.[5] If this happened and they had already announced their support for the principle of the Bill, they would be politically completely isolated, a fact made clear to them when Campbell-Bannerman excluded all Leaguers from the Liberal committee to plan opposition to the Bill.[6]

An additional, internal factor affecting the attitude of the League was the view of Perks, chairman of the nonconformist parliamentary council and very hostile to the Bill. Although Perks was a methodist, the nonconformist denomination with the largest number of voluntary schools, he

---

[1] Rosebery in Colchester, *The Times*, 16 May 1902.
[2] 4 H, cxv. 935 (2 Dec. 1902).
[3] Bannerman to Sinclair, 24 Sept. 1902, CBP 52517, n.f.
[4] Gladstone to Liberal M.P.s, 31 Oct. 1902, HGP 46105, f. 323.
[5] EHD, 7 Sept. 1902, and Rosebery to Grey, 17 Aug. 1902, RP, Letter Book.
[6] Asquith to Gladstone, 30 Apr. 1902, HGP 45989, f. 68; Bannerman dismissed Asquith's protest as 'hysterical' (HGP 45988, f. 12).

was determined to use the Bill to unite and establish nonconformity as the dominant political pressure group within
the Liberal party.[1] Such an achievement was his principal
aim in politics, and his association with Rosebery was largely
designed to make Rosebery the leader of such a group. If
any issue offered a chance for the nonconformists to gain
such a position in the party, it was the Education Bill of 1902.

Perks therefore put great pressure on Rosebery to withdraw his support from the Bill, which he did. Rosebery
argued that while on 'the abstract principle of the Bill' he
was 'in discord' with most Liberals, the political realities of
the situation were that the Bill's 'operative effect could or
should be to reunite the Liberal party'.[2] Rosebery appeared
with Fowler, Asquith, and, on Perks's initiative, Lloyd George
at a large protest meeting.[3] He described Haldane's support
for the Bill as 'picturesque' and condemned the Bill as 'a Bill
which, I venture to say without rhetorical expression, will do
more to stunt the educational development of the country
. . . than almost any measure we can conceive possible'.[4]

Arguments for and against the Bill went on within the
council of the League during the summer of 1902. Though
there was considerable private support for the Bill, the only
League M.P.s to support it publicly were Haldane, C. M.
Douglas, and Munro-Ferguson. Thus the League, launched
as a body to support 'national efficiency', found itself at its
first crisis supporting one of the oldest cries of the 'Tory
Liberals' whom Rosebery had previously denounced: the
nonconformist view of the voluntary schools. The Haldane–
Webb wing of the League saw these concessions to the
nonconformists as disastrous, for the result was 'that the
reputation of the Liberals as an education party is damaged,
and it was one of their best assets'.[5]

[1] See 4 H, cx. 1011 (7 July 1902) and his speech 'Free Church Councils and the
Education Crisis', *Free Church Year Book* (1902); the methodists split on the Bill
(M. Edwards, *Methodism and England, 1850–1932* (1943), pp. 124–5).

[2] Rosebery on 23 May and 30 May 1902, LLP 9 and LLP 12.

[3] Perks to Rosebery, 23 May 1902, RP, box 40; Perks persuaded Rosebery to
ask Lloyd George for speech information (Perks to Rosebery, 8 Aug. and 29 Nov.
1902, RP, box 40); Freeman-Thomas to Lloyd George, 4 Dec. 1902, LGP A/1/9,
summons him to Dalmeny.

[4] Rosebery in London, *The Times*, 11 June 1902

[5] S. Webb, 'How to Attain Liberal Unity', *New Liberal Review*, Oct. 1902.

The Education Bill of 1902 marked the start of the return of most Liberal Imperialists to harmonious relations with their party, and certainly served to reunite the party after the bitter arguments over imperialism. But this unity was bought at the expense of the promotion of 'efficiency'. The League leaders had hoped the League would do two things: promote the cause of 'efficiency', and act as a rallying-point for Liberals, including Liberal Unionists, who believed in 'the larger patriotism'. The Education Bill of 1902 exposed the fact that these two aims were by no means as easy to reconcile as the League leadership had at first supposed. The creed of 'national efficiency' had brought within the League some of the most progressive political thinkers of the day, but 'the larger patriotism' was also praised by many who were in almost all other aspects 'Tory Liberals'. Of these Perks was the effective representative, and he did not let his chance slip by. To reconcile these two groups, if it were possible at all, required a more competent, resolute, and courageous leader than Rosebery.

More difficulties for the League

By the end of 1902 the League faced other difficulties as well as that of its argument over education. One difficulty was, as ever, Rosebery. Though it was thought early in 1902 that Rosebery would 'never retire into his shell again—he was definitely committed to them', it became clear that this was no longer so.[1] Rosebery refused to participate in the choosing of Kimberley's successor as Liberal leader in the Lords,[2] and spent much of the summer abroad, returning briefly to address meetings on education. He told Grey, from Paris, that 'it is humanly speaking impossible that I should ever hold office again', and gave the same impression to other M.P.s.[3] As a result, as Lord Carrington told Hamilton, 'R's supporters won't stand this attitude of shillyshallying much longer. Many are already dubbing R a "rotter".'[4]

---

[1] Haldane's remark to Hamilton, EHD, 7 Apr. 1902.
[2] See Spencer to Rosebery, 16 Apr. 1902, Rosebery to Spencer, 20 Apr. 1902, RP, box 49.
[3] Rosebery to Grey, 17 Aug. 1902, RP, Letter Book; see also EHD ,10 Oct. 1902.
[4] EHD, 14 Oct. 1902; Carrington was a League member.

Rosebery's answer was that he was working for a policy, not
for his own ambition. But, as Hamilton observed, 'it is the
man, not the policy they want.'[1] This was true of some like
Perks; others, like Haldane, wanted both. Over education,
Rosebery had cast aside the policy; he seemed also to be
withdrawing the man.

With the end of the war, and with, for the most part,
harmony over education, Irish policy increasingly seemed
the dividing line between League members and other
Liberals. The Liberal Imperialists' campaign on Ireland had
some success in winning over Unionists, and in eliminating
Ireland as a major source of division between the Liberals
and the Unionists. In the 1890s the tendency had been for
Liberals to continue to join the Unionists over Ireland.[2] This
flow was now reversed, and some liberally-inclined Unionists
such as Lord Durham, no longer felt Ireland an impossible
barrier to joining the League, if not the Liberal party. The
chief prize was the Duke of Sutherland, an important and
wealthy Scottish Unionist, won over to the League by
Haldane.[3] Rosebery was also in contact with a number of
young Unionists, particularly Churchill, who saw Rosebery
as the possible leader of 'the Gvnt. of the middle'.[4]

Haldane's conversion of the Duke of Sutherland on the
grouse moors of Dornoch illustrated another weakness of the
League leaders—their excessive preoccupation with Scotland. The Commons men had based their political careers
in the 1880s on permeation of the party leadership at the
centre, using the dinner-tables of London society as their
entrée to political power; they had not attempted to establish
a regional power base. Their weakness at Westminster
during the Boer War showed the dangers of this approach.
They hoped, therefore, to use the League to establish such
a base in Scotland as Chamberlain had in Birmingham; thus
much effort was devoted to getting Imperialist candidates
selected for Scottish constituencies. The only really active

---

[1] EHD, 10 Oct. 1902.
[2] For the case of Doughty in 1898, see below, p. 269 n. 2.
[3] Haldane to Rosebery, 22 Sept. 1902, RP, box 24.
[4] Churchill to Rosebery, 10 Oct. 1902, in Randolph S. Churchill, *Winston S.
Churchill* (1967), ii. 47; for Rosebery's earlier contacts with the 'Hooligans', see
pp. 23–7 and 34–7. Churchill was never a League member.

local League branches were in Glasgow and Edinburgh, and the majority of speeches of Rosebery, Haldane, and Asquith were made in Scotland. But though these branches had some success, and Gladstone believed that 'the League seems to occupy the field in Scotland so far as organisation goes',[1] Rosebery certainly did not control Scotland, or even the Lothians, with the iron hand attributed to him by some Englishmen. Ferguson as whip, and Rosebery and then Gibson-Carmichael as President, were quite unable to control the Scottish Liberal Association, which passed anti-imperialist motions throughout this period of opposition.

It is doubtful if Imperialists more efficient than Rosebery could have had much success in Scotland, except perhaps in Glasgow; it is certain that dealing with the lack of strength in Scotland was not the major electoral task facing the League in its attempt to restore the Liberals as the 'national party'. If the League was to have a major impact, and if the Liberals were to regain power, a firm hold would have to be gained in the big boroughs of the 'predominant partner'. In theory the League recognized this; most of its policies were designed to replace 'Celtic fringe' measures with measures relevant to the mass of the population. But in practice League leaders seemed to share that obsession with 'Celtic fringe' politics which they had so deplored in Mr. Gladstone.

This weakness was recognized by Perks and Allard, who wished to use the League to regain strength in places like London, Manchester, Liverpool, and the Yorkshire boroughs, even if Birmingham was unobtainable. They persistently requested Rosebery and his Vice-Presidents to speak more in England. Perks complained that 'our League campaign is too much confined to Scotland.'[2] Such complaints had little effect, and the strong support for Liberal Imperialism in, for example, Liverpool, Leeds, and South Wales remained unorganized and largely unrecognized by the League leaders.[3]

---

[1] Gladstone to Bannerman, 1 Oct. 1902, CBP 41216, f. 234.
[2] Perks to Rosebery, 1 Sept. 1902, RP, box 40.
[3] See the many letters from Sir Edward Russell and Sir T. Wemyss Reid in RP, box 106, and K. O. Morgan, 'Wales and the Boer War—a Reply', *Welsh History Review* (1969).

Liberal Imperialists and the tariff reform campaign

The introduction of tariff reform as the dominant issue in British politics in May 1903 caused political and ideological difficulties for the League. As professed imperialists, League members could not but give serious consideration to Chamberlain's proposals; their ideological reaction may briefly be said to range from acceptance to complete rejection.[1] Politically, Chamberlain's attack on free trade, the basic economic principle common to all late Victorian governments, had the effect of breaking up the politics of the centre which lay at the root of Liberal Imperialist thinking. Asquith, always with party unity as his priority, immediately saw this and, suspending all questions of ideology, decided to 'go bald-headed for J.C. and his swindle of a zollverein', which he did at Doncaster six days after Chamberlain's speech.[2] Other Liberal Imperialists reacted less decisively. Rosebery, in particular, hoped to maintain a bipartisan, non-party view of the question. He observed that tariff reform would affect party politics 'diagonally, and not by the ordinary separation of English party lines', and he suggested a private all-party conference to discuss the proposals, thereby retaining the chance of continuity in this aspect of imperial policy.[3] Haldane was also unwilling immediately to make a party question of it, and agreed with Chamberlain 'that it was no use going back to views . . . which were expressed fifty years ago'.[4]

But it was soon clear that Chamberlain was in no mood for private bargaining or discussion. The energy of his campaign forced all other politicians to action, even if, as with Balfour, it was action to produce inactivity. In this situation Rosebery's shilly-shallying would not work. As Herbert Gladstone observed, 'the League seems to be on the edge of a precipice. If R. does not play an astute game he is likely to come a cropper.'[5] Rosebery recognized this, and, while still trying in private to develop the middle ground,

---

[1] For this see below, pp. 161–8.
[2] Asquith to Bannerman, 18 May 1903, CBP 41210, f. 223; *The Times*, 22 May 1903.   [3] Rosebery in Burnley, *The Times*, 20 May 1903.
[4] Haldane to E. Linton, *The Scotsman*, 3 June 1903.
[5] Gladstone to Bannerman, 25 May 1903, CBP 41216, f. 270.

publicly declared his hostility to Chamberlain's proposals.[1] Rosebery tried to make the League the spear-head of the anti-Chamberlain attack and refused to join the Free Trade Union. But this attempt had to be abandoned following heavy pressure from Asquith, Grey, Ferguson, and Hamilton who urged Rosebery to join the Union.[2] Moreover, the League could hardly lead the attack, because there were significant rank-and-file defections, though not as many as Chamberlain had hoped for. A number of League members supported the anonymous 'Liberal Imperialist' when he wrote to The Times supporting retaliatory tariffs.[3] Following this J. Saxon Mills, a barrister and a League member, organized in consultation with Chamberlain the Liberal Fair Trade League on the ground that 'as the controversy grows, the number of supporters is bound to increase, especially in the Liberal Imperialist section'.[4] Mills was wrong about numbers, but the defection from the League of the Duke of Sutherland, to be President of the Tariff Reform League, of Sir Edward Reed, M.P., to the Unionists,[5] of Sir Charles Tennant, Asquith's father-in-law and one of the League's chief subscribers, to sit on Chamberlain's Tariff Commission, and of T. A. Brassey, to become a Unionist candidate, again made the League's loyalty to the Liberal party, and its President's ability to lead his followers, seem suspect.

The difficulty for the League was that once Chamberlain had begun his campaign, calm discussion of the future of imperial unity could no longer be contained within small

---

[1] Rosebery to the League, 12 June 1903, LLP 47; this followed an appeal from Grey to Rosebery (11 June 1903, RP, Box 23) to oppose Chamberlain 'not only as an individual but as a party man . . . this would strengthen both the Liberal League and your own position in respect to the party as a whole'.

[2] Asquith to Rosebery, 9, 10, 27 July 1903, RP, box 1; Grey to Rosebery, 13 July 1903, RP, box 23; Ferguson to Rosebery, 17, 25 July 1903, RP, box 16; EHD, 9, 20 July 1903.

[3] See 'Liberal Imperialist' to The Times, 2 July 1903, and Sutherland, L. S. Amery, S. Bourne, T. A. Brassey, J. C. Dobie, A. E. Firth, B. Kidd, H. J. MacKinder, J. Saxon Mills, J. Paxman, Sir C. Tennant, H. Wolmer to The Times, 21 July 1903 (League members in italics). The letter declared retaliatory tariffs a matter of 'urgent national necessity'.

[4] Mills to The Times, 5 Oct. 1903; see J. L. Garvin and J. Amery, The Life o, Joseph Chamberlain (1968), v. 305-7.

[5] See K. O. Morgan, Wales in British Politics, p. 215.

dining clubs in which rational men could agree to differ. Chamberlain's campaign 'broke the Oracles in two',[1] and also broke one of the basic rules of imperialist politics— that discussion of the details of imperial policy should not be conducted on public platforms. The Imperial Federation League had dissolved itself in 1893 rather than risk a public row on tariffs; Chamberlain had deliberately provoked such a row. In a situation like this the League's aim of educating the Liberal party from a bipartisan, central position could not work. Rosebery's point, that if the fiscal controversy *'does not unite the Liberal party, the Liberal party is past all hope'*, became self-evidently true, and League members had to stand up and be counted.[2]

Accordingly, all League leaders went 'bald-headed' for Chamberlain, thus restoring their position within the Liberal party. 'How can these fellows ever have gone wrong?' wondered Campbell-Bannerman.[3] Apart from the unifying influence of the crisis upon the Liberals, League leaders were particularly active against Chamberlain, first because it was not immediately apparent that Chamberlain would, in the long run, lose, and secondly because the tariff reform crisis gave the League leaders the chance to show that for the first time since 1886 Home Rule was not the chief distinguishing mark of a Liberal, or the line of demarcation between the parties. Liberalism, the party of free trade, was certainly more satisfactory to them than liberalism, the party of Home Rule.

Rosebery: the beginning of the end

Action was required of all, but Rosebery failed to act and was left behind. Having been deserted by his lieutenants in his feeble attempt to make the League the controlling body of resistance to Chamberlain, Rosebery began to fade from the scene.[4] He substituted for action the writing of private memoranda to explain his inactivity, from which it is clear

[1] R. Kipling, quoted by B. Semmel, *Imperialism and Social Reform*, p. 82.
[2] Rosebery to the League, 12 June 1903, LLP 47 (Rosebery's italics).
[3] See *Bannerman*, ii. 120.
[4] Rosebery told Ferguson that 'he has gone as far as he can towards the Liberal Party—let the Party join the League', Ferguson to his wife, n.d. [July 1903], FP.

that, though he considered bidding for power, he had already decided against it.[1] If Balfour resigned there were two possibilities open to the Liberals—a coalition with the Free Fooders, or a Liberal government. In July, Haldane thought that 'Balfour's Govt. may resign & a Liberal Govt. be formed.'[2] In this case, no one knew for whom the King would send, but Gladstone thought 'he *might* send for R'.[3] Morley, however, presumed 'that Lord Spencer would be sent for', and both he and Hamilton assumed that Rosebery would refuse office.[4]

The Asquith committee became increasingly impatient with Rosebery, who made no effort to hold the League together during 1903, apart from making occasional speeches. Asquith ceased communication with him after July, and Haldane was 'never sure of him now-a-days'.[5] They had not yet completely abandoned Rosebery, however, and after Asquith and Haldane had spent the weekend with the Duke of Devonshire, Haldane told Rosebery that the Duke was said 'to have intimated that if the Cabinet was broken up he was prepared to form a ministry—with yourself [Rosebery] at the F.O.'[6] Rosebery made nothing of this hint that he should make contact with Devonshire. The impetus of the post-Chesterfield days with Rosebery 'leading with his coat off' had been completely lost.

Rosebery clarified his position when he summoned Grey and Haldane to Dalmeny in early October 1903. His object was to dissuade Grey from taking office under Spencer, and to make it clear he would not do so himself. Grey reported to Asquith: 'Rosebery asked me what I thought to taking office in a Spencer Govt. I gathered that he would not think of such a thing himself & dislikes the idea of any of us doing so.'[7] Haldane told Rosebery he and Grey 'could not serve under C.B. either as P.M. or as leader in the H. of C.'[8]

[1] See Crewe, ii. 577–8, 585–7.
[2] Haldane to Mother, 18 July 1903, Hal P 5970, f. 30.
[3] Gladstone to L. V. Harcourt (copy), 24 July 1903, HGP 45997, f. 43.
[4] EHD, 12 Aug. 1903.
[5] Haldane to Mother, 12 June 1903, Hal P 5969, f. 158.
[6] Haldane to Rosebery, 10 Aug. 1903, RP, box 24.
[7] Grey to Asquith, 7 Oct. 1903, AP 10, f. 92.
[8] Haldane to Asquith, 5 Oct. 1903, AP 10, f. 90, in Jenkins, pp. 143–4.

Grey took the same view, that 'under no circumstances would I take office with C-B as Prime Minister or in any Gvnt. in which C-B was leader in the . . . Commons.'[1]

Their chief objection was thus to Campbell-Bannerman; they told Rosebery that a Spencer government would be necessary to exclude Campbell-Bannerman, unless Rosebery would form a ministry himself. Rosebery refused. Grey and Haldane stressed that 'the first condition . . . is that you [Asquith] should lead in the Commons.'[2] This did not necessarily please Rosebery, who had told Ferguson a few days before that 'shd. an Asquith Govt. be formed he might go abroad.'[3]

What emerged from these conversations was first, apparently final confirmation that Rosebery would not take office of any sort, and second, the decision of Grey and Haldane to work to exclude Campbell-Bannerman in favour of Spencer. The search for a replacement for Rosebery in the person of Spencer, a man with whom they had had little political contact, was characteristic; they would not, or could not, take the lead themselves. They had to have a 'front' man, with themselves as advisers in the background. Their objection to Campbell-Bannerman was to the tone and style of his leadership of the party and to what they regarded as his erratic and irresponsible approach to politics. No policy difference was mentioned as particularly important in itself.

For the last time, Rosebery made a successful public return, in his eagerly awaited speech at Sheffield on 13 October 1903. Whereas Asquith in his speeches attacked Chamberlain with detailed statistical arguments, Rosebery offered a wider view, struck an imperial note, and successfully suggested that he was the equal of Chamberlain in his imperial vision.[4] Morley, who regarded the Liberal campaign as boring—'People don't understand the figures of Trade'—admitted that Rosebery 'struck a first rate platform note . . . it was Empired, not Fiscals' [*sic*].[5]

[1] Grey to Asquith, 7 Oct. 1903, AP 10, f. 92 (seriously mistranscribed in K. Robbins, *Sir Edward Grey*, pp. 109, 385 n. 25).   [2] Ibid.
[3] Ferguson to his wife, n.d. [? 3 Oct. 1903], FP.
[4] Rosebery in Sheffield, 13 Oct. 1903, LLP 90; see Asquith in Cinderford, *The Times*, 9 Oct. 1903.
[5] Morley to Spender, 23 Oct. 1903, SP 46391, f. 121.

Rosebery's speech was a notable contribution to the Liberal campaign,[1] but the periodic 'big speech' was not enough. As Lord Crewe remarked, 'the reception still accorded to him [Rosebery] is due to the firm belief that he is one who can be counted on in the long run, to lead.'[2] The 'committee' had ceased to count on Rosebery in this way, and were discounting him in their thoughts about the future ministry. This naturally weakened the League which, Gladstone thought, somewhat exaggerating, had by this time 'no position and no following'.[3]

The problem of the Free Fooders

The League leadership had, therefore, a lack of cohesion just at the moment when solidarity and co-operation were most needed, for the political situation had developed to that to which many of the Leaguers had looked forward since the end of the Round Table conference of 1887—the possibility of the return of a substantial number of Unionists. Chamberlain's autumn campaign made a good deal of progress—victory for free trade was by no means assured. In the north of England Haldane found: 'Chamberlain is making progress up here—he is a demagogue & understands all the cuts.'[4] In the south, by-elections at Dulwich and Lewisham did not produce the expected Liberal gains.[5]

In this precarious situation, the position of the Free Fooders was of importance.[6] Individual League members were already in contact with the Free Fooders. Ferguson and Douglas had conferences with Seeley and Goschen, the Free Food secretaries, and in August with Beach, and also with Churchill 'who represents himself rather than his colleagues'.[7] In August it was agreed that 'things must go

[1] See *Daily Chronicle*, 15 Oct. 1903, which saw Rosebery 'in the van of the Liberal attack'.
[2] Crewe talking to Hamilton, EHD, 20 Oct. 1903.
[3] Gladstone to Bannerman, 16 Nov. 1903, CBP 41217, f. 35.
[4] Haldane to Mother, 24 Nov. 1903, Hal P 5970, f. 162.
[5] *Daily Chronicle*, 16 Dec. 1903, thought there was 'a distinct advance but not yet any tidal wave'.
[6] Haldane told Perks, 'I am coming to doubt very much whether we can win . . . without an alliance with the Duke's party' (24 Dec. 1903, RP, box 40).
[7] Ferguson to Rosebery, 10 Aug. 1903, RP, box 16.

much further before we can cooperate except as regards dates for meetings and the duplication of candidates.'[1] By Christmas 1903 things had gone much further with the resignations from the government, the decay of the Free Food League, and the vigour of Chamberlain's campaign. The impending session of parliament required action. Rosebery appeared to take the initiative by writing to Devonshire to congratulate him on a speech. Devonshire took this as a call for the start of discussions, and replied at length, suggesting discussion about 'support or toleration' for Free Fooders to retain their seats, and calling for 'communication . . . between us . . . especially those with whom you act'.[2] Rosebery made no attempt to give a lead in this matter, and immediately passed Devonshire's letter to Asquith.

The Asquith committee was already involved in negotiations. Asquith himself tried, and failed, to 'collect these fellows [Free Fooders] (or at any rate the most difficult of them) round a dinner table'.[3] Haldane held a dinner on 12 December 1903 to discuss tactics.[4] Perks, who in other circumstances would have been very favourable to an alliance with the Free Fooders, gave absolute priority to the education question, and said 'it was idle to expect the noncons to support such candidates [Free Fooders] unless they will agree to vote for the drastic amendment of the Education Act.' Perks was determined to prevent a compromise on the education question, and dissuaded Asquith from making a public appeal for a middle position on education which would have helped co-operation with the Free Fooders.[5]

When Asquith, having received Devonshire's letter from Rosebery, went to discuss the situation with the melancholy Lord James of Hereford, he knew that Rosebery would not take the lead, and that there was substantial nonconformist

[1] Ferguson to Rosebery, 10 Aug. 1903, RP, box 16.

[2] Devonshire to Rosebery, 12 Dec. 1903, RP, box 78.

[3] Asquith to Gladstone, 3 Dec. 1903, HGP 45989, f. 86; Asquith was also negotiating with Lord Hugh Cecil about an amendment to the Address (Cecil to Asquith, 6 Dec. 1903, AP 10, f. 100).

[4] Perks to Rosebery, 12 Dec. 1903, RP, box 40; fourteen Leaguers attended (Haldane to Mother, 11 and 12 Dec. 1903, Hal P 5970, ff. 191–3).

[5] Perks to Rosebery, loc. cit., and see below, pp. 234–5.

hostility to any pact with Free Fooders unless there were very substantial Unionist concessions on education. Asquith, therefore, had little room for manœuvre, and he and James agreed that 'there are insuperable difficulties in the way of forming for general electoral purposes any fusion of the Free Traders in the Unionist & Liberal Parties.' They hoped, however, to 'remove the antagonism' between two free trade candidates at a local level, and agreed that 'a consultative body' should be formed between the two sides.[1] Asquith was against any 'open or general declaration of policy', for he thought that 'sooner or later, being as they are between the devil & the other thing, the Free Fooders will be either squeezed out of existence or come over to us.'[2] Thus, although a conference was eventually held between Asquith and Gladstone for the Liberals, and James and Lord George Hamilton for the Unionists, no general agreement was reached.[3]

All the early stages of these discussions were conducted by members of the League; Campbell-Bannerman did not learn of them until the end of December 1903. But the League members were not acting in their capacity as League officials, but rather as ordinary members of the Liberal party. The League completely failed to act as a body in these negotiations. There was no meeting of the League officials to discuss the situation, and Grey and Fowler, both League Vice-Presidents and the men most likely to reassure the Free Fooders by their 'responsible' views, played no part in the negotiations. There were two main difficulties. First, the failure of Rosebery to give any lead meant that the League, as such, was virtually impotent.[4] Secondly, the League now paid the price of its support for the nonconformist view of the 1902 Education Act. What was needed was a broker between the main body of the Liberal party and

---

[1] Memorandum by Lord James, 21 Dec. 1903, AP 10, f. 124.
[2] Asquith to Bannerman, 28 Dec. 1903, CBP 41210, f. 227.
[3] See R. A. Rempel, 'The Unionist Free Traders, 1903–1910', pp. 169 ff. (unpublished Oxford D.Phil. thesis, 1967).
[4] At about this time Rosebery lost the support of the Harmsworth Press, previously a strong ally; see R. Pound and G. Harmsworth, *Northcliffe* (1959), pp. 185–7, and Perks to Rosebery, 22 and 24 Nov. 1902, 28 Feb., 23 Sept. 1903, and 18 Oct. 1903, RP, box 40.

the Free Fooders on the education question. But the League could not even attempt this difficult task, because it was itself, through its strong hostility to the Act, already one of the parties to the dispute. A further difficulty was the composition of the Free Fooder group. Most of the 'efficiency' men in the Unionist party went with Chamberlain. An alliance between the League and the Free Fooders would not be an alliance between two 'efficiency' groups to produce a national party of 'efficiency'. The Free Fooder leaders were men like Devonshire, James, and Beach who were likely to be antagonistic to the Webbite 'efficiency' ideas of the League.[1]

Rosebery had thus lost his chance, supposing he wished to take it. The period from September 1903 to January 1904 was the nearest the League members got to a fluid political situation in which they could make a substantial impression upon the organization of British politics. The moment passed, and as the Liberals began in 1904 to win by-elections, the importance of the Free Fooders correspondingly decreased. Appeals were still made to Rosebery to return, but not by the League's Vice-Presidents.[2] Though contact was maintained, the Asquith committee went its own way. Haldane made a half-hearted attempt at reconciliation, but found Rosebery had 'drifted out of the usual lines, and for the time seems to have no place'.[3] Haldane told Hamilton in April 1904 that 'for the first time the outlook as regards Rosebery was bad, & that he had nearly given him up as hopeless'.[4] Even the faithful Perks complained to Rosebery of his slackness, and from June 1904 onwards assumed that Rosebery would not be a member of a Liberal ministry.[5]

Liberal Imperialists and the making of the Liberal cabinet

When parliament met in 1904, the 'general feeling' was at first 'that the Govt. cannot last long'.[6] But after the govern-

---

1 None of the Free Fooders who crossed the floor joined the League.
2 A big campaign was mounted by the party leaders to get Rosebery to attend the beginning-of-session dinner; he would not. See Spencer to Rosebery, 30 Dec. 1903, RP, box 49, and Ripon to Rosebery, 7 Jan. 1904, RP, box 46.
3 Haldane to Mother, 23 Mar. 1904, Hal P 5971, f. 128.
4 EHD, 26 [? 27] Apr. 1904.
5 Perks to Rosebery, 12 Apr. and 22 June 1904, RP, box 41.
6 Haldane to Mother, 11 Feb. 1904, Hal P 5971, f. 62.

ment survived the session, and there was no substantial defection of Free Fooders, the view was that 'the Govt. are distinctly in much smoother waters, & the general election seems a good way off.'[1] The Asquith committee assumed throughout 1904 that Balfour would stay in office despite his difficulties; they made no definite plans lest he should resign. They may have discussed such a situation, perhaps in terms of the talk of Grey and Haldane with Rosebery in October 1903, when they said they would not accept Campbell-Bannerman even as Leader of the Commons in a Spencer ministry. Campbell-Bannerman's health was known to be poor, and the possibility of his moving to the Lords, where he would be subordinate to Spencer, had already been considered.[2] The news had put Asquith 'in great spirits', but in 1904 no move was made by the 'committee' to encourage Campbell-Bannerman to leave.[3]

In 1904 there was something of a reunion between the more extreme Imperialists and the leadership. The Imperialists had virtually abandoned support for Milner's South African policies, and did not provide a 'cave' on the Chinese labour question.[4] Even Haldane, who was more favourable to Chinese labour than most, did not attend the debate in March, and paired 'so that my party was not worse off'.[5] Haldane had repaired his relations with Campbell-Bannerman in February 1904 when they had 'a long friendly talk . . . the first for a long time'. As Haldane remarked, 'things go smoother by degrees.'[6] The position of Grey and Haldane within the party was publicly consolidated when they 'were included among the six to represent the Opposition Cabinet' at a state dinner.[7] Asquith had already restored his reputation for reliability by his leading role in the campaign against Chamberlain.

The year 1904 also saw the confirmation of Campbell-Bannerman as the probable future Liberal Prime Minister.

[1] Haldane to Mother, 27 Apr. 1904, Hal P 5971, f. 172.
[2] Gladstone to Asquith, 29 Oct. 1903, AP 10, f. 98.
[3] Haldane to Mother, 31 Oct. 1903, Hal P 5970, f. 124.
[4] See below, pp. 186 ff.
[5] Haldane to Mother, 22 Mar. 1904, Hal P 5971, f. 126.
[6] Haldane to Mother, 25 Feb. 1904, Hal P 5971, f. 82.
[7] Haldane to Mother, 17 Nov. 1904, quoted in Maurice, *Haldane*, i. 144.

Any expectation that Rosebery would be summoned passed.[1] In June 1904 Perks supposed that 'Spencer and C-B will form a Ministry', and Perks expected 'that two, if not three of the League Vice-Presidents will be in it'.[2] Either Spencer or Campbell-Bannerman could be summoned, but Knollys spread about the information that 'the King had quite made up his mind to do the strictly constitutional thing & to send for C. Bannerman whenever he had to change his Govt.'[3] During the winter of 1904–5 the Asquith committee came to assume that Campbell-Bannerman would be summoned.[4]

Their aim was not to prevent this, but to ensure their own control of the Commons. At a dinner in March 1905 with Morley, 'with much frankness they [Asquith, Grey, and Haldane] suggested that CB shd. be PM in the H of L & Ld. S. For Sec., Asquith C of E & Haldane Ld. Ch. R. wd. not come in', no post for Grey apparently being mentioned.[5] This was a quite open, if indirect, appeal to Campbell-Bannerman, for Morley was certain, as he did, to pass on the information. Morley was not a confidant of the 'committee' at this time, having only recently been reconciled with Asquith, and having dined at Haldane's for the first time 'for eight years at least'.[6] It was not an isolated appeal, nor was it only of Liberal Imperialist origins, for Labouchere told Campbell-Bannerman that Lloyd George was 'explaining . . . a plan for you to go to the Lords'.[7] Campbell-Bannerman took these hints seriously and at first 'seemed as if he were disposed to fall in with this idea'. Soon, however,

---

[1] The 'committee' made no appeal in 1904 to Rosebery. Brett and Spender, however, were very energetic in appealing to Rosebery to return; see Brett to Rosebery, 4 Oct. 1904, RP, box 6; Spender to Rosebery, 22 Oct. 1904, and Spender, Memorandum, 2 Nov. 1904, SP 46387, ff. 50–3.

[2] Perks to Rosebery, 22 June 1904, RP, box 41. In conversation with Perks, Haldane also assumed at this time that Spencer would be summoned, but by the spring of 1905 he had altered his view (Perks to Rosebery, 8 July 1904, RP, box 41).

[3] EHD, 30 June 1904.

[4] See Sommer, *Haldane of Cloan*, p. 143.

[5] Gladstone, Memorandum, 29 Mar. 1905; HGP 45988, f. 161; Grey had already put this view to Morley on 13 Feb. 1905 (Trevelyan, *Grey of Fallodon*, p. 96).

[6] Haldane to Mother, 3 Feb. 1905, Hal P 5973, f. 35.

[7] Labouchere to Bannerman, 21 Feb. 1905, CBP 52518, n.f., in P. Rowland, *The Last Liberal Governments* (1968), p. 5.

'he said that after consideration he had firmly come to the conclusion that (a) he cd. not go at once to the H of L as PM (b) that in any case nothing wd. induce him to supplant Lord S. as leader in the H of L.'[1]

The Liberal Imperialists had made no secret of their views, though they did not tell Morley whether acceptance of the suggested positions was a condition of their joining the ministry. They had altered their position of October 1903 to the extent that they would accept Campbell-Bannerman as Prime Minister. Previously Grey had written that 'under no circumstances would I take office with C-B as Prime Minister or in any Gvnt. in which C-B was leader in the . . . Commons.'[2] They made no mention to Morley of any claims for themselves to the offices from which specifically imperialist policies could be pursued, despite the King's hint to Haldane 'that there should not be any "wild cats" in it [a Liberal cabinet] & that in particular he was concerned about the F.O., C.O. & W.O.'[3] With their request for Asquith at the Exchequer and Haldane as Lord Chancellor, they showed that they aimed at an over-all control of the tone of the administration.

Although so often disappointed by Rosebery, and although Rosebery had recently refused an appeal from the King to take office,[4] Asquith, Grey, and Haldane made a last attempt to persuade Rosebery to return, for this still seemed the best solution to their difficulties. In July 1905 all three visited him for 'a political talk'.[5] Haldane made all the old appeals 'about a candidate for the leadership of the nation', but the talk was 'singularly futile and fruitless'.[6] Since his failure to act during the winter of 1903–4, relations between Rosebery and the Asquith committee had been restrained; they now ceased to tell him of their plans, either for policy changes or for political manœuvres. It would be wrong to

[1] Gladstone, Memorandum, 29 Mar. 1905, HGP 45988, f. 161.

[2] Grey to Asquith, 7 Oct. 1903, AP 10, f. 92; see above, p. 104.

[3] Gladstone, Memorandum, 29 Mar. 1905, HGP 45988, f. 161; this passage records a different talk between Haldane and Morley.

[4] Edward VII visited Mentmore; Rosebery's only suggestion was that he should send for Spencer and Bannerman together; EHD, 18 Feb. 1905.

[5] Haldane to Mother, 18 July 1905, Hal P 5974, f. 30.

[6] Rosebery to Haldane, 18 and 20 July 1905, Hal P 5906, ff. 185–6.

say that the committee had abandoned Rosebery completely, for annually since 1900 they had given him up as 'hopeless' only to return to make yet another appeal. But between July 1905 and December 1905 they did not take Rosebery into their confidence. Though they maintained amicable personal relations, Haldane told Asquith that the plan they developed in September 1905 'should be kept absolutely from Rosebery . . . his interest would be to wreck it'.[1]

The Asquith committee decided to adhere to the proposals they made to Morley in March 1905. During the summer Haldane informed Knollys, the King's secretary, of these.[2] Haldane had developed a close relationship with the Court after successfully dealing with the Prince of Wales's settlement in 1903. From December 1903 onwards he frequently visited the Palace, and became accustomed to discussing the political situation with Knollys and with the King, who expressed to Haldane 'his apprehensions about a Liberal Govt.'[3] Haldane now hoped to make use of this foothold in the Court.

During the annual trek to the Scottish moors, Asquith, and possibly Grey, visited Haldane at Cloanden, his seat near Auchterarder, on 2 September 1905.[4] On 9 September Haldane stayed with Grey at Relugas, a fishing-lodge on the Findhorn in Morayshire. On 11 September Haldane visited Asquith, who was staying near by, and on that day, or the next, they both visited Grey.[5] From this series of meetings came the famous so-called 'Relugas compact', though Haldane referred to it in December 1905 as 'the policy of the Cloanden gathering'.[6]

It was already well known within the party leadership that there was a strong opinion, not only held by Liberal Imperialists, that Campbell-Bannerman should go to the Lords. There were two new elements decided by these

[1] Haldane to Asquith, 27 Sept. 1905, AP 10, f. 144.

[2] Haldane to Knollys, 12 Sept. 1905 (draft copy), Hal P 5906, f. 190 in Sommer, op. cit., pp. 145–7: 'We had, *as you know*, formed the view strongly that Sir HCB might . . . go to the Upper House' [my italics].

[3] Haldane to Mother, 28 Mar. 1905, Hal P 5973, f. 122.

[4] Cloanden guest book; information by courtesy of T. G. N. Haldane.

[5] Haldane to Mother, 8 and 10 Sept. 1905, Hal P 5974, ff. 86–8. Haldane's later recollections give a slightly different sequence of events; see Haldane, pp. 158–9.

[6] Haldane to Mother, 8 Dec. 1905, Hal P 5974, f. 186.

Scottish conversations: first, the conversion of the suggestion that Campbell-Bannerman should go to the Lords into
the definite proposition that he *must* go to the Lords if
Asquith, Grey, and Haldane were to take office, otherwise
'we shall stand aside'; secondly, the decision 'to take a
definite step in defence of our policy'. This 'definite step'
was to take two forms—a visit by Haldane to Balmoral, and
a visit by Asquith to Campbell-Bannerman to confront him
with the proposition that he must go to the Lords. Haldane's
idea was that Asquith should 'insinuate early' to Campbell-
Bannerman these views and 'propose to Sir HCB the tenure
of these offices as a condition of our joining hands with him'.[1]

Haldane gave Knollys an impression of unity and strength
of intention amongst the committee which was not wholly
accurate. Haldane thought that Campbell-Bannerman must
be directly confronted—he mentioned to Knollys an 'ultimatum'—and also thought the King should put pressure on
Campbell-Bannerman to accept the conditions. Haldane saw
early action as the essential prerequisite to success, for 'to let
things drift is to let them crystallize adversely',[2] and 'to
succeed it is essential that we should approach him early and
firmly'.[3] From the start Grey and Asquith, though they
accepted the plan, were much less keen about the 'definite
step' needed to execute it. Grey thought 'that it is too soon
to put a pistol to CB's head', and merely suggested to
Asquith: 'feel your way & use an opening, if you get it.'[4]
This would hardly amount to the rapid ultimatum desired
by Haldane. Grey was already troubled by the conflict between personal friendship and political expediency which
worried him throughout the crisis. Although Grey accepted
the plan, he also felt 'quite friendly and loyal' to Campbell-
Bannerman![5] Grey was keen that Asquith and Campbell-
Bannerman should meet, not to deal with the plan, but to
discuss the autumn campaign.[6] Grey was also 'a little

---

[1] Haldane to Knollys, 12 Sept. 1905, Hal P 5906, f. 190. 'These offices' were
'the leadership of the House of Commons with the Exchequer for Asquith, either
the Foreign or Colonial Office for Grey and the Woolsack for myself'.
[2] Ibid.
[3] Haldane to Knollys (draft copy), 19 Sept. 1905, AP 10, f. 141.
[4] Grey to Asquith, 2 Oct. 1905, AP 10, f. 148.   [5] Ibid.
[6] Asquith to Haldane, 27 Sept. 1905, Hal P 5906, f. 212.

doubtful of the expediency of approaching the throne at
this stage'.[1] The tone of Asquith's letter to Haldane giving
Grey's views suggests that Asquith did not dissent from
them. He intended to see Campbell-Bannerman 'sooner or
later', but obviously saw no urgency about it.[2]

Haldane visited Balmoral early in October, and reported
to Asquith that 'the plan is thoroughly approved in all its
details.' Haldane expected the King to put pressure
on Campbell-Bannerman, and hoped that this, plus
Asquith's apparently independent discussions, would persuade Campbell-Bannerman to become Earl of Belmont.[3]
Spencer's severe illness of 13 October meant that Campbell-
Bannerman was certain to be Prime Minister. It also
facilitated the working of the plan, for Campbell-Bannerman
had been unwilling to supplant Spencer in the Lords.
Haldane thought it was now 'almost necessary that Sir
HCB shd go to the H of L to fill the gap'.[4] In his letter to
Knollys of 17 October, Haldane discussed future offices in
detail, mentioning Grey for the Foreign Office, Elgin for
the Colonial Office, Morley for the Exchequer, Asquith as
First Lord and Leader of the Commons, but he did not say
that any of these was a condition of other Imperialists taking
office.

Campbell-Bannerman returned from Marienbad on 11
November fortified by what he rightly understood to be
royal approval of his future premiership.[5] Asquith saw him
on 13 November. Asquith wrote no account of his talk, but
according to Margot Asquith's diary, Campbell-Bannerman
mentioned that 'it has been suggested by that ingenious
person Richard Burdon Haldane that I should go to the
House of Lords . . .'[6] Asquith does not seem to have taken
this opportunity to say either that he agreed with Haldane,
or that such a move was a condition of office. Haldane
understood from Asquith that he 'gently opened matters

[1] Asquith to Haldane, 27 Sept. 1905, Hal P 5906, f. 212.   [2] Ibid.
[3] Haldane to Asquith, 6 Oct. 1902, AP 10, f. 153; Haldane told Asquith that
C-B must not 'surmise any connection' between Asquith's confrontation and the
Court's pressure.
[4] Haldane to Knollys (draft copy), 17 Oct. 1905, Hal P 5906, f. 222.
[5] See *Bannerman*, ii. 174–8.
[6] Jenkins, pp. 162–4.

about the 3 offices. CB is not hostile, but the outcome is pretty dubious'; none the less Haldane thought: 'It looks well as regards Grey, & CB is apparently thinking of the Lords.'[1] Perhaps Asquith thought Campbell-Bannerman would go voluntarily to the Lords, and that there was no need for threats, or perhaps Asquith had already ceased to take the plan seriously.

By the end of November 1905 Haldane's plan of September had largely failed. It had been based on the necessity of arranging matters before the crisis of the rush for place and before the situation began to 'crystallize adversely', and it depended on resolute action by both Asquith and the Court. The Court made no move at all to influence Campbell-Bannerman before he was formally summoned to the Palace; in weeks of conversation at Marienbad, Edward VII made no hint to Campbell-Bannerman about the Lords.[2] Haldane had clearly exaggerated the impact of his visit to Balmoral. Asquith's references to this subject to Campbell-Bannerman had been only oblique; they were certainly not an 'ultimatum'.

Rosebery's speech on Ireland at Bodmin on 25 November 1905 made public the breakdown in communication at the top of the League.[3] None of the Vice-Presidents discussed the matter with Rosebery; it was left to J. A. Spender to visit the Durdans and find Rosebery 'in a savage & despairing mood', denouncing 'A & G in unmeasured terms, accusing them of having abandoned him'.[4]

Rosebery's speech increased the probability of Balfour's resignation, and politicians gathered in London. Grey and Haldane returned to London with the likelihood of office in their minds. Grey told Rosebery: 'Asquith, RBH & I have gone too far to refuse office unconditionally & I go to hear whether the conditions, which I consider the essential minimum, are conceded . . . It isn't yet certain that I shall not stay out but I guess & fear.'[5]

[1] Haldane to his sister, 21 Nov. 1905, Hal P 6011, f. 14.
[2] See *Bannerman*, ii. 174–8.
[3] See below, pp. 284–5.
[4] Gladstone to Bannerman, 30 Nov. 1905, HGP 45988, f. 204, in James, p. 456.
[5] Grey to Rosebery, 3 Dec. 1905, RP, box 23. Grey came to London on 3 Dec. to stay with Haldane.

Haldane wrote: 'I do not know where I may have to go, but I imagine I shall have to go somewhere.' Haldane had abandoned hopes of the Woolsack, but recognized: 'I may be forced by public duty (Grey & I agree on this) to go elsewhere.'[1]

On 4 December Grey and Asquith saw Campbell-Bannerman, Asquith at Campbell-Bannerman's request,[2] and were, according to Campbell-Bannerman, 'very amicable & reasonable'. They discussed Ireland, and said nothing about the Lords.[3] The same evening, however, Grey returned alone to Campbell-Bannerman and said he 'could not join the Govt. unless Asquith leads the Commons . . . he had made up his mind that it [his position] was final.' He also told Campbell-Bannerman that 'R should be asked to join the Govt.' and that 'the new Govt. shd. be started by the announcement that CB wd. be in the Lords.'[4] But Grey immediately wrote to Asquith absolving him from any obligation to abstain from office.[5] Grey had thus abandoned whatever was left of the tripartite September agreement, even before Campbell-Bannerman became Prime Minister. Grey's 'conditions' were his alone; he did not claim to represent or to speak for his friends.

When Asquith saw Campbell-Bannerman on the morning of 5 December he pressed him to go to the Lords, and, according to Margot, told him 'that it was placing him (Henry) in a cruel and impossible position if under the circumstances Edward Grey refused to take Office', but Asquith made no conditions.[6] On the afternoon of 5 December Campbell-Bannerman became Prime Minister, and Asquith immediately, without discussion with Grey or Haldane, accepted the Exchequer. The Foreign Office was

---

[1] Haldane to Mother, 2 and 4 Dec. 1905, Hal P 5974, ff. 175–7; this was despite a long letter by Asquith to Bannerman, 25 Nov. 1905, CBP 41210, f. 247.

[2] Bannerman to Asquith, 3 Dec. [1905], AP 10, f. 184.

[3] Spender, Memorandum, 4 Dec. 1905, SP 46388, f. 59.

[4] Gladstone, Memorandum, noon, 5 Dec. 1905, HGP 45992, f. 122.

[5] Grey to Asquith, 4 Dec. 1905, AP 10, f. 180. Grey told Asquith next day not to confine himself 'to . . . the things that rankle with me . . . (1) the discourtesy of forming a Govt. without giving Rosebery the chance of expressing regret that he can't join it (2) the slighting of RBH' (5 Dec. 1905, AP 10, f. 186).

[6] Jenkins, p. 154.

offered to Cromer, to whom Grey and Haldane could not have objected, who refused it.[1]

Campbell-Bannerman refused to go to the Lords, despite further suggestions from Asquith.[2] On 7 December he offered Haldane merely the Attorney-Generalship, though allowing for further discussion of other offices. Through the medium of Asquith, he offered Grey the Foreign Office and Haldane the War Office.[3] Grey wrote refusing, and said he could not join the ministry.[4] At this point Asquith abandoned hope of his friends joining the ministry and returned to Hatfield where he was staying.[5]

During the evening of 7 December Haldane spoke to Lady Horner, an old friend, and he and Grey discussed the whole question with Acland, summoned to London for this very eventuality by J. A. Spender, who had foreseen a cabinet-making crisis involving the Liberal Imperialists.[6] As a result of these talks, first Haldane, and then Grey, decided to join the cabinet. That evening Haldane saw Campbell-Bannerman, explained Grey's change of mind, and offered himself for service. On 8 December, Grey accepted the Foreign Office and took a formal offer of the War Office to Haldane which was accepted, thus concluding this pro-tracted, comic, and notorious crisis.[7]

Haldane recollected that 'the real narrative, while it shows how C-B got us into his Government, also shows that he accomplished this in large measure, though not wholly, on our own terms.'[8] It is hard to see that 'the real narrative' shows this. The committee had achieved hardly any of their original aims. Campbell-Bannerman was not in the Lords, Asquith was not Leader in the Commons, Haldane was not Lord Chancellor. Grey was Foreign Secretary, but this had not consistently been one of their conditions of office. The committee certainly occupied some of the ministries

---

[1] *Bannerman*, ii. 197–8. Bannerman then thought of 'other possibilities' before thinking of Grey.

[2] Jenkins, p. 155.   [3] Jenkins, p. 156.

[4] Grey to Bannerman, 7 Dec. 1905, CBP 41218, f. 44.

[5] Jenkins, p. 158.

[6] Spender, Memorandum, 3 Dec. 1905, SP 46388, f. 59.

[7] Haldane to Bannerman, 8 Dec. 1905, CBP 41218, f. 161.

[8] Haldane, p. 182.

necessary to secure control of foreign policy and defence—
the Treasury, the Foreign and War Offices. But this was,
from their point of view, largely accidental. It had never been
their primary aim to capture departmental control; they had
aimed at a general supervision of the tone and style of the
government, and had even been prepared to see Morley as
Chancellor, who wanted to make the Exchequer an effective
anti-imperialist organ.[1]

The 'Relugas compact' affair has become known as a
classic intrigue, but it may be questioned whether a 'Relugas
compact' really existed. Asquith later claimed that 'from
first to last there was nothing in the nature of an intrigue.'[2]
This is too strong, but it is true in the sense that the view
that Campbell-Bannerman should go to the Lords was
always openly canvassed. Such 'intrigue' as there was
centred on the involvement of the Court, and this was mainly
Haldane's idea, and never came to anything. The conversations at Cloanden and Relugas decided that the committee
should demand certain conditions, but in September the
idea was to settle the whole question before the resignation
crisis began. What Haldane called at the time 'the policy of
the Cloanden gathering' was not intended to be a compact
binding in a last-minute crisis in the closet.[3] Campbell-
Bannerman's absence abroad and Grey's and Asquith's
reluctance to act had destroyed during October the policy
agreed to during the September conversations. Asquith,
Grey, and Haldane did not come to London with any cut-
and-dried 'compact'. Asquith had no hesitation in accepting
office; Grey and Haldane came to London expecting to take
office.

The last-minute crisis of December seems to have been
caused largely by Grey's highly personal sense of 'honour'.
Grey felt the total exclusion of Rosebery deeply, and seems
to have influenced Haldane. In matters of personal relationships, Haldane was much affected by Grey's character,
Grey's trump card in all crises. Haldane's December letters

---

[1] See Hamer, *John Morley*, pp. 311–17.
[2] Oxford and Asquith, *Memories and Reflections*, i. 196.
[3] Haldane to Mother, 8 Dec. 1905, Hal P 5974, f. 186. 'Relugas compact' seems
to have been a retrospective phrase (see Haldane, p. 159).

are full of comments that 'E. G. is like steel . . . his display of character is immense . . . it shines out.'[1] Haldane's remark that 'we hate the prospect' of office shows a very strong Grey influence; normally Haldane was extremely keen about any new outlet for his remarkable energies.[2]

Grey's nostalgic recollection that he was influenced by his wife in his decision to take office does not bear scrutiny, for Grey had no contact with his wife on the crucial evening of 7 December.[3] That evening Grey and Haldane were in an isolated position. Throughout their political life, Asquith had been the man to catch, and at the vital moment they had lost him. Their argument was that 'we should not keep our characters if we accepted office.'[4] Their manœuvring exposed them to the ridicule of posterity, but at the time Haldane's argument that 'we were thinking too much of our reputations & too little of our nation' carried the day, for to Grey 'this was a new moral argument.'[5]

To the uninformed public, the Liberal League seemed to have won a considerable victory. Of those who might have taken office, only Rosebery, Perks, and Ferguson were outside the ministry.[6] Concern was voiced about the effect the Vice-Presidents, who, almost despite themselves, were in positions of great importance, might have on policy, especially in the inner cabinet.[7] Despite its internal difficulties, the League put on a bold, even challenging public front, and indicated its intention to continue to exist by holding a League reception and council meeting on 11 December 1905, attended by all the office holders including those now in the cabinet, eleven peers, sixteen M.P.s, and twenty-three Liberal candidates.[8] Rosebery presided.

The election of 1906 increased the number of League M.P.s from about twenty-five to fifty-nine.[9] During the

---

[1] Haldane to Mother, 4, 5, and 8 Dec. 1905, Hal P 5974, ff. 177–86.
[2] Haldane to Mother, 8 Dec. 1905, Hal P 5974, f. 186.   [3] Grey, i. 63.
[4] Haldane to Mother, 7 Dec. 1905, Hal P 5974, f. 183.
[5] Haldane to Mother, 8 Dec. 1905, Hal P 5974, f. 186.
[6] Leaguers in the government were: Asquith, Grey, Fowler, Haldane, Carrington, Freeman-Thomas, Kearley, Runciman, Lawson Walton, Robson, and Ure. As Asquith recollected, Bannerman was very generous to the League in his appointments (Oxford and Asquith, op. cit. ii. 16).
[7] See, for example, W. T. Stead, *Review of Reviews*, Jan. 1906.
[8] *The Times*, 12 Dec. 1905.   [9] See Appendix II

Trade Disputes Bill crisis of 1906, the Vice-Presidents actively encouraged the League to 'remain in fully organised shape "to form the nucleus of the 'Middle party'"'.[1] But after this crisis was resolved, the Vice-Presidents had little to do with the League, which became increasingly dominated by its 'anti' elements—anti-Home Rule and, particularly, anti-socialist. Rosebery abandoned any attempt to construct ideas of 'efficiency', and became a consistent and purely negative critic of the Liberal government.[2] This criticism culminated in Rosebery's attack on the 1909 Budget. After some characteristic and embarrassing confusion, involving resignation and counter-resignation, Rosebery resigned as President, and the Liberal League was eventually dissolved in May 1910.[3]

There seem to have been no recriminations amongst the members of the committee about their handling of the crisis of December 1905. The main regret of Grey and Haldane was, despite his consistent unreliability over the years, the absence of Rosebery. Haldane visited Rosebery on 10 December 1905, writing: 'I cannot let them prevent me from coming to see the Chief of my choice—whom I would fain be under at this moment.'[4] Grey wrote that in his first days as Foreign Secretary he kept writing 'R' by mistake on dispatches![5] Less sentimentally, Asquith wrote to say that, though he hoped their personal friendship would continue, it was, none the less, a 'new era'.[6]

So the 'new era' of Liberal government began. While these three chapters have chronicled the remarkable rise of Asquith, Haldane, and Grey to almost the top rank of their party, they have also shown the sad decline of their leader and patron. For Liberal Imperialists in general, these ten opposition years were for the most part years of political failure. As Ferguson wrote, 'the fact is that none of us came

[1] Perks to Rosebery, 3 Apr. 1906, RP, box 41.
[2] Rosebery in *The Times*, 13 Mar. 1907.
[3] Rosebery in Glasgow, *The Times*, 11 Sept. 1909. For the end of the League, see Asquith to Rosebery (copy), 11 Sept. 1909, AP 46, f. 37, and the Report of the final meeting of the League Council, 31 May 1910, RP, box 106.
[4] Haldane to Rosebery, 10 Dec. 1905, RP, box 106.
[5] Grey to Rosebery, 26 Dec. 1905, RP, box 23.
[6] Asquith to Rosebery, 25 Dec. 1905, RP, box 1.

very well out of the last ten years & the less one thinks of them the better, or of the final debacle.'[1] In their attempts to promote the reform of the Liberal party, the Liberal Imperialists had not shown a sure or effective political touch, and had certainly not become the politically dominant group within the party. These were years of confusion, disorganization, and disappointment. 'Had I to do it again I am afraid I should not do it', concluded Rosebery.[2] Commenting on the League's history, Ferguson wrote: 'it has been an awful debacle for the League from every point of view save one, but that one is the essential consideration in the public interest, viz., Policy. The League policy has been at length adopted by the Liberal Party. . . .'[3]

What that policy was will be discussed in the second part of this book.

[1] Ferguson to Rosebery, 15 May 1906, RP, box 16.
[2] Rosebery to Ferguson, 18 May 1906, RP, box 16.
[3] Ferguson to Rosebery, 6 Jan. 1906, RP, box 16.

PART II

IDEAS AND POLICIES

IV

LIBERALISM AND THE NATURE OF
THE LIBERAL PARTY

P ART I of this book has shown the political manœuvres of a group of men whose personal and political relationships remained remarkably constant over a period of nearly twenty years, from about 1888 to 1905. The bond which united them, and which sustained them despite their obvious and continual inability to act together effectively, was a common view of how the Liberal party and liberalism ought to develop.

Asquith, Grey, and Haldane had never been elected to a parliament with an independent Liberal majority; Rosebery had 'never known what may be the sweets of place with power'.[1] By 1905, the Asquith committee had spent a total of sixteen years in opposition, and had been in the minority party in England in four consecutive general elections. It was not therefore surprising that their primary interest should be the condition of their party, and how it was to be improved. As Grey said in 1901, he saw 'the best years of his life slipping away'.[2]

Disease and diagnosis

As the Roseberians saw it, the leadership of Gladstone after 1886 had been disastrous, because Gladstone in his devotion to Home Rule had accepted 'every Bill presented to him', by every faction in the party, however small.[3] Under Gladstone's leadership the party had become 'a mass of fiery fanaticisms',[4] a 'herd of Gadarene swine running down a steep plane headlong to destruction'.[5] As Haldane wrote:

---

[1] Rosebery to the Eighty Club, 2 July 1895, Eighty Club Publication.
[2] Grey at the party meeting, *The Times*, 10 July 1901.
[3] Rosebery to Lord Farrer, 13 Aug. 1895, RP, Letter Book.   [4] Ibid.
[5] Rosebery to Holmes Ivory, 10 Aug. 1895, RP, Letter Book.

'Mr. G. thoroughly demoralised the Liberal party by the policy of sop-throwing in the two years before 1892.'[1] Ferguson put the view at its most extreme: he had 'had enough of being dragged about the country after an old lunatic.'[2]

The error that Gladstone had made was to surrender to 'the faddists' in the National Liberal Federation.[3] The Roseberians objected very strongly to the idea of programmes imposed upon the government by the associations, for both electoral and theoretical reasons. Electorally the Newcastle programme was harmful because 'it alienated many by its content and more perhaps by the gay ease with which it was accepted.'[4] Theoretically, programmes were undesirable because they cut across the Roseberians' view of how government should be conducted. Asquith deplored 'the political fashion which has been in vogue that is equally injurious to both parties of the State, of presenting to the country . . . not a policy but a catalogue'.[5] Privately Asquith envied the Tories because their caucus had 'never been regarded as a programme spinning machine, and confines itself, wisely, to academic discussion and to the work of organization'.[6]

To accept programmes was to accept 'the surrender of govnt. to democracy'.[7] The function of government was to bring an independent and untrammelled judgement to bear upon the national problems of the day. The essential faculty of the true statesman was a sound judgement; the Liberal party, by its espousal of programmes, prevented the exercise of that judgement. Asquith argued that the Liberal party must be

compatible with the strategic and tactical exigencies of men who have to live not *in Platonis republica* but *Romuli in faece* . . . [Liberals should have] an attitude of hopefulness, of faith, of confidence . . . It is the being possessed at all times by this temper and spirit, rather than the

1 Haldane to Rosebery, 24 Apr. 1895, RP, box 24.
2 Ferguson to his wife, 24 July 1893, FP.
3 Rosebery to Hamilton, 23 Oct. 1895, EHP 48611, n.f.
4 Rosebery to Brassey, 7 Feb. 1896, RP, Letter Book.
5 Asquith at Auchtermuchty, *The Times*, 13 Oct. 1896.
6 Asquith to Harcourt, 17 Nov. 1896, HP 9.
7 Perks to Rosebery, 3 Apr. 1906, RP, box 41, reporting Asquith's remarks.

possession at any particular moment of a carefully catalogued creed or programme, that constitutes the mark of the party of Progress.[1]

The effect of the Newcastle programme on the 1892–5 government had been to limit the exercise of this judgement and to force it to spend its energy in 'dissipation in more or less futile efforts in the simultaneous pursuit' of fruitless schemes.[2]

But the fact that 'the faddists' of the Federation could have so wide an influence was merely a symptom of a wider problem: the Liberal party had ceased to be a national party. It had become 'an army of dervishes each carrying a separate flag'.[3] The Liberals always charged the Tories with being a party of interests, unable to govern 'without being diverted or deflected by compromising alliances with particular classes and particular interests', such as the drink trade, the anglican church, and, increasingly, big business.[4] But this was exactly what the Roseberians saw the Liberal party becoming after 1886. Gladstone had left the party with 'a Welsh-Irish, Dilke and Stanhope foundation',[5] which meant that if liberalism 'could only appeal to one part of the nation . . . it must lose its qualification for what . . . it has always been and must really be . . . the national party'.[6]

Liberal Imperialists felt very deeply on this point. They believed that a 'national' Liberal party was vital to the future stability of Britain. They believed the essential function of the Liberal party to be to contain within itself all classes of society. They, as the ruling élite of the party, would act as a referee between those classes which would otherwise break out in open conflict. Fowler feared that the influence of the N.L.F. would mean 'the disruption of the Liberal party and the ultimate division of parties into the Haves and the Have-Nots'.[7] This would mean an extreme competition of interests,

[1] Preface by Asquith to H. Samuel, *Liberalism. An Attempt to State the Principles and Proposals of Contemporary Liberalism in England* (1902), pp. viii–ix.
[2] Asquith in Stockton, *The Times*, 16 Dec. 1897.
[3] Rosebery to Lord Farrer, 13 Aug. 1895, RP, Letter Book.
[4] Asquith in Leicester, *The Times*, 25 Nov. 1896.
[5] Perks to Rosebery, 8 Oct. 1896. RP, box 37.
[6] Rosebery in Scarborough, *The Times*, 19 Oct. 1895.
[7] Fowler to Morley, 14 Jan. 1898, in E. H. Fowler, *The Life of Henry Hartley Fowler* (1912), p. 439.

as Rosebery saw happening on the Continent: 'It is always possible that there may happen here that which has happened in Belgium—the elimination of Liberalism, leaving the two forces of socialism and Reaction face to face.'[1]

Democratic liberalism prevented such a confrontation. Asquith justified the extension of the franchise in the past on the whiggish grounds that 'by broadening the foundations of our constitutional structure, and thereby diffusing to the widest possible degree the sense of responsibility, it provided the only efficient safeguard both for social and political stability'.[2] By being a 'national party', liberalism in the past had allowed political emancipation, and at the same time 'preserved everything which was fundamental and integral to the social structure of England intact and unbroken'.[3] It was therefore the duty of politicians not to appeal to interests, nor to class feeling, nor to arouse the passions of the mob. Asquith deplored the brewers' supposed defeat of Harcourt at Derby in 1895 on the ground that 'if politics are to become the battleground of these organised interests . . . we are entering upon an era of demoralisation in British politics',[4] and he asked voters thinking of supporting I.L.P. candidates

to remember that in English public life and in English history we have hitherto always had parties which did not represent, or which, at any rate, did not profess to represent, particular classes, but which looked at the interests of the community from the point of view of the community as a whole.[5]

Liberal Imperialists strongly supported working-class Liberal M.P.s to make the party 'national', but were equally strongly hostile to Labour separatism. They therefore, from the 1880s onwards, supported payment of M.P.s,[6] deplored the influence of 'unconscious Tories' who controlled the 'Liberal Associations run by middle class men in the

---

[1] Rosebery to Scott Holland, 21 Aug. 1895, RP, Letter Book.
[2] Asquith to Edinburgh University Liberal Association, 10 Jan. 1900, *Pamphlets and Leaflets*, Liberal Publication Department.
[3] Asquith in East Fife, *The Times*, 18 July 1895.
[4] Asquith in East Fife, *The Times*, 18 July 1895.
[5] Asquith in Hull, *The Times*, 23 Jan. 1895.
[6] See Asquith, Grey, and Ferguson supporting M.P.s' payment, 3 H, cccxxxiv. 1179 ff. (29 Mar. 1889).

interests of middle class ideas', and called for constituency associations to adopt working men as Liberal candidates as the London Progressive party did.[1] After 1902 they recognized that Liberal associations would not select working men in any substantial numbers, and that Labour expectations had outrun the Liberal organizations' ability to assimilate them. They were not privy to the Gladstone/MacDonald negotiations in 1903, but the weakness of their party position made them accept them.[2] Haldane, however, warned that he 'strongly deprecated the formation of [Labour] representatives into groups to act independently of the Opposition . . . the real policy of those who were interested in the cause of Labour must always be to have their views well represented in the Liberal party'.[3] Labour measures and working men as Liberal M.P.s were welcome; a separate party founded on a class principle was not, for this would encourage class hostility and social disintegration.[4]

The obvious faith which Chamberlain had in 'the masses' and his readiness to appeal to them appalled the Liberal Imperialist M.P.s.[5] Asquith denounced Chamberlain's handling of the 1900 election as 'the worst fit of vulgar political debauch since 1877–8', and thought Chamberlain 'has the manners of a cad and the tongue of a bargee'.[6] Grey thought Chamberlain's tariff schemes brought with them the risk of revolution and a threat to social stability, for if Chamberlain succeeded 'there will be no going back; vested interests will spring up . . . men in despair do not see clearly enough to take long views . . . they seek redress in revolution.' In such a situation, Grey believed, the Liberal party would be the first casualty.[7]

Having such a gloomy view of the fragile nature of democracy, Liberal Imperialists were concerned about the fragmentation of the Liberal party for national as well as

[1] *Liberalism and Labour*, LLP 10, 1902; ? by J. M. Paulton.
[2] The ex-cabinet discussed the pact in Sept. 1903; see Grey to Gladstone, 18 Sept. 1903, HGP 45992, f. 100; Grey was more ready than other Leaguers to welcome L.R.C. candidates; see K. Robbins, *Sir Edward Grey*, p. 113.
[3] Haldane at West Calder, *The Scotsman*, 19 Oct. 1904.
[4] Moreover, L.R.C. candidates were almost invariably anti-imperialist.
[5] For Rosebery's views, see below, p. 147.
[6] Asquith to Gladstone, 7 Oct. 1900, HGP 45989, f. 42.
[7] Grey, 'The Autumn Campaign', *Independent Review*, 2 (1904).

personal reasons. As they diagnosed it, especially after 1895, the chief problem was the absence of 'moderate', mainly middle-class, support both at the polls and as an influence on liberalism generally.

In the 1880s, the situation had not been so clear. Socialism appeared to be a major threat to the Liberal party, and the Fabians argued that 'nothing but a generous and frank adoption of a "Labour Programme" will win the confidence of the London masses.'[1] The socialist threat seemed to lessen in the early 1890s, and the poor showing of Labour candidates in 1895 seemed to confirm this impression; between 1895 and 1903 Liberal Imperialists paid virtually no attention to the Labour voters as such.

Even in the late 1880s, Haldane was putting forward the 'middle-class' diagnosis:

What, apart from a party point of view, Liberals must aim at, if they desire to be supported by a majority of the electors, is to accomplish two distinct things. They have to keep not merely the bulk, but the great bulk of the Labour vote. They have also to get back the support of that minority of the upper and middle class, which does naturally, but at present does not, vote with them.[2]

After the electoral disaster of 1895, the expression of this view became a commonplace. The loss of moderate support was dated to 1886. Posing the question of why Glasgow had seven Liberal M.P.s in 1885, but seven Unionist M.P.s in 1901, Haldane reasoned that 'what might be called the centre, the great mass of voters . . . had voted pretty solidly for the other side.'[3] Rosebery told the City Liberals that 'when I say Liberalism I say quite frankly I do not mean sectional Liberalism, but the old Liberal spirit which existed before the split of 1886.' Rosebery believed that 'until you have a new party which will embody all the elements which existed before 1886, you will never achieve that predominance.'[4] Ferguson likewise saw a lack of moderate support, and looked to 'the wider unity which was shattered

---

[1] S. Webb, *Wanted: a Programme; an Appeal to the Liberal Party* (1888).
[2] Haldane, 'The Liberal Party and its Prospects', *Contemporary Review*, Jan. 1888.
[3] Haldane in *The Scotsman*, 19 Oct. 1901.
[4] Rosebery to the City Liberals, *The Times*, 6 May 1899.

in 1886 between the Party and the great mass of British public opinion'.[1] Asquith diagnosed 'a large and a continuous and a growing abstention from the polls of those who in days gone by were among the standard-bearers and the most stalwart in the rank and file of the Liberal party'.[2]

This centre vote was not regarded as entirely middle-class, but the organization of the Liberal League and the type of pamphlets which it produced suggest that it was the middle-class element which was seen as particularly important. The sophistications of the clean slate appealed to the educated; the constituency of Liberal Imperialism was the middle-class mind, reached through the agency of the quality national press.[3]

Little attempt was made to prove the centre diagnosis statistically. Rosebery claimed to have arrived at his electoral theories 'not as a result of intuition, but of investigation and inquiry', but there is no evidence that any of the Roseberians or the League officials attempted detailed electoral studies.[4] Beatrice Webb thought Haldane had misdiagnosed the problem:

Haldane was still keen on winning the centre, a term he regards as synonymous with the non-political voter, in whose ultimate power we believe. In reality those two sections . . . are entirely different . . . What Haldane sees is the moderate politician: the capitalist or professional man who desires little social change and the Empire maintained. But the class we wish them to appeal to is the great lower middle and working class.[5]

Lack of middle-class activity in the party organizations was a further cause of the decay of the party. Rosebery argued that lack of middle-class support was a reason for the lack of suitable candidates, and for the lack of funds to support them. At the national level the lack of party funds

---

[1] Ferguson in *The Scotsman*, 29 Oct. 1902.

[2] Asquith to the Liberal League, 31 July 1902, LLP 20.

[3] Haldane, for example, told the Eighty Club (12 May 1904): 'the audience I love to have in politics is what is called an academic audience.'

[4] Rosebery in London, 23 May 1902, LLP 9. R. E. Dell, 'Cleaning the Slate', *Monthly Review*, 7 (1902), statistically investigates the League's electoral plans, concluding that they will have little substantial impact; apart from this their theories were assertions of opinion rather than of fact. The middle-class vote was, of course, proportionately more important than after 1918.

[5] B. Webb, *Our Partnership*, p. 225 (1 Nov. 1901).

allowed the Unionists to buy up much of the Liberal provincial press.[1] Rosebery's reservations on Harcourt's Budget of 1894 were mainly based on the argument that the Budget would frighten money away from the party, for it was 'difficult to over-estimate the resources of property as a political engine'.[2]

The lack of centre support continued, the Roseberians argued, for three reasons: the excessive influence of the 'faddists' of the Federation, the Liberal alliance with the Irish, and the Liberal position on imperial affairs. The influence of the 'faddists' has already been discussed. The 1886 split was obviously partially connected with the Liberals' Irish policy, and the Liberal Imperialists all declared their separation from the Irish alliance, although they varied in the degree of their renunciation of Home Rule.[3] But the 1886 split was not only, in their view, over Ireland. Rosebery argued that the divisions in the cabinet between 1880 and 1885

were far more in what I call foreign and Imperial questions . . . than on Irish questions . . . it has always been part of my diagnosis that the separation which took place in 1886 was in reality due more to the foreign policy of the Government from 1880 to 1885 . . . than to any particular animosities in regard to the Irish question.[4]

Haldane attributed the unpopularity of the party with 'moderate' voters both to Gladstone's Irish policy and 'to the period between 1880 and 1885, when it lost the confidence of the country in foreign affairs'.[5] Even during Rosebery's handling of imperial affairs from 1892 to 1895, Haldane thought that 'the Liberal Party as a whole was not credited with administrative capacity, regarding our external relations.'[6]

It was not so much the policy itself that was wrong, although Rosebery had reservations about its conduct from

---

[1] Rosebery in *The Times*, 18 Oct. 1895.
[2] Rosebery's 'Memorandum on Harcourt's Death Duties', 3 Apr. 1894, RP, box 96. For an endorsement of the Roseberians' view of the loss of wealth in 1886, see P. W. Clayden, *England under the Coalition* (1892), p. 150.
[3] See below, Chapter VIII, *passim*.
[4] Rosebery to the City Liberals, *The Times*, 20 July 1901.
[5] Haldane to the Liberal Forwards, *Daily Chronicle*, 29 Nov. 1899.   [6] Ibid.

1880 to 1885, but rather the way the party 'as a whole' had presented itself and its policy to the electorate. Roseberians did not deny that there was a place within the Liberal party for opposition to imperialism. Asquith accepted that 'there have always been in the Liberal party, and there always will be, different schools of thought as regards our relationship to the Empire.'[1] Asquith himself had been in private a strong critic of Rosebery's policy.[2] They did not even deny that liberalism constituted to some degree the natural party of protest on such matters. Haldane agreed that 'the unbending Radical—of the H. F. Wilson type—must be respected. He is an institution and cannot be expected to change.'[3]

What annoyed the Liberal Imperialists was what they saw as the excessive degree to which the party had become a party of protest. Before the 1880 government, the Little England view had been a harmless ideological luxury; by 1895 it seemed to be becoming the majority opinion within the party. As E. T. Cook put it: 'Though Bright and Palmerston were both Liberals, and though they represented contradictory schools of thought, there was never any doubt as to which school prevailed.'[4] The large body of Little England opinion within the party was much exploited by the Unionists, who represented it to the electorate as characteristic of the whole party. There was no doubt that the Unionists had successfully established themselves as the 'Imperial Party', partly by their skilful use of propaganda, and partly through the Liberals' persistent habit of being in fact imperialist (in Egypt and Uganda) but in appearance and presentation anti-imperialist.[5] In the period after 1895 when imperial questions were in exceptional prominence, the Liberal Imperialists believed that it was above all because of the attitude of the party as a whole to such questions that it had lost the confidence of the centre. Liberalism had alienated

---

[1] Asquith in London, 19 July 1901, Liberal Publication Dept.
[2] See above, p. 16.
[3] Haldane to Gladstone, 8 Nov. 1899, HGP 41215, f. 133.
[4] Cook, 'Lord Rosebery and the Liberal Party', *New Liberal Review*, July 1901.
[5] For examples of Unionist propaganda, see R. T. McKenzie and A. Silver, *Angels in Marble* (1968), pp. 52–9. The *Daily News* commented on 6 May 1899 that on the question of an 'unpatriotic' appearance 'Liberals are often their own worst enemy.'

'the silent voters'[1] since it seemed to have dissociated itself from 'the new Imperial spirit'.[2] Thus while there were few London Liberal M.P.s, the liberal Progressives controlled the L.C.C. The anti-imperialism of Liberal candidates was identified as the differentiating factor. Grey argued that:

. . . if anyone ever succeeded in foisting upon the Liberal party the title of 'anti-Imperialist', then the Liberal party could not only lose all prospect of office, but it would also be displaced from its recognised position.[3]

Roseberians believed they alone prevented this disaster.

Finally, the Liberal Imperialists diagnosed a lack of relevance in the content of liberalism itself. Liberalism had become excessively dominated by the policy of political and religious emancipation which it had followed in the past. It was not denied that Welsh disestablishment, Irish Home Rule, and franchise reform were desirable in principle, but the former were reforms which directly affected only a small proportion of the population, and it was doubtful whether further franchise reform would benefit the Liberals. Such reforms were not worth the major, divisive, and time-consuming crises which they provoked in parliament, crises of which Asquith and Fowler had great experience, having been respectively in charge of the abortive and highly contentious Bills for Welsh disestablishment and of the Parish Councils Act.

Continual adherence to these as the major Liberal targets prevented, they felt, liberalism being 'progressive in opinion and catholic in scope'.[4] Roseberians argued that 'there had never been a formula in the Liberal creed corresponding to the old test of ecclesiastical orthodoxy, *Quod semper, quod ubique, quod ab omnibus.*'[5] But they felt that Liberals who argued, as Campbell-Bannerman did, that 'we had better walk quietly along the old Liberal paths' were congealing the party in a jelly of Gladstonianism, which was bad in principle and bad electorally.[6] Liberals who thought that, if they kept 'a fixed political faith', 'sooner or later, and soon

[1] Haldane in *Daily Chronicle*, 29 Nov. 1899.
[2] Rosebery in *The Times*, 6 May 1899.
[3] Grey in London, *The Times*, 21 Mar. 1900.
[4] Asquith in London, *The Times*, 2 May 1903.   [5] Ibid.
[6] Bannerman in *The Times*, 23 Mar. 1899.

more probably than late, our doctrines, because they are doctrines of truth, will prevail' were stultifying the natural development of Liberal thinking.[1] Haldane, discussing such men in 1896, 'was reminded of what happened to Lot's wife. There were a good many pillars of salt among their old friends.'[2] These Liberals were Rosebery's 'Tory Liberals',[3] who had made liberalism 'a fixed dogma graven long ago on a rock',[4] and who 'neutralise and render impotent the force of Liberalism'.[5]

The Roseberians thus identified four malicious forces within the party, the faddists of the Federation, who were wrongly trying to democratize the party, the Celtic fringe which drowned the party in a flood of contentious marginalia, the Little England group which made the Liberals seem unpatriotic, and the Tory Liberals, often the ageing chairmen of the constituency associations, wealthy and cautious about any change from the 'good old days', who made liberalism an irrelevant and inflexible creed.[6]

Remedies

The diagnosis contained the suggestion for the remedy. The party must become national, embracing all elements of society, particularly adding the centre, mainly middle-class, element lost in 1886; it must be freed from the influence of the faddists; it must be seen to be patriotic, pragmatic, and flexible in its approach, progressive enough to give justice to the oppressed, moderate enough to retain the support of the wealthy. Above all, it must allow the Roseberians a position within the party from which their judgement would be allowed free play over the problems of the nation.

Liberal Imperialists saw the Liberals caught in a circular situation; the centre would not support the party because it was irresponsible, the party was irresponsible because it lacked centre support. Their challenge was to break the

---

[1] Bannerman in London, *The Times*, 13 Jan. and 23 Mar. 1899.
[2] Haldane, 'The Future of Liberalism', *The Scotsman*, 30 Dec. 1896.
[3] Rosebery to the City Liberals, *The Times*, 20 July 1901.
[4] Rosebery to a correspondent, *The Times*, 29 Nov. 1895.
[5] Rosebery in *The Times*, 20 July 1901.
[6] See 'Liberalism and Labour', LLP 10, 1902.

circle. They did not doubt that this was possible, if the party would listen to them. Fowler refused to admit 'that the Liberal party is in a permanent minority'.[1] Rosebery held that 'Liberalism . . . is the national spirit of the country, but it is dormant in a cave.' Moreover, Rosebery believed that 'there is, however, in existence, probably, a bugle somewhere destined to blow the note that will break the spell.'[2] The problem was to find the bugle, and then to blow it effectively. The Liberal League was the bugler, Liberal Imperialism the note it played.

The essential and distinctive ideological feature of the Roseberians was their pragmatism, and it was this which they felt constituted their main contribution to liberalism. Rosebery's metaphor of the clean slate depicted their pragmatism in its most graphic form.

The concept of the clean slate was most articulately developed by Haldane. Haldane believed, after the experience of the 1892–5 government, that liberalism 'was in the process of adaptation and recasting'. The old Gladstonian principles were quite inadequate to revive the doctrine. Haldane thought Liberals saw two courses open to them. Given that 'the temple was shattered', some Liberals believed 'there remained some corners, some walls of the temple still standing, and that they could shelter there from the weather, and go on as before'. This view was, Haldane said, 'futile'. It was necessary 'to be bold—to clear the ground and to put on the site of the old temple a new building'.[3] Haldane did not accept any abstract theory of 'right' as a criterion, for 'the truth was that the truth itself must change, must develop, as generation succeeded to generation.'[4] Haldane therefore did not even look for political rights, let alone expect to find any. He stated his views at great length in the Gifford Lectures given in 1902 and 1903, when the League's clean slate campaign was at its height. In these he attacked 'unconscious dogmatism', and concluded: 'It is the nature of mind that it is free from the dilemmas that affect the

---

[1] Fowler in *The Times*, 28 Jan. 1896.

[2] Rosebery to Professor Knight, 31 Oct. 1897, RP, Letter Book.

[3] Haldane in *The Scotsman*, 14 Oct. 1896.

[4] Haldane, *The Pathway to Reality* (1904), i. 13, ii. 114. Haldane found 'the cleansing of the slates is not always an easy or wholly agreeable process' (i. 13).

object-world, and that it neither stands still nor is mere change. Its nature is to be permanence in change and change in permanence.'[1] Given this, principles were not abandoned, but merely altered in changed circumstances. Therefore liberalism's 'watchwords had represented the truth for their own times, but it did not follow that they represented the truth for the wholly different and developed times in which they lived.'[2]

Other Liberal Imperialists expressed similar views in less philosophical form. Fowler thought the party must adapt 'to the pressing and constantly freshly developing emergencies of today. They were not prepared to go on munching . . . the dry biscuit of an old political economy.'[3] Asquith, who thought Haldane did 'all the brain work of the Liberal party',[4] found in the clean slate the 'same doctrine which I have preached to you for years past in less picturesque language, the doctrine of selection and concentration'.[5] Grey put the implication of the doctrine in its bluntest form: 'it was not their business to produce a definite programme.'[6]

Rosebery, in a sustained campaign in 1895 and 1896 designed to 'make . . . the faddists furious', declared that liberalism 'is necessarily a moving adaptable creed, to be adjusted to the wants of a rapidly changing age'.[7] Rosebery even denied the relevance of the historical Liberal tradition, to most Liberals an important part of their approach: 'it is nothing to us what Pym, or Walpole, or Fox would say of 1895, for we have to deal with the spirit of our times.'[8] Rosebery wanted 'to start with a *tabula rasa*'.[9] He returned

---

[1] Ibid. ii. 114.

[2] Haldane, 'Political Ideas in the Twentieth Century', *Dundee Advertiser*, 11 Oct. 1901.

[3] Fowler in *The Times*, 19 Dec. 1901.

[4] Asquith to 'a friend', 1901, in Maurice, *Haldane*, i. 112.

[5] Asquith to his constituency chairman, *The Times*, 3 Mar. 1902.

[6] Grey at Newcastle, *The Times*, 21 Oct. 1897; Grey was disconcerted by this intellectual freedom, telling B. Webb: 'Politics have completely changed . . . formerly you had your cause made for you, and all the politicians had to do was to preach it; now you have to *make your cause*' (Webb, op. cit., p. 226 (28 Feb. 1902)).

[7] Rosebery to Hamilton, 23 Oct. 1895, EHP 48611, n.f., and in *The Times*, 29 Nov. 1895.

[8] Rosebery, *The Times*, 29 Nov. 1895; for other speeches denouncing programmes and advocating pragmatism, see Rosebery in *The Times*, 18 Oct. 1895; 3, 12, 30 Mar., 28 Apr., 16 May 1896. [9] EHD, 16 Oct. 1896.

to the *tabula rasa* theme in July 1901, emerging from retirement to advise the party to 'start with a clean slate as regards those cumbersome programmes with which you were overloaded in the past'.[1] He developed the concept further in his Chesterfield speech and in his speeches of 1902 as an aspect of what he called 'common sense' and 'sane Imperialism'.[2]

The clean slate offered ideologically a prerequisite for redefining Liberal thinking on matters of policy in all fields, and politically a way of reducing the power of the faddists and of allowing the Liberal Imperialists free play as regards party policy. It was not denied that the party should have a policy, but a clear distinction was drawn between a policy and a programme. A policy was a general criterion, an attitude to progress; a programme was a series of specific commitments. If the centre was to be regained, the Liberals must have something to offer, and the Roseberians certainly did not argue that the clean slate meant a blank mind.

The object of the Roseberians was to find a policy which would regain the support of the centre and simultaneously unite the warring factions within the party, for, as Harcourt observed, 'who will deny that the Party is hopelessly split up not only on Foreign Policy but on all great domestic questions?'[3] The Gladstonian tactic, analysed and supported by Morley, had been to 'focalize' the party and public opinion on a 'single great issue', thus uniting the party in support of a specific political proposal.[4] The 'single great issue' left as a legacy by Gladstone in 1894 was the question of the Lords. At first the Roseberians tried to continue this 'focalization', and in the 1895 election Asquith, Haldane, Fowler, and Ferguson all followed Rosebery in making the Lords question, 'the primary question for all Liberals', the main point of their electoral appeals.[5] The Lords question was, however, quite unsuitable as a rallying-cry in opposi-

---

[1] Rosebery to the City Liberals, *The Times*, 20 July 1901.

[2] Rosebery in Glasgow, LLP 3.

[3] Harcourt to Morley, 24 Dec. 1898, HP 10.

[4] See D. A. Hamer, *John Morley*, pp. 89–95 for an analysis of Morley's development of this concept.

[5] Rosebery in Scarborough, *The Times*, 19 Oct. 1895; see also H. Jones, *Liberalism and the House of Lords* (1912), pp. 88–93.

tion, especially in view of the Lords' inactivity during the Unionist government. After 1895 it was hardly mentioned.

Whereas Morley had looked to a specific issue to bring the party together under an 'umbrella', the Roseberians were attracted by their dislike of programmes and by their pragmatism to what was basically a totally different approach. They hoped to unite the party and solve its electoral and ideological problems not by a specific proposal, but by the 'umbrella' of a concept which implied no single specific legislative proposal, but rather general agreement about a common approach to politics.[1]

The 'umbrella' developed by Liberal Imperialists was the idea of 'sane Imperialism', coupled with 'national efficiency'. 'Sane Imperialism' and the 'larger patriotism' were deliberately vague phrases. Applied to the actual problems of the empire, they were virtually meaningless. But their function was primarily domestic—to offer a concept which could unite the various Liberal factions and attract the centre vote. Imperialism was to restore to the Liberal party the reputation for patriotism which it had had under Palmerston and which under Gladstone it had lost to Disraeli.[2] National efficiency was simultaneously to be used as a criterion for assessing national and imperial needs and for developing a positive rather than a negative liberalism.

In the 1880s the Roseberians believed that 'the Liberal party has accomplished the main part of what it has to do in the way of establishing more freedom from interference for the individual.' Its function was next 'to win for him the condition of freedom in a more subtle and far-reaching sense'.[3] Grey thought that 'the advanced party must occupy a point of view so comprehensive that it embraces all questions of social welfare and property.'[4] Even at this time Haldane deplored the concentration 'on single questions', and hoped to steer it into a general positive policy.[5] In the

[1] See Haldane, 'The New Liberalism', *Progressive Review*, Nov. 1896, p. 141.
[2] Unionists were sensitive to this potential threat; see Anon. [J. L. Garvin], 'A Palmerston—with Nerves', *Fortnightly Review*, July 1899.
[3] Haldane, 'The Liberal Party and its Prospects', *Contemporary Review*, Jan. 1888.
[4] Grey, *Rural Land* (1892), Eighty Club Pamphlet.
[5] Haldane, 'The Liberal Creed', *Contemporary Review*, Oct. 1888.

1880s it was 'the individual' who was their yardstick. As the Roseberians became concerned in the 1890s about the industrial position of Britain, they altered their criterion from the individual to the nation. As Haldane put it: 'Belief in the state as real equally with the individuals in whom it is realised and whom it controls, this is the foundation of orderly government.'[1] It was the function of the state to develop 'not measures of emancipation but measures of construction'.[2] 'Liberty (in a political sense) is not only a negative but a positive conception.'[3]

This concept of the state as the progenitor of a 'positive conception' of liberalism suggested that the state was organically composed, and that the rights of the individual must be subordinate to the efficient functioning of the whole. Criticizing the clean slate and the Chesterfield speech, J. A. Hobson correctly stated the Liberal Imperialists' position :

> The conception of society as a moral organism negates the old Democratic idea of political equality based on the notion that every member of a political society had an inherent right to the same power as every other in determining the action of society. The idea of natural individual rights as the basis of Democracy disappears.[4]

As Asquith put it, reform must be looked at not as a benefit to the individual 'but as a question of social and Imperial efficiency'.[5]

This was a departure from the traditional Liberal individualism of which J. S. Mill was regarded as the typical exponent. C. M. Douglas, League M.P. and lecturer in philosophy in Edinburgh, attacked Mill for regarding 'truth as an objective standard'.[6] Mill's philosophy showed conclusively 'the difficulty of erecting a theory of knowledge and action on a basis of individualism'.[7] Mill's difficulty, Douglas thought, was that he had inherited the English

---

[1] Haldane's Edinburgh Rectorial, 10 Jan. 1907, in *Army Reform and other Addresses* (1907), p. 297.

[2] Rosebery in Glasgow, 10 Mar. 1902, LLP 3.

[3] Asquith in H. Samuel, op. cit., pp. vii–ix.

[4] J. A. Hobson, 'The Re-Statement of Democracy', *Contemporary Review*, Feb. 1902.

[5] Asquith in London, *The Times*, 17 July 1901.

[6] C. M. Douglas, *John Stuart Mill* (1895), p. 45.

[7] Ibid., p. 12.

empiricist tradition: such successes as he had had came late in his life through the possibly unconscious absorption of Hegelianism, which produced 'tendencies, which may be inconsistent with his avowed principles, but which are genuinely characteristic of his thinking'.[1] Douglas did not succeed, however, in showing how Hegel's views could apply in a Liberal democracy, and it cannot be said that he or Haldane succeeded in doing more than adumbrate in very vague terms a British neo-Hegelian theory of the state.

Liberal Imperialists did not stress the rights of individuals and, during the Boer War, were ready to support conscription, whose absence was regarded by most Liberals as one of the most valuable attributes of Liberal Britain.[2] But this aspect of their thought should not be overstressed. They called for a moderate reduction of wholesale nineteenth-century individualism. They believed that the intense individualism of most Britons was a sufficient safeguard against any dangerous intrusion into personal liberty, and that the debate, especially characteristic of the 1880s, about 'The Man *versus* the State' was of theoretical rather than practical significance.[3] Haldane conceded: 'Like all valuable principles that of the duty of organisation may be ridden too hard, but into this danger our national characteristics are not likely to let us fall.'[4]

If the clean slate called for a radical rethinking of all aspects of Liberal policy, national efficiency offered a criterion for this rethinking, because of all the questions facing Britain and the empire, 'the greatest . . . is efficiency, because it combines them all.' Efficiency was

the condition of national fitness equal to the demands of our Empire—administrative, parliamentary, commercial, educational, physical, moral, naval and military fitness—so that we should make the best of our admirable raw material.[5]

Thus the criterion for the value of a future Liberal policy

[1] Ibid., pp. 92–6; see also Haldane, 'Hegel', *Contemporary Review*, 1895 and on T. H. Green in 'The New Liberalism', *Progressive Review*, Nov. 1896.
[2] See Grey to the City Liberals, *The Times*, 21 Mar. 1900.
[3] The title of Herbert Spencer's famous 1884 pamphlet.
[4] Haldane, *Army Reform*, pp. 298 ff.
[5] Rosebery in Glasgow, 10 Mar. 1902, LLP 3.

was whether it contributed to 'everything, in short, that tends to national, communal, and personal efficiency'.[1]

Haldane told the Dundee mock-parliament that 'all political controversy is circumscribed within a certain ambit.' The idea of efficiency would narrow the activity of a Liberal government to the area of national concern. The Roseberians assumed that there was basic agreement amongst intelligent men about national priorities; discussion would centre on details, not on principles. In answer to the question 'were not the political ideals the different ideals of different parties?' Haldane answered that this was not so, and said that 'the nation . . . indicated the limits within which it was going to allow party controversy to occur.'[2]

During the Boer War such a central consensus did seem to exist, but it was fragmented by the tariff reform campaign of 1903, which simultaneously caused 'the welding of the Liberal party'.[3] Politically, opposition to tariff reform proved to be the effective bugle-call to reunite the factions within the party and to win over the centre. But while this was electorally good, it jeopardized the future of efficiency, for it caused, the Imperialists thought, a general Cobdenite revival, based on free trade but including general hostility to state action, 'a narrow, fanatical, vindictive . . . and retrograde Liberalism'.[4] In their attempts to defend free trade, even some League members fell back on purely negative arguments. Asquith

abstained now from developing the positive side of the Liberal programme. Even if they had to confine themselves to . . . opposition to the Education Act and to Tariff Reform, there would be abundant justification for the country returning them to power.[5]

This sort of talk appalled the Webbs who 'sat and listened with consternation to "our leader" [Rosebery] declaiming against public expenditure *per se*'.[6] Haldane was alarmed that the Liberals should appear to be making only a negative

---

[1] Asquith in H. Samuel, *Liberalism*, p. x.

[2] Haldane in *Dundee Advertiser*, 11 Oct. 1901.

[3] Haldane at Drem, *The Scotsman*, 6 Oct. 1903.

[4] Rosebery to the Liberal League, 10 June 1904, LLP 144.

[5] Asquith in Leven, *The Times*, 14 Oct. 1904; see C. Chesterton, *Gladstonian Ghosts*, n.d. [? 1904], *passim* for attacks on this attitude.

[6] B. Webb's Diary, 26 Nov. 1903, L.S.E., Passfield Papers.

appeal, and told the League there was an 'absolute necessity for the Liberal Party stepping forward, not resting content on a mere negative victory against Protection', but Haldane became an increasingly lone voice.[1]

But if hostility to tariffs formed the umbrella after 1903, it was national efficiency which was intended to be the umbrella in the years when the party's fortunes were at their lowest.

Politically, national efficiency was to be the bugle-call for a rejuvenated and united Liberal party. Since it was national it could appeal to Tory Liberals usually reluctant to accept extension of the state's power; its concept of state action would appeal to Fabians, socialists, and the labour voter, since its domestic suggestions would be largely concerned with improving the quality of the race; to the patriotic middle class it could appeal because it implied an intimate involvement of the Liberal leadership in 'sane Imperialism'. It would not appeal to the Celtic fringes of the nation, but these could hardly vote other than Liberal, and, the Roseberians hoped, would have their influence in the party diminished by the regained centre vote.

The possibility of party disintegration

The objective was to create 'progressive, practical and National Liberalism', but it was recognized that it might be impossible to achieve this within the Liberal party.[2] All Liberal Imperialists had as their primary aim the resuscitation of the Liberal party, but they varied in their optimism about their probable success. The less optimistic had, therefore, a continual eye on possible alternatives.

Of the four leading Roseberians—Rosebery, Grey, Haldane, and Asquith—only Asquith was an obvious party man who firmly and positively believed in the party system of government. Asquith's paramount aim was the unity of his party. He believed that party government was 'the best system which the political genius of mankind had invented for organising opinion and translating it into action'. Parties

---

[1] Haldane to the Liberal League, 13 Apr. 1905, LLP 191.
[2] Asquith's Liberal League memorandum; see Appendix III below.

were 'functions which were essential to the working of a free state'; without party, democracy risked 'completely falling into decay'.[1] Asquith took his stand in the centre of the English parliamentary tradition, and throughout this period did not doubt that the Liberal party would pull through intact.

In principle, Grey agreed with Asquith. He hoped that Goldwin Smith's opinion that 'the party system was likely to disappear altogether . . . was not true,' for if it was true, then 'the whole Parliamentary system would have to be modified . . . they would have politics split into groups, and they would have an unstable government.'[2] But Grey felt that, regrettable though this would be, it might happen.[3] He found the 'Liberal party is disintegrated everywhere', and thought that early in 1902 the Liberals might split and that 'perhaps a corresponding split may come amongst the Conservatives and a large middle party come into being for a while.'[4] Later in 1902 Grey, expecting Balfour's resignation over the Education Bill, hoped Rosebery might lead a central ministry appealing to the nation 'with the credit both of Liberalism and Efficiency in Affairs, the latter helped I hope by having Kitchener in the Cabinet and perhaps Milner'.[5] Grey had, however, a curious passivity, and, despite his presidency of the I.L.C., did not see himself as a positive agent in the construction of a coalition.[6]

Whereas Grey and Asquith saw the Liberal party as a glory in itself, and stayed with it all their lives, Haldane was different. Haldane was a political activist, always with a project in mind. As Lloyd George perceptively remarked:

Haldane was a baffling personality . . . with all his loquaciousness he was a doer of things . . . A combination of ideas and energy is tiresome to the complacent . . . the indolent cannot distinguish between intrigue and action—so Haldane passed for an intriguer.[7]

[1] Asquith in Oxford, *The Times*, 26 Feb. 1900.
[2] Grey in Hexham, and in Glasgow, *The Times*, 6 Feb. 1899, and 29 Nov. 1901.
[3] Grey was ready to join and lead the I.L.C., a possibly disruptive body, earlier than Asquith; see above, p. 75.
[4] Grey to Milner, 16 Mar. 1902, MP 40, f. 111.
[5] Grey to Rosebery, 11 Aug. 1902, RP, box 23.
[6] The same was true in 1910, when Grey approved of, but did little to assist, Lloyd George's coalition proposals (Grey to Asquith, 26 Oct. 1910, AP 12, f. 214).
[7] D. Lloyd George, *War Memoirs*, 2nd ed. (1938), i. 603.

Haldane was thus, as he said, not 'a very good party man'. He was a Liberal because he was 'intensely interested in certain ideals of Liberalism'.[1] For all its shortcomings, Haldane saw the Liberal party as the best available party of progress; however, he seems basically to have believed that the ideal would be a Fabian-controlled party of the 'centre'.[2] But his own inadequacies as a politician prevented him from starting such a party, and Rosebery, Asquith, and Grey, through whom he had to work, persistently refused to work hard in that direction. In 1902 Haldane believed that 'the sense of the nation is working towards the construction of a great centre party.' But, he warned, to achieve this 'clear thinking and firm action are the essentials.'[3] But these qualities were just those that he could not count on from the intended chief of his centre party, Rosebery.

Rosebery's views on party

Rosebery's views on party and politics are so remarkable for a man who was a Liberal Prime Minister, and are so basic to an understanding of his persistent reluctance to act, that they require separate examination.

Whereas men like Asquith regarded political activity as good in itself, Rosebery doubted the value of the whole British political structure. He regarded the Lords, to which he was permanently condemned, as incompetent and in need of reform, but he also had 'long thought that the H. of Commons was in the nature of a dangerous and life long disease'.[4] Politics was a charade in which 'we are all of us . . . in politics eloquent men, first debaters . . . able to prove our opponent to be either a nincompoop or a knave.' British emphasis on debating skill meant that politics were 'a monotony and a groove', irrelevant to the real problems of the nation. The effect of this was 'the impotence of all governments to carry any great measure in the teeth of

---

[1] Haldane, *Constructive Liberalism*, 12 May 1904, Eighty Club Pamphlet.
[2] Haldane was greatly disillusioned with the Unionist progressives by their failure to support him over a Catholic university for Ireland.
[3] Haldane to Rosebery, 6 Oct. 1902, RP, box 24.
[4] Rosebery to Ferguson, 21 July 1899, RP, box 15.

opposition'.[1] The 'obstruction of Parliament ... the obstruction of privilege ... the obstruction of prejudice' were such that 'governments prefer to patch up and botch up any immediate difficulty ... and pass on until some worse difficulty falls on them.' The result of all this was that 'we do not proceed by scientific methods.'[2]

Rosebery had long believed that the qualifications for being an M.P. should include education in the technical matters of government,[3] and that party loyalty was used as a substitute for independent thought. During the Boer War he felt that the defects of party government had been exposed, for he saw

few needs of our nation which are more clamant than the need for independent thought. The nation was like a man emerging from the eighteenth century in periwig and ruffles, unable to understand why he is out of touch with his neighbours, assuming that it is he who is correctly dressed.[4]

In 'apathy' the nation slept on, unawoken by its legislators who carried on their games in remote impotence.

Rosebery suggested two remedies. First, he called for the removal of the old-style politicians from government. He promoted the Cromwell Statue project after 1895 and used the revival of interest in Cromwell to call for dictatorial methods. He announced that 'we could find employment for a few Cromwells now.'[5] The twentieth-century Cromwell should take the form of a 'dictator, a tyrant ... a man of large mind or iron will who would see what had to be done and do it'.[6] If there was not to be a tyrant, then Rosebery suggested 'a Cabinet ... in which no politician should be permitted ... a Government in which, perhaps, no member of an existing or former Government should be included'. This

---

1 Rosebery in Edinburgh, *The Times*, 15 Nov. 1901.
2 Rosebery at Chatham, *The Times*, 24 Jan. 1900.
3 See Rosebery in 1874, in *Lord Rosebery's Speeches* (1896), p. 23.
4 Rosebery in Birmingham, *The Times*, 16 Oct. 1901.
5 Rosebery at the Cromwell Tercentenary celebration, *The Times*, 15 Nov. 1899.
6 Rosebery in London, *The Times*, 14 Nov. 1899; see also my contribution to the *Past and Present* colloquium on 'Cromwell and the Nineteenth Century'.

cabinet would be made up 'entirely of business men'. Rosebery mentioned Andrew Carnegie, Sir Thomas Lipton, and Sir Richard Moon as possible members.[1]

Alternatively, Rosebery hoped that 'the nation' might be mobilized to force the legislators into fruitful action, since 'the model race' could only be perfected by a direct appeal to the people to abandon 'the strange, crippling apathy . . . which appears to veil the thoughts of the nation'.[2] In 1900 Rosebery told the Shoreditch electors that 'the power is not in these borough councils that we are going to elect, but rests in yourselves', and he raised an almost Chartist cry: 'What power London could not exert if it chose to put it out! Five millions of people surrounding the Parliament and the centre of the Empire!'[3] Rosebery's confident appeal to the mob contrasted strongly with his Commons friends' nervous acceptance of democracy.

Rosebery not only disliked party government; he believed it was disappearing. He dated 'the gradual disintegration of party to Disraeli and 1867'.[4] The extended franchise would not accept the frivolities of party games, and a future generation 'will nerve themselves without regard to those persisting Shibboleths for some great national effort in which party machinery will be both useless and forgotten'. But Rosebery did not see himself as the catalyst for this great event; he therefore contented himself with advising the Liberal party, for the time being 'a necessary evil'.[5]

But since he held these views, Rosebery gave his advice without confidence and without enthusiasm, more as a commentator than a participant. How seriously Rosebery accepted his own opinions is unclear. They amounted to a formidable indictment of British party and parliamentary government, but Rosebery made no attempt to act upon them, except perhaps in his half-hearted leadership of the League. In his actual political behaviour Rosebery was as punctilious as anyone about the forms and niceties of British

[1] Rosebery in Edinburgh, *The Times*, 15 Nov. 1901.
[2] Rosebery in Birmingham, *The Times*, 16 Oct. 1901.
[3] Rosebery in Shoreditch, *The Times*, 27 Oct. 1900.
[4] Rosebery to Goldwin Smith, 18 Mar. 1902, RP, Letter Book.
[5] Rosebery in Edinburgh, *The Times*, 15 Nov. 1901.

public life, but in his political ideas he pointed the way to more ferocious attacks on the tenets of democracy.[1]

This disagreement about the value, function, and future of the Liberal party explains much of the lack of effective co-operation apparent in Part I of this book. Theoretically, these arguments pointed to some sort of coalition. Thoughts of coalition run implicitly and sometimes explicitly through the correspondence, though hardly ever through the speeches, of the period. But there is no indication that Liberal Imperialists thought a coalition imminent or practicable, and they did not work to achieve one. They realized that their destiny lay, for the foreseeable future, within the Liberal party, and they never seriously tried to do otherwise than work within the party to gain control of it. Given this practical necessity, they felt a substantial and distinctive measure of agreement. They had a common vision of a Liberal party, patriotic and national in scope, moderate but progressive in policy, élitist and pragmatic in its leadership. They assumed, almost as a matter of right, that they would lead this party, and most of their contemporaries accepted this assumption.

The bugle-call of Liberal Imperialism was thus to summon to the colours a unified, expanded Liberal party, and an extended view of liberalism. Part I of this book has shown the Imperialists' political failure to establish themselves as the Orthodox Church within the Liberal tabernacle; they always seemed to be dissenters, plaintiffs rather than defendants. They were accepted as part of the party leadership for their personal qualities, in spite, rather than because, of their ideas. Their hope of fusing 'left' and 'right' to produce 'a practical policy on which progressive opinion can unite' was unrealized.[2] They had failed to persuade their party that imperialism was progressive. To most Liberals national efficiency seemed 'right wing', and men like Morley, who with their *laissez-faire* Gladstonian ideas had in the early 1890s seemed 'right wing' and reactionary,

---

[1] Similar indictments were often made in this period, but by men like Milner, Arnold White, and Belloc, men on the bank, not in the main political stream. For them to be persistently expressed by a Liberal ex-Prime Minister was remarkable.

[2] *The Liberal League*, n.d. [1902], LLP 18.

again emerged as standard-bearers of the 'left'. The confusing effect of imperialism on the 'left/right' distinction was noted by Beatrice Webb:

The cleavage about the war runs right across the cleavage on economic affairs: the old 'Illingworth set' being again on the left of the Liberal party whilst some of the most progressive reformers are flirting with Imperialism and even talk well of Milner.[1]

At the same time as they were trying to permeate, control, and revive their party, Liberal Imperialists were attempting to apply the concepts of the clean slate, national efficiency, and 'business methods' to the problems of policy, both imperial and domestic. Their analysis of these problems, and their attempts to offer solutions, are discussed in subsequent chapters.

[1] B. Webb's Diary, 20 Feb. 1900, L.S.E., Passfield Papers. Percy Illingworth was a prominent Little England, *laissez-faire* Yorkshire M.P.

V

LIBERAL IMPERIALISTS
AND THE EMPIRE

SOME Liberal Imperialists, like Rosebery and Brassey, were veterans of the Imperial Federation League of the 1880s. Their careers had been largely built around their interest in the empire, an interest that had created rather than followed the fashion of imperialist rhetoric in *fin de siècle* Britain. The Liberal Imperialist group in the Commons, however, was largely composed of men with little interest in the empire before about 1892. Fowler, later one of the most strident imperial rhetoricians, had taken the view that 'the happiness and progress of our home population is of vastly more importance than any foreign policy, than any extended Empire. You may call it a parochial policy—call it what you like.'[1] Asquith had opposed Rosebery's Uganda policy.[2] Haldane opposed the parliamentary grant for the 1887 Jubilee, regarding it as a 'ridiculous sum to waste'.[3] As late as 1896, Haldane, speaking as 'an advanced Liberal', said 'he did not stand there as an out-and-out advocate of all the political creed which was associated with the name of Lord Rosebery. He was one of those who had thought in the past . . . that Lord Rosebery was apt to take courses which were bold even to the point of rashness.'[4]

Of the group in the 1880s, only Ferguson and Buxton had any sustained interest in imperial questions, or spoke on them in the Commons. Once having been in office, or acquainted with office through his friends, each became, as Asquith wrote to Rosebery, 'an Imperialist in your sense'.[5] This was the result partly of their natural pragmatism, partly of their analysis of how liberalism ought to develop, partly

---

[1] Jan. 1880 (E. Fowler, *Life of H. H. Fowler*, p. 115).
[2] See above, p. 16.
[3] Haldane to Mother, 17 May 1887, Hal P 5939, f. 115.
[4] Haldane in N. Berwick, *The Scotsman*, 14 Oct. 1896.
[5] Asquith to Rosebery (not sent), 6 May 1899, in Jenkins, pp. 111–12.

of their general desire for continuity of government.[1] It was also the result of their view that the empire was facing 'an exceptional array of difficulties'.[2] The series of crises facing Britain in the Near and Far East, India, and in various parts of Africa dominated press and parliament, their prominence encouraged by the lack of Unionist domestic legislation. The Commons men had thus become involved in imperial affairs because such affairs were prominent, not because they were inherently interesting, or because, like Grey and Fowler, they were appointed to offices in which they had previously had no interest. They were involving themselves in what seemed the spirit of the age; as Haldane wrote to Milner: '"Get Geist" was the injunction which Matthew Arnold left . . . its truth is beginning to be badly felt.'[3]

The hope of using imperialism to restore the unity and fortunes of the Liberal party encouraged Roseberians to vague and rhetorical statements, the best-known of which is Rosebery's peroration:

How marvellous it all is! . . . Human, and yet not wholly human, for the most heedless and the most cynical must see the finger of the divine . . . Do we not hail in this less the energy and fortune of a race than the supreme direction of the Almighty?[4]

This was itself a gloss on Gladstone's claim, often quoted by Imperialists, that the empire 'is a part of my being . . . of my heart and soul . . . a trust and function given by God'.[5] Such statements were for electoral consumption; they had little to do with practicalities of policy. But Liberal Imperialists also believed that the empire 'is not merely a question for perorations, but it is a question of the most vital and practical politics'.[6] It was clearly important to distinguish between rhetoric and reality, and to remember that a purple passage, convincing to a domestic audience, could well distort clear thinking about policy. The Liberal Imperialist electoral strategy was aided by as wide a definition of imperialism as possible: 'definitions . . . so elastic that

---

[1] See Ch. IV, *passim*.   [2] Asquith in Glasgow, *The Times*, 7 Dec. 1899.
[3] Haldane to Milner, 3 Mar. 1901, MP 39, n.f.
[4] Rosebery's Glasgow Rectorial, 16 Nov. 1900, in W. L. Langer, *The Diplomacy of Imperialism 1890–1902*, 2nd ed. (1960), p. 94.
[5] Gladstone in Midlothian, 17 Mar. 1880; used as definition of 'sane Imperialism' in LLP 37.   [6] Rosebery at Imperial Institute, *The Times*, 8 July 1898.

they were capable of any interpretation', as Lloyd George observed.[1] To solve imperial problems, Liberal Imperialists hoped to use a 'business' approach; they claimed to be practical men, seeking out 'efficiency' and introducing it where it was absent. They saw imperial, and also domestic, politics as a series of soluble problems: they did not try to develop a theory of imperialism, or to counter Hobson's famous analysis, *Imperialism: a Study*.[2] Such a pragmatic approach required a careful definition of what 'efficiency' was, and their failure to produce one led the Liberal Imperialists into many difficulties.

The empire confronting the Imperialists was complex in its structure, containing almost every known type of non-republican constitution. Liberal Imperialists saw it as a three-tier system, each tier having distinctive problems, and each tier being only by accident of government related to the other two. Grey illogically but typically analysed the empire:

> The idea of Empire was not the idea of one race domineering over another race. The first thing was the attachment of our self-governing colonies and the splendour of having created them. The next thing was the rule of India. That no doubt, was the ruling power of one race, but a power which in latter years had ruled India as it had never been ruled before. In regard to uncivilized countries he thought our hand had been forced. It had been forced in Africa by the pace at which other nations had gone.[3]

The empire was therefore first white; secondly and as an accepted anomaly, Indian; thirdly, 'uncivilized' and expanding. Grey's semi-racial, semi-regional analysis will be used as a basis for discussion, starting with his third category.

An expanding empire?

In the late nineteenth century, expansion seemed the most obvious characteristic of the 'uncivilized' empire. Was such expansion inevitable? Explaining the occupation of the

---

[1] Lloyd George to Ruskin Debating Society, 23 Nov. 1901, LGP A/10/1/36.
[2] Thus both Haldane, *Education and Empire*, 1902 and T. A. Brassey, *Problems of Empire*, 1904 are collected speeches.
[3] Grey in Berwick, *The Times*, 31 May 1901.

Sudan, Asquith observed 'natural and economic causes' at work,[1] and claimed that

> there was a process of expansion which was as normal, as necessary, as inseparable and unmistakable a sign of vitality in a nation as the corresponding processes in the growing human body . . . we might control it and direct it . . . we could not arrest it.[2]

Asquith's use of fashionable Darwinian ideas was not entirely accepted by his political colleagues at this time, who were at pains to show that imperialism did not imply continual, though it might involve spasmodic, expansion. Rosebery thought: 'Imperialism should have for its main object the maintenance and consolidation of the Empire: extension should be avoided if possible.'[3] The empire, in their view, was not expanding under its own momentum, as Asquith's analogy, borrowed from Benjamin Kidd, suggested; a certain element of choice existed. None the less, the concept of inevitability was frequently used, particularly with reference to Africa. The expansion in Africa in the 1880s and 1890s was seen as a defensive move, the result of the initiatives of other European powers by whom 'the pace has been made for us'.[4] But given that competition to exist, Britain's share in it was, to use one of Grey's favourite words, inevitable:

> Individual men may hold that it is undesirable that we should enter into free competition for the development of Africa, but that competition exists and . . . it was inevitable from our powers, from our tendencies, from our capacities and from our histories that we should take part in it . . . the share we have taken in it . . . we could not have avoided.[5]

Britain's expansion in East Africa was also inevitable, given the premiss of Egyptian occupation. Grey argued: 'we entered Egypt years ago and when the late Liberal government came into power, I held that they had no free choice as regards Uganda.'[6] Expansion into the Sudan was therefore merely the last step of this policy; to ignore the logic of the situation was 'academic'. Grey thought Morley's attempt to

[1] Asquith in Fife, *The Times*, 1 Oct. 1897.
[2] Asquith in Lancashire, *The Times*, 28 Jan. 1899.
[3] Rosebery to Spender, 2 Nov. 1899, RP, Letter Book.
[4] Grey in 4 H, lxvii. 491–5 (24 Feb. 1899).   [5] Ibid.   [6] Ibid.

revive Cobdenist thinking on expansion was not so much wrong as totally unrealistic: 'even he [Morley] must think that it [occupation of the Sudan] has become inevitable.'[1] Rosebery thought Leonard Courtney's views on Africa absurd, and told him: 'You do not, I think, take sufficient account of the changed conditions of the world since Cobden's Liberalism affected the minds of men.'[2]

The new factor was the activity of other powers. As Rosebery put it: 'So long as we were free to develop . . . without any particular concurrence, there was no conflict of interest . . . but now almost all these empires have developed a colonial policy of their own.' Liberal Imperialists were unclear about the forces which had caused this new activity. Rosebery thought them uncontrollable, and said: 'you must not blame the European states for their attitude towards us. It is wiser to explain it by natural reasons.'[3] These 'natural reasons' were commercial. There had been expansion 'not in the least because Great Powers wish to flatter themselves with territorial expansion on the map, but because they are lured on by the hope of commercial expansion'.[4] This was also the public reason given for British East African expansion and the expense involved therein, though without much conviction. Grey claimed that 'we shall justify that expenditure when . . . within a few years these great territories become self supporting . . . Africa . . . when it is settled must lead to a large increase in the volume of our trade.'[5] This was an argument for domestic consumption. Grey skilfully included the Sudan, almost wholly desert, and occupied for essentially strategic reasons, with those parts of Africa suitable for white settlement, to which Rosebery referred as 'new areas for our surplus population'.[6] Though there was an element of 'pegging out claims for posterity',

---

[1] Grey in 4 H, lxvii. 491–5 (24 Feb. 1899); for Morley's attempt at a Cobdenite revival, see Hamer, *John Morley*, ch. 21.

[2] Rosebery to L. Courtney (Unionist pro-Boer M.P.), 21 July 1901, RP, Letter Book.

[3] Rosebery at the Imperial Institute, *The Times*, 8 July 1898.

[4] Rosebery in London, *The Times*, 22 Mar. 1901.

[5] Grey in 4 H, lxvii. 497 (24 Feb. 1899) (Sudan debate).

[6] Rosebery in London, 5 July 1895, in (ed. anon.) *The Foreign Policy of Lord Rosebery* (1901). For the Nile valley policy, see R. Robinson and J. A. Gallagher, *Africa and the Victorians* (1961), pp. 306–38, and G. N. Sanderson, *England, Europe and the Upper Nile, 1882–1899* (1965), pp. 98–113.

the Liberal Imperialists' lack of interest in economic development in Africa does not suggest that it had priority.[1]

Expansion in tropical Africa was therefore seen more as
a fulfilment of the pledge of continuity of policy than as an
expansion desirable in itself. Though most Liberal Imperialists knew Cecil Rhodes and admired his energy in an
abstract way, they had not much enthusiasm for the drive for
commercial expansion which was his motivating aim, and
they did not work as a group to help him.

By 1895 partition was largely over; as Rosebery remarked, 'how very little of the world in a very short time
there will be to divide!'[2] The main area for future expansion
lay in Asia, and it was here that Liberal Imperialists, working
as a group, had their chance to advocate expansion, should
they so desire. The 1892–5 Liberal government's Asian
policy was uncertain, and left no clear legacy. Over the
Sino-Japanese war the Liberals reversed their earlier policy
and left the Concert to side with Japan over the Shimonoseki
settlement.[3] The integrity of Siam had been preserved, but
Rosebery's policy of a buffer state to keep the French away
from Burma and to safeguard British entry to the Yangtze
basin had virtually failed by 1895.[4] Kimberley told Rosebery
in April 1895: 'I feel at present on almost all the most
important questions of the present moment we are really
without any definite policy.'[5] Liberals in opposition were
therefore not bound to any clear position on Asia as they
were on East Africa.

Some Liberal Imperialists had high hopes of imperialism
in China. Henry Norman's authoritative book on the Far
East argued that 'the rest of the world is parcelled out like
an allotment-ground. In the Far East alone an unworked
mine awaits us.'[6] Norman, writing in 1895, expected and
welcomed partition: 'In Asia will be founded and will

[1] See below, p. 158.
[2] Rosebery at Imperial Institute, *The Times*, 8 July 1898.
[3] Langer, op. cit., pp. 174, 182–6.
[4] Langer, op. cit., pp. 43–6; and A. J. P. Taylor, *The Struggle for Mastery in Europe 1848–1918* (1954), pp. 343–4.
[5] Kimberley to Rosebery, 6 Apr. 1895, RP, box 54.
[6] H. Norman, *The People and Politics of the Far East* (1895), p. 599. For praise of the book see Langer, op. cit., p. 413; for Norman, soon a Liberal Imperialist M.P., see Appendix I.

increase a great Empire . . . *Be Asiatic, there lies the future.*'[1]
He suggested an 'Anglo-Russian-Japanese understanding'
to organize partition. 'The maintenance of the status quo'
was 'old fashioned'; Britain must be first in the field to peg
out her claims.[2]

Norman's views were publicized by Reginald Brett, a
close friend of Rosebery, who wrote that 'England . . . if her
place . . . is to be maintained, must be primarily an Asiatic
Power.'[3] Joseph Walton, Liberal Imperialist M.P. for
Barnsley and an 'Old China Hand', thought China offered
better commercial prospects than India and wrote that
whilst 'we should do all in our power to increase the trade
between Britain and our Indian Empire, the fact still remains
that China is the neutral market which offers the greatest
possibilities for trade expansion'.[4] These Liberal Imperialist
experts thus offered the basis for an aggressive policy in
China, should their leaders wish to develop one.

Norman's book ends with a call to Rosebery to take the
lead in promoting Britain's Far Eastern greatness. He was
to be disappointed. After 1895 Rosebery hardly mentioned
Far Eastern affairs. He showed no enthusiasm for China as
a territorial or commercial Far Eastern India. He did not see
in the 'Old China Hands' and their railway concessions the
equivalents of Rhodes, Goldie, and Mackinnon. Grey was
similarly unreceptive to Norman's hopes for Liberal pressure
on the government. Grey was quite ready to accept
Salisbury's abandonment of the buffer-state policy. He
observed that Salisbury had made 'great concessions' in
Indo-China, but said that if the concessions brought friendship with France, 'we shall have a *quid pro quo.*'[5] This was
the first airing of Grey's general theme: the need for a general
détente with the Dual Alliance, if necessary at the expense of
local interests and concessions.

When the Far Eastern question became acute at the end
of 1897, Grey made no attempt to force the government's
hand. The *Daily News* agreed that this 'is no time, if it can

---

[1] Norman, op. cit., p. 597.   [2] Norman, op. cit., p. 402.
[3] R. Brett, 'The Far Eastern Question', *Contemporary Review*, Mar. 1895.
[4] J. Walton, *China and the Present Crisis* (1900), p. 321.
[5] Grey in 4 H, xxxix. 343 ff. (27 Mar. 1896).

possibly be avoided, for indulging any Gargantuan thirst for more Empire'.[1] Grey supported the 'open door' policy. The situation was, he said, 'the very opposite' to the Powers' policy of tariff barriers in Africa.[2] But the basic question was, could the door remain 'open', given Chinese decay and European activity?[3] Grey mixed optimism with necessity:

> The policy of the open door is one I still regard with hope, for it seems the only policy in the Far East by which it is possible to reconcile the interests of this country with the interests of the other Great Powers.[4]

But Grey was ready enough to see the door closed by Russia. He urged a *détente* with Russia in the Far East, and showed no interest in Britain's commercial interests in China. He was willing to see Russia take northern China, and he was especially concerned that Britain should not in any way occupy the Yangtze basin, for 'territorial influence . . . would be disastrous.' The British government should be very wary that a sphere of influence did not 'carry with it that sort of obligation which is bound to be carried with it in Africa'.[5] Grey agreed that the Anglo-Russian agreement of 1899 was a poor one looked at from the view-point of Britain's local interests in China, but that was not, in Grey's view, the main point. He welcomed the agreement 'not so much for what is contained within the four corners of it, but because it is the beginning of a policy of frank communication between the two countries'. 'For the sake of relations between the two countries', Grey accepted the violation of China's integrity.[6]

Liberal Imperialist leaders thus ignored the advice on Asia of their locally interested colleagues; they were hostile to expansion and were ready to encourage the sacrifice of local British commercial interests in return for the further-

[1] *Daily News*, 1 Jan. 1898.

[2] Grey in 4 H, liii. 148 (8 Feb. 1898).

[3] See N. A. Pelcovits, *Old China Hands and the Foreign Office* (New York, 1948), p. vii; Pelcovits misnames Joseph Walton as 'John Walton, M.P. for Middlesborough', *passim*.

[4] 4 H, lvi. 280 (5 Apr. 1898).   [5] 4 H, lxvi. 237–41 (8 Feb. 1899).

[6] 4 H, lxxii. 817 ff. (9 June 1899). Walton had meanwhile split the quiescent China Association to organize support for vigorous defence of commercial interests (Pelcovits, op. cit., p. 268). But Perks, as a financier, told Rosebery: 'We are likely to do an enormous trade with Russia—it seems madness indeed to quarrel . . .' (29 July 1898, RP, box 39).

ance of their primary concern, a *détente* with the Dual
Alliance. They saw China as an exercise in foreign and
diplomatic policy; imperialism, in the sense either of govern-
mental control or the informal development of commerce,
was to be avoided, almost at all costs.

'Undeveloped estates'

If Liberal Imperialist leaders showed little positive concern
for commerce in China, they showed not much more for
economic imperialism and Chamberlain's policy of developing 'undeveloped estates'.

In a famous remark in 1893, Rosebery said: 'We are
engaged "in pegging out claims for the future" . . . We have
to consider what countries must be developed either by ourselves or some other nation.'[1] But the Liberals in office
showed themselves much more interested in denying the
claims of others than in developing their acquisitions.
Though ready to speak the rhetoric of economic expansion
for the benefit of domestic audiences, Liberal Imperialist
leaders had little understanding of or interest in economic
development. Rosebery was ready when in office to sacrifice
most of relatively prosperous West Africa to gain security
in the sandy Sudan.[2] It is true that security in the Sudan was
seen as a vital aspect of security in India, but Liberal
Imperialists had no plans for the development of India,
though they had, under heavy pressure from India, introduced cotton duties there in 1894. In Africa little economic
benefit was expected from recently pegged out claims.
Asquith thought 'there was very grave reason to doubt
whether some of our more recent adventures . . . in Africa
were likely to prove in the long run remunerative.'[3] Nor did
the Liberal Imperialists see direct Colonial Office control as
an aid to development. The *Daily News* thought Chamberlain wrong to see it so, and argued that Colonial Office
control in Nigeria would produce less development than the
Royal Niger Company.[4]

---

[1] Quoted in Langer, op. cit., p. 78.
[2] See Robinson and Gallagher, op. cit., p. 333.
[3] Asquith in Birkenhead, *The Times*, 20 Jan. 1898.
[4] *Daily News*, leader, 24 Aug. 1899.

Though Rosebery in 1896 had urged the end of the 'pegging out' of claims and the start of development and 'consolidation', he had not indicated how these were to be achieved.[1] Such development was likely to raise awkward questions of fiscal orthodoxy for Liberals. This proved to be the case in Grey's attempts to grapple with the economic stagnation of the West Indies. Chamberlain asked Grey in 1896 to serve on the West Indies Royal Commission with Sir David Barbour and Sir Henry Norman. Rosebery, Asquith, and Morley tried to dissuade Grey, on the ground that he 'might be let in for something such as differential duties, which could not be justified on the wide ground . . . though it might be the only remedy for the sugar producing colonies'.[2] None the less, Grey joined the Commission, and soon found himself in the position his colleagues had feared.

Only the application of countervailing duties, or the negotiation of the removal of the bounty in Europe, could save the West Indian sugar industry. The latter was assumed to be impossible.[3] The commissioners therefore agreed that 'the levy of countervailing duties is practically the only remedy', but disagreed as to whether the remedy should actually be applied.[4] Grey and Barbour opposed countervailing duties because of 'the loss to the British consumer that would result from any rise in the price of sugar; the inconvenience to trade . . . and the danger of departing from what had hitherto been considered to be the settled policy of the United Kingdom'.[5] Norman supported such duties in a minority report.

There was no clean slate for Grey in the West Indies, but he did not, as some Liberals did, oppose negotiations to remove the bounties, and he did support grants to assist the colonies. The Colonial Loans Bills of 1898 and 1899 facilitated these grants, and met persistent Little England opposition, Labouchere opposing assistance on the ground

[1] Rosebery in Edinburgh, *The Times*, 10 Oct. 1896.
[2] Grey to Ferguson, 16 Dec. 1896, in Trevelyan, *Grey of Fallodon*, p. 71. Harcourt told Morley Grey 'had better jingoise in England than Zollvereinise in the Indies' (13 Dec. 1896, HP 10). Sir H. Norman was a colonial servant, *not* the Liberal M.P.
[3] See R. W. Beachey, *The British West Indies Sugar Industry in the Late 19th Century* (1957), ch. viii, *passim*, and p. 169.
[4] The Commission's Report, Parl. Papers 1897, 1 (C. 8655).
[5] Ibid., para. 49.

that 'a Crown Colony is a Colony which is thoroughly rotten'.[1] Perks denounced Labouchere's views and urged: 'we must not hesitate to lend the credit of this country.'[2] The Liberals consistently split on the question of development loans, but before the 1902 budget these splits were of minor importance.[3] This budget made protection a major issue; to support Chamberlain's schemes now would seem to condone his protectionist views. Moreover, Chamberlain unexpectedly succeeded in negotiating the removal of the sugar bounties.[4] This had been Grey's solution, but his party was opposed to the rise in the sugar price expected from it. Grey was clearly embarrassed. He supported the 1902 interim grant to the West Indies, but would not discuss its general implications, despite the taunts of the Little Englanders.[5] He stayed away from the 1903 sugar debates, when his friends voted against the convention.

While ready to make minor concessions to fiscal unorthodoxy, Liberal Imperialists were not ready to make imperial economic development a major priority, or a major point of difference with their party.

India

Liberal Imperialists showed remarkably little interest in India, the second tier of Grey's analysis. Gibson-Carmichael and Freeman-Thomas were not preparing themselves for the central roles that, as Lords Carmichael and Willingdon, they were later to play in governing India.

Henry Fowler was the Leaguer most involved in Indian matters, and this was merely the result of his appointment in 1894 to the Indian Office, to which post he brought, Curzon observed, an 'unfettered judgement'.[6] Fowler dramatically overruled the Indian government's desire to expand permanently to Chitral on the northern frontier, and he was involved,

---

[1] 4 H, lxii. 190 (18 July 1898).
[2] 4 H, lxxv. 1192 (2 Aug. 1899).
[3] See Div. list in 4 H, lix (16 June 1898), lxiii (2 Aug. 1898), lxxv (2 Aug. 1899), cxii (31 July 1902).
[4] J. L. Garvin and J. Amery, *The Life of Joseph Chamberlain* (1951), iv. 247 ff.
[5] 4 H, cxii. 304 ff. (31 July 1902).
[6] See E. Fowler, *H. H. Fowler*, p. 286.

conciliatorily, in the cotton-duties dispute.[1] But his main aim was to resist the demands for constitutional reform from Congress and its Westminster representatives, Sir William Wedderburn and Dadabhai Naoroji, the Parsee Liberal M.P.[2] Though forced to allow an inquiry into Indian expenditure, he refused any general inquiry into the structure of Indian government and regarded Wedderburn's reforming ideas as 'thoroughly rotten . . . impracticable and absurd'.[3] Believing that a firm hand could stop the Congress movement, which he saw as an Indian version of the National Liberal Federation, Fowler was more stridently anti-Congress than the Unionists, and earned the Unionist government's public thanks.[4] He supported Curzon through his stormy Viceroyalty and claimed, to vociferous opposition from his own party, that Curzon 'in the main character of his administration . . . had the confidence of all Parties'.[5]

Fowler's main constructive work for India was done in opposition as chairman of the committee on Indian finance.[6] The committee's aim was to resolve the chronic instability of the rupee, a major barrier to growth in the Indian economy. Fowler's solution was cautious and orthodox. His committee in 1898 recommended 'the ultimate establishment of a gold *currency* in India as well as a gold *standard*'.[7] The committee specifically rejected A. M. Lindsay's plan for an internal paper currency as impractical and unorthodox.[8] But within a few years Lindsay's plan was in operation, for it proved the only workable solution, and Fowler's considerable labours were proved unimaginative and sterile.[9]

The development of the 'Union of sympathy'

When Liberal Imperialists spoke of 'the empire', they almost always meant the top tier of Grey's analysis, the areas of

---

[1] See P. Harnetty, 'The Indian Cotton Duties Controversy, 1894–1896', *E.H.R.* (1962).

[2] See M. Cumpston, 'Some Early Indian Nationalists and their Allies in the British Parliament, 1851–1906', *E.H.R.* (1961).

[3] Fowler to Harcourt, 30 Mar. 1895, HP 3.

[4] 4 H, xlv. 541 (26 Jan. 1897).   [5] 4 H, cxl. 441 (12 Aug. 1904).

[6] See A. Godley's opinion in Fowler, op. cit., p. 290.

[7] See J. M. Keynes, *Indian Currency and Finance* (1913), p. 34.

[8] Ibid., pp. 4–5.   [9] Ibid., p. 34.

white settlement. The empire was 'composed of free self-governing communities, bound together, not by force, but by sentiment and affection . . . It was in essence a Liberal Empire.'[1] Rosebery, observing the difficulty of giving 'any satisfactory account to the logical mind of the basis on which the Empire rests', found its essential feature was 'the union of races'. By this he meant 'the community of memories, of work, of object and of aim'.[2] It was with this empire that the Liberal Imperialists were largely concerned.

'Race' was defined culturally, not biologically. Rosebery thought the 'sympathy of the race' was based on linguistic, 'moral, intellectual and political influences'. Immigration from 'foreign races' was acceptable as long as it was assimilated. Thus Americans were part of the 'British or Anglo-Saxon' race.[3] Theoretically anyone could become part of this cultural unit in time. But Rosebery did not expect this actually to happen. He compared the Russian to the British empire, and expected the former to become homogeneous; the latter would remain fragmented since the British lacked 'the magic faculty of assimilation'.[4] India could never be British in the sense that Siberia would become Russian. In a dangerous world, Britain must look for strength, in the long run, to that which 'is the essence and root of the matter—the union of sympathy'.[5] For Rosebery the vital feature of the Boer War was colonial participation, which was

not so much the work of governments as the spontaneous impulse of the peoples themselves . . . If with all our reverses we have purchased only the fact that the Empire is a united Empire . . . we should have made a profitable transaction.

The empire would be 'henceforth a supreme factor in the balance of the world'.[6]

The issue facing all imperialists was, could and should this 'union of sympathy' be developed into something more cohesive and regulated? In the 1880s Rosebery took a dynamic view:

---

[1] Grey in Berwick, *The Times*, 27 Sept. 1900.
[2] Rosebery in Australia, 1884, in *The Foreign Policy of Lord Rosebery* (1901).
[3] Rosebery in London, *The Times*, 8 July 1898.
[4] Rosebery in London, *The Times*, 5 Mar. 1896.   [5] Ibid.
[6] Rosebery in Chatham, *The Times*, 24 Jan. 1900.

It is absolutely impossible for you to maintain in the long run your present loose and indefinable relations to your Colonies . . . Britons will have to make up their minds what footing they wish their colonies to occupy with respect to them, or whether they desire their colonies to leave them altogether.[1]

As President of the Imperial Federation League, Rosebery played a major part in putting these questions to the public and in emphasizing the League's 'non-party character'.[2] But the Liberals showed little interest. Of the eighty-three M.P.s on the League's council in 1888, only six were Liberals.[3]

To avoid a public row over Imperial tariffs, the I.F.L. dissolved itself in 1893, but in the late 1890s schemes for imperial unity were much to the fore; Chamberlain in particular showed he hoped for developments. Liberal veterans of the I.F.L., and those becoming interested in imperial affairs, like Asquith, Haldane, and Grey, had to decide whether to continue the non-party principles of the League by supporting Chamberlain, or whether to advance their own plans.

Constitutional, fiscal, and defence plans were the most obvious means of strengthening the 'union'. When Prime Minister and opposition leader, Rosebery made no attempt to develop plans in any of these directions. He abandoned his dynamic views and said in 1896: 'we may say of the British Empire at this moment, that never was its unity so fully comprehended . . .' Rosebery believed that 'the mechanical union of that Empire' was less likely than ten years previously, but this was not regrettable—existing bonds were sufficient:

I . . . should not earnestly strive to bring the unity of the Empire very much nearer than it is at present, because it seems to me to rest at present on a liberal and affectionate comprehension—and what surer basis of an Empire is there than that?[4]

Asquith hoped in 1896 for 'machinery for joint consultation and for concerted action' on defence,[5] but he agreed on the

[1] Rosebery in Leeds, 11 Oct. 1888, in *Lord Rosebery's Speeches 1874–1896*, p. 53.
[2] J. E. Tyler, *The Struggle for Imperial Unity 1868–1895* (1938), p. 112.
[3] Lord Brassey, *Papers and Addresses: Imperial Federation and Colonisation* (1895), appendix iii. The Liberals were: J. A. Bryce, S. Buxton, Ferguson, H. L. W. Lawson, McArthur, Alfred Thomas. For Ferguson's later work, see below, p. 221.
[4] Rosebery to South Australians in London, *The Times*, 5 Mar. 1896.
[5] Asquith in Reading, *The Times*, 11 June 1896.

main point with Rosebery. 'The more time and the more thought' Asquith gave to unity schemes the more he believed 'that the loose and informal connexion which at present exists . . . might perhaps in the long run be found to be the best and surest safeguard for the permanence of our Imperial unity'. This view was partly based on the obvious difficulties involved in major amendment of the British constitution, and on the feeling that strengthening 'visible and mechanical bonds' might overstrain 'the whole structure'.[1] But for Liberals there was the additional difficulty that major constitutional change would be likely to involve fiscal change also.

The 1892–5 Liberal government found itself frequently on the brink of protectionism. Ripon, the Colonial Secretary, suspected the government generally, and Buxton and Rosebery particularly, of 'leanings to fair trade'.[2] Fowler had subsequently to admit that there was 'an element of protection in the duties' he introduced in 1895 for Indian cotton.[3] The cabinet was split over whether the registration of sellers of foreign meat would condone protection.[4] The 1894 'subsidiary' Ottawa conference called for mutual differential duties between Britain and the Colonies.[5] Ripon pointed out the traditional objections to this, that British taxation would increase, that colonial trade was only a small part of Britain's total trade, and that British trade would suffer. He agreed, however, that

a Customs Union comprising the whole Empire, whereby all the existing barriers to free commercial intercourse between the various members would be removed . . . would certainly prove effective in cementing the unity of the Empire.[6]

There were also fiscal complications in southern Africa, over an attempt by Cecil Rhodes to 'insert the thin end of the

---

[1] Asquith in Reading, *The Times*, 11 June 1896.
[2] L. Wolf, *Life of the First Marquess of Ripon* (1921), ii. 218.
[3] 4 H, xliv. 799 (13 Aug. 1896).
[4] See the sundry comments on Mundella's memorandum, n.d. [1894], RP, box 36.
[5] *C.H.B.E.* iii. 412; and J. E. Kendle, *The Colonial and Imperial Conferences 1887–1911* (1967), p. 18.
[6] Ripon to Governors-General, 28 June 1894, in Parl. Papers 1895, lxx (c. 7824); see R. A. M. Shields, 'Imperial Policy and the Ripon Circular of 1895', *Canadian Historical Review*, vol. 47, no. 2 (1966).

wedge for the introduction of the Protectionist policy of differential duties within the Empire'.[1]

Despite these opportunities the 1892–5 government, including Rosebery, consistently maintained free trade as best they could. Chamberlain's proposals after 1895 thus came to men who had already squarely faced these questions in office. When Chamberlain proposed a Zollverein in 1896, Buxton, surprisingly, strongly supported him in public, on the ground that unity could only 'be decided on the basis of the German Zollverein'; Britain would have to be 'prepared to place duties on the imports of foreign food and raw materials'.[2] Buxton claimed to be maintaining 'continuity of policy'.[3] Here was a call for a modification of Liberal policy, should others wish to follow. None did. Asquith expressed his 'most emphatic dissent . . . the proposal was . . . unsound in principle, unworkable in practice and chimerical as an ideal.'[4] This was a clear rebuff to 'continuity', and from a man who was becoming more 'imperialist' in his interests.

Rosebery made no comment on Chamberlain's proposal at this time. Liberal Imperialists showed no particular enthusiasm for the 1897 Colonial Conference, though they made much of the Jubilee celebrations. The *Daily News* welcomed the Canadian preference tariff of 1897 as 'a far reaching event', but the Commons men kept well clear of the issue.[5] Rosebery replied to Chamberlain in November 1897. He reaffirmed his belief that the empire had 'marched with seven league boots' on the basis of sympathy, which basis must continue: 'anything in the direction of an Imperial commercial league would weaken this Empire internally and excite the permanent hostility of the whole world.'[6] Whereas Asquith's chief objection was to an increase in British prices, Rosebery placed his main emphasis on the world situation. While a 'local' empire, such as that of Russia or Germany, could effectively run a customs

[1] Ripon to Rosebery, 12 Apr. 1894, RP, box 46.
[2] Buxton, *The Times*, 10 June 1896.
[3] Ibid.; the *Daily News*, 10 June 1896, gave Buxton strong support.
[4] Asquith in Reading, *The Times*, 11 June 1896.
[5] *Daily News*, 19 and 31 July 1897.
[6] Rosebery in Manchester, *The Times*, 2 Nov. 1897.

union, 'an Empire spread all over the world with a uniform
barrier of a Customs Union . . . would be . . . a perpetual
menace, a perpetual incentive and irritation to war.'[1]
Chamberlain's union would amount to a 'new Empire'
which might fulfil Rosebery's fear that 'the next great war
. . . will be a war for trade and not for territory.'[2] Rosebery
also strongly objected to such a 'new Empire' since it would
exclude the U.S.A. which he saw as a vital part of the future
'union of sympathy'. Rosebery therefore tried to dampen the
ardour of the Federationalists in Canada, telling G. R.
Parkin to avoid 'hindering a good understanding between
Great Britain and the United States' by supporting
Zollverein proposals.[3]

When the tariff issue again came to the fore with the 1902
Budget, it was fairly clear that the Liberal League leaders were
unlikely to support fiscal union. Rosebery had a long commitment against it which had become the more pronounced the
more the question was publicly discussed. He made a brief
and half-hearted attempt to apply the principles of the clean
slate, arguing that free trade was not 'part of the sermon on
the mount' and declaring that he would not 'hastily reject
without mature consideration, any plan offered on high
authority and based on large experience for really cementing
and uniting the British Empire'.[4] But Rosebery put forward
these views more as a hope of maintaining continuity and
decorum in the discussion of imperial affairs than because
of any genuine feeling for imperial federation with a tariff
basis.

If Rosebery had by 1903 reached a virtually passive
position with regard to the development of the empire, this
was not so of all Leaguers, and it is clear that by 1902 some
Liberal Imperialists were toying with the idea of a bipartisan
introduction of tariffs. Some important Leaguers did in fact
join Chamberlain in his 1903 campaign, but none was a
member of the inner group of League leaders.[5] Haldane,
who applied the idea of efficiency more seriously and con-

---

[1] Rosebery in Manchester, *The Times*, 2 Nov. 1897.
[2] Rosebery in London, *The Times*, 8 July 1898.
[3] Rosebery to Parkin, 24 Nov. 1899, RP, Letter Book.
[4] Rosebery in Burnley, *The Times*, 20 May 1903.
[5] See above, p. 101.

sistently than his colleagues, tried to consider the problem dispassionately. He was the least committed to free trade and the most willing to attempt an unbiased assessment. He joined a 'small dining club . . . to discuss Commercial Federation',[1] and after Chamberlain's speech in May 1903, visited Clinton Dawkins, Milner's protectionist friend, to 'talk about the tariff question'.[2]

Haldane saw two problems facing Britain and her empire: the question of future imperial unity and the question of Britain's poor economic performance. Chamberlain's proposals were designed to solve both problems by imperial federation linked with imperial preference. Haldane had only become deeply interested in imperial questions during the Boer War, which set him 'thinking about the machinery of the Empire'.[3] But though he believed that the country wished to 'provide better machinery for holding the nation and her colonies together', he did not think this could be achieved at a stroke; those who called for immediate and complete imperial federation were 'faddists . . . misunderstanding the political ideals of the times', and especially the ideals of the colonies.[4]

Haldane was ready to consider fiscal unity as a possible solution to Britain's economic difficulties. He appointed Percy Ashley, brother of William Ashley, the protectionist, as a research assistant and instructed him to

make a dispassionate study of the argument for and against the scheme, examining particularly the defence of their own Zollverein by the German economists, & determining how far they have put it on economic grounds at all.[5]

From this inquiry, Haldane reached two conclusions—first, that 'there is really no analogy in the German case', and

---

[1] Haldane to Mother, 9 Dec. 1902, Hal P 5968, f. 164; the Coefficients club was 'to discuss preferential tariffs within the Empire' (ibid., 20 Jan. 1903, Hal P 5969, f. 13); on the basis of the recollections of very junior members, the club is given exaggerated importance in B. Semmel, *Imperialism and Social Reform* (1960), pp. 75–82; the club is not mentioned in B. Webb's Diary, Passfield Papers, and is not so named by Haldane.

[2] Haldane to Mother, 15 June 1903, Hal P 5969, f. 162.

[3] Haldane in East Lothian, *The Scotsman*, 6 Jan. 1903.

[4] Haldane, 'Political Ideals of the 20th Century', *Dundee Advertiser*, 11 Oct. 1901.

[5] Haldane to P. Ashley, 1 June 1903, Hal P 5905, f. 38.

secondly, that 'this problem is for the German economists and statesmen no merely economic one.' But for Britain 'the root problem *is* an economic one.'[1] Haldane thus agreed with Chamberlain that there were two problems—political federation and British economic improvement—but he did not see the problems as interrelated, and he therefore could not accept Chamberlain's proposals. Haldane believed, as did other Liberal Imperialists, that social reform, not protection, was the answer to Britain's economic problems. He believed that a Zollverein 'would seriously endanger the stability of the Empire', because the growth of interests resulting from protection would cause corruption and moral decay in society.[2] Haldane's basic antipathy to protection was, however, moral, not economic or even rational, as he himself admitted in a statement characteristic of all Liberal Imperialists who did not join Chamberlain: 'I own I hate the unhealthy influence of a protection system. I will back almost any effort to deal with what I admit to be a situation that needs attention, by other means.'[3]

Haldane's reaction to the tariff question was therefore emotional, almost religious. By November 1903 he felt 'like [his] grandfather preaching the gospel', so deeply rooted had the once empirical support of free trade become amongst Liberals.[4]

Haldane and constitutional evolution

Haldane believed that the various proposals for immediate and complete federation were impractical, whether they were of the fiscal sort proposed by Chamberlain or of the constitutional sort suggested by T. A. Brassey. Brassey's proposal was to achieve federation in one massive bill, which would set up a whole series of new legislative assemblies and administrative departments.[5] Milner supported Brassey, and Brassey's proposals also gained some Liberal

---

1 Haldane to Ashley, 27 Sept. 1903, Hal P 5906, f. 53; their conclusions are in P. Ashley, *Modern Tariff History* (1904), preface by Haldane.
2 Haldane in East Linton, *The Scotsman*, 6 June 1903.
3 Haldane to Ashley, 20 Sept. 1903, Hal P 5906, f. 46.
4 Haldane to Mother, 18 Nov. 1903, Hal P 5970, f. 152.
5 T. A. Brassey, *Problems of Empire* (1904), pp. 52 ff.

support.[1] Haldane rightly believed that any such proposal was certain to fail, and favoured an evolutionary approach— the same 'step-by-step' approach as he was developing for achieving Irish Home Rule. The first step should be made, he thought, through the Judicial Committee of the Privy Council, where he did much of his legal work. More colonial judges should sit on the J.C.P.C., and they should also sit as life peers in the Lords, thus forming a *de facto* Imperial Court of Appeal.[2] Subsequently the J.C.P.C. would join the Lords judicial committee to form a complete Imperial Court of Appeal, 'a real step towards the only kind of imperial federation which seems possible'.[3] Even this modest proposal soon ran into difficulties over the vexed case of clause 74 of the Commonwealth of Australia Constitution Bill. This clause dealt with the right of appeal from the Australian courts on constitutional issues; the Australians wished to deny any appeal beyond the highest Australian court, a desire which would clearly frustrate the development of a Court of Imperial Appeal in London. In January 1900 Haldane declared that the only solution to the question of appeals was for Britain to offer 'the finest court of Ultimate Appeal that the Empire can produce'; if this were done, the Australians and others would accept it.[4] During the 1900 debates on the Australia Bill, Haldane and Asquith both urged this. Haldane, taking 'a somewhat different point of view than that taken by some of his hon. friends', supported Chamberlain's last-minute attempts to alter clause 74 to allow appeal, though he stopped short of calling for the amendment of the Bill without the Australian delegates' consent.[5]

Haldane realized that the 1900 Australia Bill debates had shown that the J.C.P.C.'s status was too lowly to appeal to the colonies, and that even its elevation into an Imperial Court of Appeal, while a valuable reform, would be insufficient. He therefore suggested that the House of Lords be

[1] Milner to Brassey, 25 Feb. 1901, MP 33, f. 111; Bannerman to Gladstone, 26 Dec. 1900, HGP 45987, f. 157.
[2] Haldane in Pencaitland, *The Scotsman*, 30 Aug. 1899.
[3] Haldane to Scots Law Society, Jan. 1900, in Haldane, *Education and Empire* (1902), pp. 145–6. [4] Ibid., p. 150.
[5] 4 H, lxxxiii. 99–102 (14 May 1900), and 4 H, lxxxiii. 769 (21 May 1900).

made into an Imperial Senate. This would help the empire, and incidentally help the Liberal party by solving the Lords problem, for the Lords 'would no longer represent a party in a majority of 10 to 1, but the Empire at large'. This reform would produce

an Imperial Council, which would deal with Imperial questions, in which the views of the Colonies would be expressed about navy and army reforms, about the policy of war . . . and about things which concerned our great Empire as a whole.[1]

When the bipartisan Pollock committee was formed under Sir Frederick Pollock in 1903 to promote moderate and evolutionary steps towards constitutional federation, Haldane's views were already substantially developed.[2] As a member of the committee Haldane altered his stress on the position of the Lords, adhering to the committee's view that the Privy Council was the most readily available agency for an Imperial Council, but he still hoped to see the Lords as the 'Senate House of the Empire'.[3]

Haldane believed his proposals were a realistic alternative to Chamberlain's. The essential difference between them was that Chamberlain saw tariffs as a solution both to Britain's economic problems and to the problem of imperial unity, whereas Haldane, regarding the problems as quite separate, had a step-by-step constitutional solution to the latter and a domestic solution to the former. But Haldane failed to get general Liberal Imperialist support for his proposals. Grey attended meetings of the Pollock committee, but Asquith came only once.[4] Rosebery, whose support, especially from his progressively non-party position, would be useful, showed no interest. He still supported the need for 'the affectionate relations of kinship', but he did not support the Pollock proposals.[5] Privately, he was hostile to them, and

---

[1] Haldane in Glasgow, *The Scotsman*, 24 Oct. 1900.
[2] For the Pollock committee, see Kendle, op. cit., ch. iv.
[3] Haldane, 'The Cabinet and the Empire', 9 June 1903, *Proceedings of the Royal Colonial Institute*, xxxiv, pp. 325–52.
[4] F. Elliot to Rosebery, 27 Oct. 1904, RP, box 79.
[5] Rosebery in Stourbridge, *The Times*, 26 Oct. 1905.

tried to dissuade Haldane from supporting them. Ferguson urged that 'we who fight for our seats as Imperialists have to define some clear notions of what we consider practical policy in contrast to preference', but, probably through Rosebery's hostility, the Liberal League never made any positive statement on imperial unity.[1] Thus what could have become a major Liberal Imperialist initiative remained the suggestion of a few individual Liberal Imperialists.[2]

A regional problem within the 'union of sympathy': South Africa

The South African problem was complex in itself, and in its implications for the Liberal party.[3] It marked the height of notoriety of the Liberal Imperialists and involved them in a major power struggle in their party. The war and its settlement brought together the various concepts of inevitability, continuity, trust in judgement, and the clean slate through which they approached problems, and it demonstrated the danger of applying any of these concepts too rigorously.

Those who became most notorious for their South African views—Asquith, Grey, Haldane, and to a lesser extent Rosebery—knew very little about South Africa.[4] Rosebery never visited the Cape on his voyages, and he understood its problems 'rather in gross than in detail'.[5] Asquith and Rosebery were not on the Cabinet Council on South Africa in 1892–5, and Asquith's clash with Chamberlain during the 1900 election on the question of past Liberal policy suggested he had taken little interest in the problem at that time.[6] Grey and Haldane also knew very little, and Milner wrote to them as 'to those who do not know the

---

[1] Ferguson to Rosebery, 12 June 1905, RP, box 16.
[2] Haldane hoped to become Lord Chancellor in 1905 to further these proposals; see Haldane, p. 174.
[3] For British reaction to the war, see *C.H.B.E.* iii. 354–77. Liberal attitudes are examined in J. Butler, 'The Liberal Party and South Africa, 1895–1902' (Oxford D.Phil. thesis, 1963).
[4] This applied to the other extreme of the party also, e.g. Lloyd George.
[5] Rosebery to Ripon, 16 Oct. 1894, Rip P 43516, f. 161.
[6] Council members were 'Ripon, Kimberley, Bryce, Acland, assisted by S. Buxton and Meade', all of whom took a moderate line in the war; Ripon to Asquith, 24 Sept. 1900, Rip P 43518, f. 205. For Asquith's clash with Chamberlain, see ibid.

local circumstances'.[1] Asquith, Grey, and Haldane consistently turned down positions which would have increased
their knowledge, Asquith refusing to serve on the Jameson
raid inquiry and on the commission of inquiry into the war,
Haldane refusing to serve on the concessions commission,
Grey refusing the Cape governorship.[2] They appear to have
made little attempt to take advice from their more experi-
enced colleagues such as Ripon and Buxton. As the 1899
situation worsened, Haldane 'got up' the South African
question as he would a brief, using Fitzpatrick's polemic,
The Transvaal from Within, as his main source.[3] Rosebery
recommended this book as 'the mark of truth', though
Fitzpatrick clearly stated that his aim was 'to state the case
for the Uitlanders'.[4]

The Liberal Imperialists had an unusual source of information in Alfred Milner. Though a Liberal Unionist,
Milner had gained considerable Liberal trust by his work
on the 1894 death duties budget, and he went to South
Africa with 'the general consensus' of the Liberal party that
he was the man for the job.[5] This consensus included Morley
and Stead, later two of Milner's strongest opponents.[6]
Milner's mastery both of detail and of strategy, his forceful
and clearly outstanding intellect, his willingness to think
and plan conceptually, and his lucid, dramatic, and persuasive letters and dispatches made a profound appeal to the
élitist predilections of the Liberal Imperialists. They saw in
Milner the personification of all that seemed best and right
in an imperial ruling élite. Once on the spot, Milner would
do the job. The Liberal Imperialists therefore at first made
no attempt to formulate a South African policy by their own
expertise; they trusted to Milner's judgement. This was
consistent with their general view that judgement was the
vital factor in statesmanship. Their judgement was that

---

[1] Milner to Grey, 7 Aug. 1899, in Headlam, i. 476.

[2] See Asquith to Balfour, 6 July 1902, Bal P 49692, ff. 74–6; Haldane to Milner,
31 July 1900, Headlam, ii. 127; Grey to Chamberlain, 3 Dec. 1900, JC 11/39/70.

[3] Haldane to Mother, 11 Oct. 1899, Hal P 5962, f. 91.

[4] Rosebery in Bath, *The Times*, 28 Oct. 1899; J. P. Fitzpatrick, *The Transvaal
from Within* (1899), p. vii.

[5] Asquith to Milner, 15 Feb. 1897, MP 31, n.f.

[6] Morley to Milner, 15 Feb. 1897, MP 31, f. 116; Stead in *Review of Reviews*,
Mar. 1897.

Milner's assessment would be correct. Asquith made it clear that it was Milner's judgement, rather than the details of his policy, that he supported: he would defend Milner's judgement 'whatever may be the ulterior aims of his policy'.[1]

Asquith, Grey, and Haldane made much of their friendship with Milner. Asquith had known Milner since their Oxford days; Haldane worked with him on the 1894 Budget and had known him since the early 1880s. Asquith, Haldane, and Milner visited France together in the 1880s.[2] But during Milner's service in Egypt from 1889 to 1892 no letters passed between them, and after 1892 Milner's diary does not suggest he was more than an irregular acquaintance of Asquith, Grey, and Haldane.[3] The subsequent story suggests either that they had totally misunderstood Milner's character, thus condemning their own judgement, or that they were less friendly with him than they said they were.

Public affirmation of friendship for Milner had one great advantage; it enabled the Asquith committee to support the war without supporting Chamberlain, thereby giving them, at first, a better chance of keeping the Liberal party a 'national' party on the war issue. Support for Chamberlain would certainly split the party, support for Milner might not. But support for Milner proved equally divisive, breaking the consensus and eventually going beyond what even Haldane could accept. Once tied to Milner, however, it was difficult to abandon him without appearing 'unpatriotic'.

Almost up to the start of the war, most Liberal Imperialists assumed both that a peaceful solution was possible and desirable, and that Milner would pursue it. Chamberlain, if anyone, was expected to go 'jingo'. Asquith warned Chamberlain that 'there is no place where the ingredients of a political explosion are more perilously congregated' than South Africa, and called for 'prudence of language and calmness of temper'.[4] Rosebery told Chamberlain 'we have had too much of precipitation' in South Africa.[5] E. T. Cook

[1] Asquith to Bryce, 28 Sept. 1899, BP, box A; see Asquith in Northumberland, *The Times*, 27 Nov. 1899.
[2] Haldane, p. 83.
[3] Milner's diary in MP fully records his social intercourse.
[4] Asquith in York, *The Times*, 1 May 1897.
[5] Rosebery in Rochdale, *The Times*, 29 Apr. 1896.

sponsored the Uitlanders' claims in the *Daily News* after 1896, but he received no public support from Liberal Imperialist M.P.s. They could not be accused of 'jingoism' before the war began. Even in September 1899, Asquith maintained 'there is nothing in the situation . . . which cannot and ought not to be safely solved by firm and prudent diplomacy.'[1] Asquith and Haldane both pointed out that the Transvaal was a 'self governing and independent country', and Haldane said it was wrong 'to think that the British were entirely in the right and the Boers entirely in the wrong'.[2]

This was no public front; Asquith and Haldane took the same view in private. Haldane was 'pretty sure the govt. do not wish to fight in the Transvaal—there is no justification for it and they know that'.[3] Asquith thought in August 1899 that 'everything . . . points to a pacific arrangement on the basis of give and take.'[4] Grey and Rosebery did not altogether agree. Grey from 1897 thought that 'it looks as if the use of force could not be avoided', and Rosebery, who 'sought to shut my eyes to all this business', believed 'this issue will have to be fought out by bullets sooner or later.'[5] But though Grey and Rosebery both regarded some eventual conflict as probable, they did not believe this position had been reached in 1899, and they both thought Milner and Chamberlain had bungled the 1899 diplomacy. Rosebery found 'the present ground for war . . . extremely slender'.[6] While publicly supporting Milner, Grey privately criticized his policy, telling him in July that he was 'not convinced that war now . . . would be either right or wise'. Grey showed how far he was from appreciating Milner's real policy by telling him that 'Kruger's last franchise plan should be accepted . . .'[7] Grey thought the seven years franchise should

[1] Asquith in Leven, *The Times*, 4 Sept. 1899.
[2] Haldane in Pencaitland, *The Scotsman*, 30 Aug. 1899.
[3] Haldane to Mother, 26 June 1899, Hal P 5961, f. 188.
[4] Asquith to Harcourt, 4 Aug. 1899, HP 9.
[5] Grey to Milner, 9 Apr. 1897, Headlam, i. 33; Rosebery to Grey, 7 Sept. 1899, RP, Letter Book.
[6] Rosebery to Grey, 7 Sept. 1899, RP, Letter Book.
[7] Grey to Milner, 13 July 1899, MP 16, f. 357A. For Milner's reply, see Headlam, i. 476–9. For Milner's determination to precipitate war, see G. H. L. Le May, *British Supremacy in South Africa 1899–1907* (1965), ch. i.

be seen to fail before further action was taken. Even when war was imminent, Grey told Milner: 'I am hampered by the feeling that better diplomacy might have avoided war.'[1]

The lack of understanding of Milner's policy was shown by the belief of Asquith, Grey, and Haldane that 'the whole responsibility rests with Kruger and his obstinate burgers [sic].'[2] Grey thought the concluding British demands were 'very moderate'.[3] In fact, Milner 'deliberately precipitated a crisis which was inevitable before it was altogether too late', and had been intent on war since 1898.[4] Haldane knew from Balfour 'that it is Milner and not Chamberlain who had been leading in these last weeks', but the significance of the remark seems to have escaped him.[5] Their assumption that Milner desired a peaceful solution in South Africa 'on the basis of give and take' was totally wrong.

Once the war began, the Liberal Imperialists, determined to play a 'patriotic' role, and fearful that the new electorate might be apathetic or even hostile to the first major war with white men since the Crimea,[6] called for the nation 'to stand together with an unbroken front'.[7] For public consumption, they presented the war in black and white terms.[8] Rosebery continued privately to think 'the whole affair has been greatly bungled'.[9] What is curious is that the others completely abandoned their previous position. Grey told Milner: 'the end has justified the view you have taken of the South African question from the beginning', and, quite contrary to his pre-war assessment, thought 'it is better that it should be faced and had out now than deferred by further negotiation.'[10]

---

[1] Grey to Milner, 4 Oct. 1899, in Headlam, i. 560.
[2] Haldane to Spender, n.d. [Oct. 1899], SP 46388, f. 141 (wrongly catalogued under 23 Sept. 1899).
[3] Grey to Rosebery, 30 Sept. 1899, RP, box 23.
[4] Milner to Roberts, June 1900, in Le May, op. cit., p. 1; see also J. S. Marais, *The Fall of Kruger's Republic* (1961), pp. 206–10.
[5] Haldane to Spender, 23 Sept. 1899, SP 46388, f. 141.   [6] Ibid.
[7] Asquith in East Fife, *The Times*, 13 Oct. 1899; see also Rosebery in *The Times*, 12 and 28 Oct. 1899.
[8] See above, p. 42.
[9] Rosebery to Grey, 21 Oct. 1899, RP, Letter Book.
[10] Grey to Milner, 1 Nov. 1899, Headlam, i. 561.

Haldane no longer thought that 'the faults of the diplomacy of the govt. have made any great difference'; the war was 'inevitable'.[1]

This complete change of front suggests that Haldane, Grey, and Asquith had no real conception of the South African situation, or of the government's policy. They accepted British diplomacy at its face value. Haldane drew heavily on Fitzpatrick's book; Asquith thought the war was to achieve 'equality of treatment' for the Uitlanders; Grey saw the war's first aim as 'the right to protect our fellow subjects in the Transvaal'.[2] The government's war aims were only incidentally to do with the Uitlanders' rights. Fowler, never a correspondent of Milner, was much nearer the Milner/Chamberlain position: the war was for 'the absolute supremacy of the Crown', on which 'depends the civil and political freedom of South Africa, and the honour and integrity of the British Empire throughout the world'.[3]

Asquith, Haldane, and Grey soon broadened their base of support for the war. The Uitlanders were unsatisfactory for long-term propaganda. They were associated with the generally unpopular Jameson Raid, and they were made up, Haldane thought, of 'a great deal of the scum and the very dregs of the population' of South Africa, 'driven there by the lust for gold'.[4] Moreover, to see the Uitlanders as the main cause of the war was to accept, in some degree, the view that the war was 'a capitalists' job'.[5] Liberal Imperialists were keen to deny this theory. 'It was not a war that had been caused by financiers', said Grey, though he 'regretted . . . the trail of the financier . . . in South Africa'.[6] Fowler strenuously attacked the 'capitalist plot' theory.[7] None the less, though discounting direct capitalist influence on British policy, after the war began they discovered causes for it which accepted

[1] Haldane to Spender, n.d. [Oct. 1899], SP 46388, f. 141.

[2] Haldane in *The Scotsman*, 11 Oct. 1899; Asquith in Dundee, *The Times*, 12 Oct. 1899; Grey in Glasgow, *The Times*, 26 Oct. 1899.

[3] Fowler in Wolverhampton, *The Times*, 30 Nov. 1899; for government policy, see Robinson and Gallagher, op. cit., pp. 434–7, 454–5; and Le May, op. cit., pp. 25–6.

[4] Haldane in East Lothian, *The Scotsman*, 11 Oct. and 30 Aug. 1899.

[5] 'Is the war a Capitalists' job?', *Daily News*, 4 Nov. 1899.

[6] Grey to City Liberals, *The Times*, 21 Mar. 1900.

[7] Fowler in Wolverhampton, *The Times*, 20 Apr. 1900.

capitalist activity as the main cause, though in suitably flattering terminology. Grey found

great causes at work . . . The fact was that there had been a great pressure of industrial progress around the Transvaal on every side . . . The moment that they [the Boers] admitted that stream of industry . . . then the very condition of their independence was that they should assimilate modern ideas of democracy. Those were the great causes at work . . . The issues about the franchise and about the joint inquiry were only apparent causes.[1]

But if such a long-term historical analysis was true in November 1899, it must also have been true in July 1899, when Grey thought war 'neither right nor wise'. Certainly these arguments were for public consumption, but the energy with which they were urged and the lack of private contrary assessments suggest that the Liberal Imperialists believed them. At what point did wars become 'inevitable' through social forces? What was the role of individuals in the development of such forces? Liberal Imperialists did not face up to such questions. They seem to have made no attempt to recognize or assess their complete change of front; their ignorance of the actualities of the South African situation did not allow them to do so. Asquith, who did not 'belong to either of the fashionable schools of fatalism', fully accepted this point, arguing 'that upon the matter as to the time for intervention he attached considerable weight to the authority of Sir Alfred Milner'.[2]

The Boer ultimatum and invasion saved those Liberal Imperialists who expressed the 'inevitability' view (Rosebery, Haldane, Grey, and Fowler were the most prominent) from having to think seriously about the relationship of diplomacy to economic and social forces. Grey argued, and apparently believed, 'it is a war which has been forced upon this country', just as the partition of Africa had been forced upon Britain.[3] In each case Grey thought Britain had played a passive role.[4]

[1] Grey in Peebles, *The Times*, 6 Nov. 1899.
[2] 4 H, lxxviii. 734 (6 Feb. 1900), and Asquith in Northumberland, *The Times*, 27 Nov. 1899.
[3] 4 H, lxxviii. 378 (1 Feb. 1900).
[4] Milner's object was to employ the imperial factor positively, Le May, op. cit., pp. 20–6.

The effective opening Boer campaign raised the general question of British supremacy in southern Africa, the real concern of Milner and Chamberlain throughout. Liberal Imperialist M.P.s had given no attention to this before the war, though it had been an important aspect of the *Daily News* case.[1] Fowler stated the argument clearly:

> It was not a war for the obtaining of the franchise, nor for the rights . . . of the Uitlanders, but . . . for nothing less than British supremacy in South Africa. That supremacy meant their Indian Empire . . . it meant our continuance as one of the Great Powers of the world.[2]

This eschatological view came to be generally adopted by Liberal Imperialists. It was this view, and its corollary that 'we are Englishmen first, and Liberals and Conservatives after', which especially irritated other Liberals.[3] Was it possible to give full support to the government without becoming 'laudatores Josephi', as Campbell-Bannerman put it?[4] One solution was to support Milner, but this did not face the basic question, for it assumed that Milner's policy would be supportable—that Milner would remain within an ambit acceptable to reasonable men.

Reluctant annexation

Asquith and Haldane in 1899 thought the function of the war was merely to enforce pre-war British diplomatic demands. They both explicitly excluded annexation as a war aim.[5] They did not see that the fact of war totally altered the South African situation. Grey was more cautious, but still called for 'no sign of vindictiveness' in the settlement, and in December 1899 supposed that 'the govt. can hardly propose anything but a Liberal settlement on equal lines for both races . . .'[6] Rosebery, however, from the start said publicly: 'there is no conceivable government . . . which could repeat

[1] e.g. *Daily News*, editorial, 9 Sept. 1899.
[2] Fowler in Wolverhampton, *The Times*, 20 Apr. 1900.
[3] Fowler in Wolverhampton, *The Times*, 30 Nov. 1899.
[4] Bannerman to Gladstone, 9 Dec. 1899, CBP 41215, f. 165.
[5] Asquith in Dundee, *The Times*, 12 Oct. 1899; Haldane in East Linton, *The Scotsman*, 11 Oct. 1899.
[6] Grey in Glasgow, *The Times*, 26 Oct. 1899; Grey to Haldane, 4 Dec. 1899, Hal P 5904, f. 212. Grey's meaning of 'Liberal' here is unclear.

. . . the policy which concluded peace after the reverse of Majuba Hill.'[1]

As the Boers' strength was revealed, the 'Liberal settlement' had to be combined with imperial security. Speaking for the Liberal Imperialists, Grey said in February 1900 that there were now two war aims: 'the first is equal rights between white men in South Africa . . . the second is this—that never again . . . shall it be possible for an arsenal to be formed . . . under any control except British control.'[2] Liberal Imperialists were reluctant to admit that to secure these two aims it would be necessary to go to the extent of annexation. Asquith had repeated his view that there was no 'design on the internal independence of their republics'.[3] He said this while still supporting Milner, and while criticizing Campbell-Bannerman strongly for an attack on Milner for his alleged remark that he intended to 'break the power of Afrikanderdom'. Asquith assumed that the remark so totally misrepresented Milner's aims that he 'never attached to it the slightest importance'.[4] In fact, as Asquith admitted, Milner's denial was only in 'general' terms; breaking the power of Afrikanderdom was exactly Milner's real objective.[5]

None the less, Milner's Liberal supporters began to think in annexationist terms with extreme reluctance. Haldane illustrates the trend:

We have to secure equal treatment & get rid permanently of the Transvaal's arsenal. If these two things have been accomplished . . . then it would be the height of folly to ask for more for conquest's sake. But what I find difficult is to lay down in advance the means by which we can accomplish the two objects . . . I do not disguise from myself that the last, especially, *may* imply the Queen's flag . . . I cannot say whether it will be safe to do more than offer complete self government under that flag . . . It is certainly not a thing that we ought to desire, the putting up of that flag . . . I shall hold it to be an evil if it turns out to be necessary.[6]

---

[1] Rosebery to a correspondent, *The Times*, 12 Oct. 1899.
[2] 4 H, lxxviii. 376–7 (1 Feb. 1900).
[3] Asquith in Northumberland, *The Times*, 27 Nov. 1899.
[4] Asquith to Bannerman, 23 Nov. 1899, CBP 41210, f. 177.
[5] Ibid., and Le May, op. cit., pp. 34, 52–3. See below, p. 183.
[6] Haldane to J. R. Thursfield, 19 Feb. 1900, Hal P 5905, f. 20.

Grey was reaching a similar conclusion,[1] but he discouraged its public recommendation, for 'any fool can annex. Annexation did not take them one step out of the difficulty.'[2]

Liberal Imperialists were thus genuinely reluctant annexationists. Publicly they were not in the van on this issue; privately they were slow to recognize the implications of government policy. They might thump the patriotic drum to make the Liberals seem a 'national' party, but this had much more to do with British party politics than with South Africa. On the basic issue of imperial policy in South Africa, they were cautious: Campbell-Bannerman was the first Liberal leader publicly to support annexation.[3]

Relations with Milner

As to the settlement of the annexed areas, there were two main problems, assuming a swift end to the war: what was to be the form of the settlement and who was to administer it? Being already committed to Milner, the Liberal Imperialists were bound to support him, assuming he wished to be the administrator. They defended his appointment throughout the 1900 election campaign. During 1900, however, Liberal Imperialists were coming to realize that Milner meant what he said about complete British supremacy, and that he did not at all share Campbell-Bannerman's view of 'our chief aim . . . the conciliation and harmonious cooperation of the two European races'.[4] The spirit of Milner's policy is shown by his remark: 'The Boers die hard, and what is worse, they have never been properly beaten.'[5] Even Kitchener found Milner's views 'vindictive'.[6] If this was Milner's view, could the Liberal Imperialists maintain continuity? One way out was to persuade Milner to refuse the post of administrator. Given Milner's character, this was a delicate matter. Haldane cast a fly in this direction in March 1900 through Philip Gell, Milner's closest personal friend, who wrote to Milner: 'the view that he [Haldane] put to

---

1 Grey to Haldane, 4 Dec. 1899, Hal P 5904, f. 212.
2 Grey to City Liberals, *The Times*, 21 Mar. 1900.
3 *Bannerman*, i. 278–83.
4 Bannerman in Glasgow, 7 June 1900, in *Bannerman*, i. 281–2.
5 Quoted in Le May, op. cit., p. 84.   6 Ibid., p. 99.

me—(very seriously!)—was whether *you might* not have so far alienated Dutch feeling, that (Oh! Good Lord!) it might be politic for you to leave the settlement to—someone else.'[1] Milner ignored this.

Between October 1899 and June 1900 there was no correspondence between Milner and the Imperialists. When it became clear there would be no quick end to the war, Milner, anxious about support for his settlement, began a long correspondence on this subject.[2] Milner's aim in writing was to establish a non-party basis of support for a substantial period of non-parliamentary government in the annexed states *and* at the Cape. For their part, the Liberal Imperialists hoped to support Milner, but also to contain him within the ambit they could accept.

Milner had two specific aims: 'one is to start the conquered countries on right lines; the other is to break up the rebel party at the Cape.' To achieve the first he wanted 'paternal despotism'; to achieve the second he wanted 'to suspend the [Cape] constitution altogether', or failing that 'to disenfranchise the rebels'.[3] Entirely contrary to the normal Liberal view, Milner regarded political activity as in itself divisive, arguing that 'if it were not for the existence of constitutional government . . . the two races would gradually live together in harmony.'[4]

Following reports such as that of Haldane that 'there is no doubt that the country here is getting tired of fighting', Milner became increasingly nervous that the Liberals would occupy 'some half-way house between Imperialism & pro-Boerism'.[5] Milner feared the Imperialists would join in 'attacking the govt. whenever necessity compelled it to run counter to any humanitarian or constitutional fad'.[6] The

[1] Gell to Milner, 23 Mar. 1900, MP 29, n.f.
[2] H. W. McCready, 'Sir Alfred Milner, the Liberal Party and the Boer War', *Canadian Journal of History*, vol. 2, no. 1 (1967), reviews and quotes these letters at length, mainly from Milner's view-point; my emphasis differs from his on a number of points.
[3] Milner to Hamilton, 24 June 1900, EHP 48627, n.f.
[4] Ibid. In South Africa 'racial problems' meant Briton/Boer.
[5] Haldane to Milner, 3 Mar. 1901, MP 39; Milner to Haldane, 1 July 1901, Hal P 5905, f. 75.
[6] Milner to Haldane, 1 July 1901, Hal P 5905, f. 75, partially quoted in Headlam, ii. 264–5, and in McCready, op. cit., p. 24.

'fad' which Milner feared the Imperialists would refuse to
support was suspension of the Cape constitution, 'a particularly dangerous point', as men in both parties would oppose
it. Milner played on the Liberal Imperialists' frequent claim
to place imperial questions above party, and suggested that
suspension would be both 'national' and 'liberal', since he
was himself 'at bottom, a Liberal'![1] When in London in
June 1901, Milner gave tutorials to the Asquith committee,
arguing that 'formal suspension . . . was unnecessary'; *de
facto* suspension by not summoning the Cape parliament
would be sufficient.[2]

Chamberlain was hostile to suspension at the Cape, but
told Charles Boyd that 'if I had my assurance that they [the
'Limps'] would support suspension . . . it might influence
my own policy.'[3] It was thus vital for Milner to win such
support; he accordingly put pressure by letter and through
Boyd, Jameson, and Lewis Michell in London on to
Rosebery, Grey, Haldane, and Asquith.[4] He then tried to
force everybody's hand by making a speech advocating
suspension.[5]

The Liberal Imperialists confronted with this situation in
1902 had gone a long way in their public support for Milner
and for the government. They had made little effort,
despite their reversal of front in 1899, to improve their
knowledge of South Africa. For them, the war fought itself
out amongst the Councils, Leagues, and arguments within
the Liberal party. For the most part, they had accepted
Rosebery's advice: 'you do well to trust the man at the helm
when you are passing through a storm.'[6] In 1900 they
supported the government on the amnesty for Cape rebels
and on unconditional surrender, and in 1901 they backed
the Kitchener policy of camps and block-house clearing. 'I
could not support censure of the men on the spot without

---

[1] Milner to Haldane, 1 July 1901, Hal P 5905, f. 75.

[2] Milner to Haldane, 17 July 1901, Hal P 5905, f. 87.

[3] C. Boyd to Milner, 10 May 1902, MP 33, f. 178. For Chamberlain's views see
L. M. Thompson, *The Unification of South Africa* (1960), pp. 8–9.

[4] Boyd to Milner, 10 May 1902, MP 33, f. 178, and Milner to Haldane, 8 June
1902, Hal P 5905, f. 189.

[5] Thompson, op. cit., p. 8, and Garvin and Amery, op. cit., iv. 104.

[6] Rosebery in Bath, *The Times*, 28 Oct. 1899.

the strongest evidence of wanton & unprovoked brutality', Grey told Campbell-Bannerman.[1]

They praised in Milner qualities rather than policies; they liked his comprehensiveness, his steadfastness, his thoroughness; that is, those qualities which had seemed lacking in past Liberal administrators. It was these qualities which the Liberal Imperialists hoped their efficiency campaign would introduce into the Liberal party. It was this attitude which G. B. Shaw's *Fabianism and the Empire* praised: 'what the British Empire wants most urgently in its government is . . . brains and political science.'[2] Rosebery and Haldane were 'both delighted with the Fabian manifesto . . . one of the most brilliant and incisive analyses' which Haldane had seen.[3] They supported in South Africa the application of the method of efficiency, rather than any detailed policy, but they gave little thought as to what efficiency ought to mean in practice, or as to what Milner meant by it.

It gradually became clear to them that Milner's efficiency was much more thorough than their own. Milner's efficiency was his only criterion; their own was tempered by compromise and humanitarianism. As they realized this, they became increasingly alarmed. Haldane followed up his indirect suggestion that Milner should not be the administrator with a series of pleas for conciliation of the Boers. In December 1900 he asked Milner 'to make a friendly utterance to the Boers'.[4] This was the least Haldane could ask, but Milner immediately pointed out that even this struck at the heart of his policy: the Boers must first be 'completely beaten'. Milner intended not only to have 'smashed up the armies of the enemy and the political organisation', but to smash the social structure of Afrikanderdom. The war dragged on because

with their primitive social & political condition the Boers can go on merrily for a long time . . . just as low types of animal organisations will long survive injuries wh. wd. kill organisms of a higher type outright. They die, too, in the long run, but it takes time.[5]

[1] Grey to Bannerman, 17 Nov. 1900, CBP 41218, f. 8.
[2] Anon. [G. B. Shaw], *Fabianism and the Empire* (1900), p. 93.
[3] Haldane to Shaw, 15 Oct. 1900, Shaw Papers 50538, n.f.
[4] Haldane to Milner, 22 Dec. 1900, MP 29, f. 281.
[5] Milner to Haldane, 21 Jan. 1901, Hal P 5905, f. 53.

Haldane must have realized from this remarkable letter, if he had not before, the extent of Milner's thoroughness. Considerably alarmed, Haldane replied, increasing his demands: Milner must give public evidence 'that a firm course with the Boers does not mean the setting up of an alternative form of Uitlander or Rhodes ascendancy'.[1] Haldane saw that Milner's extremism jeopardized continuity. 'To the doctrine of what was called continuity . . . there were limits',[2] and Milner was about to step outside them. Haldane anticipated an imminent Liberal government; he was therefore 'anxious to see . . . a policy being pursued when it [Unionist govt.] does go out, in South Africa which men like Asquith & Grey and probably Rosebery would find no difficulty in carrying on in its continuity [sic]'. Haldane urged in March 1901: 'note the Bogey of Rhodes ascendancy . . . It is this I am anxious to put forward now that you may keep it in view for the days that are ahead.'[3] This was a clear warning to Milner that he must not go too far, and that if he did, continuity could not be maintained, as indeed it was not.

Haldane's pleas got no concessions out of Milner. But these private pleas were indicative of a general movement of Liberal Imperialist opinion. At the Rugby N.L.F. meeting in February 1901 Perks and other junior Imperialists joined with Lloyd George in a motion hostile to unconditional surrender; in July 1901 Rosebery privately tried to negotiate an end to the war.[4] The senior Commons men, whose colours had been most conspicuously nailed to Milner's mast at the start of the war, found themselves increasingly isolated. They began to adopt an attitude to the Boers which, while not 'conciliatory' in Campbell-Bannerman's sense, suggested their resolution was limited. Grey declared: 'unconditional surrender I do not believe to exist.'[5] Asquith told the Commons: 'there is no step whatever . . . that we ought not gladly to face and to advocate for the purpose of bringing this controversy to an end.'[6] Asquith attacked Kitchener's

---

1 Haldane to Milner, 3 Mar. 1901, MP 39, n.f.
2 Haldane in Pencaitland, *The Scotsman*, 30 Aug. 1899.
3 Haldane to Milner, 3 Mar. 1901, MP 39, n.f.
4 James, pp. 427–9.   5 Grey in 4 H, xcviii. 1158 (2 Aug. 1901).
6 Asquith in 4 H, xcix. 1039–41 (15 Aug. 1901).

'banishment proclamation' of August 1901, which Milner supported. Asquith thought the proclamation was legally unconstitutional, and practically 'not consistent with the usages of war or the dictates of humanity'; after the war the proclamation would be 'capable of amendment, revision, and even reversal'.[1]

These rather timid concessions to conciliation did not amount to public disavowal of Milner. The Asquith committee depended on Rosebery's Chesterfield speech to rescue them from their isolation. Rosebery had the authority to break down the entrenched positions in which the various Liberal groups were embattled. He did this brilliantly with his suggestion of an 'apparently casual meeting in an inn' which would form the basis for a negotiated settlement. Rosebery was never interested in the details of the South African situation, and his reasons for the need of a quick end to the war show his priorities:

In the first place it [the war] is an open sore through which is oozing much of our strength. In the next place it weakens our international position . . . In the third place it stops all domestic reform, and in the fourth place it adjourns and embitters the ultimate settlement of South Africa.[2]

In his views on party government, Rosebery was close to Milner, but in his views on the end of the war he was much closer to Campbell-Bannerman. Rosebery's view that there should be 'a regular peace and a regular settlement' and his explicit mention of the 'exiled Boer government' showed that he regarded the war as being between two separate states, and not, as after annexation it technically was, a civil war. This was completely contrary to Milner's grand design of total social and political defeat of the Boers,[3] and Milner, anticipating Rosebery's position, wrote to urge that the Boers must have no 'chance of recovering by political intrigue what they have lost in arms'.[4]

---

[1] Ibid. For the proclamation, see Le May, op. cit., p. 104.

[2] Rosebery at Chesterfield, 16 Dec. 1901, *National Policy* (1901).

[3] Stead, in *Review of Reviews*, Jan. 1902, notes that most contemporaries ignored this basic difference.

[4] Milner to Haldane, 8 Dec. 1901, Hal P 5905, f. 132.

Asquith, Grey, and Haldane had moved away from the full rigour of Milner's position; probably they had never wittingly supported it. They all endorsed the Chesterfield proposals, and not merely publicly.[1] Grey told Milner that 'the sketch he [Rosebery] gave there of a possible settlement seemed to me to be satisfactory.'[2] In January 1902 Asquith was involved in plans for a secret negotiation to end the war.[3] The *Liberal League Manifesto* gave general support to the Chesterfield proposals, but did not mention South Africa specifically, except in the context of War Office reform.[4] In 1902 the Liberal Imperialists did not disavow Milner publicly; they ignored him.

It was in this context of diminishing support that the Liberal Imperialists received Milner's letters on suspension of the Cape constitution, and met his envoys. Charles Boyd found Asquith 'very sympathetic',[5] but after Vereeniging, Asquith came out strongly against suspension. Privately he wrote to Chamberlain deploring the suggestion of suspension, commenting: 'I hope that Milner himself will see that this is, in the altered circumstances, the course of wisdom.'[6] Publicly he congratulated Chamberlain for 'wisely' averting the 'proposed suspension'; Asquith 'had found nothing . . . which suggested . . . any doubt as to the justice and good policy of allowing that Parliament to resume its constitutional duties'.[7]

Milner's campaign had failed; he had stepped outside the ambit of acceptable continuity. Correspondence ceased.[8] Liberal Imperialists no longer trusted Milner; Milner had nothing to gain from them. The Asquith committee's flirtation with and subsequent abandonment of 'Milnerism' seem to have led to no immediate heart-searching on their

---

[1] See above, p. 81.

[2] Grey to Milner, 16 Mar. 1902, MP 40, f. 111.

[3] J. Herbert to Asquith, 7, 8, and 9 Jan. 1902, AP 10, ff. 56–67.

[4] *Liberal League Manifesto*, May 1902, LLP (no number).

[5] Boyd to Milner, 10 May 1902, MP 33, f. 178.

[6] Asquith to Chamberlain, 28 June 1902, in Garvin and Amery, op. cit. iv. 115. Milner told Haldane that recent 'events . . . do not make the slightest difference' (8 June 1902, Hal P 5905, f. 189).

[7] Asquith in Tayport, *The Times*, 4 Oct. 1902.

[8] Except Milner to Haldane, 14 Nov. 1902, Hal P 5905, f. 254; Milner briefly regrets he has no time to write.

part. Haldane came to 'doubt whether Milner . . . was the best man for South Africa' and came 'in the end to wish that the negotiations . . . had been in the hands of a man of more diplomatic temperament'.[1] The Asquith committee had, in effect, made a gross miscalculation, in terms both of imperial policy and of party politics. They found themselves almost driven out of their party because of their attachment to a man and a policy both of which they did not, in the long run, support. Something had clearly gone badly wrong, but no attempt seems to have been made to discover the nature of the difficulty. The Asquith committee had placed their faith in a man whom they did not really know and, through their pragmatism, in a policy which they did not understand and for which they had no satisfactory criterion of evaluation.

The settlement of the Transvaal

South Africa remained an important and controversial question, especially with reference to the settlement of the annexed territories. This raised the question of whether 'paternal despotism', representative, or responsible government was to be the form of government, the question of the security of British supremacy and of future federation, and the question of the position of the natives. Probably there was no formula which could in the long term resolve all these questions. Liberal Imperialists made no serious attempt to find one. They frequently stated quite irreconcilable aims, with no attempt at a resolution of their contradictions. Fowler typically said the settlement must contain

the establishment of the supremacy of the Queen throughout South Africa . . . equal rights, civil, political and religious, for all white men . . . self government on the widest basis . . . provision to secure just and humane treatment of the native races.[2]

In the Boer states the Liberal Imperialists at first supported continued military occupation rather than 'a name such as Crown Colony that would lead to the idea that a definite settlement would be deferred'.[3] Soon they became

[1] Haldane, pp. 135–6.
[2] Fowler in Wolverhampton, *The Times*, 20 Apr. 1900.
[3] Grey to City Liberals, *The Times*, 21 Mar. 1900.

vaguer, Asquith advocating 'no quarrelling about phrases until we are certain of our facts'.[1] When Chamberlain in December 1900 said that 'for the sake of a name we will call it Crown Colony government', Asquith, following him, had no objections.[2]

Milner wanted Crown Colony government to last at least until there was a majority of British voters. Liberal Imperialists did not; they never seriously considered a party row over as swift a return as possible to self-government. They always justified their case for a tough prosecution of the war by pointing out the future benefits for all of British rule: 'The fact that the Boers were fighting for independence rendered it all the more necessary to make clear . . . the alternatives; under the British flag free institutions, equal laws, responsible government.'[3] Grey said that the government's suggestion of long-term delay before self-government was 'not within the region of practical politics'.[4] Haldane used an argument of necessity; since the Transvaal whites wanted Chinese labour (he thought) and the British people did not, the question must be resolved by immediate self-government:

We had the responsibility for these colonies on our hands. Our duty was to make them self-governing as soon as we can, and get rid of the odious necessity of having to pronounce, it might be against them, on such a question.[5]

Haldane attacked the Lyttelton Constitution of 1905 on the Canadian analogy that 'representative as distinguished from responsible government has always been a failure', and told Ashley to get up a historical case against Lyttelton.[6]

The long-held view that in 1906 'the Imperialists finally yielded' is thus unsubstantiated.[7] Asquith told Spender in 1912 that 'the notion that CB was opposed in the Cabinet or "won it over" in regard to the Transvaal settlement is a

---

1 Asquith to City Liberals, *The Times*, 26 Apr. 1900.
2 4 H, lxxxviii. 259 ff. (7 Dec. 1900).
3 Asquith at Oldham, *The Times*, 25 Nov. 1901; see also Haldane in Haddington, *The Scotsman*, 5 Oct. 1901.
4 Grey at Eighty Club, *The Times*, 21 Feb. 1901.
5 Haldane in North Berwick, *The Scotsman*, 6 Apr. 1904.
6 Haldane to Ashley, 29 Apr. 1905, Hal P 5906, f. 163.
7 G. B. Pyrah, *Imperial Policy and South Africa 1902–1910* (1955), p. 173.

ridiculous fiction . . . There was never the faintest difference of opinion about it in the Cabinet.'[1] Asquith's recollections seem to square with Liberal Imperialist views before 1906.[2] This was quite consistent with their abandonment of Milnerism during 1901–2.

Liberal Imperialists hoped to mitigate the effects of responsible government by federation and by increasing the number of Britons in the Boer territories.[3] They therefore supported not only British urban settlement, but also the purchase of Boer farms for British colonists.[4] Rosebery's only correspondence with Milner during the war was about a Mr. Stevenson who hoped to combat the Boer birth-rate by British child settlement.[5] This was also Milner's scheme and he supplied material for speeches on it.[6]

Milner's plans were to be financed by rapid expansion of the mining industry. When shortage of labour prevented this, Milner reluctantly decided to import Chinese labour. Normally this could probably have been done; there were a number of Liberal and Conservative precedents for roughly similar ordinances, though on a smaller scale, unnoticed by the public and by most politicians.[7] The unusual circumstances of the day caused the issue to become a major controversy, almost spontaneously, the politicians being as surprised about the agitation as they were about constituency hostility to the Education Bill.[8] The question soon became involved with the xenophobic agitation for an Aliens Bill, and as H. G. Wells observed:

[1] Asquith to Spender, 15 June 1912, in B. B. Gilbert, 'The Grant of Responsible Government to the Transvaal: More Notes on a Myth', *Historical Journal*, vol. 10, no. 4 (1967); see also R. Hyam, 'Smuts and the Decision of the Liberal Government to grant Responsible Government to the Transvaal, January and February 1906', *Historical Journal*, vol. 8, no. 3 (1965).

[2] Grey to Selborne, 22 Dec. 1905, in Trevelyan, *Grey of Fallodon*, p. 88.

[3] Grey in Pyrah, op. cit., p. 146, and Asquith to the British Women's Emigration Association, *The Times*, 20 Mar. 1902.

[4] Grey in Bristol, *The Times*, 12 Dec. 1901.

[5] Rosebery to Milner, 16 Mar. and 17 June 1901, MP 39, f. 143; Rosebery to Chamberlain, 31 July 1902, RP, Letter Book.

[6] e.g. Milner to Hamilton, 26 June 1900, EHP 48627, n.f.

[7] The most recent, roughly similar, precedent was the British Guiana Labour Ordinance, approved by the Liberal government in 1894.

[8] Haldane in North Berwick, *The Scotsman*, 6 Apr. 1904. Herbert Samuel, one of the main campaigners, against Chinese labour, found public response astonishing' (Visc. Samuel, *Memoirs* (1945), p. 45).

The Market place roared with delight, but whether that delight expressed hostility to the Chinaman or . . . to their practical enslavement no student of the General Election of 1906 has ever been able to determine . . . one of the most effective posters on our side displayed a hideous yellow face, just that and nothing else.[1]

Except for Haldane, Liberal Imperialists reacted straightforwardly, publicly opposing first the proposal, then the ordinance.[2] They did so on the ground that 'We subordinate every other aim to that of making the Transvaal a white man's country . . . No solution of the Transvaal labour difficulty which is likely to conflict with that . . . can be tolerated.'[3] Their difference with Milner lay in their support for quick responsible government. Immediate responsible government meant the priority was British settlement; Milner's priority was rapid economic expansion. Liberal Imperialists therefore called for slower expansion, using unskilled whites. This was not the stock Liberal moral objection to Chinese 'slavery' as such; indeed the League pamphlet suggested the 'temporary admission' of 20,000 coolies to 'avert a crisis'.[4] It was intended to be a 'realistic' argument, though the labour shortage was so acute that its successful resolution by mainly white immigration was improbable.[5]

Haldane's different view was based on a different approach to the question of security. Haldane never strongly pressed the view that the Transvaal could be filled with Britons; he sought security through federation. All gave lip-service to federation, but Haldane went further. He attacked the government for not 'laying before Parliament proposals for a new Act, under which, when the time came, the constitution of South Africa might be worked out'.[6] This Act was to replace the plan of the 1877 Act, which, Haldane said, 'was wholly unfitted for the purposes of the settlement which was to be effected in South Africa', because its structure was too loose and would give the Boer states too much latitude:

[1] H. G. Wells, *The New Machiavelli*, 2nd ed. (1911), p. 278.
[2] McCready, op. cit., pp. 38–40, and see below, pp. 193–4.
[3] Anon., *A White Man's Land: Liberal Imperial Policy on Transvaal Labour*, LLP 135 (Mar. 1904).
[4] Ibid.   [5] Le May, op. cit., p. 158.
[6] Haldane in Haddington, *The Scotsman*, 5 Oct. 1901.

If South Africa was to be welded into a whole, it was necessary it should have a constitution in which the parts should be brought together more closely, and in which there should be more possibility of common control than was the case under the Act of 1877.[1]

Haldane was working towards the solution of Union eventually adopted by South Africans in 1910, but it is interesting that he thought in terms of a federal constitution imposed, like that of 1877, by Westminster. He soon discontinued this line of thought, but still saw federation as the main means of security.[2]

Not requiring a British majority in the Transvaal to achieve security, Haldane was readier to accept Chinese labour, and abstained in the censure debate of 21 March 1904, mainly on the basis of colonial self-determination:

The Chinese labour question is very intricate. Practically the whole of the nonconformist ministers out there are very bitter against us for saying it is a moral question. Their reply is that we do not understand the facts . . . and that the proposal is the alternative to the black slavery which prevails elsewhere . . . I do not feel myself able to be so confident about the facts as to be capable of overruling the people on the spot.[3]

The 'black slavery' mentioned by Haldane already concerned the Liberal Imperialists. Milner's first letter to them from South Africa had argued that the native question was the basic question in South Africa, and that only the employment of the imperial factor could solve it.[4] Liberal Imperialists always mentioned 'just treatment' for the natives as one of many aims in South Africa, but they failed to face the fact that even British-dominated 'responsible government' was most unlikely to produce 'just treatment'. The insistence of most Liberals on the priority of Boer conciliation added to the problem. Of the Liberal Imperialists Asquith showed most interest in the native question. When the settlement was discussed during the war, he brought forward this question, which he said was 'quite as important as the future of administration' of the Boers. He

---

[1] Ibid.   [2] See Haldane, 'Chinese Labour', *The Scotsman*, 6 Apr. 1904.
[3] Haldane to Mother, 23 Mar. 1904, Hal P 5971, f. 128.
[4] Milner to Asquith, 18 Nov. 1897, part in Headlam, i. 177–80; this important letter is analysed in J. Butler, *Boston University Papers in African History* (1964), i. 245–70.

pointed out that Little Englanders were harming the natives' cause by excessive concentration on Boer grievances, but, though he argued that this question was 'of immense importance as regards the ultimate settlement of these territories', he offered no solution.[1] Like other Liberal leaders, Asquith made no criticism in 1902 of the 'franchise' clause in the Vereeniging peace.[2] Asquith remained worried about the natives, and told the N.L.F. in Hull in 1903:

> Many and serious as were the problems which confronted them [in South Africa] the most urgent and the hardest to solve were for the moment those not connected with the relations of Britons and Boers, but those connected with the relations of both to the coloured population.

But Asquith still had no solution to offer, for 'it was only a charlatan who could pretend to have in his pocket a solution to the native question in South Africa.'[3]

Asquith was mainly interested in the social, not the political, position of the Africans. There was, he observed in 1897, no 'natural force at work in the direction of a better treatment of the natives'.[4] The only available force was the imperial government. After a brief and decisive war, imperial power might have been used on the Africans' behalf. But the effect of pro-Boer propaganda, and later of the hostility to Chinese labour, was that the use of imperial power to solve problems in South Africa was discredited, and the only force likely to defend the Africans' rights was largely withdrawn.

On imperial questions the Liberal Imperialists had tried to achieve a compromise between those who, like Chamberlain and Milner, sought to employ the imperial factor in a dynamic role on a wide number of fronts, fiscal, economic, and strategic, and those who, like Campbell-Bannerman, saw the empire in essentially static terms, instinctively mistrusting the application of the imperial factor. The Liberal Imperialists had failed to find a concept which would offer a general solution to the various imperial problems of the

---

[1] 4 H, xcix. 1043–5 (15 Aug. 1901).
[2] Thompson, op. cit., pp. 11–12, and Pyrah, op. cit., p. 92.
[3] Asquith in Hull, *The Times*, 29 Jan. 1903.
[4] Asquith to Milner, 12 Jan. 1898, in Headlam, i. 180–1.

day, and which may be identified as a coherent doctrine of Liberal Imperialism. There were attempts to clean the slate of traditional Liberal views and to apply the criterion of efficiency to imperial questions. But these were hardly successful. Tentative movements towards fiscal unorthodoxy were checked before any major step was made. Local commercial interests in the West Indies, West Africa, and China were consistently sacrificed for the sake of the consolidation of the empire as a whole. Though some individual Liberal Imperialists had plausible ideas about imperial constitutional development, the group as a whole had nothing specific to offer. The Liberal Imperialists were hesitant about the thorough application of their own premiss of efficiency, and, when faced with such an application in the form of Milnerism in South Africa, drew back alarmed, discovering the distinction between rhetoric and policy too late to save themselves from inconsistency.

The Liberal Imperialist often berated Campbell-Bannerman for sitting on the fence. But on the major imperial crisis of the day, Campbell-Bannerman's view that the Boers could and should be conciliated had a respectable ancestry.[1] Milner's view that a rigorous application of the principles of 'thorough' would solve the problem also had a coherent, if not very British, doctrine behind it.[2] It was the Liberal Imperialists who balanced uneasily between Campbell-Bannerman and Milner, and who in the end seemed to betray the latter without persuading their contemporaries of their full allegiance to the former.

Note on the Liberal Imperialists, Milner, and Chinese labour

In *The Milner Papers*, Headlam states that Milner only approached Lyttelton with his plan for Chinese labour when 'as a result of a conversation with the moderate section, he had been assured that those Liberals who had supported him during the war, would continue to do so . . .'[3] On the basis of these remarks, it has been generally assumed that such assurances were given, and that the vote against the ordinance in the Commons marks the start of a private as well as public break

[1] D. M. Schreuder, *Gladstone and Kruger* (1969), pp. 469–70.
[2] See E. Stokes, 'Milnerism', *Historical Journal*, vol. 5, no. 1 (1962), pp. 47–60.
[3] Headlam, ii. 477 and n. 1.

with Milner. But Headlam's remarks are, as Gollin observes, 'undocumented'.[1]

Milner dined with Haldane and L. S. Amery at Sir Clinton Dawkins's house on 27 October 1903, when they 'sat up talking till a late hour'. On 29 October 1903 Milner dined with Asquith and afterwards 'talked a good deal to Asquith, Grey and Haldane'. Milner again met Haldane for a 'long talk' on 30 November, and had a chance meeting with Asquith on 21 November 1903.[2] None of the letters which mention these meetings gives any idea of the content of the talks, far less of any specific assurance. Milner did not, as he did in the summer of 1901, follow up his tutorials with letters to prevent any possibility of misunderstanding.

No doubt the labour question was discussed, but Milner knew that the Liberal Imperialists were by this time far removed from him on the general question of tariff reform and the future of the empire, that Asquith and Grey were already publicly on record as hostile to such a solution to the labour problem,[3] and that on previous questions, such as unconditional surrender and the suspension of the Cape constitution, they had not, in the long run, taken his side. Moreover, with the rise of the tariff issue, the position of the Liberal Imperialist group was even weaker in the Commons than it was in the war years. In such circumstances it was improbable that Asquith, Grey, and Haldane should as a group give Milner a blank cheque for his labour policy, or that he should make their supposed support the decisive factor in his decision to go ahead with it. Asquith and Grey may have expressed support for a limited number of temporary coolies under a 'Liberal' ordinance, as the Liberal League pamphlet did.[4] Milner certainly felt he had been let down, but there is no evidence that the Liberal Imperialists thought themselves under any obligation to him in this matter.[5] Perhaps there was a misunderstanding on Milner's part. Throughout the war, the Liberal Imperialists had underestimated Milner's 'thoroughness'; perhaps he now underestimated their 'liberalism'.

[1] A. M. Gollin, *Proconsul in Politics* (1964), p. 63 n. 1. See also McCready, op. cit., p. 38, and A. M. Gollin, 'Asquith: a New View', in M. Gilbert (ed.), *A Century of Conflict, 1850–1950, Essays for A. J. P. Taylor* (1966), p. 109.

[2] Haldane to Mother, 28 Oct. 1903, Hal P 5970, f. 117; Milner's Diary, 28 Oct. 1903, MP 265; Asquith to Milner, 19 Oct. 1903, MP 41, f. 6; Milner's Diary, 21 Nov. 1903, MP 265; Haldane to Mother, 30 Oct. 1903, Hal P 5970, f. 121.

[3] See McCready, op. cit., p. 39.

[4] Anon., *A White Man's Land: Liberal Imperial Policy on Transvaal Labour*, Mar. 1904, LLP 135. See above, p. 190.

[5] Professor McCready, in charging Sir E. Grey with having 'a thoroughly cynical attitude', wrongly attributes to Sir E. Grey a letter by Lord Grey to Milner supporting the labour policy. See McCready, op. cit., p. 40 n. 117, and Lord Grey (i.e. Albert Grey) to Milner, 19 Mar. 1904, MP 41.

VI

FOREIGN AND DEFENCE POLICY

Continuity and its implications

IN their approach to foreign policy the Liberal Imperialists
accepted Rosebery's view that there should be 'continuity of policy'. Rosebery had adhered to this view in
the period between his foreign secretaryships, and he reaffirmed in 1895 in his pre-election speech that 'whatever
our domestic differences may be at home, we should preserve
a united front abroad.'[1] 'Continuity' for the Liberal Imperialists meant in effect the admission that Unionist foreign
policy was reliable and that the radical dissenters, the
majority of whom were to be found at this time in the Little
England group of Liberals, must be excluded at all costs,
even at the cost of not having a Liberal government at all.
As Haldane said, 'continuity of policy was more important
than party victories.'[2] 'Continuity of policy' also meant an
absence of detailed comment on foreign policy, or at least
its confinement to minor criticisms. This was reinforced by
a general feeling amongst moderates on both sides of the
House that the less said in public about foreign policy, the
better. As one of the leading Liberal foreign policy spokes-
men, Grey was expected to comment on developments in
this field, but he greatly disliked doing so. He wrote to
Rosebery that he (Grey) 'must talk about foreign affairs
which it is hateful to discourse upon from a platform'.[3]

Support for continuity and for absence of serious public
criticism was no mere patriotic gesture. The Liberals before
1900 could make little electoral ground on domestic questions because of the paucity of Unionist measures to criticize.
Foreign affairs were to the fore partly because of a lack of

[1] Rosebery in the Albert Hall, *The Times*, 6 July 1895.
[2] Haldane introducing Rosebery at the Eighty Club, 2 July 1895 (Eighty Club
Pamphlet).
[3] Grey to Rosebery, 15 June 1896, RP, box 23.

domestic controversy. There was therefore a strong temptation to make capital out of Unionist mistakes abroad. Such
criticism could easily have been presented as 'patriotic', since
Unionist mistakes consisted, so many Unionists themselves
argued, in giving too many concessions in Asia, Madagascar,
and Venezuela. Attacks on these concessions coupled with
an attack on Salisbury's Near East policy could have considerably damaged the government. Such attacks, Rosebery
commented, 'would, Heaven knows, have been easy enough',
but the Liberal Imperialists avoided the temptation.[1]

The Liberal Imperialists did not try to gain 'patriotic'
support by showing the Unionists to be incompetent guardi-
ans of the national interest in foreign policy. The real test of
continuity would come, however, when they actually disagreed with the fundamentals of Unionist policy. For most
Liberal Imperialists this problem did not arise; Grey in
particular had no difficulty in maintaining continuity in
public and in private. For Rosebery the problem did arise:
he was clearly suspicious of the Japanese alliance of 1902,
and definitely hostile to the Entente of 1904.[2] In both
cases, however, he limited his public opposition to a brief
announcement of his suspicion and hostility. He refused to
discuss his reasons or to repeat his opinions at any length.
In taking this position on the 'new course' of British policy,
Rosebery took his view of continuity to its logical extreme
by saying that 'the second rate foreign policy which is continuous is better than the first rate foreign policy which is
not.'[3] It was better to be 'continuous' than to be right. In
maintaining his priority of continuity even when he believed
the continued policy to be seriously wrong, Rosebery
showed a consistency not to be found in other aspects of his
career.

The concept of continuity suggested that those who professed it were not looking for a specifically 'liberal' foreign
policy. The Liberal Imperialists denied that this was either
desirable or possible, a position which particularly annoyed
the radical wing of the party, which saw what the Liberal

1 Rosebery to a correspondent, *The Times*, 20 Jan. 1896.
2 His views are discussed later in this chapter.
3 Rosebery in Stourbridge, 25 Oct. 1905, LLP.

Imperialists regarded as a lack of options as a conspiracy by the 'governing classes'.[1] Liberal Imperialists assumed that the natural course of British foreign policy would be clearly indicated by the circumstances, and that individuals could not expect to change the direction of its flow. Rosebery agreed

that the policy of Great Britain is not dictated in reality by this man or that; it is dictated by broad considerations which compel any Minister who holds the office of Secretary of State for Foreign Affairs and which practically compel any Government that holds office in this country to be animated by considerations by which they must be animated.[2]

This rather determinist view accorded with Grey's rather passive approach to imperialist expansion. Grey agreed that 'in questions of foreign policy . . . the question between the two sides of the House is not one . . . of alternative policies',[3] but merely of the competence of the government in executing the agreed policy.

In identifying what the national policy ought to be, criteria to be applied should be realistic rather than moral. In keeping with their view that natural rights did not exist, and that the doctrine of the clean slate must be applied in ever-changing circumstances, Liberal Imperialists did not see foreign policy in moral terms. The criteria to be applied were 'business' criteria. Haldane told Paul Cambon that 'there were two extreme parties in England—one the Jingo party of Ashmead Bartlett in its extreme form—the other a peace under almost any circumstances party—represented by my friend John Morley.' Neither of these extremes, according to Haldane, represented British policy, or the views of the Liberal Imperialists. The latter, Haldane told Cambon,

looked at foreign relations as matters not for copy book maxims but for business men—that while desiring peaceful or pleasant relations with everybody, as all sensible people must, they were of opinion that

[1] See A. J. P. Taylor, *The Trouble Makers* (1964), pp. 95–104; and the argument between Haldane and Labouchere in 4 H, xlvi. 1489 (2 Mar. 1897).
[2] Rosebery in London, *The Times*, 10 Mar. 1905.
[3] 4 H, lvi. 275 (5 Apr. 1898).

those could only be maintained by conducting affairs on a business-like footing.[1]

Business criteria did not wholly exclude moral actions in foreign policy, but they did mean that such actions could only be taken when they could be executed with the support of other European powers.

'Business' criteria and the Near East, 1895–1897

This view was well illustrated by the Near Eastern crisis of 1895–7, the occasion of Rosebery's resignation from the party leadership. Under heavy pressure from the Armenian lobby, headed by Bryce and W. E. Gladstone, Rosebery and Kimberley had, when in office in 1895, gone some way along the path of humanitarianism in trying to obtain reforms in Turkey beneficial to the Armenians, but had stopped short of taking substantial independent action.[2] Their gesture was something of a sop to the humanitarian lobby in exchange for Rosebery's virtually free hand in imperial questions. Rosebery had little enthusiasm for the Armenians' case and greatly offended W. E. Gladstone by telling him: 'I do not see why we should bear the whole burden of this astute if pious race.'[3] In opposition after 1895, Rosebery consistently opposed independent action by Britain and also independent action by the Liberal party. There was to be no recrudescence of Midlothian.[4] Asquith stated the Liberal Imperialists' position most effectively. 'Speaking as a practical man', Asquith said that he was

not prepared to gratify the noblest and most philanthropic sentiment ... We cannot forget that we are trustees of a great Empire, inhabited by men and women of our own flesh and blood, that our first duty, as well as our first interest, is to do nothing which will imperil the security of that priceless possession.

[1] See Haldane to Rosebery, 4 Jan. 1899, RP, box 24 for a report of this conversation.

[2] K. H. W. Hilborn, 'British Policy and Diplomacy in the Near East during the Liberal Administrations, August 1892–June 1895' (Oxford D.Phil. thesis: conclusion).

[3] Rosebery to W. E. Gladstone, 10 Aug. 1893, GP 44290, f. 170; Grey agreed (Grey to Channing, 14 Aug. 1893, PRO FO 800/39, f. 201).

[4] See Rosebery's letters in *The Times*, 30 Dec. 1895, 2 and 20 Jan., 20 Aug., 14, 19, and 28 Sept. 1896.

Asquith recognized that Britain had a special treaty obligation in the Near Eastern question, but thought that 'as
practical men' the British should play down the extent of
their obligations.[1]

The objection that the Radicals raised to this approach
was that Rosebery had been prepared to risk war over Siam
—in the Radicals' eyes an 'obscure' issue—but would hardly
lift a finger in the Near East to help what the Radicals
regarded as an obviously just cause. In their eyes Rosebery's
policy was what the *Chronicle* called 'a kind of *reductio ad
Rhodesiam*', an extreme example of the triumph of expediency over morality.[2]

There was some truth in this Radical view, but it ignored
a vital factor which the Near Eastern crisis illustrated.
Questions like Siam, South Africa, and even Fashoda were in
a completely different category from Turkey. The existing
strength of the British navy, augmented by the Spencer naval
programme of 1894, bought time for the British to consolidate the imperial gains they had made since 1882.[3] Up to
and including the Boer War, European powers could make
no effective threat to Britain's imperial interests. Even the
invasion scare of 1900 was shown to be wholly without
foundation.[4] It was expected that the sort of war that might
occur with France on an imperial question would be a purely
naval war, in which Britain would avoid invasion and isolate
the enemy's colonies.[5] But any British action in Turkey, for
whatever reason, could not be executed by the fleet alone; if
British troops were involved in the mainland of Europe, the
situation would be completely transformed and 'a European
war would be a scene of universal carnage and ruin', quite
different in kind from a naval war.[6] The Near Eastern crisis
was, in the years between 1895 and 1905, the unique case
of a crisis within Europe. All the other crises of these years

[1] Asquith, *The Times*, 13 Oct. 1896. This powerful statement of the anti-
interventionist position contrasted very strongly with Asquith's speech in Leven,
The Times, 2 Oct. 1896, virtually advocating independent British intervention.
[2] *Daily Chronicle*, 11 Oct. 1896.
[3] A. J. Marder, *The Anatomy of British Sea Power*, Connecticut, 1964 ed., ch. xv.
[4] Ibid., pp. 378–9.
[5] Ibid., appendix ii.
[6] Rosebery to a correspondent, *The Times*, 28 Sept. 1896.

took place in an imperial setting, though they had important European implications.

Rosebery and 'splendid isolation'

The traditional pattern of British foreign relations since the invasion of Egypt had been an uneasy reliance on support from the powers of the Triple Alliance. This had achieved its most concrete form in the Mediterranean Agreements of 1887 and the Anglo-German Agreement of 1890. The exchange of Heligoland for security in East Africa, the 'back door' of the Nile, and for German recognition of the Nile valley as a British sphere of influence indicated British priorities. Rosebery was not as favourable as Salisbury to very close co-operation with the Triple Alliance, and wrote to Gladstone

of the paramount necessity of our holding aloof from the Triple Alliance, or any other such engagement; for the same reason for which I am hostile to the Channel Tunnel:—that I am anxious to obtain the full advantage of the insular position with which providence has endowed us. In saying this I lean neither to the right nor to the left— neither to Germany nor to France.[1]

The history of the Rosebery–Kimberley Foreign Secretary-ship bore out this statement of Rosebery's isolationist intentions. Relations with Germany sharply declined in 1892–3, and there was no corresponding increase in good relations with France.[2] The conclusion of Rosebery's ministry found Britain in an isolated position. Negotiations with France had broken down over the Nile valley question, and attempts to co-operate with the Triple Alliance had collapsed through the German attitude to the Anglo-Congolese treaty and through German failure to support Britain at the Straits.[3] Detailed study of Rosebery's policy has produced the conclusion that 'the Liberals' record was one of failure piled upon failure.' This failure, however, in the long run proved beneficial, as it provided the context in which the Spencer naval programme became a vital necessity.[4]

---

[1] Rosebery to W. E. Gladstone, 16 July 1891, GP 44289, f. 140.
[2] See A. J. P. Taylor, *The Struggle for Mastery in Europe 1848–1918*, p. 342.
[3] Ibid., pp. 346–55.   [4] Hilborn, op. cit., p. 394.

The world situation was therefore thought to be critical, and the Liberal Imperialists faced the future with little of the brash confidence usually regarded as typical of the period.[1] Rosebery humming *Rule Britannia* to keep up his spirits was a better indication of their state of mind.[2] Asquith contrasted the pomp of the 1897 Jubilee celebrations with the actual perils of the situation, for 'while we have been concerned in this great Imperial commemoration we have only to lift our eyes in order to find ourselves confronted in almost every quarter of the political horizon with dark menacing clouds.'[3] The reason for the general world hostility to Britain was, Rosebery thought, the antagonism caused by the process of imperial expansion. In 1888 Rosebery said that 'a very great change has come over the whole of our foreign policy in the last twenty years, and I think you will see a much greater change in the next twenty years.' Rosebery thought that 'our foreign policy has become more of a colonial policy', in the sense that 'formerly our foreign policy was mainly an Indian policy', but that now 'the colonial influence must necessarily overshadow our foreign policy', partly because of the increasing strength of the white colonies, but mainly because in Africa and Asia 'instead of your policy being an insular foreign policy, you are now a Power with boundaries adjoining those of three or four European states.'[4] The consequence of this colonial policy, necessary though it was, was first that 'you have excited to an intolerable degree the envy of other colonising nations ... you can reckon not on their active benevolence, but on their active malevolence', and secondly, as a corollary to this, that 'the foreign policy of Great Britain, until its territory is consolidated, filled up, settled, civilised, must inevitably be a policy of peace.'[5]

Throughout this period Rosebery took a traditional view, often supported by Liberals, that Britain should avoid close attachments to either of the continental alliance groupings.[6]

[1] See M. Beloff, *Imperial Sunset* (1968), i. 20–1.
[2] Robinson and Gallagher, op. cit., p. 311.
[3] Asquith in East Fife, *The Times*, 1 Oct. 1897.
[4] Rosebery in Leeds, 11 Oct. 1888, in (ed. anon.) *The Foreign Policy of Lord Rosebery* (1901).   [5] Rosebery in Edinburgh, *The Times*, 10 Oct. 1896.
[6] For this view, see C. H. D. Howard, *Splendid Isolation* (1967), p. 35.

But at the same time he had supported intervention in Africa and Asia. He now feared, in the years after 1895, that Britain's commitments, to which he had himself contributed, might become so extensive that she might be forced to compromise her independence to maintain her security. One way in which this could be avoided was to expand as little as possible until the international atmosphere became more calm. Rosebery was therefore very hostile to the start of the reconquest of the Sudan, not because he objected to it in principle, but because of its unpropitious timing.[1] Asquith supported this view, and asked in March 1896, 'why choose this moment of all others . . .?'[2] At the start of the Boer War Rosebery pointed out that 'we stand in a parlous position' as regards other powers,[3] and told the Lords: 'I confess I watch the situation in Europe and elsewhere more closely than I watch the situation in South Africa.'[4] But once such enterprises had got under way, Rosebery had no option but to support them, because of his principle of continuity and his belief that Liberals must appear to be patriotic. Moreover, in the case both of the Sudan and of South Africa, the government had acted because of the local situation, and in each case they had been justified by events. The discovery of Marchand at Fashoda and the revelation of Boer military strength showed that the government's argument of an immediate local threat to British security was in both cases correct. Rosebery therefore accepted the Sudanese and South African situations as necessary but regrettable exceptions to his general rule that to avoid clashes with other European powers, further expansion was undesirable.

Rosebery was not entirely hostile to agreements between Britain and other European countries, but he saw such agreements only in terms of themselves; agreements which might have further-reaching implications and involvements he distrusted. Rosebery wanted Britain to be in a sufficiently friendly position to make bargains, but not be so friendly with one power that others felt excluded: independence of

1 See above, p. 27.
2 Asquith in Swansea, *The Times*, 23 Mar. 1896.
3 4 H, lxxviii. 36 (30 Jan. 1900).
4 4 H, lxxix. 31 (15 Feb. 1900).

action must be preserved. He commented on Goschen's statement on 'splendid isolation':

I agree with Mr. Goschen that it is not possible in our conditions, and still less is it desirable, to enter into a system of alliances. There I am entirely with him, but between a system of alliances, and a system of isolation, splendid or otherwise, there seems to me to be a very wide chasm.[1]

Grey and Britain's 'new course'

Grey did not embrace isolation quite so readily as Rosebery, though before the Boer War there was no obvious public split between them. Grey thought that in the future 'we must not use such language as he [Goschen] used some time ago about "splendid isolation" . . . We must not look to isolation. We must find a common ground of interest with other Powers.'[2] But Grey's desire to find a 'common ground of interest' was a development from his position during the 1892–5 Liberal ministry. At that time he had favoured a strong line, almost regardless of the position of other powers, and on the Sudan he had been particularly adamant, even more so, perhaps, than Rosebery. He had made the famous 'Grey Declaration' independently of Rosebery and Kimberley, and in the closing months of the ministry supported the start of a movement into the Sudan.[3] Grey regarded the unauthorized advance of a small British military group into the Sudan as 'a direct interposition of Providence', and urged that although the officers had defied their instructions, they had 'done the right thing and started the policy which soon must have been declared'.[4] It was perhaps to this sort of attitude that Rosebery was referring when he told the Eighty Club that he had been 'to some degree under his [Grey's] guidance and presidency'.[5]

In 1896 Grey did not share Rosebery's reluctance to support advance into the Sudan; his comments were limited to suggestions about the route to be taken.[6] But when the

---

[1] Rosebery at the Eighty Club, *The Times*, 4 Mar. 1896.
[2] 4 H, lvi. 281 (5 Apr. 1898).   [3] For the declaration, see above, p. 15.
[4] Grey to Rosebery, 24 Apr. 1895, RP, box 23.
[5] Rosebery, *The Times*, 4 Mar. 1896.
[6] Robinson and Gallagher, op. cit., p. 353.

crisis at Fashoda came in 1898, Rosebery and Grey had exchanged positions. Grey put his emphasis on the positive point that the Sudan must be under British–Egyptian control; Rosebery stressed the negative point that the French must be kept out and that the French were committing 'an unfriendly act'.[1] This was not a fundamental difference, but it was indicative of the start of such a difference. Certainly there is no evidence that Grey went as far as Rosebery is recorded as having done in suggesting that 'a war with France would simplify differences in the future.'[2]

The reasoning behind what Rosebery regarded as Grey's 'mild statement' at the time of Fashoda must to some extent have been conditioned by Grey's attitude to Asian problems.[3] On the Asian question, Grey consistently reiterated and developed the view adumbrated by the 1892–5 Liberal government, that Britain must reach an accommodation with Russia.[4] Indeed, shortly after leaving the Foreign Office in 1895, Grey had decided that, in a friendless world, the accommodation of Russia should become the chief priority of British policy. Such an accommodation could come either in the Mediterranean or in Asia. Grey outlined to Buxton in a remarkable letter the views which he was to hold at least until he returned to the Foreign Office in 1905:

... The fact is that the success of the British race has upset the tempers of the rest of the world, & now that they have ceased quarrelling about provinces in Europe & have turned their eyes to distant places, they find us in the way everywhere. Hence a general tendency to vote us a nuisance & combine against us. I am afraid we shall have to fight sooner or later, unless some European apple of discord falls amongst the Continental Powers, but we have a good card or hand to play yet & I think a bold & skilful Foreign Secretary might detach Russia from the number of our active enemies without sacrificing any very material British interests. I have never been very devoted to the blue eyes of the Mediterranean & if old Sarum [Lord Salisbury] has the pluck to

---

1 Grey, *The Times*, 14 Nov. 1898; Rosebery in Epsom and in Perth, *The Times*, 13 and 24 Oct. 1898.

2 M. V. Brett (ed.), *Journals and Letters of Reginald Viscount Esher* (1934), i. 222 (Journal, 28 Oct. 1898).

3 Rosebery to Grey, 15 Nov. 1898, RP, Letter Book.

4 This policy was, in 1894–5, mainly directed towards Armenia; see C. J. Lowe, *The Reluctant Imperialists* (1967), pp. 187–95. Grey welcomed accommodation with France in Indo-China (see above, p. 156).

do a bold stroke of policy & play the dog in the manger there less, I for one should be glad.

... Unless Russia is bent on annexing Persia, room could easily be found for her wants and ours both in Asia and Europe: & if Russia stands aside we ought to be able to deal easily with any combination of European navies, which is possible at present.[1]

In the circumstances of the day the Far East was the area in which Russia's 'wants' could most easily be gratified, and after 1895 Grey continually urged such an accommodation by direct negotiation with Russia, bypassing the nominally sovereign Chinese government, and at the expense of local British interests.[2] Thus he thought the government were right to agree to a Russian warm-water port, and wrong to argue after the event about Port Arthur, which should have been the start of an Anglo-Russian agreement.[3] During the 1898 race for concessions, Grey continued to call for concessions for Russia 'in the most friendly spirit', and to deny that Russia wanted 'a Protectorate over the whole of China'.[4] Early in 1899 he continued to regret the absence of such an agreement,[5] and he therefore particularly welcomed the Anglo-Russian agreement of April 1899, regardless of its effect on local British interests.[6]

But accommodation with Russia in the Far East could not occur in isolation from developments in policy elsewhere. As Asquith said, 'you cannot segregate your foreign policy into watertight compartments . . . The solidarity of international relations is now complete'; it was therefore illogical to look for a *détente* with Russia in Asia while quarrelling with her ally in Africa.[7] But Grey held that security on the Nile was a vital priority in itself. There was therefore no option but to go through with the Fashoda affair. Grey's movement towards France should not be pre-dated; it followed by a number of years his movement towards Russia. Asquith,

[1] Grey to Buxton, 31 Dec. 1895, Buxton Papers.
[2] See above, p. 157.
[3] 4 H, lvi. 1653 (29 Apr. 1898); 4 H, lxvi. 231 ff. (8 Feb. 1899); *The Times*, 14 Apr. 1898.
[4] 4 H, lxvi. 237–41 (8 Feb. 1899).
[5] 4 H, lxviii. 1449–50 (20 Mar. 1899).
[6] See above, p. 157, and 4 H, lxxii. 817 ff. (9 June 1899); for the agreement, see Langer, op. cit., pp. 682–5.
[7] 4 H, lvi. 1346 (10 June 1898).

as well as making the usual Liberal comments about good relations with France at the time of Fashoda,[1] thought that that crisis had cleared the air, and called for an agreement with France which would 'be a lasting foundation for the settlement of our future relations in the northern part of the great continent of Africa'.[2] Grey was not, before the Boer War, ready to take as friendly an attitude to France as this. He was not as quick to call for an Entente policy in North Africa as he was in Asia.

During the Boer War, Grey remained uncommitted to either alliance:

... he was not a friend of 'splendid isolation' and he would like to see us on good terms with every nation, but he did believe that widespread as our interests were, so long as we kept up the strength of the Navy it was in our power to have more free play ... in our foreign policy and friendships than any other nation except the United States.[3]

But in Grey's view it was becoming increasingly difficult to be friendly with Germany. Grey never showed any enthusiasm for Germany in this period. Though he was ready to sacrifice British interests in China for the sake of good relations with Russia, he adopted a completely different attitude to the Anglo-German Yangtze Agreement of October 1900. Whereas he had ignored details and welcomed the Russian agreement as valuable in itself, he judged the German agreement strictly on its local merits. So regarded he found it 'a most one-sided Agreement . . . the more I look at this agreement . . . the more one-sided it appears to me to be'.[4] Grey gave no attention to the potential general implications of the Yangtze Agreement; his comment on it was that it showed that a continuing Anglo-Russian Agreement 'is really vital to any satisfactory state of affairs'.[5]

---

[1] Asquith in Leven, *The Times*, 14 Oct. 1898.
[2] Asquith in Newburgh, *The Times*, 13 Oct. 1899. See also Asquith's statement during the crisis that 'by dispelling once and for all a cloud of formidable and dangerous misconceptions they had enormously improved the chances of a permanent good understanding between Britain and France', *The Times*, 28 Jan. 1899.
[3] Grey in Glasgow, *The Times*, 29 Nov. 1901. Like other Liberals, Grey called for better British–U.S.A. relations (see K. Robbins, *Sir Edward Grey* (1971), p. 130), but he did not link these with his calls for *détente* with the Dual Alliance.
[4] 4 H, xcviii. 283–6 (26 July 1901).   [5] Ibid.

Grey did not welcome Chamberlain's calls for an Anglo-German alliance.[1] He regarded Chamberlain's Leicester speech of 30 November 1899 calling for such an alliance as 'disastrous'.[2] Grey and Asquith consistently opposed Chamberlain's 'new diplomacy' when it was directed towards achieving an alliance with Germany. Asquith in his first Commons speech on foreign policy denounced Chamberlain's attacks on Russia and his call for a German alliance in 1898, and asked: 'what have we done . . . that we are now to go touting for allies in the highways and byways of Europe?' Asquith singled out Germany as the main threat to Britain's Chinese policy.[3] Grey similarly attacked Chamberlain's concluding attempts at an alliance with Germany in 1901.[4] But when Chamberlain used 'open diplomacy' *against* Germany in October 1901, Grey praised him for having 'said nothing which could be regarded as offensive to the German nation . . . he held Mr. Chamberlain clear in that speech'.[5] Grey attacked the German charges against Britain in South Africa as 'a vile lie', and argued that while 'national interest' was a principal factor in international relations, 'there was a magnetism between peoples which repelled or attracted and which had its influence on the conduct of foreign affairs.'[6] By the end of the Boer War Grey had concluded that Britain must make a move towards France. He wrote to Herbert Gladstone:

I am glad that Italy has arranged her own affairs with France, because it makes it possible for us to get on good terms with France too, which is much better than clutching at the skirts of the Triple Alliance, considering the feelings of the Germans about us.[7]

---

[1] Langer's argument that Grey spoke in favour of a German alliance in 1898 is based on a misreading of Grey's speech which Langer quotes (pp. 497–8). Grey was referring to the continuance of the Concert in China. He stressed that Britain had similar commercial interests to Japan, the U.S.A., and Germany, and that out of this 'may come political agreement'; this is far from suggesting a general alliance with Germany alone.

[2] Grey to Haldane, 4 Dec. 1899, in Trevelyan, op. cit., p. 77.

[3] 4 H, lvi. 1348–50 (10 June 1898); Asquith's case was very carefully prepared; see his Memorandum of 26 Jan. 1898, AP 19, f. 37.

[4] *The Times*, 31 May 1901.

[5] Grey in Glasgow, *The Times*, 29 Nov. 1901.   [6] Ibid.

[7] Grey to Gladstone, 2 July 1902, HGP 45992, f. 96.

In 1902, therefore, Grey believed that 'we were in a critical period', 'a very delicate time, when a wrong step might prejudice future policy'.[1] In this situation 'the first thing he should like to see striven after was whether we could not better the relations that had existed in the past between France, Russia and ourselves.'[2] But any such improvement had to take account of the 1902 Anglo-Japanese alliance, which seemed to go against Grey's priority of friendship with Russia. He made no public comment on this alliance in 1902. He did not speak in the adjournment debate in February. On that occasion Harcourt and Campbell-Bannerman were both cautiously hostile to the alliance, on the general ground of avoiding alliances. Henry Norman, the Liberal Imperialist who moved the adjournment, quoted Grey's views on a Russian understanding and said: 'It is quite useless to deny that this treaty is aimed at Russia.'[3] In his speech in November 1902 Grey seemed to allude to the alliance when he said 'we had got into the habit of making concessions without making friends. He wanted the country to be careful, if it was no longer to be splendid isolation, to make alliances and not entanglements.'[4] Grey made no actual attack on the alliance of 1902, and he accepted it in its renewed, extended form in 1905.[5]

Whatever his opinion of the Japanese alliance, Grey became more and more apprehensive about Germany. In February 1903, during the Venezuelan crisis, Grey said 'he must say that he was not surprised that co-operation with Germany was not popular in this country at the present time.' He then rehearsed the list of failed attempts at co-operation with Germany on imperial questions, dwelling especially on the Yangtze Agreement. Grey now seemed to see an 'either/or' situation developing:

[1] Grey in Sheffield and in Weymouth, *The Times*, 8 and 26 Nov. 1902.
[2] Ibid., 26 Nov. 1902.
[3] Norman in 4 H, cii. 1278 (13 Feb. 1902).
[4] Grey, *The Times*, 8 Nov. 1902.
[5] Grey publicly accepted the alliance on continuity grounds in 1905 (see Trevelyan, op. cit., p. 90). Privately, he feared that it might have a 'bad effect on native opinion in India', and thought 'if we are to run the risk of having to go to war on behalf of Japan in the Far East, there ought to be some corresponding risk undertaken by her on behalf of us' (Grey to Asquith, 2 Oct. 1905, AP 10, f. 148).

We had hitherto cultivated our good relations with Germany at the expense of our good relations with Russia and with France, and we were now cultivating them at the expense of . . . our good relations with the United States.[1]

The view that Britain must choose was new in Grey's thought: he had not maintained in 1898 that bad relations with France meant a search for good relations with Germany. Grey made no explicit reference to German naval plans, but in November 1902 he observed that 'other navies were growing up all around us, and peace in coming years would depend not only on the strength of the British Navy, but upon the relations into which we entered with other powers.'[2]

The Anglo-French Entente of April 1904 thus fitted clearly into the line of thought which Grey was developing. He welcomed the Entente, not from the point of view of a bargain about extant imperial questions, but from the point of view of general policy. The agreement meant, he said, 'a change in policy'. Looked at as a bargain, he admitted that France gained greatly from the Entente 'both sentimentally and materially', but Grey did not grudge France this, for he regarded, as he had regarded the start of Anglo-Russian co-operation, the fact of the existence of the agreement as more important than the details it settled. He also thought the Entente would be 'a working model for other cases', referring presumably to Russia.[3]

Grey's whole-hearted support for the Entente as 'a change in policy' was to be of vital significance for future British policy. Grey was ready to sacrifice continuity to defend it, telling Ferguson in 1905 that 'if any government drags us back into the German net I will oppose it openly at all costs.'[4] Before taking office he said that better relations with Germany could only come so long as they did nothing 'in any way to impair our existing good relations with France'.[5] Grey privately thought in October 1905 that 'we are now

[1] Grey in Berwick, *The Times*, 7 Feb. 1902.
[2] Grey in Sheffield, *The Times*, 8 Nov. 1902.
[3] 4 H, cxxxv. 516 ff. (1 June 1904). Grey's speech established him clearly as opposition spokesman on foreign affairs.
[4] Grey to Ferguson, 13 Aug. 1905, in Trevelyan, op. cit., p. 84.
[5] Grey in the City, *The Times*, 21 Oct. 1905, and in P. Knaplund (ed.), *Speeches on Foreign Affairs 1904–1914* (1931).

running a real risk of losing France and not gaining Germany, who won't want us if she can detach France from us.'[1]

What was so bad about 'the German net'? Grey's view seems to have been to some extent sentimental: his speeches continually urge that not only national interest but national sentiment is an important factor in determining foreign policy.[2] Whatever caused Grey's hostility to the Germans—the destruction of his papers makes it difficult to trace its private development—it was not the result either of profound study or of Foreign Office pressure. Grey recalled in 1910 that in opposition he 'followed foreign affairs only to the extent which it was necessary to enable me from time to time to take the part which was expected from me in the House of Commons'.[3] There is no indication that Grey had any regular intimate contact with the Foreign Office staff, when in opposition. He entered the Foreign Office in December 1905 having already held for some years the suspicions about German policy which his advisers later encouraged. Grey seems rather to have drifted into this position, but once having taken a position, he was, as Acland wrote of him, a man 'of very fixed opinions'.[4] The necessity for the 'new course' was, Grey thought, self-evident. It had been dictated more 'by the persistent pressure of circumstances than by any definite plan'. Grey believed 'there is in great affairs so much more ... in the minds of the events ... than in the minds of the chief actors.'[5] This statement accorded well with the passive attitude with which Grey looked at politics generally. As in imperial affairs, Grey denied freedom of choice to Britain: Kruger and the Kaiser had the initiative.

Rosebery sticks to the 'old course'

Rosebery by 1905 was completely isolated from the rest of the Liberal party on foreign affairs.[6] Most Liberals regarded

---

[1] Grey to Spender, 19 Oct. 1905, SP 46389, f. 8.
[2] For examples see *The Times*, 29 Nov. 1901, 26 Nov. 1902, 8 Nov. 1904; 4 H, cxxxv. 516 ff. (1 June 1904).
[3] Trevelyan, op. cit., p. 64.
[4] Acland to Spender, 20 Nov. 1899, SP 46391, f. 52.   [5] Grey, i. 36, 51.
[6] Hamilton found the Entente 'approved as much by the "outs" as by the

the Entente with France as the natural result of common democratic impulses. As Campbell-Bannerman observed:

Friendship with France is, to the Liberal party, something more than a cherished ideal or an historical tradition . . . to Liberals it has been given to a special degree to appreciate the incalculable benefits which the great nation of France has bestowed upon mankind.[1]

Rosebery had none of this sympathy for the French. He disliked the Foxite tradition within English liberalism, and he disliked even more the French revolutionary tradition it supported. He regarded the Third Republic as unreliable and aggressive, and thought that Salisbury's policy of concessions in Siam and Madagascar had encouraged France to play England 'a dirty trick' at Fashoda.[2] British success on the Nile in 1898 did not make Rosebery less anti-French. In September 1899 Haldane found him 'vehemently anti-French—the Dreyfus case has made him more so than ever'.[3] Rosebery's hostility to the French did not make him 'pro-German' in any positive political sense; he regarded German commercial competition with alarm, and he never gave support to the various proposals for an Anglo-German alliance. When Chamberlain attacked France and suggested an alliance with Germany in November 1899, Rosebery rebuked him for 'this flouting of foreign nations'.[4]

Rosebery did not openly attack the alliance with Japan, though 'he should prefer a looser but perhaps more intimate understanding.' He was more concerned with the alliance as a precedent, and as the first step towards European involvement. He believed the alliance could not be considered only on its own merits; its implications would 'be felt not merely in the Far East, but all over the world'; the treaty 'having been made . . . cannot be the last', for when a nation began treaty-making, 'it lost the response it usually

---

"ins" ' and thought Rosebery would become 'a complete outsider' because of his view of it; EHD, 11 June 1904.

[1] Bannerman in Portsmouth, 11 Nov. 1902, Liberal Publication Dept. Paradoxically, he advocated a similar *détente* with the Russians in his next sentence.
[2] Rosebery to Herbert Bismarck, 15 Nov. 1899, RP, Letter Book.
[3] Haldane to Mother, 13 Sept. 1899, Hal P 5962, f. 77.
[4] Rosebery in Edinburgh, *The Times*, 2 Dec. 1899.

had to those who proposed them; viz. that it did not make treaties.'[1]

Rosebery saw the Anglo-French Entente as the unfortunate result of this policy. He objected both to its details and to its implications. He denounced almost all the agreements made by the government since 1895 as 'one-sided'. Agreements with Germany over Samoa, China, and Venezuela had been 'wholly one-sided', but 'no more one-sided agreement was ever concluded between two powers at peace with each other' than the Anglo-French agreement,[2] which was 'a disastrous transaction'.[3] Its specific terms offered a 'dangerous and needless' concession in Morocco, and Rosebery hoped that Britain 'may never regret having handed Morocco over to a great military Power'.[4]

But the implications of the Entente upset him even more than the details of its provisions. He publicly attacked Grey for his view that the agreements, 'if they may be one-sided, will produce a friendly feeling'.[5] He thought that Britain's new diplomatic obligations to France meant that 'this unhappy Agreement is much more likely to promote than to prevent unfriendliness in the not too distant future.'[6] Rosebery accepted that the rules of continuity meant that the 'next government' would have to stand by the terms of the agreement, but he regarded the Kaiser's visit to Tangier in March 1905 as an illustration of his fears, and wrote to Spender: 'perhaps you may also be beginning to say that I was not mad when I said that the Anglo-French agreement was "much more likely to lead to complications than to peace".'[7]

Rosebery's view of the European situation was based on his fear of German strength and his simultaneous mistrust of the French government. '"You are leaning on an aspen" he said in tragic tone, "and the German Emperor has four

---

[1] Rosebery in Liverpool and Burnley, *The Times*, 15 Feb. 1902 and 20 May 1903.

[2] Rosebery in London, 10 June 1904, LLP.

[3] Rosebery to a correspondent, *The Times*, 22 Aug. 1904.

[4] Ibid.   [5] Rosebery in London, 10 June 1904.

[6] Rosebery, *The Times*, 22 Aug. 1904; Lloyd George recalled this as Rosebery's immediate reaction to the agreement (*War Memoirs*, i. 1).

[7] Rosebery to Spender, 20 June 1905, SP 46387, f. 58. Many Liberal Leaguers took Rosebery's warnings lightly; he repeated them in more detail at a private meeting at Perks's house in July 1905 (Perks to Rosebery, 20 July 1905, RP, box 41).

millions of soldiers and the second best navy in the world.' '[1] Rosebery emerged as the sole public supporter of the old isolationist view of British policy. Grey appeared to have reverted to the Liberal, non-imperialist view that Britain and France were natural friends.[2] But Grey was not so much pro-French as instinctively anti-German, and was, with Haldane, about to put on an 'official' level the nascent military conversations, implying a military involvement on the Continent which was very far from any traditional Liberal policy.[3]

The difference between Rosebery and Grey was profound. Both had arrived at their conclusions more by intuition than by calculation. Despite their pleas for efficiency, they do not seem to have made an attempt to resolve the differences between them, or to have tried to assess the basis of their different view of the national interest, or to have discussed how two men who had worked so amiably together on foreign affairs in 1892–4 were now in the position that if one held office, the other was virtually, by his disagreement on policy, excluded.

Haldane's views

Haldane occupied a position midway between Rosebery and Grey on the Entente policy, but took a more extreme view than either of the alliance with Japan. Haldane came close to breaking the continuity rule over the Japanese alliance. His view of this alliance was that 'of all the rash proceedings in the history of our foreign policy the alliance with Japan was one of the rashest', because of the risk of British involvement in the Russo-Japanese war.[4] He modified this position on the grounds of continuity in 1905, and approved of the revised alliance as giving security 'in the Indian frontier'.[5]

Haldane was favourable to the Entente with France. He had never been much interested in the details of North

---

[1] Grey to his wife, 12 July 1905, Trevelyan, op. cit., pp. 83–4.

[2] C. Spring-Rice thought the Japanese alliance and the Entente policy 'were in their inception Liberal policies and in strict conformity with Liberal principles'; Rice to Spender, 13 Sept. 1905, SP 46391, f. 156.

[3] For the conversations, see K. Robbins, op. cit., p. 146.

[4] Haldane in Macmerry, *The Scotsman*, 14 Oct. 1904.

[5] Haldane in Tranent, *The Scotsman*, 14 June 1905, and in Haddington, *The Scotsman*, 11 Oct. 1905. Ferguson took the same view in Leith, *The Scotsman*, 1 May 1905.

African imperialism, but he regarded the conclusion of disputes in that area with satisfaction.[1] He also saw the Entente as 'stemming the tide of militarism' in Europe.[2] But he did not, as Grey did, see the friendship with France as an end in itself, or the maintenance of this friendship as Britain's first priority. He regarded the Entente as only the first step in a series of reconciliations with European powers, and thought 'it would be the completion of a large policy if we could establish better relations with Germany and Russia.' Good relations with Russia were part of Grey's plan, but the tone of Grey's City speech in 1905 was very different from Haldane's view that 'it was one of the great bits of work before the Liberal party to establish a better understanding with Germany.'[3]

Haldane had an ambivalent attitude towards Germany. Whereas Grey could look with relative dispassion (and ignorance) at the continental scene, Haldane's thoughts, both of fear and trust, naturally turned first to Germany, the country where he was partially educated and which he visited annually before 1906. He recognized a dynamic quality in German life which expressed itself both in 'militarism' and in admirable progress in all fields of domestic life; this dynamism was the result of the application of 'scientific method'.[4] No Liberal Imperialist ever quoted France as the model of the social future, but German ideas were making an impact on British thinking on military, social, economic, and educational reform. Haldane was one of the leading British exponents of these ideas, and of the school of German philosophers whose thinking lay behind the ideas. He therefore both admired and feared Germany. Sentiment, and appreciation of the power of German organization, made him reluctant to abandon his position, even after the Tangier incident, that the 'paramount duty of Britain and Germany

---

1 Haldane in East Lothian, *The Scotsman*, 14 Oct. 1905. In 1897 Haldane and Asquith went to Paris to improve their knowledge of French and of French politicians; Grey did not accompany them (Haldane to Mother, 6 June 1897, Hal P 5957, f. 183).

2 Haldane in Ealing, *The Scotsman*, 12 Nov. 1904.

3 Haldane in Haddington, *The Scotsman*, 11 Oct. 1905.

4 Haldane in Ealing, *The Scotsman*, 12 Nov. 1904, and Haldane to the Edinburgh German Society, *The Scotsman*, 18 Oct. 1904.

was to be at peace with one another, whose interests were in the same direction, and for both of whom there was room.'[1]

By accepting the Entente with enthusiasm, however, Haldane indicated that he regarded Anglo-French friendship as the base from which Britain must in future work towards finding friendship with Germany. He therefore found no difficulty in co-operating closely with Grey over the military conversations during the crisis following the start of the 1905 Liberal ministry, and though he continued when in office to try to promote better Anglo-German relations, he never entered a serious caveat against Grey's policy.[2]

Interest in defence

The corollary of foreign policy was defence policy. Behind the changes in foreign policy lay anxiety about the defence of the vast empire for whose security Britain was solely responsible, though she could draw on the small contributions of the white colonies and the substantial reserve of the Indian army. Imperialists had long seen that Britain's defence position required overhauling. The Liberal Imperialists of the Liberal League came relatively late to this movement. They had played little part in the agitations of the 1880s for improved defence arrangements, and, apart from Rosebery, had played no significant role in the controversy about the navy programme of 1894.[3] Before the Boer War, defence was hardly ever mentioned in their speeches. During the war, however, the urgent need for reform, especially of the War Office, but also of the navy, became an important theme in their speeches. This linked Asquith, Grey, and Haldane with an older generation of imperialists in the Liberal party —men like Stead and Dilke who, while they had been wary of Liberal support for colonial expansion, and were positively hostile to Liberal Imperialist plans for the development of the Liberal party, had always maintained their interest in the priority of an effective defence policy.

[1] Haldane in Haddington, *The Scotsman*, 11 Oct. 1905.

[2] See G. Monger, *The End of Isolation* (1963), p. 250. See ibid., pp. 298 ff. for Haldane's attempts to moderate Grey's suspicion of Germany. These should not be exaggerated. Since Haldane controlled the British end of the military conversations, he could have used their cessation as a weapon against the Foreign Office had he felt hostility of principle rather than of tone to Grey's policy.

[3] See Stansky, pp. 19–25.

The navy and the 'blue water' policy

Haldane was the leading Liberal Imperialist most closely interested in defence. From his membership of the Explosives Committee set up by Lansdowne during the Boer War, he had intimate knowledge of the new techniques available both to the army and to the navy.[1] Haldane was also closely connected with the Fisher school of naval thinking through his intimacy with J. R. Thursfield, *The Times* leader-writer on naval affairs. Most of Haldane's statements on the navy were drafted by Thursfield.[2] Haldane also introduced Asquith to Thursfield, whom Asquith wished 'should stoke him' with naval information.[3] Based on Thursfield's information, Haldane argued that

> that which had been called the 'Policy of the Blue Water School' seemed to him to be the true principle of naval and Imperial defence . . . Not only was the Navy a great source of economy to us . . . but it was really the principal instrument by which our Empire had been made a great Empire.[4]

To gain priority for this view, which most people nominally agreed to, Haldane organized and chaired a conference at the Palace Hotel in February 1903. Leo Maxse was the secretary and Dilke, Spenser Wilkinson, and other well-known civilian defence experts attended. By Haldane's disavowal that 'we had no hostile feeling towards Germany' as well as a strongly anti-German letter from George Meredith, which was read out, it was clear that the real object of the conference was to consider the problems raised by German naval expansion. The conference concentrated on the menace of the German navy programmes, and the need for a North Sea fleet and base to meet the challenge.[5]

[1] See Haldane, pp. 164–5, and Lansdowne to Haldane, 1, 10, and 15 Apr. 1900, Hal P 5905, ff. 24–8.

[2] Haldane to Thursfield, 25 Aug., 16 Sept., 7 Oct. 1901, 5 Jan., 5 Mar. 1903, Hal P 5905 and 5906. For Thursfield, see Appendix I.

[3] Haldane to Thursfield, 18 Oct. 1901, Hal P 5905, f. 112. For Thursfield's intimacy and accord with Fisher, see A. J. Marder (ed.), *Fear God and Dread Nought* (1952), i. 198–262.

[4] Haldane at Prestonpans, *The Scotsman*, 6 Jan. 1903.

[5] See the conference report in *The Scotsman*, 17 Feb. 1903.

This was a period of dispute within the navy as to how 'an invincible Navy', as Haldane called it, could best be achieved. In this dispute the Liberal Imperialists supported Fisher. Rosebery visited Fisher at Malta in 1901 and was enthusiastic about his plans;[1] a number of Fisher's views appeared in the Liberal League pamphlet *Unionist Muddle and Waste: the Tories and the Navy*.[2] In 1902 Grey visited him, partly to try to persuade him to return to the Admiralty.[3] Haldane gave strong public support to Fisher's controversial proposals to scrap out-dated ships, and asked 'why the Admiralty had not long ago adopted the reforms which had signalised the arrival of Lord Fisher to the Department. Our Navy had obviously been encumbered for a long time with useless ships . . .'[4] The corollary to the scrapping of old ships was the building of the Dreadnoughts, and Haldane strongly supported this. His Explosives Committee was involved in the development of long-range guns, and Haldane, as early as 1901, publicly advocated the need for Britain to be first in this field.[5] Haldane, Thursfield, and Fisher also strongly agreed on the need for every officer 'to be trained in science just as the manufacturer must be if he is to hold his own in competition'. This applied to all officers, but especially to 'those in high office'.[6]

Fisher's reforms appealed to the Liberal Imperialists because they were not only efficient but cheap. Like everybody else the Liberal Imperialists were worried about rising expenditure, but as Liberals they had the additional worry that in office they could expect substantial demands for reduced defence estimates from their own parliamentary

---

[1] Fisher to Rosebery, 10 and 22 May 1901 in Marder, *Fear God*, i. 188–96; Fisher was also in frequent contact with Rosebery in 1904 (see RP, box 79).

[2] LLP 29 (1902). After leaving the *Daily News*, E. T. Cook spent time 'writing leaders for Fisher' (J. Saxon Mills, *Sir Edward Cook*, p. 220).

[3] Fisher to C. Fisher, 5 Aug. 1902, in Marder, op. cit. i. 276. Grey was also involved in naval reforms, though less intimately than Haldane, through his chairmanship of the Naval Reserves Committee which reported in Jan. 1903 (Parl. Papers 1903, xl (Cd. 1491)).

[4] Haldane at the Eighty Club, *The Scotsman*, 18 Jan. 1905.

[5] Haldane in Haddington, *The Scotsman*, 5 Oct. 1901.

[6] Ibid. Haldane told Thursfield he was 'in full correspondence with the breezy Fisher about Education' (5 Jan. 1903, Hal P 5906, f. 1). *The Urgent Need for a Definite Naval Policy*, LLP 21 (1902), almost certainly by Thursfield, gives an admirable and very detailed statement of the whole Fisher case.

supporters.[1] As a result of Fisher's 'thinking', Haldane said, there had been made possible an efficient and economic navy.[2]

A navy founded on efficiency called into question the two-Power standard, which stressed size rather than efficiency. It has been correctly observed that 'the two-Power standard had taken firm hold of popular imagination.'[3] For a party to disavow it led, therefore, to an easy charge of lack of patriotism. Grey and Haldane indicated that they were working towards a recognition that the two-Power standard, which Dilke frequently argued was too lenient a margin, might be too vigorous and excessive.[4] Grey and Haldane excluded the United States as one of the two Powers, on the grounds both of friendship and necessity.[5] Grey argued that

when they talked of the two-Power standard, the committee ought to bear in mind that that standard must always have a reasonable interpretation, and that circumstances might arise under which policy would have to take the place of the maintenance of the two-Power standard.

Even before the signing of the Entente, Grey hoped that Britain and France could sign a 'mutual agreement . . . with regard to stopping the increase in the Fleets'; such an agreement would necessarily involve, on the British side, security against the expanding German fleet.[6]

Army reform

Given Liberal Imperialist enthusiasm for Fisher's methods, it was natural for Haldane to say 'he wished we could get another Sir John Fisher at the War Office', for War Office reforms were slow and confused.[7]

[1] See, for example, F. W. Hirst, 'An Ideal Budget', *Independent Review*, Dec. 1905, which expected to cut the army estimates from £32½m. to £20m. and the navy estimates from £40m. to £24m. by 1908.

[2] Haldane in East Lothian, *The Scotsman*, 11 Jan. 1905.

[3] E. L. Woodward, *Great Britain and the German Navy* (1935), appendix ii, p. 461. The standard demanded a navy superior (usually by numerical definition) to a combination of any two Powers.

[4] After 1900 Dilke frequently advocated a three-Power standard (Marder, op. cit., p. 509).

[5] Haldane, 4 H, cxxx. 1301, quoted in Woodward, op. cit., p. 468, and Grey, 4 H, cxxx. 1404 ff. (1 Mar. 1904).'

[6] Grey, ibid. Asquith used Grey's speech when preparing to speak on the standard in 1909 (AP 21, f. 266).   [7] Haldane, *The Scotsman*, 18 Jan. 1905.

One problem was that the function of the army was unclear. Campbell-Bannerman thought Liberals should 'demand a well thought out system based on our actual needs'.[1] But what were the actual needs? Liberal Imperialists were quite clear what was *not* the function of the army. It was *not* 'to provide for the failure of the navy' and it was *not* for the army 'to provide against invasion and to garrison coast defences and ports on a large scale'.[2] Defence against invasion was to be left entirely to the navy at sea. The army was not to be designed on the assumption that the navy would fail. Liberal Imperialists, therefore, joined strongly in the attacks upon Brodrick's scheme for six army corps as a 'fatuity' because it was mainly concerned with home defence.[3]

It was easy enough to shoot holes in Brodrick's plans; it was less simple to suggest an alternative. Assuming that the navy could be made fully efficient, Britain, Haldane thought in 1901, should have

a comparatively small Army—one extremely efficacious and capable for foreign service which would be mobile for service at home, but which need not compete with the enormous armaments of Europe that fought under totally different conditions.[4]

Haldane thus supported 'a small and efficient Army for service abroad and the maintenance of the Volunteer force', but before 1905 the details of such an army did not much interest him, for 'he wanted our efforts to be concentrated on keeping our sea power.'[5] This view was common to most leading Liberal Imperialists; they were deeply involved in the details of naval reform, but they kept well clear of the intrigues within the army.[6] Haldane, before 1905, while recognizing that a small, efficient army would serve 'abroad',

[1] Bannerman to Gladstone, 9 Feb. 1903, HGP 45988, f. 32.

[2] *The Urgent Need for a Definite Naval Policy*, LLP 21. See also Haldane, *The Scotsman*, 6 Jan. 1903, and Asquith in 4 H, cxviii. 765 ff. (24 Feb. 1903).

[3] LLP 21, and Asquith in London, *The Times*, 4 May 1901, and Asquith in 4 H, xciv. 312 ff. (16 May 1901).

[4] Haldane in Haddington, *The Scotsman*, 5 Oct. 1901; see also Asquith in 4 H cxviii. 765 ff. (24 Feb. 1903).

[5] Haldane in Dunbar, *The Scotsman*, 3 Oct. 1902.

[6] Even Ferguson, with his Guards background, kept clear of military controversies; see *The Scotsman*, 5 Feb. 1903.

seems to have regarded 'abroad' as meaning abroad within the empire. Although Grey's views on foreign policy were beginning to point towards military involvement in Europe, Haldane did not publicly or privately contemplate this before going to the War Office in 1905.

At first the solution proposed for the army difficulties was to 'put at the head of the War Office a man who knows his own mind and can get his own way'.[1] The suitable man was, according to Rosebery and Haldane, Kitchener.[2] Kitchener was, Rosebery said, 'a man of genius . . . a great organiser, such a boon as is not given to a nation twice in a century'.[3] Yet Kitchener had been 'exiled' to India, although he was obviously 'the man for the crisis'. Rosebery said Kitchener should be given a completely free hand: 'none of the flimsy formulas which have been urged should be allowed to prevail against his judgement.'[4] Rosebery knew nothing of Kitchener's opinions on military reorganization, but his reputation as a ruthless ignorer of 'red tape' appealed to Rosebery's notions of 'efficiency'.[5] He thought the difficulties of a military Secretary of State could easily be got over, but Gladstone thought the 'Kitchener idea won't be congenial to Asquith and seems designed to keep him out of office.'[6]

There were very strong military objections to this idea. Esher wrote to Rosebery on 2 September 1903 to stress in private the importance of the memorandum he had written for the War Commission. He emphasized that Rosebery's support was vital to the scheme's popularity, and argued that 'the "one man rule" cannot be depended upon', but Esher thought that 'with a military "Cabinet" or "Board" you stand as good a chance as ever with Kitchener at the top.'[7] Rosebery wrote a public letter of 10 September 1903 which suggested that full powers be given to Kitchener; but he

---

[1] Asquith, *The Times*, 17 Sept. 1900.

[2] Haldane in Dunbar, *The Scotsman*, 3 Oct. 1902.

[3] Rosebery in Edinburgh, 1 Nov. 1902, LLP 33.

[4] 'Rosebery to a Correspondent on the Report of the Royal Commission on the War', 10 Sept. 1903, LLP 76.

[5] Kitchener wrote to Rosebery that many people assumed they were in close contact, whereas in fact they never corresponded (12 Sept. 1903, RP, box 78).

[6] LLP 76, and Gladstone to Bannerman, 19 Sept. 1903, CBP 41217, f. 16.

[7] Esher (Reginald Brett) to Rosebery, 2 Sept. 1903, RP, box 6.

assumed in this letter that Kitchener would use those powers to set up 'a Board as in the case of the Admiralty'.[1] Kitchener, however, immediately wrote opposing the idea of an army board or council.[2] Rosebery again advocated the use of Kitchener's talents in 1904, but offered no comment on the army council idea.[3]

Haldane did not continue his support for Kitchener.[4] Like Grey and Asquith he was enthusiastic about a planned, 'scientific' approach to defence problems, and looked to the proposals of the Esher committee for the best expression of this sort of view. The Liberal Imperialists made no very clear criticism of the 1904 proposals of Arnold-Foster, which Asquith found 'a vague and experimental scheme'.[5] The Liberal Imperialists claimed that it was impossible to evaluate the Arnold-Foster proposals since little parliamentary time was given to their exposition, and it was unclear whether the government would actually support Arnold-Foster in his proposals.[6] Rather than expect the War Office to produce satisfactory reforms from within, the Liberal Imperialists looked to the Committee of Imperial Defence for military salvation.

The Committee of Imperial Defence fulfilled a long-standing Liberal Imperialist aim. When the Imperial Federation League was dissolved in 1893, Ferguson started an *ad hoc* committee to keep the necessity of the integration of imperial defence before the public, and in the 1892–5 administration Asquith had worked with Dilke and A. J. Balfour to start a 'Defence Committee of the Cabinet'.[7] The C.I.D. would, if efficiently run, combine many of the virtues which the Liberal Imperialists wished to develop throughout the civil service. It would provide an 'element of continuity' through its permanent secretariat, it introduced 'business

[1] LLP 76.
[2] Kitchener to Rosebery, 18 Sept. 1903, RP, box 78.
[3] Rosebery in Lincoln, 20 Sept. 1904, LLP 161.
[4] Haldane soon came to regard Kitchener as a potential obstacle to reform. See Sommer, *Haldane of Cloan*, p. 165.
[5] Asquith in 4 H, cxxxix. 1432 ff. (8 Aug. 1904).
[6] Ibid.; Asquith in 4 H, cxliii. 60 ff. (15 Mar. 1905); Grey in 4 H, cxliv. 171 ff. (3 Apr. 1905).
[7] See S. Gwynn and G. M. Tuckwell, *The Life of Sir Charles Dilke* (1917), ii. 454–7.

talent' into government,[1] it would co-ordinate the functions of the army and the navy 'and consolidate these two separate demands into one great demand for Imperial defence', it would help to make possible 'efficiency and economy'.[2] It would act as a precedent for institutional co-operation between Britain and the Colonies. Most important, however, would be its symbolic effect: 'at least in one department of Government we had now got something like a scientific approach to a great problem.'[3] The Committee would serve as a model for the extension of this approach to other departments, starting with the Foreign and Colonial Offices.[4]

Liberal Imperialists thus looked to the Committee of Imperial Defence as the linchpin of future defence planning. Their main fear was that the Committee would not be strong enough to control the traditionally independent tendencies of the War Office and the Admiralty. Grey feared that the Esher Committee was being over-optimistic in its claims for the Committee and thought that a Ministry of Defence, though rejected by the Esher Committee, was 'a possible alternative well worthy of consideration'.[5]

With the exception of Rosebery's championing of Kitchener, which did not develop into a major issue, Liberal Imperialist co-operation on defence was more coherent than their co-operation on other questions of imperial and foreign policy. The main reason for this was that they studied the question in more detail than most other imperial questions, and they found in Fisher an expert whom their judgement could back, whose policy could satisfy the needs of the imperial situation without forcing its supporters, as had become the case with Milner, to move outside the area which could reasonably be called 'liberal'.[6]

The policy of strong support for the Entente, which through the default of Rosebery became Liberal Imperialist foreign policy, demanded a closer involvement in European

---

[1] Haldane in 4 H, cxlvi. 118 ff. (11 May 1905).
[2] Grey in 4 H, cxxxix. 622 ff. (2 Aug. 1904).
[3] Haldane in 4 H, cxxxix. 633 ff. (2 Aug. 1904).
[4] Haldane in 4 H, cxlvi. 118 ff. (11 May 1905).   [5] As n. 2 above.
[6] LLP 21, *The Urgent Need for a Definite Naval Policy*, is the only League publication to analyse in detail and to propose solutions to an imperial problem.

affairs than Foreign Secretaries between 1874 and 1900 would have thought desirable. Though both Ententes were superficially bargains about non-European matters, they had profound European implications. It is unclear to what extent the Liberal Imperialists realized this. They had not, when they took office, realized the full implications of the position, for it implied a British army equipped and reserved to fight in Europe. Such an army had played no part in their defence plans, which they still saw largely in terms of the navy. On the other hand, they appreciated that the 'mind of events' had changed, and Grey, more by instinct than calculation, seemed to sense that his role as Foreign Secretary would be very different from that played by Lord Salisbury only a few years before.

VII

THE HEART OF THE EMPIRE: DOMESTIC POLICY

National inefficiency

LIBERAL Imperialists shared the general concern felt about Britain's trading position in the 1890s. Anxiety about the competence of British institutions and of British industry to meet the challenge of increasing world competition reached its height during and after the Boer War, but it was no sudden phenomenon. In 1896 Rosebery, calling for a commission of inquiry into Britain's trading position, pointed out that 'year after year our consuls and our various officials of the Board of Trade have called the attention of the community to the fact that we are no longer, as we once were, undisputed mistress of the world of commerce.'[1] Asquith, a man of normally sanguine temperament, reviewed Britain's strategic and commercial world position in gloomy terms at the time of the 1897 Jubilee,[2] and during the Boer War became even more alarmed. He compared Britain's position in 1900 with that of the Britain of Tennyson's *Locksley Hall* and the confident optimism of Harriet Martineau's *History of England during the Thirty Years Peace*. He found a 'grave and rude disappointment'. The world

hardly seemed to be as yet within a measurable distance of the ideal of the past . . . it certainly bore little resemblance to the pacific triumphs of reason over prejudice . . . so far from enjoying the undisputed hegemony which was so confidently predicted for British trade fifty years ago, there was now not an inch of ground in any one of the international markets for which we were not fighting with all our available strength.[3]

The deterioration of Britain's position in the world production tables was a theme constantly urged, not only by Liberal Imperialists, in the 1890s. But it was not until

[1] Rosebery in Epsom, *The Times*, 25 July and 2 Oct. 1896.
[2] Asquith in Ladybank, *The Times*, 1 Oct. 1897.
[3] Asquith in Leeds, *The Times*, 24 Nov. 1900.

Chamberlain made it a central reason for his call for tariff reform in 1903 that the subject received more than spasmodic public attention. Liberal Imperialists deplored Chamberlain's fiscal solution to the nation's economic problems, but they praised him for successfully drawing public attention to the problem. To Haldane it was 'a matter for rejoicing that this matter should at last have come to the front. Some of us have been going up and down and preaching it to very moderate audiences for years past . . .'[1] Chamberlain had 'stirred us up to take stock of our industrial position in a fashion we have not done for many a long day'.[2]

There was, therefore, no doubt amongst the Liberal Imperialists that there was need for 'much thought, political, commercial and military, if we are to maintain our national power; and national power in these days is synonymous with national safety'.[3] Thus the criterion for the Liberal Imperialists' view of domestic policy must be, because of the urgency of the situation, whether a measure would substantially assist the development of 'national power'.

Given their premiss that British 'methods and machinery are out of date, and even decayed', the Liberal Imperialists had to diagnose the nature of the decay.[4] Hamilton, contemplating from his vantage point in the Treasury the 'breakers ahead', diagnosed the 'principal dangers' as: '(1) politically finance, (2) economically trade unions and (3) socially plutocracy'.[5] To these Rosebery said he would add:

(1) the badness of our educational system (2) our cock-sureness and insolence (3) the idiotic way in which our manufacturers set their face against keeping up to date . . . and our farmers decline to adapt to altered circumstances.[6]

Other Liberal Imperialists concurred in this diagnosis and added, as Rosebery did on other occasions, temperance, housing, and the inability of parliament as then constituted to act as an effective legislative machine. With the exception of finance, this was an analysis of social and political decay; it was likely to call for social and political, rather than fiscal,

---

[1] Haldane in London, Nov. 1903, in *Army Reform and other Addresses* (1907).
[2] Haldane, 'The Lesson of the Free Trade Controversy', in *World's Work*, Mar. 1904. [3] Rosebery in Birmingham, *The Times*, 16 Oct. 1901.
[4] Ibid. [5] EHD, 1 Jan. 1901. [6] EHD, 7 May 1901.

remedies. It was not an analysis which pretended to much originality. Haldane tried to approach the problem systematically, and he used the London School of Economics to provide statistics to support his views, but other leading Liberal Imperialists made little attempt to investigate the problems which they identified, either as to how they could be solved, or whether problems such as temperance and housing were indeed the fundamental questions which needed solution if greater national prosperity and competitiveness were to be achieved. This was an age when statistics on such subjects were notoriously unreliable, but the League as a whole made little attempt to use the readily available expertise of the Webbs, nor did it try to use the growing body of research by men like Booth and Rowntree to assess the relevance of its social policies.

There were two complementary reasons for this: the Liberal Imperialists' belief in political judgement, and their hostility to programmes. They believed, as we have seen in Chapter IV, that the function of a cabinet minister was to allow his judgement to play unfettered upon the issues of the day, and to arrive at a calm judicial decision on the basis of the data provided. This was, given the way British government worked, a plausible approach, and indeed was the approach assumed by most British politicians. But it ill accorded with the stated view of the Liberal Imperialists that what was needed to identify and deal with a problem was not 'haphazard energy', but a business approach involving consistent inquiry and expert evaluation based on long and detailed experience.[1] If the content of liberalism was to be 'everything . . . that tends to national, communal, and personal efficiency', it was desirable that the exponents of this 'efficiency' should, in their own approach to politics, give some lead towards it.[2] Yet what contemporary could look to the Liberal League as a shining example of method or efficiency in politics?

In addition to this, the frequently declared Liberal Imperialist hostility to programmes placed the League in a tactical difficulty. Since one of their main objectives was to clean the slate of the Newcastle programme, it was difficult, without admitting their opponents' case, to put forward positive specific suggestions of their own. For some Liberal Imperialists this argument became something of an excuse for avoiding serious thought. For others, like Haldane and Webb, it was an argument which was not to be pushed too far. Webb became tired of the League's unwillingness to put forward specific programmes, and after 1902 became less and less connected with it.[1] Haldane began to promulgate his own programmes, on the ground that back-benchers but not ex-cabinet men should put forward detailed legislative proposals.[2] It was therefore not to be expected that the League would produce a 'Chesterfield programme'. But the efficiency men within it hoped none the less to persuade their party that certain areas of reform must take priority in a future Liberal government, and the identification of these areas owed nothing to the traditional idea that retrenchment and reform should extend the political rights of the individual.

In looking at the condition of the nation, the Liberal Imperialists were alarmed, but not despondent. There were, they believed, a number of problems facing society which prevented its efficient functioning, but these problems were taken to be both definable and soluble, an assumption which conditioned their entire approach to domestic policy. The malfunctionings within British society could be specified, examined, and cured without altering the general social and economic structure of the nation. This was what Liberal Imperialists and most other Liberals meant when they spoke of 'social reform'.

Though they recognized that there might be social upheaval if such problems were ignored, Liberal Imperialists did not see either the problems they identified or the solutions they proposed as requiring a re-alignment of social classes, except in the long run through increased education opportunities. It was certainly not their primary intention to promote such a re-alignment, nor did they see the function of Liberal social reform as being more than to provide spare parts for a basically sound and well-designed machine.

---

[1] See above, p. 93 n. 4 and *New Liberal Review*, Oct. 1902 for Webb's call for 'a dozen Opposition planning committees'.

[2] Haldane in North Berwick, *The Scotsman*, 6 Apr. 1904.

Education

Of all the factors impairing the efficiency of the nation, the Liberal Imperialists believed that the lack of a suitable education system was the most serious and the most urgent: 'they might be sure that the one chance they had as a nation of maintaining their supremacy, industrially and politically . . . lay in their giving the largest and widest possible development to their system of national education.'[1] Fowler believed that in a competition between two manufacturing nations, it was superiority of the education system which would give one country a decisive advantage.[2] This stress on the vital economic role of education was based on the German analogy. Germany was 'creeping up to us', and at a rate which could conceivably put her ahead of Britain. The cause of German expansion was that Germany was, 'above all, a systematic nation . . . a scientific nation'; German system and science had been particularly applied to the production of the 'most perfect system of technical education in the world'.[3] In order to meet the German challenge Britain must therefore equal Germany in quality and quantity of education.

This argument received a particular impetus from Haldane, who analysed the question in much greater depth than other Liberal Imperialists. He believed that educational reform was essential, not so much in the field of working-class education, as amongst the managerial class in the economy. Haldane argued that the lack of scientific knowledge amongst 'our middle classes' was responsible for Britain's poor performance relative to Germany and America. The middle classes were depending on 'courage, energy and enterprise', out-of-date virtues which were as useless in a scientific age as 'the splendid fighting of the Dervishes against the shrapnel and the Maxims at Omdurman'. The expansion of education must be designed to equip future leaders of industry with the ability to 'apply science to industry' in a modern manner.[4]

[1] Asquith in Oxford, *The Times*, 28 Feb. 1896.
[2] Fowler in Wolverhampton, *The Times*, 16 Jan. 1896.
[3] Rosebery in Epsom and Colchester, *The Times*, 25 July and 21 Oct. 1896.
[4] Haldane, 'Great Britain and Germany: a Study in Education', *Monthly Review*, Nov. 1901, and in *The Scotsman*, 5 Oct. 1901.

Haldane's educational interest was therefore mainly centred on higher education. He believed that British higher education was woefully deficient, both in type and in quantity. He argued that there must be a major movement away from the traditional syllabuses of the universities which aimed 'at teaching people for only three professions—medicine, the church and the law'. University education must be much more utilitarian. Although Haldane supported the view that 'a Liberal education' should be the basis on which the scientific structure should be built, he regarded it as 'only the beginning for a colonising and commercial nation like ours'. The traditional virtues of an English liberal education should be obtained in the secondary school, not the university. The universities must give 'courses adapted to the special needs of the people they were teaching'. The university, or the 'institution on a level with the university', such as the technical high school, must move away from its present aim of producing 'character and public spirit . . . the power of getting on with men and of ruling them', and must produce 'in every department of life more science'. Haldane guarded himself against the criticism that his views would produce a wholly materialistic society, 'subordinated to utilitarian considerations'. The forces existing in British society would in themselves prevent this, and in any case 'the Germans have shown us how the university can fulfil a double function without slackening the effort after culture.'[1]

Higher education must also be greatly expanded, in the form both of universities and of other institutions. Haldane had no patience with the view, held by many Liberals, that such expansion would mean a fall in standards: 'How ridiculous it is to dread that such universities would prove Lilliputian!'[2] 'In Germany there were seven Professors for every one in this country', and no one had shown that the Germans had lower standards.[3] The weakness of secondary

[1] Ibid., and Haldane, 'Education and Imperial Policy', in S. C. Goldman (ed.), *The Empire and the Century* (1905), p. 163, and in Edinburgh, *The Scotsman*, 18 Oct. 1904. Haldane argued that secondary schools should offer a choice between 'culture' for intending professionals and 'scientific knowledge' for future 'captains of industry'; see 4 H, cvii. 706 (5 May 1902).

[2] *Monthly Review*, Nov. 1901. [3] *The Scotsman*, 5 Oct. 1901.

education meant that entrance qualifications might have to be variable, but 'elasticity of standard is quite compatible with a high standard'.[1] This expansion of higher education could not be efficiently executed without massive state aid, for 'until we made it our business to do what none but the state could do we should not make much progress'—the state should ideally pay for at least seventy per cent of the expansion.[2] The state must also see that there was no wastage of intellect; it must give an 'equal chance to the son of the duke and to the son of the working man'. This must be done by a massive scheme of state grants, linked to a means test.[3]

Haldane expected that educational reform would transform the economy. He also believed it would transform society. 'He knew of no other way to break down the barriers that separated class from class', but simultaneously, through the moderation that came from being educated, 'to establish stability in the constitution'.[4] But Haldane also thought that reforms of this sort would produce a new class structure, based on achievement in education:

... the elementary school raises our people to the level at which they may become skilled workers. The secondary school assists to develop a much smaller but still large class of well-educated citizens. But for the production of that limited body of men and women whose calling requires high talent, the University or its equivalent alone suffices.[5]

Haldane hoped, therefore, that the educational changes he proposed would produce a managerial élite which would be the foundation of Britain's future economic strength. His educational priorities were firmly based on what he took to be the needs of the nation, with only incidental attention to individual self-betterment. His view of educational reform was clearly worked out and far-reaching in its effect. He was supported in it spasmodically by Rosebery, who acted as a figurehead in fund-raising for university extension; by Webb, with whom he worked closely on the 1898 London University Act and the 'Charlottenburg scheme' of 1902–3

[1] Haldane to Thursfield, 30 Dec. 1902, Hal P 5905, f. 261.
[2] *The Scotsman*, 5 Oct. 1901.
[3] Haldane in East Lothian, *The Scotsman*, 1 Sept. 1899.
[4] Haldane in North Berwick, *The Scotsman*, 12 Oct. 1905.
[5] Haldane's Edinburgh Rectorial, 10 Jan. 1907, *Selected Addresses and Essays* (1928), p. 13.

for the expansion of London technical education; and by
Ferguson, who supported him over the Education Bill
during his period of unpopularity in 1902.[1] But the
Liberal Imperialists did not succeed in working together
for the cause of education, important though they all
claimed it to be.

The disruptive factor was the dispute about the degree to
which efficiency, in theory the absolute criterion, should be
applied in practice, and the issue was raised dramatically by
the various Unionist attempts at legislation, culminating in
the monumental Bill of 1902. During the 1892–5 government Acland had made considerable progress, especially in
elementary education, by skilful use of administration within
the existing legislative structure; he had attempted no
major reforming Bill.[2] Recognizing that secondary education
was the battleground of the future and knowing the Liberal
government would soon fall, he staked out a future Liberal
position by appointing the James Bryce Commission on
secondary education. The Bryce Report recommended the
establishment of yet another educational authority—on this
occasion to be controlled by the county council—to oversee
secondary education only; it did not foresee the end of the
elementary school boards.[3] The abortive Bill of 1896
retained the school boards, created the new authority, but
gave it a rather unclear authority over the boards as well as
over secondary education. The Liberal Imperialists all
opposed this as unworkable. The 1902 Bill in its amended
form abolished the school boards, set up as a single authority
for secondary, technical, and elementary education a committee of the county or borough council, and retained the
voluntary schools, but within the new framework, receiving
direct assistance from the rates.

Haldane and Webb supported the 1902 Bill on political
and educational grounds. Politically they welcomed it

[1] See Rosebery in London, *The Times*, 22 Mar. 1901; Haldane to Rosebery, 21
Mar. 1901, RP, box 24, and to Ashley, 31 May 1902, Hal P 5905, f. 81; Ferguson
in Glasgow, *The Scotsman*, 12 Sept. 1902; see also R. Morant to Haldane, 25 May
1902, Hal P 5905, f. 175.
[2] See Gillian Sutherland, 'Some Aspects of the Making of Policy in Elementary
Education . . .' (Oxford D.Phil. thesis, 1970), pt. III, sect. 9.
[3] Parl. Papers 1895, xliii (C. 7862).

because they believed that a Liberal government would never be able to pass a major Education Bill. The strength of non-conformist feeling was such that any major Liberal Bill would have to attack the voluntary schools; any Bill which did so would never pass in the Lords. For Haldane, therefore, the Bill was, quite apart from its educational merits, 'the last effectual attempt to remedy a national evil for years to come'.[1] Educationally they welcomed the Bill because they approved of the idea of the single authority. Though recognizing the value of Acland's administrative work, Haldane believed that the multiplicity of boards, committees, and *ad hoc* authorities led to confusion and inefficiency; he praised the new structure as being both simple and potentially effective. Moreover, he saw the single authority as typical of the application of 'scientific principle', for 'education ought to be treated as an organic whole . . . you can no more separate secondary from primary education than you can separate the head from the hand.' Indeed Haldane wished to link tertiary education directly with the single authority so that the whole unit would be 'permeated from the top with the intention of the university'.[2]

Haldane and Webb thus had no difficulty in supporting the Bill. They saw education in essentially utilitarian terms and they had little patience with the nonconformists and anglicans, both of whom thought the aim of education was primarily to produce a good nonconformist (or a good anglican) rather than a skilled worker. But for Liberal Imperialists with no detailed interest in or views on education, yet with a general sympathy for its improvement, the situation was confusing. The Bill had obvious attractions in its boldness and thoroughness, but it raised political difficulties.[3]

Asquith had the latter foremost in his mind. He told Acland:

I have been getting more and more apprehensive for some time about this cry for a 'single authority' . . . there will be infinite confusion and division among us, if, as is probable, he [Devonshire] seeks to set up

---

[1] Haldane to his sister, 26 May 1902, Hal P 6010, f. 196.
[2] 4 H, cvii. 703 ff. (5 May 1902).   [3] See above, pp. 94–7.

for both primary and secondary education the much demanded 'single authority'.[1]

Asquith called on the party to prepare 'to defend the School Board system in the large towns'; 'popular representation and popular control' were the only safe principles.[2] But there was no necessary link between direct popular control and educational efficiency. Once it was clear that the government was determined to pass the Bill, with no repetition of the 1896 fiasco, when the Bill was withdrawn, Liberal Imperialist support for the school boards waned.

Asquith recognized that 'in many of the great urban centres . . . the new authority would probably do a great deal', and Grey said 'he never thought school boards an ideal way of dealing with education.'[3] Liberal Imperialists had realized that they might become committed to repealing the Act when again in office. They deplored this possibility —a sure way of 'ploughing the sands', as the various Liberal Education Bills in 1906–7 showed—and consistently opposed any suggestion that the ex-cabinet should so commit itself.[4] They therefore tried to make the Bill into a reasonably acceptable Act, by amending it in committee, and they then tried to see that the Act was so effectively in operation that it could hardly be repealed by a subsequent Liberal government.

Liberal Imperialist amendments had little success, though they earned Grey a reputation as an education specialist![5] But the potential effectiveness of the Bill was greatly increased by the amendment of Henry Hobhouse, a Liberal Unionist, making compulsory the previously voluntary demise of the school boards. On a free vote, Asquith, Haldane, Ferguson, and Emmott voted for this amendment, and Grey and Fowler abstained.[6]

---

[1] Asquith to Acland, 30 Oct. 1901, Acland Papers, MS. Eng. Lett. d. 81.

[2] Asquith in Oldham, *The Times*, 25 Nov. 1901.

[3] Asquith in Barnsley, Grey in Cambridge, *The Times*, 19 Apr. and 10 May 1902.

[4] Ferguson to Rosebery, 18 Oct. 1902, RP, box 16; Grey to Gladstone, 3 Aug. 1903, HGP 45992, f. 97; Fowler, *Life of Fowler*, pp. 139 ff.

[5] R. Farquharson, 'The Compleat Member', *New Liberal Review*, Apr. 1902, and 4 H, cviii. 1343 (3 June 1902).

[6] 4 H, cx. 1295 (9 July 1902).

Once the Act was passed, League members, with the exception of Perks, worked to prevent what Asquith called the 'miasma of sectarian controversy' upsetting its efficient operation.[1] Their aim was to persuade the nonconformists to accept the Act by arranging local compromises over the religious difficulty. Asquith strongly opposed non-co-operation in the working of the Act: 'it was clearly their duty to make the most they could of such facilities as the new Acts gave for the popular control of education.'[2] Public exhortation of this sort could have only a limited effect. A better line of approach was private discussion with the nonconformist leaders. Haldane and Acland both wrote to Rosebery, whom Haldane called 'the one man who can handle the situation', to ask him to arrange a compromise between the nonconformist leaders and the anglican clergy.[3]

Rosebery was well placed to act as arbitrator. In his speech against the Bill in the Lords he ignored all considerations of efficiency and, as Perks said, 'very rightly put the nonconf. case'.[4] Rosebery, however, did not act directly himself, and unwisely allowed Perks to be his representative at a series of meetings of nonconformist leaders after Easter 1903.[5] Negotiations reached a critical stage during the winter of 1903–4. But it was Lloyd George, not Perks, who was arranging a compromise. When Lloyd George revealed at a meeting of the nonconformist committee the 'Educational Compromise' which he was arranging with the Bishop of St. Asaph, Perks 'was the first to break the prolonged silence pointing out first that a compromise such as he suggested would be a surrender that would take the heart out of the Dissenters, and as in 1874 they would return to their tents and liberalism would lose its most vigorous

[1] Asquith in Barnsley, *The Times*, 19 Apr. 1902.

[2] Asquith in Hull, *The Times*, 29 Jan. 1903.

[3] Acland to Rosebery, 5 Sept. 1902, RP, box 77; Haldane to Rosebery, 8 Nov. 1903, RP, box 24.

[4] Perks to Rosebery, 7 Dec. 1902, RP, box 40; for Rosebery's speech see 4 H, cxvi. 98 ff. (5 Dec. 1902).

[5] Perks to Rosebery, 4 Apr. 1903, RP, box 40: Perks, Lloyd George, and Robertson Nicoll met 'to formulate our Educ. plan'; Perks, though bitterly hostile to the Act and to a compromise with anglicans, did not actively support refusal to pay rates (Perks, 'Free Church Councils and the Education Crisis', *Free Church Year Book* (1902)).

fighters'.[1] Perks had no intention of supporting any compromise and was furious both with Lloyd George and with the Revd. Reginald Campbell, a member of the Liberal League council, who was trying to arrange a compromise with Chamberlain.[2]

Perks effectively wrecked the Liberal League as a movement for the introduction of efficiency into education, although Haldane, C. M. Douglas, and Ferguson organized Liberal Imperialist support for the Scottish Education Bills of 1903–4.[3] Liberal Imperialists continued to argue for a 'sane Imperial policy' whose main feature would be education reform, but they were very cautious in their suggestions, confining themselves mainly to proposals about school meals and the health of the children.[4] They had not, as a body, resolved the conflict between the administrative convenience developed in education by Morant's view of efficiency, and the traditional Liberal idea of popular control. Nevertheless, the Acts of 1902–4 had brought about the sort of change in orientation in national policy which even the Liberal Imperialists who had opposed it called for in their more abstract moments. For, as Webb noticed, by those Acts 'Public education has . . . come to be regarded not as a matter of philanthropy undertaken for the sake of the individual children benefited, but as a matter of national concern undertaken in the interest of the community as a whole.'[5]

Social reforms

If education was to be the corner-stone of the attempt to stop the decay of Britain's commercial position, it was to be buttressed by reforms which could ensure that the labour-force,

[1] Perks to Rosebery, 1 Apr. 1904, RP, box 41. For Perks's earlier attempts to prevent a concordat, see Perks to Rosebery, 23 Dec. 1903, RP, box 40, and Perks to Asquith, 23 Dec. 1903, AP 10, f. 118.

[2] Ibid.; see also K. O. Morgan, *Wales in British Politics*, pp. 187–92, for Lloyd George's attempted concordat.

[3] See *The Scotsman*: Ferguson, 7 Feb. 1903, Haldane, 4 June 1903; Bannerman to Gladstone, 2 Jan. 1905, HGP 45988, f. 139.

[4] See Rosebery to the League, 13 Apr. 1905, LLP 191; Grey to B. Bosanquet, 23 Jan. 1905, in J. H. Muirhead (ed.), *Bernard Bosanquet and his Friends* (1935), p. 101. For the significance of this interest, see B. B. Gilbert, *The Evolution of National Insurance in Great Britain* (1966), ch. 3.

[5] S. Webb, *London Education* (1904), p. 9.

once educated, was in a fit shape to work efficiently, for 'the Imperialism that . . . ignores the conditions of an Imperial race, is a blind, a futile, a doomed Imperialism.'[1] The question was not whether the labour-force was unhappy in the conditions in which it lived and worked, but rather whether the poverty of its conditions impaired its economic effectiveness.

The view that social reform was an essential element in the pursuit of national efficiency linked the Liberal Imperialists with a number of other groups. It linked them first with their own past. Whereas their interest in defence and imperial questions was for many of them a new interest in the late 1890s, interest in social reform for the sake of efficiency was merely an extension of the long interest they had had, from a humanitarian point of view, in the standards of factory conditions and in the general condition of labour. In the early 1890s they had thought it was the function of the State 'to mitigate the harshness' of industrial life because such harshness was 'an injustice';[2] the Liberal objective was that of 'securing for each member . . . an equal level of opportunities for making the best of himself'.[3] Liberal Imperialists were now concerned with national rather than individual progress, but the measures which they argued were necessary to achieve this were based on the collectivist ideas which they had begun to develop as young M.P.s in the 1880s. The social reforming aspect of their imperialism also linked them with a large, loose grouping of Liberals who found the imperialist aspects of the Liberal League unnecessary, but not wholly repugnant. The views of this group were most effectively represented by Herbert Samuel in his *Liberalism* (1902), and in the leading articles of J. A. Spender's *Westminster Gazette*.

By their attempt to use the criterion of 'efficiency' in social reform, Liberal Imperialists were also linked with a stream of thought on the Unionist side, which advocated a similar interest in the 'efficiency' of the race, but pushed its ideas of the ruthless aspect of efficiency a good deal further

[1] Rosebery in Liverpool, 14 Feb. 1902, LLP 3.
[2] Asquith in Cambridge, *The Times*, 21 Mar. 1895.
[3] Asquith in Nottingham, *The Times*, 4 Apr. 1895.

than the Liberal Imperialists. The ideas of this school of thought were seen at their most moderate in Balfour, and in their more extreme form in the writings of Arnold White, a defence reformer, a jingoist, and a popularizer of the growing cult of eugenics. His writings on 'efficiency' contained a strong element of anti-semitism and carried the priority of racial fitness much further than politically active Liberal Imperialists were prepared to accept.

White, however, was not unwelcome to the League. The *New Liberal Review*, the Liberal Imperialist periodical sponsored and edited by the Harmsworths, thought that 'if any man ought to join the Liberal League as a fire escape from . . . Unionism, Mr. Arnold White is the man . . . he is preaching the true Liberalism without protesting it.'[1] White's book *Efficiency and Empire* (1901) was one of the fullest statements of the extreme efficiency school, but it also contained something of a Liberal *imprimatur* in the form of a memorandum on education by J. H. Yoxall, a Liberal M.P. White sent a copy to Rosebery, who replied that he was 'in substantial agreement' with much of the book. Rosebery's comment on White's proposal to 'sterilise the unfit' was merely that it was 'an impracticable recommendation'.[2]

In legislation, the successive attempts of the government to pass an Aliens Bill reflected in part the influence of the school of which White was representative. The Bill received strong support on anti-semitic grounds from some Liberal Imperialists outside parliament.[3] Liberal Leaguers in parliament, however, were unanimously hostile to the Bill.[4] Rosebery, whose wife had been a Rothschild, opposed anti-semitism in any form. Asquith said the Bill of 1904 was based on 'the most absurd and fantastic exaggeration', was

---

[1] A review of White's pamphlet 'For Efficiency' in *New Liberal Review*, March 1903. He addressed joint Liberal Imperialist/Liberal Unionist meetings in Hampstead, see *Daily Chronicle*, 19 Dec. 1901.

[2] Rosebery to White, 24 Oct. 1901, RP, Letter Book.

[3] See Anon., 'Alien Immigration', *New Liberal Review*, Feb. 1903. This review was closely involved in arousing concern about the unfitness of the race, and published many articles similar to H. F. Trippel, 'National Physique and National Training', Apr. 1903.

[4] For the League case, see *The Alien Bogey*, LLP 167.

'only protection in a disguised form', and was 'wrong in principle'.[1] Thus parliamentary Liberal Imperialists tried to avoid the anti-semitism which was widely prevalent in this period, and which distorted the attitude of some Unionists to social reform, and of some radicals to imperial questions.[2]

In their own quest for racial efficiency, the Liberal Imperialists laid the main stress on temperance and, to a lesser extent, housing, as being the problems whose solution was most vital. As Haldane put it:

> Of all the problems that lie in front of the Liberal party, there is probably no one which signifies more for the national well being than that of temperance. In temperance reform, if anywhere, is to be made a first step towards national efficiency.[3]

Like education, temperance was a subject fraught with difficulties for the Liberals, because of nonconformist pressures which had a moral rather than a pragmatic basis on the one hand, and the small but wealthy group of Liberal brewer and grocer M.P.s on the other.

Local Veto had been one of the main domestic proposals of the Rosebery administration. Harcourt's Local Veto Bill of 1895 was strongly supported by Fowler and Asquith, as attempting to solve the drink question by an extension of local democracy.[4] But Rosebery was unsympathetic to the Bill, hardly even giving it nominal support.[5] The Bill was a liability to the Liberals in the 1895 election, and the source of dispute during the election between Rosebery and Harcourt. Liberal Imperialists subsequently made little reference to the temperance question until the start of the Boer War. The increase in interest in racial fitness which came with the war, and the publication of the final report of the Peel Commission on licensing reform in 1899, aroused Liberal Imperial interest in the subject.[6]

---

[1] Asquith in Reading, *The Times*, 20 Jan. 1904. Eight East London Liberal M.P.s supported the 1905 Bill; none was a Leaguer (*The Times*, 1 May 1905).

[2] See H. Belloc's 'Verses to a Lord' in his *Collected Verse* (1958), and A. White, *Efficiency and Empire*, pp. 79–80.

[3] Haldane's preface to *National Efficiency and the Drink Traffic*, by A Ratepayer, 1906.

[4] Ferguson to his wife, 17 June 1895, FP, and Fowler to Harcourt, 20 Jan. 1895, HP 12.   [5] Rosebery in Cardiff, *The Times*, 19 Jan. 1895.

[6] Royal Commission on Liquor Licensing Laws, Parl. Papers 1899, xxxv (C. 9379).

Liberal Imperialists were determined that the extreme demands of the nonconformist temperance view should not commit the party to an impractical position, as they felt had been done in the case of Harcourt's Local Veto Bill. From the criterion of efficiency, any licensing reform was better than none: as Rosebery put it, 'my principle in regard to temperance legislation is to take what you can get.'[1] Therefore the first aim of the Liberal Imperialists was to wipe Local Veto from the slate. They were assisted in this by Peel's minority report which took the view that while 'there is a strong demand for some measure of local control', it was impractical to 'recommend the adoption of a direct popular measure'.[2] Campbell-Bannerman and Asquith cautiously accepted the general view of the minority report, without committing themselves to details.[3] Asquith and Haldane decided, however, that it must be made clear that the religious aspects of the temperance movement, which placed as much emphasis on the way temperance was achieved as on its actual achievement, must not be allowed to dominate Liberal thinking in the future.

The result of the hostility to compromise of the advanced temperance men was that 'the question was no further advanced than it was when they commenced their work.'[4] In 1900 Haldane therefore revived proposals he had made in 1896 and 'formally substituted a temperance programme which Asquith and I [Haldane] had made out . . . excluding local veto and giving compensation, for the Harcourt Bill'.[5] Haldane denounced the 'all or nothing' religious attitude of the advanced temperance men, and argued that the Liberals must take a pragmatic view and take what they could get.[6] This position was reinforced by Rosebery who argued that Liberals must not regard even the Peel scheme

[1] Rosebery in Glasgow, 10 Mar. 1902, LLP 3.
[2] Minority Report, p. 279.
[3] Bannerman in Aberdeen, *The Times*, 20 Dec. 1899; Gladstone to Bannerman, 4 and 12 Dec. 1899, CBP 41215, ff. 153–69; Asquith to Bannerman, 20 Dec. 1899, CBP 41210, f. 179; Gladstone feared brewer and grocer defections from the Liberals.
[4] Haldane in Prestonpans, *The Scotsman*, 18 Sept. 1900.
[5] Haldane to Rosebery, 18 Sept. 1900, RP, box 24; see Haldane in Dunbar, *The Scotsman*, 31 Dec. 1896.
[6] *The Scotsman*, 18 Sept. 1900.

as a minimum, but if necessary 'take something less'. He was therefore not prepared to put forward any conditions which Liberals should regard as essential.[1]

The Unionist Licensing Bill of 1904 came within Rosebery's terms. The Liberal Imperialists were in a difficult position. On their own arguments, they were required to support the Bill. But the capitulation of most Liberal Imperialists to the nonconformists over the Education Bill two years previously, and the growing effectiveness of the opposition after the start of the tariff reform campaign, made it difficult to discuss the Bill from the efficiency viewpoint. Asquith, who opposed the Bill for the League,[2] attempted to draw a distinction between a solatium, which he supported, and the proposed 'compensation' which he opposed, thus lamely trying to maintain the view that Liberals should take what they could get, without excessively offending the nonconformists.[3]

Education and temperance were the problems which Liberal Imperialists claimed needed immediate legislative action. In both cases their reaction to legislation seemed flabby and inconsistent. The basic reason for this was their failure, in the years before 1902, to build up a sufficient body of strength within the Liberal party to enable them to put the full case for efficiency to the party.[4] Haldane's view at the start of the Unionist government, that 'the functions of Opposition were something more than to oppose . . . they might prove to be functions of cooperation' on domestic matters, was unrealistic, given the strong political position of the nonconformists within the party.[5] Most Liberals wanted a hard-hitting opposition of the traditional type.

Allied to the temperance question as a cause of racial inefficiency was thought to be the question of housing, 'insanitary and insufficient homes, which lie so much at the root of the drink'. Poor housing caused the bulk of the population to feel, as Rosebery quaintly put it, 'below par',

---

[1] Rosebery in Glasgow, 10 Mar. 1902, LLP 3.
[2] Ferguson to his wife, n.d. [1904], FP.
[3] 4 H, cxxi. 413 ff. (24 Apr. 1903) and cxl. 90 ff. (29 July 1904).
[4] Perks's presence in the League increased this difficulty, though he was less fervent on temperance than on education.
[5] 4 H, xxxvi. 98 (15 Aug. 1895).

and therefore unable to work efficiently. Rosebery, Asquith, and Haldane were especially interested in the housing question. Rosebery, with his L.C.C. experience and his ability to sense the mood of the masses, thought it particularly important. In his Glasgow speech he strongly attacked housing exploitation, and his phrase 'make these slum lords skip' looked forward to Lloyd George's Limehouse speech.[1]

Liberal Imperialists regarded housing reform as purely the function of local government: the role of the national politician could therefore only be exhortatory;[2] the essential thing was to overcome 'the apathetic resignation of public opinion'.[3] Rosebery tried to achieve this by intervening in the borough elections in Shoreditch in 1899, and Asquith was chairman of a conference organized by Canon Scott Holland.[4] No detailed proposals came out of this interest in housing, though Liberal Imperialists helped to increase interest in the subject, and made it clear that the problem must be solved by government rather than by charitable or individual action. Asquith very scathingly attacked 'the spasmodic invasion of unorganised philanthropy' in the East End.[5] Haldane showed that the Liberals were hostile to the Unionist view, which was to set up artisans as small freeholders, and that the alternative was for local authorities to buy up land and let it to workers for a small rent, but this was no more than an indication of the broad outlines along which local authorities should move.[6]

The housing question, which the Liberal Imperialists placed, with education and temperance, as one of the three measures to be inscribed upon the cleaned slate, was part of the land question, which the Liberal Imperialists did not, in their Liberal League days, promote so prominently, doubtless because of the number of extremely wealthy landowners who subscribed to the League. Land policy had been one of the major interests of the Commons group before 1892, and Haldane's Land Bill of 1892 had been their major legislative

---

[1] Rosebery in Glasgow, 5 Dec. 1904 and 10 Mar. 1902, LLP 174 and LLP 3.
[2] Rosebery in Glasgow, 10 Mar. 1902, LLP 3.
[3] Asquith in *Commonwealth*, Dec. 1899, p. 369.   [4] Ibid.
[5] *The Times*, 22 Nov. 1895.
[6] Haldane in 4 H, xxxviii. 146 (4 Mar. 1898).

initiative.[1] Land reform was seen as the prerequisite both to an efficient housing policy in the towns, and to a start 'to ameliorate the condition of agriculture'.[2] Whereas on most subjects their views altered considerably, Liberal Imperialists' views on this subject remained constant before 1906.

They made three main proposals, summed up by Asquith in 1899:

... you ought to give to the local authority of every urban community vastly larger powers than it at present possesses for the compulsory acquisition of land. Secondly there was needed such a reform of the law of local rating as will make it impossible for a man to withhold land from public use ... lastly, and most important of all, we want a system of municipal taxation, under which it will be possible ... to throw an appreciable and just share of the cost of works on the owners of the soil instead of as at present, throwing the whole of the burden on the occupiers.[3]

This was what Haldane's private Bill of 1892 had given, and this was what Liberal Imperialists were urging in 1905.[4] Such a programme was daring in 1892, but by 1905 it was beginning to seem inadequate. 'Municipal Socialism' of this type was beginning to seem too indirect and too slow to solve the social problems of the day.

Industrial relations

The question of housing also linked the Liberal Imperialists with the much wider question of 'the condition of labour'. In their early days in the Commons the Rosebery group had been greatly concerned about labour relations: 'The relations of labour and capital are what puzzle us', reported Ferguson to Rosebery in 1888.[5] They believed that excessive concentration by the party on Ireland was isolating it from reality

[1] See above, p. 10.
[2] Asquith in Cambridge, *The Times*, 21 Nov. 1904; see also Sir E. Grey, *Rural Land* (1892), and R. M. Ferguson, 'The Drift of Land Reform', *Contemporary Review*, Oct. 1893.
[3] 4 H, lxvi. 543–4 (10 Feb. 1899). Similar, suitably adapted proposals were made for rural land, see Grey, *Rural Land*, Eighty Club Pamphlets 1892, and Asquith in Cambridge, *The Times*, 22 Nov. 1904.
[4] See 4 H, iv. 66 (4 May 1892), Local Authorities (Purchase of Land) Bill, and Haldane in Paisley, *The Scotsman*, 20 Oct. 1905.
[5] Ferguson to Rosebery, 20 Sept. 1888, RP, box 14.

and from urgent domestic questions; Fowler believed that 'while we play with politics great social questions are rising which before long may let loose a deluge over us.'[1] Haldane spent much of his spare time before 1892 lecturing to working-class clubs on the dangers of 'the Socialistic theories of Lassalle and Karl Marx', of Henry George's erroneous ideas about land taxation, and of Cunninghame Graham's version of socialism which was 'doing a great deal of mischief all over Scotland'.[2] Haldane did not, however, doubt the existence of the problem; it was the function of liberalism not to ignore 'the magnitude and importance of the problem with which Karl Marx and the socialists have sought to deal in so courageous a fashion', but to tackle the problem from a national rather than a class view-point.[3]

The answer to the problem must lie in improvements at a local level in the working man's housing and his personal life, and at a national level through effective administration to improve his working conditions. As Home Secretary, Asquith denounced 'socialists' for showing 'ignorance of the elementary conditions of human nature and the inexorable laws which govern the action of communities'. Nevertheless, he believed that the state, while accepting 'our existing industrial system', could and must intervene at the margin 'to compel some employers to level up until they are brought into harmony with those who have accepted the required principle'.[4] Thus the function of the state was to use 'every legitimate means . . . so far as the law can legitimately and effectively intervene, to mitigate the harshness'. Unless this was seen to be done, the state would be unsuccessful in justifying the system to the workers, and that way, Asquith implied, lay revolution. But, Asquith argued, the state must not interfere too blatantly; its function was 'not to initiate but to supervise'.[5]

---

[1] Ferguson to Rosebery, 30 Aug. 1887, RP, box 14; reporting Fowler.

[2] Haldane to his aunt, 24 Jan. 1882, Hal P 5902, f. 5; to his sister, 17 Oct. 1883, Hal P 6010, f. 17; and to Mother, 25 Oct. 1887, Hal P 5940, f. 101.

[3] Haldane, 'The Liberal Party and its Prospects', *Contemporary Review*, Jan. 1888.

[4] Asquith in Cambridge, *The Times*, 21 Mar. 1895; for Asquith's Home Office work, see Spender and Asquith, pp. 85–6.

[5] *The Times*, 21 Mar. 1895.

Asquith's oblique approach was seen in his Employers' Liability Bill of 1893. Asquith hoped to deal with the question of factory accidents by removing the doctrine of common employment. This doctrine having been removed, the employer would be forced to prevent accidents in order to avoid liability. Asquith's Bill was withdrawn after mutilation by the Lords. The moderation of the Bill had been in part designed to avoid such destruction by the Lords, but Asquith also believed his approach was correct in principle.[1] The Unionist Bill of 1897 dealt with the problem from the opposite view-point, giving financial compensation for accidents. Though he did not deny the rightness of compensation, Asquith continued to think the oblique approach the best.[2] Haldane disagreed with him in this, and wanted a vast extension of the Unionist Bill, 'a complete system of compensation such as obtained in Continental countries'.[3] Asquith and Haldane discussed their differences and decided to work together for the extension of the measure;[4] Haldane negotiated with Balfour and Chamberlain to extend the provisions of the Bill to various groups of workers not originally covered by it.[5]

Haldane's enthusiasm for compensation was perhaps the result of his liking for German schemes, for on other labour issues he favoured the oblique approach. This was clear in the Liberal Imperialists' approach to trade unionism. The Liberal Imperialists were by no means opposed to state interference on principle; indeed, as has been seen, the reverse was the case. They were, however, opposed to excessive state interference; they regarded the state as an interferer of last resort.

This was evident in their early days in parliament over the question of the Eight Hours Bill. Morley was opposed

[1] Asquith, 4 H, xlviii. 1433 (3 May 1897).
[2] Ibid.; Asquith in Battersea, *The Times*, 8 May 1897, and Asquith's preface to Anon., *Employer's Liability* (1897).
[3] Haldane, 4 H, xlviii. 1443 (3 May 1897); *The Times* rightly thought Asquith had been 'thrown over by his colleagues': leader, 12 May 1897.
[4] EHD, 4 May 1897; Hamilton found them 'taken aback by the drastic nature of the Bill'.
[5] Haldane to Mother, 6 June 1897, Hal P 5957, f. 183. For a comparison of the Asquith and Chamberlain Bills, see D. G. Hanes, *The First British Workmen's Compensation Act* (1968), *passim*.

to the Bill on principle;[1] Haldane was opposed to it because
he thought it unnecessary, for 'the evidence appears to be
that there is practically little or no compulsion to work for
more than eight hours, except in a few pits.'[2] Haldane was
prepared for such interference if it was necessary, but where
he thought it unnecessary he was not prepared to see the
state forced into a token gesture. Moreover, Haldane
believed that a struggle to achieve an eight-hour day would
increase the efficiency of the unions.[3] Liberal Imperialists
approved of efficient trade unions. Given that it was part of
progress that the industrial worker should want 'to live at a
higher level', and that increased efficiency would come from
such a desire, the place of efficient trade unions was extremely
important. Trade unions were 'a great blessing to the working classes, enabling the weak to bargain collectively in
something like an equal footing with the strong'. Trade
unions were also a great blessing to the state, and especially
to the Liberal party, with its large labour vote, because they
were the main agency in 'encouraging the working classes
to provide for their own necessities'.[4] The trade unions,
therefore, by being able to balance the strength of the
employers, saved the state, and particularly the Liberal
party, from having to intervene much more than it already
did on the worker's side in labour questions.

The effect of the union movement was that there were
'two great standing armies'.[5] The function of the state was to
act as a mediator and arbitrator between them. The success
of this view was illustrated by the successful mediation by
Rosebery in the coal strike of 1893 and in the Scottish coal
strike of 1894. Prompted by Haldane, Asquith wrote to
W. E. Gladstone to propose the 'Government taking some
active step' to settle the coal strike of 1893, and suggested
Rosebery as the man to take charge of arbitration.[6] Rosebery,

[1] See Hamer, *Morley*, ch. 17.

[2] Haldane, 'The Eight Hours Question', *Contemporary Review*, Feb. 1893.

[3] Haldane, 3 H, cccxix. 901 (17 Aug. 1887). When an Eight Hour Bill was
proposed in 1893, Haldane abstained in concert with Grey and Ferguson (Haldane
to Mother, 3 May 1893, Hal P 5949, f. 129).

[4] Haldane in the Lothians, *The Scotsman*, 24 Oct. 1903, 11 and 12 Oct. 1905.

[5] Asquith in Rochdale, *The Times*, 11 Nov. 1897.

[6] Asquith to W. E. Gladstone, 9 Nov. 1893, GP 44517, f. 305; see also Haldane
to Mother, 7 Nov. 1893, Hal P 5950, f. 152.

assisted behind the scenes by Haldane, achieved settlements in 1893 and in 1894.[1] This view of the state as a referee between two roughly equal teams depended on both unions and employers taking a conciliatory and not an intransigent attitude. As Asquith argued during the engineering lock-out in 1897, failure to reach a swift compromise would be 'a reproach to English common sense'.[2]

Asquith and Haldane believed that there was always a reasonable answer to an industrial dispute, and that it was the state's function to find it. Asquith did not, however, believe that the state should be compelled to intervene in every case: he had 'always been strongly opposed to any attempt to establish . . . a system of compulsory arbitration'. But this was because the state's fluid and impartial position might be compromised. He did, however, argue that when 'the conflict covers a substantially wide area', the Conciliation Act of 1896, embodying the *de facto* procedure worked out by the Liberals in 1892–5, should be employed to reach an agreement.[3] This reliance on 'English common sense' was to prove insufficient in the early years of the twentieth century, but it was the nearest the Liberal Imperialists got to a theory of industrial relations.[4]

Any likelihood of the approximate equilibrium between employers and unions which the Liberal Imperialists felt desirable was shattered by the series of legal judgements which culminated in the Taff Vale judgement of 1901 which made unions and their officers liable for all the damages from the tortious actions of their agents. For their theory to work, the position of the unions had to be restored, and Asquith and Haldane played an important part in drawing the attention of parliament to 'the state of absolute confusion in which the law is at present'[5] as a result of the judges' decision, and in urging that 'as regards a question like this, which goes down to the very roots of the

[1] Haldane to Mother, 15 Aug. 1894, Hal P 5952, f. 103.
[2] Asquith in Stockton, *The Times*, 16 Dec. 1897.
[3] Asquith, 4 H, cxxi. 482 ff. (27 Apr. 1903), on the Bethesda dispute; Haldane strongly supported Asquith's position (ibid., cols. 528 ff.).
[4] Grey was the only leading Liberal Imperialist directly and professionally involved, through his railway directorship, in industrial relations, but he seems to have made no political contribution in this field.
[5] Haldane, 4 H, cviii. 320 ff. (14 May 1902).

economic and social conditions of the people, Parliament and Parliament alone should be the real judges.'[1]

The Liberal Imperialists thus appeared to be on the side of the unions. Haldane was retained for the unions in the Taff Vale appeal case, and in the debate of 14 May 1902 which raised the question for the first time in the House, 'the Labour members were united in asking me [Haldane] to put their case.'[2] Asquith, Haldane, and Reid attended a conference with the Labour Representation Committee arranged by Asquith and Dilke to discuss suitable union tactics.[3]

Asquith and Haldane soon, however, made it clear that they were not in complete agreement with the unions which in principle wanted the reversal of all the recent judgements hostile to them. Asquith suggested that 'there should be two Bills: one to deal with funds, and the other with picketing etc.',[4] and Haldane regarded the *Quinn* v. *Leatham* decision, which effectively prevented union action to force a closed shop, as more serious for the unions than Taff Vale.[5] The reason for both these views was that in the Liberal Imperialist lawyers' view

the common sense of the community would not be easily convinced that an association of persons—whether technically incorporated or not made not the slightest difference—wielding great powers, controlling considerable funds, should not be answerable for the conduct of agents acting under their authority.[6]

Asquith would therefore support a Bill restoring the unions' picketing position, but not one which included a complete reversal of Taff Vale, though he agreed the latter's potentially devastating effect on union funds should be limited and modified.[7] These conditions were met by the

[1] Asquith, ibid., col. 327.
[2] Haldane to Mother, 15 May 1902, Hal P 5967, f. 148.
[3] Asquith to Dilke, 15 and 24 Oct. 1901, 5 Nov. 1901, DP 43877, ff. 23–6; and Haldane to Dilke, 19 Oct. 1901, DP 43917, f. 60.
[4] Asquith to Dilke, 5 Dec. 1901, DP 43877, f. 27; the legality of picketing had been questioned in *Lyons* v. *Wilkins*.
[5] Haldane to Dilke, 19 Oct. 1901, DP 43917, f. 60.
[6] Asquith to Eighty Club, *The Times*, 7 Feb. 1903, following Haldane's line at the Glasgow Liberal League (*The Scotsman*, 4 Oct. 1902).
[7] Asquith's proposal was typically oblique: a reform of the law of agency limiting liability to that section of the union directly involved; see H. A. Clegg, A. Fox, and A. F. Thompson, *A History of British Trade Unions since 1899* (1964), i. 369.

unions, and the Bill introduced in May 1903 by Shackleton did not attempt to deal with Taff Vale.[1] Haldane supported verbally, though he voted for the Bill, the government's alternative proposal to set up a Royal Commission, and he was successful in seeing that the supposed supporter of the unions on the Commission was Sidney Webb, who in fact took the Haldane view of Taff Vale.[2]

The lawyers seemed to have gained the initiative, but they were soon to be frustrated by the younger members of the League. J. M. Paulton, Secretary of the League and M.P. for a mining constituency, introduced a Bill in 1904 which dealt with picketing, conspiracy, and Taff Vale, reversing the latter. Clearly embarrassed, neither Asquith nor Haldane spoke, and Reid, who had hitherto supported their position, mildly supported Paulton's reversal of Taff Vale.[3] Haldane and Asquith, publicly frustrated, developed their policy in private, and Haldane's Trade Disputes Memorandum, of April 1905, which was a draft of a Bill to embody their proposals for a reform of the law of agency, represents the fullest expression of their views.[4] They were determined that the unions should have some liability for damages.

Haldane and Asquith regarded the trade union controversy as of great importance. Their proposals on trade disputes were the only detailed and fully worked out proposals on any aspect of domestic policy which they took with them into the 1905 cabinet. The dramatic defeat which they suffered from the Labour group and Campbell-Bannerman during the 1906 Trade Disputes Bill debate was a major rebuff, not merely at the personal level, but also for their conception of liberalism.[5] For their view of trade disputes was not primarily a legal view. Believing that the essence of the Liberal party was that it should be a national party, unsubordinated to any class or interest, Liberal Imperialists

[1] For Asquith's and Haldane's speeches, see 4 H, cxxii. 232 ff. (8 May 1903).

[2] B. Webb, *Our Partnership*, p. 268; Haldane told his mother he 'was strongly on the side of the men', 11 May 1903, Hal P 5969, f. 120.

[3] Paulton secured the publication of his Bill and of his speech in LLP 140, *To Protect Trade Unions*; it thus became in a sense official League policy.

[4] Haldane, Trade Disputes Memorandum, Apr. 1905, AP 92, f. 9.

[5] See Halévy, *The Rule of Democracy* (1961), pp. 96-7.

deplored extra-legal concessions to the unions. Granting the
unions a permanently privileged position made the Liberals
appear to be the captives of an interest. As Asquith said in
1895, 'the root and spring of Liberalism' was that 'the
interests of the community as a whole ought to be paramount
over the interests of any class, any interest, or any section.'[1]
Campbell-Bannerman's sudden acceptance of the Labour
amendment to the Trade Disputes Bill in 1906 was, Asquith
believed, the 'surrender of gvnt. to democracy', a distinction
which, perhaps above all else in politics, Liberal Imperialists
believed must be maintained.[2]

Support for state arbitration suggested some state
responsibility for generally facilitating the smooth working
of the economy. Such a responsibility was also being accepted
by the Liberal Imperialists in the field of unemployment.
In this they worked with the party organization, and it was
on Herbert Gladstone's initiative that the issue was raised.
Asquith took the view that responsibility for unemployment
should fall 'not on the charitable, nor on the specially
affected districts, but on the whole community'. The state
should make permanent provision for public works which
could be executed 'when the problem of unemployment
became acute'.[3] He was therefore accepting a permanent
degree of some unemployment, with the state dealing only
with spasmodically high unemployment, and disagreed with
Gladstone's proposal for national workshops, which would
be continually in use, and suggested instead periodic
employment in forestry.[4]

Haldane's view was more extensive. He thought the
whole question 'must be raised', and argued that it was the
function of government to eradicate the causes of unemployment through ill health by better housing, to provide a
national, not a local, scheme of 'work and relief', and to
strike at the root of unemployment by providing 'systematic
organisation of the means of employment', as was done in

[1] Asquith in Newcastle, *The Times*, 31 Jan. 1895.
[2] Perks to Rosebery, 3 Apr. 1906, RP, box 41, reporting Asquith.
[3] Asquith to Bannerman, 1 Jan. 1905, CBP 41210, f. 241.
[4] This was perhaps at Ferguson's suggestion, who supported large-scale forestry
nationalization, as in 'Forestry—a "Depressed Industry"', *Independent Review*,
May 1904.

Germany.[1] Thus while Liberal Imperialists felt an obligation on the part of the state to intervene in the economy, they had no clearly marked out plan, nor did they regard the problem of unemployment as a chief priority. Nevertheless, Haldane's rough ideas pointed the way forward to the Liberal proposals in power.

Such were the proposals of the Liberal Imperialists on social reform and industrial relations. Accepting that the British commercial position was threatened, they regarded these proposals, taken together, as the best way of ensuring 'their efficiency as a fighting nation, their efficiency as a model nation, their efficiency as an intelligent nation'.[2] They believed that Chamberlain's programme of tariff reform was superficial in that it did not strike at the fundamental evils of ill-educated management and ill-nourished workers, but attempted to bypass needed reforms by an interference with the actual commerce of the nation.[3]

Liberal Imperialists regarded a free market economy as the best means of industrial progress. Their reforms were intended to facilitate the working of that economy, not to change it. They looked to parliamentary social legislation, not to fiscal management, for an oblique, indirect, and long-term solution to economic questions. The working of the fiscal economy must not be subjected to direct interference: 'let them be careful what they did to affect that organism.'[4]

Social legislation was linked with two other problems, the solution of which Liberal Imperialists regarded as vital to national efficiency: government finance and the administrative and legislative machine.

Government finance

Throughout the period, but especially after 1898, Liberal Imperialists were concerned with the problem of government finance. Hamilton, contemplating the return of the Unionists in 1895, believed 'that the great crux ahead for the

[1] Haldane in North Berwick, *The Scotsman*, 12 Oct. 1905.
[2] Haldane in Prestonpans, *The Scotsman*, 11 Jan. 1905.
[3] See *Wanted! Efficiency not Tariffs*, LLP 64, and *We Want Efficiency—not Tariffs*, LLP 158.
[4] Haldane to Liberal League in Glasgow, *The Scotsman*, 30 Nov. 1903.

present government is finance'.[1] There was no doubt that
ten years of Tory rule showed a considerable increase
in ordinary expenditure, from £94 million in 1894–5 to an
expected £144 million in 1904–5.

Liberals were able to make a great deal of political
capital out of this rise, especially after the start of the tariff
reform campaign, and the Liberal League made the size of
government expenditure an important feature of its popular
tabloid pamphlets.[2] Typical of this approach was Asquith's
view that the worst thing the Unionists were doing was 'not
tariffs . . . but the enormous and progressive increase in what
the State took, and was taking, by taxation and by borrowing
out of the pockets of the people'.[3]

But the position of the Liberal Imperialists was much
more complex than this. Politically, they were assailed from
both sides. The anti-imperialists argued that the increase
was the result of imperialist policies. Harcourt believed that
'the growth of normal expenditure is the result of Jingoism',[4]
and Hobson's view that imperialism led to general extrava-
gance and hence to tariffs was a stock criticism made by
all anti-imperialists.[5] To meet this argument the Liberal
Imperialists had to show that extra expenditure on imperial
activities was abnormal and that the Unionists had been unnecessarily wasteful. They attempted to show this by arguing
that the incompetence of the Unionists had made the South
African war excessively expensive, and that the army could be
efficiently run at considerably reduced estimates. The charge
that jingoism caused an increase in *normal* expenditure was
as hard to refute as it was to substantiate.

Liberal Imperialists were also under fire from the Unionists, who argued it was illogical to support the government
in the war and simultaneously to oppose increases in indirect
taxation, since this was the only area of taxation which,
Unionists also argued, was elastic. They were also likely to
run into difficulties with the wealthier members of their own
Liberal League, who tended to be hostile to any increase in

[1] Hamilton to Harcourt, 13 Sept. 1895, HP 8.
[2] e.g. *Why You Cannot Afford the Present Government*, LLP 141.
[3] Asquith in Cambridge, *The Times*, 22 Nov. 1904.
[4] Harcourt to Morley, 15 May 1901, HP.
[5] J. A. Hobson, *Imperialism. A Study*, rev. ed. (1905), pp. 83 ff.

direct taxation, and who argued that such an increase would frighten away that middle-class section of the electorate which the League was largely designed to attract.[1]

Liberal Imperialists had little doubt that 'national expenditure has been increasing of recent years with great rapidity, and there seems no likelihood of its limit being reached in the immediate future.'[2] They admitted that the increase was general and did not spring from a number of departmental estimates which could be reduced. Such an increase, Haldane thought, should be seen 'not as an isolated case, but concurrently with the rising of the national expenditure in other countries'. Its cause lay in the natural development of the organic state: 'We are spending more because we have a larger house, a larger family, a higher way of living, new necessities which have come from an improved condition of things.'[3] Moreover, Liberal Imperialist proposals, especially for social reforms, were likely to maintain the tendency to increase. The Liberal League in 1902 thought it likely that 'we shall soon be called upon to face a normal and recurring expenditure of something approaching £150,000,000 a year', whatever government was in power.[4] Even Fowler, whose inclinations in financial matters tended to extreme Gladstonian orthodoxy, believed that

there are large branches of future expenditure which will have to be met from Imperial funds for improving the general condition of the people . . . and there are many items which now stand at comparatively small figures which will have to be increased.[5]

One obvious solution to this problem was the old cry of 'retrenchment', which, Rosebery complained, not even the Cobden Club urged loudly any more.[6] Liberal Imperialists hoped to save a small amount on administrative reform, but this could only be a marginal saving; as Haldane observed, 'they could not do it merely by supervision of small details, useful as that was.'[7] Liberal Imperialists were, indeed,

1 Rosebery had taken this line over Harcourt's Death Duties Budget in 1894 (see above, p. 132) and did so again after 1905 (see James, p. 465).
2 Anon., *The Corn Tax and British Commercial Policy*, LLP 19 (1902).
3 Haldane, 4 H, cvi. 828–9 (21 Apr. 1902).
4 LLP 19.   5 4 H, lxix. 1031 (13 Apr. 1898).
6 Rosebery at the Eighty Club, *The Times*, 4 Mar. 1896.
7 Haldane in Gullane, *The Scotsman*, 7 Apr. 1904.

suspicious of the role the Treasury played in keeping down expenditure. Fowler was 'sure that a great deal of money which had been well spent in all Departments would never have been spent at all, if the decision had been left entirely to the Treasury'.[1] Expenditure could at least be kept constant by avoiding commitments to expensive extensions of policy, for, Haldane said, 'expenditure depended on policy' rather than details of administration.[2] Changes of policy in defence matters were to produce substantial army and, possibly, navy reductions. But the main area of policy where Liberal Imperialists hoped to avoid increase in expenditure, at least for a time, was that of old-age pensions.

Old-age pensions were not an aspect of national efficiency, since they applied, by definition, to those who had ceased to be efficient or productive. They were not mentioned by Liberal League pamphlets as a desirable innovation. Asquith believed in 1895 that all the suggested schemes were 'irreconcilable with the principles of actuarial calculation', and then thought that the extension of friendly societies offered the best hope for the old.[3] By 1899 Asquith was in principle in favour of a national scheme of pensions, but was 'not satisfied that any one of the schemes yet put forward is either practical or adequate'; he had no suggestions of his own to offer.[4] Liberal Imperialists, though not opposed in principle to old-age pensions, made little attempt to bring forward discussion of them, and viewed the old-age pension movement in the Unionist party with some suspicion. Hamilton thought that Chaplin's aim in supporting pensions was 'to force up the State's expenditure to such an extent as will necessitate the reimposition of a tariff'.[5] Asquith, when Chancellor, took pride in pointing out that he was in no way pledged to introduce a pensions scheme; he was able to do so only as a result of the improved fiscal position.[6]

But though some saving might be achieved, Liberal Imperialists had to face the fact that 'this expenditure to which we are committed is chronic, normal',[7] and that it was

---

[1] 4 H, li. 319 (16 July 1897).   [2] Haldane, *The Scotsman*, 7 Apr. 1904.
[3] Asquith in Leven, *The Times*, 10 July 1895.
[4] 4 H, lxx. 415 (24 Apr. 1899).   [5] EHD, 27 July 1899.
[6] 4 H, clxix. 223 (13 Feb. 1907).
[7] Fowler in 4 H, lxix. 1031 (13 Apr. 1898).

'an expenditure which would probably increase'.[1] Given this assumption, where was the revenue to come from? They believed that 'the ordinary sources of revenue seem unlikely to remain adequate.'[2] Hamilton's forecast in 1895 was that 'no amount of elasticity of present sources of revenue will keep them [the Unionists] going for long',[3] and by 1901 Haldane thought it obvious that 'we are going to be presently face to face with a time in which we cannot count on the elasticity of those sources of revenue to which we have been accustomed to look up to now.'[4] Haldane told his Scottish audience how 'profoundly impressed' he had been by Morley's account of Gladstone's financial views, but that they must recognize that this system was designed for a different concept of government, and that it was breaking down.[5] But what was to take its place?

The Unionists, and especially Hicks Beach, were wrong, the Liberal League argued, in trying to shore up the existing system by 'hand-to-mouth methods' such as the corn duty, the coal tax, and the raids on the sinking-fund.[6] What was needed was 'a new system of national finance'.[7] But Beach was fighting a rearguard action in the cabinet because many Unionists favoured precisely that: a new system, but one founded on tariffs. Liberal Imperialists were fully aware of this alternative, but condemned it on social and economic grounds. Socially, further tariffs on food would be unjust because there is 'an irreducible minimum which you ought not to tax', and economically tariffs on raw materials were unacceptable as 'endangering the position of this United Kingdom as to a large extent the workshop and as the market and clearing house of the industrial world'.[8]

Thus although a new form of government might be evolving, Liberal Imperialists held to an entirely orthodox, Liberal view on this aspect of taxation. The government was not responsible for, and could not produce, good trade, but it might produce bad trade by direct meddling in the fiscal

[1] Haldane in 4 H, cix. 379 (11 June 1902).   [2] LLP 19.
[3] Hamilton to Harcourt, 13 Sept. 1895, HP 8.
[4] Haldane, 4 H, xciv. 652 (20 May 1901).
[5] Haldane in Gullane, *The Scotsman*, 7 Apr. 1904.
[6] LLP 19.   [7] Ibid.
[8] Asquith in 4 H, cix. 1028 ff. (18 June 1902).

economy.[1] As Fowler said, 'it was altogether outside the province of governments to make good trade.'[2]

Additional indirect taxation on food and raw materials being thus excluded, the Liberal Imperialists looked to direct taxation to provide the main bulk of the expected requirements. The existing system of direct taxation still theoretically regarded the income tax as a temporary tax, to be reduced whenever possible. In a speech on the Budget of 1902, Haldane outlined the Liberal Imperialist position. Using figures prepared for him by the L.S.E., he attacked the view that Britain, even under war taxation, was a heavily taxed country. He claimed that, excluding local taxation, current French taxation was at £3. 13s. 5d. per head, German at £3. 17s. 6d. per head, and British at £3. 5s. 0d. per head. Of the major European powers, Britain was therefore 'best fitted to bear that increase of [future] expenditure'. The main field of increase was to be that of direct taxation, for Haldane was confident that Britain had not 'exhausted the resources of civilisation in respect of income tax ... I do not think we have got to the limits of direct taxation even yet.'[3]

The income-tax revenue could be substantially increased by raising the basic rate, by graduation, and by differentiation between earned and unearned income.[4] In June 1902 C. P. Trevelyan, a young League member, moved an amendment to the Finance Bill to introduce a graduated income tax, which was supported by all Liberals.[5] Reform of the income tax, and its establishment as the recognized major organ of revenue collection, must also involve much more knowledge of tax payment, for under existing methods 'there is not even a return of the number of persons paying income tax, and it is still more difficult to arrive at any estimate of the proportion of the total population which they represent.'[6] Such an inquiry would make even the existing income tax more remunerative, as there was thought to be widespread evasion.[7]

---

[1] See *Trade Depression*, LLP 120.
[2] Fowler in Moseley, *The Times*, 12 July 1895.
[3] 4 H, cvi. 827 ff. (21 Apr. 1902).
[4] In 1901 Haldane thought that the *normal* income tax 'ought to be as high as it was at the time of the Crimean War', 4 H, xciv. 655 (20 May 1901).
[5] 4 H, cix. 371 (11 June 1902); see also Grey, 4 H, cxxxviii. 459 ff. (19 July 1904).
[6] LLP 19.   [7] See Halévy, vi. 272–4.

This stress on income tax would have the effect of altering the ratio of direct to indirect taxation which was approximately 50 : 50 in the years before 1906.[1] Such an alteration would have the effect of some redistribution of wealth. Liberal Imperialists did not regard redistribution of wealth as a priority *per se*. Their object was to raise revenue to expend on efficiency. Since for various reasons they could not raise revenue on tariffs, they fell back on direct taxation. But they did not promote direct taxation as a primary engine of social reform.[2] Rosebery was concerned that 'the progress of luxury, the expenditure of luxury are assuming gigantic proportions', but he did not think that the remedy was to tax such luxury, but rather to launch 'a resolute effort on behalf of simplicity of life', though his own style of living could hardly have struck contemporaries as a persuasive lead in that direction.[3]

The income tax could be assisted by a reformed land tax, which could be used to relieve the Treasury of some of the burden of assistance to local authorities. Asquith believed that 'there was lying untaxed a large reservoir from which... a substantial contribution might be made to fertilize the country at large, and that was the taxation of land.'[4] Asquith was more optimistic than some, though without detailed inquiry it was as yet unclear how much such taxation could yield.[5] Assistance could also come from increased non-protective indirect taxation on luxuries, but this area was regarded as virtually inelastic.[6]

Other possible increases in taxation, such as further death duties, were not discussed in detail before 1905; it was anticipated that the suggested reforms in the income and land taxes would provide sufficient extra revenue. Haldane in 1903 thought that consideration of other sources was for the

[1] See Asquith, *Memories and Reflections*, i. 276; by 1914 indirect taxation produced only *c*. 30 per cent of the revenue.
[2] They did not go nearly so far as L. G. Chiozza Money, *Riches and Poverty* (1905), *passim*.
[3] Draft letter by Rosebery to *The Times*, 1898, RP 75. Although later Rosebery strongly attacked Liberal finance, he made no criticism while its foundations were being prepared before 1905.
[4] Asquith in Southport, *The Times*, 23 Jan. 1904.
[5] See Haldane in Gullane, *The Scotsman*, 7 Apr. 1904, and H. Cox, 'Shall we Tax Land Values? NO!' in *World's Work*, Apr. 1905.
[6] LLP 19.

present unnecessary: since the trade cycle 'appeared to be broken', existing taxation would yield more revenue.[1]

Direct taxation was the conscious price for avoiding protection. As Asquith wrote in 1908: 'I have realised from the first that if it could not be proved that social reform (not Socialism) can be financed on a Free Trade line, a return to Protection is a moral certainty.'[2]

Reform of the administrative and legislative machine

Behind the various schemes for efficiency in the social services and in taxation lay the idea of a general reform of the administrative and legislative system. A state playing an active and expanded role required an expanded government, central and local, to meet the new requirements. Reforming Liberals in the 1892–5 government found a good deal of administrative inefficiency and excessive orthodoxy in their departments. Asquith at the Home Office had various clashes with Lushington, the Permanent Under-Secretary who, Asquith thought, 'was bound to do all the white washing he could, as he cannot but feel that each fresh proof of the inefficiency of the Domestic Department is . . . a reflection upon himself'. To promote efficiency Asquith retired Lushington and McClintock.[3]

The nearest these feelings of uneasiness about the role of the civil service came to a systematic attempt at demand for reform was in the 'Committee of Vigilance for considering and promoting administrative reform', a feeble echo of the Administrative Reform Association of 1855, headed by Rosebery.[4] A thousand members had joined the committee by December 1901, but Rosebery refused to address a public meeting on the subject,[5] and the committee was dissolved. The reasons were clear enough. Roseberians might talk of the need to introduce 'a business element into our administration',[6] but they had no coherent idea how to go about this, and contented themselves with vague exhortations to

[1] Haldane in East Lothian, *The Scotsman*, 3 Jan. 1903.
[2] Asquith to Strachey, 9 May 1908, Strachey Papers 11/6/6.
[3] Asquith to H. Gladstone, 19 Jan. 1894, HGP 45989, f. 17.
[4] See above, p. 60, and *Nineteenth Century*, July, Aug., and Nov. 1900.
[5] J. Knowles to Rosebery, 30 Dec. 1901, RP 76.
[6] Rosebery in Glasgow, 10 Mar. 1902, LLP 3.

the government. Since they had no criticism of principle to make, their criticisms, if voiced in any detail, were likely to appear *ad hominem*.

Liberal Imperialists therefore maintained the principle of ministerial responsibility in their criticism of administrative incompetence. Moreover, though Haldane was friendly with Robert Morant, the main social contacts of the Liberal Imperialists were with the group of civil servants introduced by W. E. Gladstone. Eddy Hamilton's attitude to 'a business approach' may be assessed from his view that 'the first qualifications of a Chancellor of the Exchequer are character and being a *gentleman*. Then comes influence and financial aptitude.'[1]

Sir Arthur Godley was delighted with what Rosebery had to say about administrative efficiency, but after 1898 Godley saw his duties at the India Office as 'though not irksome or disagreeable, pure task work . . . my daily round was never part of my real life.'[2] There is no record of any feeling that such civil servants were at all inadequate; Asquith kept Hamilton, though virtually paralytic, at the Treasury until 1907.[3] Liberal Imperialists played some part in urging a reform of the Foreign Office, to include an efficient consular service to represent British trade abroad, but this was a particular reform, a part of their answer to protection, and not part of a general proposal.[4] They praised the C.I.D. as a model for the future civil service, but produced no plans for extending its principles to civilian departments.[5]

The legislative experiences of the 1892–5 government made it clear that a subsequent Liberal government would run into difficulties. The lesson to be learned was that

social legislation . . . in the long run could not be adopted upon a large and really liberal scale until they amended their political machinery in three vital respects . . . relieve the House of Commons, choked and overburdened as it was under the existing system of local business . . . refer the transaction of local affairs to local bodies . . . and thirdly the

---

[1] EHD, 6 Sept. 1900.

[2] Quoted in D. Dilks, *Curzon in India* (1969), i. 98.

[3] But the *World's Work*, Dec. 1902, did give prominence to Morant as a new and desirable type of civil servant.

[4] See Asquith in Southport, *The Times*, 23 Jan. 1904, and Grey, 4 H, cxi. 300 ff. (15 July 1902). [5] See above. p. 222.

completion and climax of the whole . . . readjustment of the function
of the two Houses of Parliament.[1]

One way to relieve pressure on the Commons was to reform
its own legislative procedure. Liberal Imperialists consistently supported the Unionists' attempts to do this.
Against the mass of the party, Grey supported Balfour's new
supply regulations in 1896, arguing that 'a time limit would
conduce to the effective discussion of matters in the House.'[2]
Fowler believed Balfour's experiment 'was a great success',
and supported its extension.[3] As John Dillon pointed out,
this was a change from the traditional position of opposition
leaders as champions of private members' rights: Fowler
was 'actually requesting the Government to make the operation of the existing Rule more oppressive'.[4] Asquith, on the
other hand, attacked the new supply regulations of 1905 as
'another stage on the journey which has marked . . . the
degradation of the House of Commons . . . from a delibera-
tive to a dependent body . . . a mere automatic machine'.[5]
Asquith thought that 'the machinery of the Commons . . .
could not be adapted to the totally different requirements of
the twentieth century by a process of mere tinkering and
patching'; his solution was 'the employment on a far larger
scale of standing committees'.[6] Devolution from the floor of
the House to committees was also supported by Grey, who
was appalled at the time and energy which 'the whole
strength of the government's debating power' had to bring
to bear upon the Education Bill in 1902.[7]

More important than reform within the Commons was
the lessening of the amount of work to be done by the
Commons. A Liberal government was likely to produce a
great deal more legislation than a Unionist one; the amount
of legislation proposed in the Liberals' Queen's Speeches in
1892–5 was manifestly far greater than an existing Commons could cope with, even with improved rules. Asquith

---

[1] Asquith in Leven, *The Times*, 10 July 1895.
[2] 4 H, xxxvii. 1293 ff. (27 Feb. 1896).
[3] Fowler in 4 H, lxvii. 312 (23 Feb. 1899).
[4] Dillon in 4 H, lxvii. 315 (23 Feb. 1899).
[5] 4 H, cxliii. 66 (15 Mar. 1905).
[6] Asquith in Leven, *The Times*, 8 Oct. 1902.
[7] Grey in Sheffield, *The Times*, 8 Nov. 1902.

appreciated this, and observed that 'the longer he sat at
Westminster . . . the more he was confirmed in the belief
that the House of Commons . . . must be prepared to
delegate some of its work.'[1] But to whom was the work to be
delegated? Any such proposal raised the question of Home-
Rule-all-round, yet Home Rule in any form was the sort of
political reform which the Liberal Imperialists particularly
wished to avoid, for it would reproduce the 1892–5 'ploughing of the sands'. The whole point of the clean slate was to
eradicate such contentious political reforms, and bring to the
fore the social legislation vital to efficiency. As Rosebery
wrote to T. A. Brassey, even the British part of Brassey's
ambitious scheme of imperial government reform could not
be considered by the Liberal party, which must become
'cruelly practical'.[2]

The solution to this dilemma was to 'rescue the Commons
from suffocation' by putting 'more trust in the great munici-
palities and county councils and through them advance
measures for social reform'.[3] But the Liberal Imperialists did
not produce any worked-out plan of how local councils could
deal with social legislation of a national kind. They hoped
that Grand Committees would deal with Scottish, Welsh,
and Irish local legislation, but these would still involve
M.P.s.[4] The proposal for greatly increased activity by
existing local authorities was put to the test in the 1902
Education Bill. Those Liberal Imperialists who opposed the
Bill did so partly on the ground that local government
would be unable to deal efficiently with education.[5] It was
difficult, therefore, subsequently to advocate extensive devolution of control of social reform to bodies which they
believed to be already overburdened. Thus trapped in a
logical impasse, the Liberal Imperialists were unable to offer
any solution to the problem of devolution, except to indicate
that they supported it in principle.

The problem of overburdening in the Commons affected
both parties, but especially the Liberals; the problem of the

[1] Asquith in Inverness, *The Times*, 22 Oct. 1904.
[2] Rosebery to T. A. Brassey, 18 Jan. 1901, RP 89; see T. A. Brassey, *Problems of Empire*, pp. 52–71.   [3] Grey, *The Times*, 29 Nov. 1901.
[4] Ferguson in Leith, *The Scotsman*, 10 Oct. 1901.
[5] See Asquith in 4 H, cxv. 1163 (3 Dec. 1902).

Lords affected the Liberals only. Reform of the Lords was thus likely to be even more contentious than reform of the Commons. The question of the Lords was not one which the Liberal opposition could expect to keep as a major vote-getter, and after 1895 it receded into the background.[1] The Lords even gained some popularity after May 1903, their value as a second chamber being illustrated by the fact that unlike the Commons they could debate tariff reform regardless of the government's wishes. None the less, the question of the Lords was 'a controversy which, when once raised, must go forward to an issue',[2] and, as Rosebery pointed out to the 'young evanescent hopes' of the Liberal League, the Liberal programme, however moderate, would run against 'the dead brick wall of the House of Lords'. Rosebery's accurate forecast was 'that in the first year of this new government you will find the House of Lords as resolutely, aggressively and defensively Tory as it has ever been in the past'.[3] It is remarkable that Liberal Imperialists, and other Liberals, gave very little thought, in public or in private, to what was likely to be a major challenge.[4]

During the 1892–5 government, members of the Rosebery group held very differing views about the solution to the Lords question. Rosebery's position before 1892 as a reformer of the structure of the Lords, and hence in some respects as a strengthener of its permanence in the constitution, was well known. During his period as Prime Minister he countered the radicals 'ending' by a proposal for 'mending' by means of a declaratory resolution, to be passed in the Commons.[5] In taking this position he was, as Salisbury observed, as much declaring war on the radicals as on the peers.[6] At the other extreme was Asquith, regarded by Salisbury as the most influential of the 'enders'.[7] Haldane

[1] See above, pp. 138–9.

[2] W. E. Gladstone in the Commons, 1894, quoted in J. Morley, *The Life of William Ewart Gladstone* (1903), iii. 512.

[3] Rosebery to the Liberal League, *The Times*, 14 Apr. 1905.

[4] Herbert Gladstone suggested the setting up of committees to produce contingency plans for virtually every domestic crisis a Liberal government might meet, but he did not include one on the Lords (Gladstone Memorandum, Nov. 1904, HGP 41217, f. 145).   [5] Stansky, pp. 135–41.

[6] Salisbury, 'Lord Rosebery's Plan', *National Review*, Dec. 1894.

[7] Ibid.

took on the difficult task of reconciling these positions and showing that 'there is no conflict between Lord Rosebery and Mr. Asquith.'[1] Whereas Rosebery saw the declaratory resolution as a tactical move, the real solution lying in reform of the structure of the House, Haldane raised it to the level of constitutional theory.

Haldane appealed to reasonable men to see that the constitution was 'not fixed but . . . evolving itself in a course of development towards democracy'. The declaratory resolution would be merely one more step in the age-old British evolutionary process of precedents 'which, professing only to declare what already exists, alter the substance while preserving the old form'. The relationship between the two Houses must be 'a question of spirit rather than of letter'. The Lords should be left with a

reserve power of veto . . . akin to that which the Home Rule Bill contemplated the Imperial Parliament should have over the Irish legislative body, a power to be exercised only when the spirit of the Constitution was being violated.

The Haldane/Rosebery scheme assumed that the Lords would recognize the inevitability of their situation and would by common sense amend their attitude. Haldane suggested that this would be assisted by a change in the Lords' function through devolution within the United Kingdom, and that 'after the question of the Veto has been disposed of', the Lords would become an imperial senate for the whole empire.[2]

Haldane's position was much nearer Rosebery's than Asquith's, and the latter soon moved nearer to his friends. He talked no more of 'ending', but said instead there were two solutions, either to 'make the veto . . . suspensory and not definitive', or 'to enable either House when there was an irreconcilable difference of opinion between them, to refer the pacific issue to the judgement of the nation', by which it was assumed that Asquith meant a referendum. Asquith stated no preference for either solution.[3]

---

[1] Haldane, 'Lord Salisbury and the House of Lords', *National Review*, Jan. 1895, from which other quotations in this and the next paragraphs come.

[2] See also above, pp. 169–70.

[3] Asquith in Stockton, *The Times*, 16 Dec. 1897.

Although Asquith asked for 'serious pondering' of the Lords question during the period of opposition, Liberal Imperialists did not respond.[1] The Liberal Imperialist position, such as it was, depended on a change of spirit by the Lords themselves. To raise the question would merely encourage radical proposals of a far more revolutionary type. The Liberal Imperialists hoped that the Lords, confronted with a 'patriotic' Liberal party, shorn of its proposals for Home Rule and Disestablishment, would recognize the need for the passing of national efficiency measures. If this was insufficient, then the declaratory resolution would be the first of a series of warnings.[2] There was an implicit bargain in this; the Liberal League would reform the Liberal party, the Lords would reform themselves. But even the League's moderate proposals contained much that was likely to offend their lordships, especially on the land question, and, apart from the specific measures, the tactical position within the fragmented Unionists after 1903 was likely to cause indiscriminate hostility to a Liberal government, as Rosebery recognized.[3] None the less, Liberal Imperialists maintained a moderate approach. Trevelyan deplored the radical suggestion that a Liberal government should obtain royal assent to create a majority of Liberal peers before taking office, and indeed deplored the mass creation of peers at any time.[4] The best that could be done, Haldane said, was to produce sensible measures, backed with a large majority, the result of which might be 'to inspire the House of Lords with awe'.[5]

Liberal Imperialists had in the concept of national efficiency produced one means of analysis to deal with the

[1] The radicals did better in A. Reid (ed.), *The House of Lords Question* (1898).
[2] See C. P. Trevelyan, one of Rosebery's 'evanescent hopes', in 'The Future and the House of Lords', *Independent Review*, Nov. 1904.
[3] Rosebery to the Liberal League, *The Times*, 14 Apr. 1905.
[4] Trevelyan, op. cit.
[5] Haldane in Haddington, *The Scotsman*, 11 Oct. 1905. After 1906 Rosebery continued his attempts to reform the Lords (see Crewe, pp. 626–31), and the Liberal Imperialists supported the moderate 'Ripon' plan, drawn up in fact by Crewe and Asquith (see C. C. Weston, 'The Liberal Leadership and the Lords' Veto, 1907–1910', *Historical Journal*, vol. 11, no. 3 (1968)). The Liberal party proceeded, in the first instance, with a declaratory resolution in 1907.

problems of the expansion of state involvement in the British economy. At the time national efficiency seemed a novel and to some an alarming concept. But the proposals put forward in its name by Liberal Imperialists, while they provided a general framework, albeit one poorly thought out in all its details, were characterized by moderation. Liberal Imperialists were seeking a minimum. Recognizing in principle the need for extended state activity, their object was to interfere only at the margin of the economy, and, for the most part, by indirect means. Underlying this approach was a profoundly conservative conviction: the Liberal Imperialists believed that the existing economic and social framework of the nation was capable, with only minor adjustments, of maintaining both itself and the structure of the empire which was linked to it. The object of national efficiency was to provide those minor, but urgent, adjustments. In believing this, the Liberal Imperialists were representative of a diminishing proportion of the nation. Most Unionists believed that the economic survival of the nation, and to a lesser extent of the empire, required a major alteration in the form of the introduction of tariffs. Many Liberals and Labour men believed that the existing social structure could not, and should not, be maintained, and that the optimistic moderation of the national efficiency proposals was insufficient to achieve a just society.

VIII

THE PROBLEM OF IRELAND

A NEW Liberal approach to the Irish question was regarded by Liberal Imperialists as essential. Their strategy of party reconstruction depended on substantial Liberal Unionist defections, and Ireland was an obvious barrier to these. The success of social reform depended on the availability of parliamentary time for legislation, and in 1892–5 the Irish question had severely restricted this. The Liberal Imperialists saw the Gladstonian form of Home Rule as a principal agent in causing an increase in inter-party bitterness and hence in breaking up the politics of the centre which they favoured.

During the 1895–1905 period of opposition, changes in Ireland and in Unionist attitudes towards Ireland seemed to make a new Liberal approach feasible. The Local Government Act of 1898 and the Irish Land Act of 1903 offered room for Liberal manœuvre. The reunion of the Irish nationalist factions under John Redmond in 1900 encouraged Liberal Imperialists to action to avoid a further period of reliance on Irish votes, but the fact of that reunion also reminded them of the Irish commitment to Home Rule.

Early attitudes

The Liberal Imperialists had voted for the Home Rule Bill of 1893. Those who had been in parliament had also voted for the Bill of 1886. But this did not mean that they had been enthusiastic supporters of Gladstone's policy. Rosebery had, from the start, been suspicious of entanglements with Parnell and had only refrained from resigning in 1882 because of personal loyalty to Gladstone.[1] None the less, in

---

[1] Rosebery Memorandum, 6 May 1882, RP, box 109.

1886 and in 1893 he and all remaining Liberals had stood up and been counted.

Liberal Imperialists as a group had brought little influence to bear upon the 1886 decision to support Home Rule; the question as it appeared to them after 1886 was, what form should future measures of Home Rule take, and what should be their position of precedence within the party programme? It was the view of John Morley in 1888 that 'Home Rule remains and must remain the dividing line' between the parties.[1] The young group in the Commons disputed this. Haldane complained that the party leadership was 'apt to regard the establishment of a Parliament and Executive in Dublin as the be-all and end-all of Liberal policy'; this might legitimately be Mr. Gladstone's overriding aim, but 'his colleagues are hardly justified in adopting substantially the same course.'[2] Asquith stressed that Home Rule for Ireland could only be justified as 'both imperial (in the true sense) and democratic' if it was seen as part of a general plan of devolution, for, 'if the issue is contracted (as Mr. G. and J. M. wd. narrow it) to one which is local, exceptional and anomalous, we are hopelessly shut in.'[3] Grey and Haldane voted with the Unionists on land purchase in 1888 and 1890, because otherwise the Liberals would seem to be 'keeping open the sore of agrarian discontent in Ireland because their agitation was based on it'.[4]

In the group developing around Rosebery in the late 1890s there was therefore the feeling that Home Rule must not continue as the sole criterion of liberalism, that Home Rule must be seen in the general context of imperial devolution, and that it must not be regarded as the only, though it might be the eventual, panacea for Ireland. None of the Liberal Imperialists was connected with the detailed planning of the 1893 Bill. An attempt by Rosebery to have future Irish plans discussed by a wider spectrum of Liberal opinion was rebuffed in 1890 by Gladstone, and, according to Asquith, neither he nor Rosebery had seen the Home Rule

---

[1] Morley to Haldane, 29 Jan. 1888, Hal P 5903, f. 77.

[2] Haldane, 'The Liberal Creed', *Contemporary Review*, Oct. 1888.

[3] Asquith to Rosebery, n.d. [*c.* 1892], RP, box 1.

[4] Grey in 3 H, cccxx. 1668 (20 Nov. 1888); see also Grey to Haldane, 8 Nov. 1890, Hal P 5903, f. 173. See above, p. 7.

Bill before its introduction in the Commons.[1] None the less, they hoped Home Rule would pass and the Irish question be thus solved; if it was not, the prospects for the future were grim. They hoped, even after Parnell's fall, as did other Liberals, that given a large Liberal majority in the Commons, the Lords would not dare to throw the Bill out.[2] The small Liberal majority in 1892 dashed these hopes, and Gladstone retired leaving his party the legacy of two failed attempts at Home Rule for Ireland.

In his famous 'predominant partner' speech in 1894, Rosebery showed one line of possible approach to the problem.[3] Rosebery's lack of resolution, combined with a poor sense of occasion, rendered this attempt at modification of Home Rule a fiasco, but there was no doubt in the Rosebery group that such modification was essential.[4] One solution was to pass Home Rule for Ireland as part of a general scheme of Home-Rule-all-round, thus simultaneously solving the nationalist problem and the problem of business congestion in the Commons. Asquith had long supported this view, and in 1894 Ferguson told his wife: 'I'm going to try and move my colleagues on a bit towards HR all round.'[5] Home-Rule-all-round enjoyed some popularity as a means of uniting the various nationalist factions within the Liberal party, and a Radical Committee on Home-Rule-all-round was established in 1896, containing, at first, Liberals of all points of view. The Radical Committee decided, however, that 'the present time was inopportune to begin programme making.'[6] Home-Rule-all-round raised as many problems as it settled. A major Bill on such lines would be highly contentious and time-consuming, and was as likely to be rejected as an Irish Home Rule Bill; the Irish Nationalist M.P.s, moreover, were hostile to any such measure.

---

[1] Rosebery's Memoranda, 7 and 9 Jan. 1890, RP, box 109; Asquith to Rosebery, 10 Feb. 1893, RP, box 1.

[2] See Grey's speech moving the 1891 N.L.F. Home Rule resolution, in P. W. Clayden, *England under the Coalition*, p. 538.

[3] For this speech and its repercussions, see Stansky, pp. 100–6.

[4] Haldane to Rosebery, 13 Mar. 1894, RP, box 34, supports the speech and attacks the 'Irish babies'.

[5] Ferguson to his wife, 13 Feb. 1894, FP; see also Ferguson's Election Address in *The Scotsman*, 8 July 1895.

[6] *The Times*, 25 Mar. 1896 (also contains a list of members).

Home-Rule-all-round attempted to embrace two quite separate questions: the devolution of Welsh and Scottish problems from the Commons to relieve congestion, which were, Haldane argued, 'much more problems of a business character than questions connected with any sentiment of nationality', and the question of Ireland, which was 'a matter of social order, based upon the fact that it was necessary to satisfy nationalist aspirations'.[1] The Welsh and Scottish nationalist movements disintegrated after 1895, and Haldane therefore rightly thought that 'there is little amalgamation between them and the question of Irish Home Rule.'[2] There was little support for Home-Rule-all-round after 1896.

Haldane's 'step by step' policy is gradually accepted

In December 1896 Haldane outlined, after discussion with Asquith, the approach which was to become subsequently that of most Liberal Imperialists.[3] Haldane started from the premiss that 'he was a Home Ruler in 1886 and he was a Home Ruler in 1896.' Haldane argued that however embarrassing Home Rule was for Liberals, the Irish question could not be wished away. None the less, the Liberals must put their own house in order; Haldane 'saw prospects of some of those who, he thought, went rashly out of the party in 1886 coming back to it, and he did not think there ought to be difficulty in the way'. The solution was:

. . . first concede the principle of an Irish Parliament and Executive as it was claimed to be in 1886 . . . and let them proceed to look at its application with one change from what it was in the mind of Mr. Gladstone. Let them get rid of the notion that they must establish a final scheme at once.

'By proceeding gradually . . . step by step', politicians of all parties might find a way out of what was 'otherwise a hopeless impasse'.[4] 'Step by step' was a call for a return to con-

---

[1] Haldane, 4 H, liv. 1701–2 (15 Mar. 1898).
[2] 4 H, liv. 1701 (15 Mar. 1898).
[3] Haldane to Mother, 6 Nov. 1896, Hal P 5956, f. 121.
[4] Haldane, 'The Future of Liberalism', *The Scotsman*, 30 Dec. 1896; H. W. McCready wrongly attributes this innovation to Grey in 1901 in 'Home Rule and the Liberal Party 1899–1906', *Irish Historical Studies*, vol. 13, Sept. 1963, p. 324.

tinuity of policy on Ireland; implied in it was the hope that
the Unionists would fall into step, and that if the extent of
devolution intended in 1893 was ever reached by a gradual
process, they would not oppose it.

The Irish Local Government Act of 1898 was, the *Daily
News* thought, 'a stage on the road to Home Rule, but it
also makes the question of Home Rule less urgent ... Home
Rule must now come by stages, and probably in the end by
consent, not by a party majority', a view which was endorsed
by Fowler.[1] But although Liberal Imperialists, and other
Liberals, might welcome the Act in this sense, there was
no explicit change in Liberal policy. Whereas the tendency
of the constituencies, exemplified by the case of Doughty in
1898, seemed to be away from Home Rule,[2] the report of
the Royal Commission on Financial Relations between
Great Britain and Ireland seemed to strengthen the case for
Home Rule. Harcourt, hitherto unsympathetic to Home
Rule, accepted the finding of the Commission that fiscally
Ireland required separate treatment, and told Morley: 'We
shall all have to stand in white sheets and confess our former
ignorance.'[3] But Fowler, despite continual and heavy
pressure from Harcourt and Morley, refused to stand in a
white sheet or to accept the recommendation of the Com-
mission, telling the government: 'you ought to deal with
Ireland upon your own principles—Unionist principles.
You cannot sever Ireland from Middlesex or Lancashire.'[4]

There was, before 1899, a lack of clarity in Liberal thinking on Home Rule. Harcourt gave no guide to his party;
Rosebery before October 1896 had wanted 'to give some
hint about the Irish question and a possible change of front
towards it', but had felt too weak to do more than hint.[5]

---

[1] *Daily News*, 19 July and 22 Nov. 1898.
[2] G. Doughty, returned as a Liberal for Great Grimsby in 1895, in 1898
accepted the Stewardship of the Chiltern Hundreds and immediately stood again
as a Liberal Unionist, his election manifesto dealing only with Home Rule; he
substantially increased his majority.
[3] Harcourt to Morley, 19 Dec. 1896, HP 10; for the Report, see Parl. Papers
1896, xxxiii (C. 8262).
[4] Fowler in 4 H, xlviii. 1671 (6 May 1897); and see Fowler, *Life of Fowler*,
pp. 409 ff.
[5] EHD, 10 May 1896 (report of a talk with Rosebery); see *The Times*, 6 July
1895 for a 'hint'.

Haldane's step by step suggestion received tacit support, especially amongst the Liberal Imperialists, but it was not yet the expressed view even of that group.

The situation was further complicated by the attitude of the Irish M.P.s. Redmond, the Parnellite leader, was prepared to take whatever he could get from the Unionists, but at the same time increased his ultimate demands. He therefore welcomed the Irish Local Government Act of 1898, and co-operated in its swift passage through parliament. Simultaneously, however, he moved an amendment to the Queen's Speech for 'an independent Parliament and Executive responsible thereto for all affairs distinctly Irish', and said that acceptance of this, and the continued priority of Home Rule in the Liberal programme, was a test of the Liberal–Irish alliance.[1] This alliance was already strained by persistent Irish support for Unionist educational proposals to assist voluntary schools. The Irish educational attitude, said Perks, 'would cause surprise and disappointment to thousands of nonconformists throughout the country'; the alliance with the Irish 'might have to be cast to the winds'.[2]

The split over English education, the different standards demanded by the Irish of the Liberals and the Unionists, and the disputes within the Irish themselves brought a *de facto* end to the alliance. The *Daily News* commented that 'if Home Rule has become unpopular with English Liberals the Irish Nationalists have only themselves to thank.'[3] But the *de facto* end of the alliance solved nothing for the future for the Liberals. Fowler, alarmed at the lack of a clear Liberal lead, wrote to Rosebery that the Irish question remained 'of the gravest difficulty, which cannot be ignored, which must be faced with a clear and statesmanlike decision'. Between the Irish and the Liberals, Fowler thought, 'the chasm cannot be bridged over. But the belief is that unless the Liberal Party secure the Irish vote its success at the polls is impossible.'[4]

Here lay the reason for the Liberal leaders' reticence. The

[1] Redmond in 4 H, liii. 371 ff. (11 Feb. 1898). For Redmond's views, see D. Gwynn, *The Life of John Redmond* (1932), ch. 2.

[2] Perks in 4 H, xl. 1204 (12 May 1896).

[3] *Daily News*, 4 Aug. 1898.

[4] Fowler to Rosebery, 5 Aug. 1898, RP, box 75.

THE PROBLEM OF IRELAND

problem for the Liberals was not merely that of Ireland itself, of the alliance with the Nationalists, or of the priority of Home Rule in the Liberal programme. Herbert Gladstone calculated that about eighty-one of the seats won by the Liberals in England and Wales in 1892 were 'dominated' by the Irish vote.[1] This meant, taken at its very worst, and assuming Irish voters in England would follow instructions, that the 80 Nationalists could control about 160 seats. Even granted that this was an extreme view, Liberal leaders had to approach any change of policy towards Ireland with caution.

Although the Liberal leadership had made no move on Ireland, the Liberal Imperialists were beginning to organize themselves. The view was gaining currency, as yet privately, that they did not 'want to see our party back in office unless we came in quite independent of the Irish vote'.[2] Haldane thought that 'what the party had to make up its mind to do, (as it would) [*sic*], was to decline to assume office after the next General Election if the only way to a majority was alliance with the Irish.'[3]

For the supporters of Rosebery such a policy might prove beneficial, for the Unionists would have to go on with a minority government, 'and would gradually go to pieces. Then would come Rosebery's chance and it would be a good one.'[4] With Rosebery inactive, however, no other Liberal Imperialist as yet felt strong enough to urge this policy publicly.

Herbert Gladstone attempted to rationalize the Liberal position in a memorandum circulated to the ex-cabinet at the end of 1899. Recognizing that 'since 1895 the alliance between the Liberals and the Nationalists has been dissolved', Gladstone argued that at the next election 'the Irish question . . . in a general sense . . . would be before the country, but it would not rank for the time being, as a practical question of politics. This line would give plenty of scope for individual divergencies.'[5] Gladstone's suggestion was the very minimum which could be proposed; it amounted to an admission

[1] H. Gladstone, Memorandum, n.d., HGP 46107, f. 28.
[2] Perks to Rosebery, 30 Aug. 1897, RP, box 37.
[3] EHD, 22 Mar. 1899.   [4] Ibid.
[5] H. Gladstone, Memorandum, 8 Dec. 1899, HGP 45987 f. 50; the memorandum is discussed in H. W. McCready, op. cit., p. 318.

that there was no Liberal policy for Ireland. Gladstone dealt neither with the question of the Irish alliance in the future, nor with what sort of Irish Bill a Liberal government should bring in.

The comments on the memorandum by the Liberal Imperialist members of the ex-cabinet were favourable, but were restricted to the tactical aspect of the problem. Fowler wrote that 'Home Rule at the present is, in my opinion, outside practical politics—I therefore agree with H. G.', and Asquith wrote: 'the sole question is—is it to be raised as an issue at the next election?'[1] The Liberal Imperialists did not wish to make Home Rule the subject of yet another dispute in an already deeply divided ex-cabinet.

But the development of the Liberal Imperialist group and the return to active politics of Rosebery were bound to lead to a raising of the Irish question, for, as Asquith mentioned in his comments on the memorandum, the Irish 'attitude on external questions e.g., Soudan, United States, the present war' produced a new barrier between Irish and some Liberal M.P.s.[2] The attempt of the Liberal Imperialists to make the Liberal party 'national' by taking a patriotic stand on imperial questions and thus winning over lost Unionist votes was bound to be jeopardized by the constant Unionist taunt that the Liberals remained tied to Irish apron-strings, for Irish M.P.s were consistently and implacably anti-imperialist. Rosebery's statement in May 1899 that 'until you have the Liberal party as it was before 1886, reconstituted in some form or other, or until you have a new party which will embody all the elements which existed before 1886, you will never achieve that predominance' carried with it the implication that a major overhaul of Liberal policy on Ireland would be one of Rosebery's main aims in returning to public life. The Boer War, the reunion of the Nationalist factions under Redmond's leadership, and their alliance with the Little Englanders on imperial questions made action by the Liberal Imperialists the more pressing.[3]

[1] Fowler to Gladstone, 12 Jan. 1900, HGP 46057, f. 257; Asquith to Gladstone, 8 Jan. 1900, HGP 45989, f. 28.   [2] Asquith, loc. cit.

[3] Rosebery to the City Liberals, *The Times*, 6 May 1899; for Nationalist reorganization, see F. S. L. Lyons, *The Irish Parliamentary Party 1890–1910* (1951), pp. 83–9.

Liberal Imperialists were, however, slow to make a move on the Irish question. During 1900 Ireland figured hardly at all in their speeches. During the election they held to Herbert Gladstone's view that it was best to allow the question to fall as far into the background as possible. It may have been that, with the end of the war expected in 1900, the Liberal Imperialists hoped to avoid a confrontation with the Irish which might force the Little Englanders, because of their alliance on imperial questions with the Irish, into a militant Home Rule mood; they may have feared that Campbell-Bannerman would leave his central position in the party if the Liberal Imperialists introduced Home Rule into the disputes.

When the war did not end, and matters came to a head in the crisis within the Liberal party in June 1901, the Asquith committee decided, as part of 'the autumn plans of campaign . . . to repudiate the Irish alliance, declare that Gladstonian H.R. is dead, but advocate conciliatory and remedial laws'.[1] The effect of the 'war to the knife—and fork', the crisis over the sundry dinners in the summer of 1901, in which Campbell-Bannerman appeared to surrender the centre group into the arms of the Little Englanders, was to precipitate a Liberal Imperialist campaign about Ireland.[2]

The campaign of Haldane, Asquith, and Grey distinguished between the constitutional needs of Ireland and the relationship between the Liberal and Irish M.P.s. 'It was vital', Haldane said, 'that there should be a Liberal party that was completely independent of the Irish.' Asquith called for 'an independent Liberal majority in the House of Commons' before a Liberal government could be formed. Asquith admitted that 'such a majority may take a long time to secure', but 'it was far more likely to come upon that footing than any other', because only in that case would the constituencies vote Liberal. Grey 'associated himself entirely with the declaration of Mr. Asquith as to the future relations of the Liberal party and the Irish nationalists'.[3]

This aspect of the campaign had little to do with Ireland;

[1] Perks to Rosebery, 8 Aug. 1901, RP, box 39.
[2] See above, pp. 72–3, for the background of this campaign.
[3] Haldane in Glasgow, *The Scotsman*, 19 Oct. 1901; Asquith in Ladybank, *The Times*, 30 Sept. 1901; Grey in Newcastle, *The Times*, 12 Oct. 1901.

it was a dissociation from the Irish in their capacity as pro-Boers. As Grey put it, 'the recent election in N.E. Lanarkshire seemed to show that the Irish vote was to be used to oust every Liberal who sided with his own country in this war.'[1] In this situation 'they would never get the confidence of the centre of the nation.'[2] These Liberal Imperialists thus committed themselves to the position of an absolute Liberal majority, partly on the ground that association with the Irish was undesirable in itself, but also on the ground that unless the *de facto* breakdown of the alliance was explicitly and publicly accepted by the Liberals, they would not win over 'the centre of the nation'.

As a solution to the actual problems of Ireland, the Liberal Imperialists introduced the 'step by step' policy adumbrated by Haldane in 1896. Step by step was not an attempt to erase Home Rule permanently from the slate. Asquith believed that the measures of the Unionists, far-reaching though they might be, would never solve the problem:

. . . the problem of Irish government is as serious and as intractable as it ever was. You cannot kill it with kindness; you cannot extinguish it by land purchase; you may shut your eyes to it but it will continue to stare you in the face . . . I believe as strongly as ever I did in the two governing principles . . . namely, first, the necessity of maintaining the universal, absolute, and unimpaired supremacy of the Imperial parliament, and, subject to that condition, the policy of giving as large and as liberal a devolution of local powers and local responsibilities as statesmanship can from time to time devise.[3]

Asquith's cautious and carefully phrased statement did not specifically mention 'step by step'. Haldane had, however, revived the policy early in 1899, and from Perks's report to Rosebery, it had evidently been discussed at the conference in August 1901.[4]

The general approach of the Liberal Imperialists having been outlined by Asquith, and his authority having been given to the 'independent majority' policy, Grey and Haldane filled in the details on Irish government. Both argued that 'they

---

1 Grey, loc. cit. For this by-election see above, pp. 74–5.
2 Haldane in Glasgow, *The Scotsman*, 19 Oct. 1901.
3 Asquith in Ladybank, *The Times*, 30 Sept. 1901.
4 Haldane in Dumbarton, *The Times*, 11 Jan. 1899. For Perks's report, see above, p. 273.

could not rest with the present measure of self government ...
but progress in that direction [Home Rule] must be made, not
in one great measure, but step by step.'[1] The result of step by
step, since it built on Unionist foundations and might reasonably hope to gain Unionist support, might be to 'get to something very like Home Rule for Ireland as complete, or, perhaps,
more complete—because there was no finality in it—than
under Mr. Gladstone's Bills'. Haldane suggested three ways
of making the first step: the informal existing association of
county council representatives might be given 'legal recognition and some administrative powers'; there might be provincial councils; there might be 'one council for the whole of
Ireland'.[2]

The step by step policy would give the Liberals a flexibility in their Irish policy which the 'final settlement' of
Gladstone had precluded. This was especially necessary in
view of the development of the Ulster problem. Haldane
visited Ulster in 1894, and found the Ulstermen 'irreconcilable ... I shall never be surprised to hear of Ulster initiating
a nationalist movement.'[3] The step by step policy would give
Ulster a feeling of security:

... let them give Ulster, if they like to demand it, a provincial assem-
blage which should deal with that difficult question of religious education
in a fashion which might remove the bone of controversy between
Ulster and the rest of Ireland.[4]

The step by step policy was a change of means rather than
of ends, and was the result of the application to the Irish
problem of the criterion of efficiency, or, as Haldane put it,
of the 'quality of effectiveness'. Behind it lay the traditional
Liberal view that they must not 'suppose that in Ireland
force was any remedy', and that the Irish problem would
remain insoluble 'so long as they insisted on the endeavour
to govern Ireland according to British ideas and not according to the ideas of Ireland'.[5]

[1] Grey in Newcastle, *The Times*, 12 Oct. 1901.
[2] Haldane in Tranent, *The Scotsman*, 4 Oct. 1901, which gives the fullest exposition of the thinking behind 'step by step'.
[3] Haldane to Mother, 9 Oct. 1894, Hal P 5952, f. 138.
[4] Haldane in Edinburgh, *The Scotsman*, 30 Dec. 1896.
[5] Haldane in Tranent and in Dunblane, *The Scotsman*, 4 Oct. and 28 Dec. 1901.
The difficulty that 'Irish ideas', as expressed by the Nationalist M.P.s, now included

Rosebery's dissent from 'step by step'

Very different was the view taken by Rosebery. In his references to the clean slate in July 1901 and at Chesterfield in December 1901, Rosebery left little doubt that Home Rule was the chief item of the Newcastle Programme which he wished to see expunged.[1] At his meeting with Campbell-Bannerman after Chesterfield, Rosebery felt that Ireland, as a cause of division between him and the Liberal leadership, was equal to, perhaps even greater than, imperialism.[2] According to Campbell-Bannerman

Ireland is of itself enough to keep him [Rosebery] away; is opposed to Home Rule in any form; might agree to provincial Councils or some Committee of H. of C.—a legislative body never. If he spoke again, wd devote his speech to this. Used all the old Unionist arguments.[3]

In his next two speeches, and in his preface to their printed version, Rosebery gave his opinions on the Irish question. He took the view 'that the conditions of the problem of Irish government have fundamentally changed', as a result of the Irish Local Government Act of 1898. Ireland must not be regarded as a special case, but must be accorded 'equality of treatment'. Rosebery surveyed various schemes of dual government in Europe, in particular those of Russia and Finland, Austria and Hungary, and Norway and Sweden, and found them all wanting. In addition he used the traditional strategic argument of the Unionists:

If Ireland were loyal and remote I would gladly give her the privilege of the self governing Colonies. What we have to remember is that this is the heart of a widely scattered Empire . . . we cannot afford . . . that there should be a Parliament hostile, which, for example, in the case of the present war, might have turned the balance between success and defeat.

Whereas the step by step policy was intended eventually to satisfy the wishes of the Nationalists, Rosebery claimed that 'you must give up any hope of satisfying the sentiment of a demand for an 'independent Parliament', a demand unacceptable to Haldane, was not resolved.

[1] Rosebery to City Liberals, *The Times*, 20 July 1901, and at Chesterfield, LLP 1.
[2] Fowler told Asquith: 'I gather the *real* difficulty is Ireland' (10 Jan. 1902 AP 10, f. 70).
[3] Bannerman to Bryce, 25 Dec. 1901, BP; see also Crewe, ii. 573.

Irish leaders in this matter.' Ireland must be ruled 'without the hope of Irish gratitude'.[1] As Rosebery said, if Irish Home Rule were the only domestic issue, he would be virtually at one with the Unionists.

Unresolved contradictions

On the future of Irish government there was a basic differ-ence of approach between Rosebery and the Commons group. Whereas the latter were, as the *Pall Mall Gazette* put it, 'only against Home Rule because it is inexpedient, not because it is wrong', Rosebery thought it both inexpedient and wrong.[2] But this difference was, at this stage, only theoretically apparent. Rosebery agreed, as did many Unionists, that it might be possible to enlarge the sphere of local government, and his proposals for doing so were much the same as, if more tentative than, those of the Commons men. But since Rosebery believed that 'we cannot afford a dualism of Parliament and of Government', and since he equated any Irish parliament with *de facto* dualism, the first step for him was also the last.[3]

Rosebery and the Commons men agreed on the indepen-dent majority and the end of the alliance. They also agreed that the Liberal party must be seen explicitly to alter its Irish policy, to remove Home Rule from the head of the programme, and to declare the alliance ended. Liberal Imperialists could therefore concentrate on these aspects of the question, and ignore their important differences on Irish government.

When the Liberal League was formed shortly after Rosebery's Liverpool speech, no attempt was made to recon-cile the two approaches to the Irish question. Liberal Leaguers in the Commons saw the Irish question as only a part of the League's work, and they underestimated the weight which Rosebery gave to it. It would hardly be extreme to say that Rosebery came to see the League as

[1] Rosebery in Liverpool, 14 Feb. 1902, and in Glasgow, 10 Mar. 1902, LLP 3; he believed dual government would be the *de facto* result of any Home Rule Act.
[2] *Pall Mall Gazette*, 3 Mar. 1902.
[3] Rosebery in Liverpool, 14 Feb. 1902, LLP 3.

primarily an anti-Home Rule organization. Rosebery's speech at Liverpool gave Haldane 'the keenest pleasure',[1] but Haldane was so accustomed to Rosebery's changes of opinion that he probably paid little attention to the details of Rosebery's argument. The overriding aim of the Commons group at this time was to attach Rosebery to party political activity; it was not a time for quibbling over details.[2]

The effect of the formation of the Liberal League, and the publicity given to Rosebery's speeches in the summer of 1902, in which he dealt continually, and in increasingly negative tones, with the Irish question, was to make Asquith, Haldane, and Grey appear more extreme on Ireland than they really were.[3] This impression was encouraged by the fact that the other two Commons League leaders, Fowler and Perks, followed the Rosebery line on Ireland. During the education debates of 1902, Perks's hostility to the Irish became almost fanatical, and Fowler, though more moderate in tone, attacked the step by step policy, and told his constituency chairman: 'I adopt the policy of Lord Rosebery. I believe it to be the only practical policy.'[4] Campbell-Bannerman's refutation of the clean slate at Leicester, his apparent, though guarded, support for Home Rule as 'the sole remedy for the condition of Ireland', and the continued allegiance of Asquith, Grey, and Haldane to Rosebery even after he had announced his 'definite separation' from Campbell-Bannerman specifically on the Irish issue, all gave an extreme impression of the position of Asquith, Grey, and Haldane.[5]

Their position remained as it had been expounded in the autumn of 1901. It was, if anything, more unified, for Asquith, attacking the 'great deal of loose rhetoric . . . current on the subject', came out clearly for the first time for

[1] Haldane to Rosebery, 16 Feb. 1902, RP, box 24.

[2] Asquith told Gladstone 'not to take too seriously what was said or supposed to be said [at the Rosebery/Bannerman interview] about Home Rule' (5 Jan. 1902, HGP 45989, f. 57).

[3] See particularly Rosebery in Leeds, 31 July 1902, LLP 20, and in Edinburgh, 1 Nov. 1902, LLP 33.

[4] Fowler, The Times, 6 May 1902.

[5] Bannerman at Leicester, The Times, 20 Feb. 1902; Rosebery to The Times, 21 Feb. 1902.

the step by step policy. Asquith's letter to his constituency chairman in 1902 was moderate in tone, entirely lacking the emphasis which Rosebery and Fowler placed on Irish 'treachery'.[1] The step by step men were also successful in getting their policy written into the League Manifesto.[2] During 1902 Asquith, Grey, and Haldane continued to state that they 'had not abandoned . . . the ends of their Irish policy', and to advocate step by step as an alternative means. They began to point out that step by step was the only positive suggestion which Liberals were putting forward, and to attack Morley and Campbell-Bannerman for their 'ostrich like tendency' of virtually admitting that a complete and immediate Home Rule Bill was an impossibility, without being prepared to abandon it in principle and to suggest an alternative policy.[3]

There was as yet no clash between the step by step men and Rosebery, and they remained agreed about the independent Liberal majority. From 1903 the fiscal controversy drove Ireland almost off the stage. The effect of the split in the Unionist party over tariff reform was that for the first time since 1886, the Liberals could with justification point to something other than Home Rule as the major dividing-line in British politics. Liberal Imperialists threw their efforts into persuading the electorate that the decisive feature of a Liberal was that he was a free-trader. In such a situation, it was obviously indiscreet to mention Ireland. This situation was assisted by the absence of controversy over the Irish Land Purchase Act of 1903, and by the indication of the Unionists, through the appointment of MacDonnell, a Liberal Catholic Home Ruler, as Permanent Under-Secretary, that a bipartisan policy might be possible. Such controversy as there was about Ireland was coming mainly from Unionists who regarded the Wyndham/MacDonnell policy as too conciliatory.

[1] Asquith to J. Scott, *The Times*, 3 Mar. 1902; and in Spender and Asquith, i. 144; the step by step policy was as yet by no means acceptable to the Liberal leadership, see Lord Spencer to Asquith, 3 Mar. 1902, AP 10, f. 74.

[2] Liberal League Manifesto, May 1902, LLP.

[3] Asquith in Fife, *The Times*, 15 Mar. 1902; Grey in Alnwick and in Oxford, *The Times*, 31 May 1902 and 30 May 1903; Haldane in Tranent, *The Scotsman*, 2 Oct. 1902.

The split in the Unionist party also transformed the context in which the Liberals discussed Ireland. The various policies of 1901 and 1902 had been enunciated in a context in which a Liberal government seemed to be only a remote possibility. By the summer of 1904 this was no longer so. Liberals might soon again have to deal with Ireland in office.

Realizing this, Rosebery was determined that the Liberals should explicitly accept his policy. He put over his views in increasingly negative form. In London in June 1904 he denounced the Irish, without suggesting any alternative proposal.[1] The intransigence of Rosebery's position was now becoming clear. In April 1904 at a private League dinner there was a row between the step by step men and the supporters of Rosebery,[2] and following the London speech, Haldane wrote to Rosebery:

> I did not agree with Perks in liking the Irish reference best. Not that I did not agree with every word you said, but I should have liked an addition. We cannot govern Ireland by coercion if the Liberal party comes in, so that in criticism means and end have to be distinguished, a broad distinction but a necessary one. For in the end I am pretty sure that a large amount of self government . . . in Ireland . . . will have to be helped to grow up.[3]

Thus while Haldane, Grey, and Asquith continued to advocate a policy intended to deal with the actualities of the Irish situation, Rosebery and Perks increasingly disregarded Irish problems, and stressed only the need for clarity about the tactical, political situation at Westminster.[4]

The policy of Dunraven, MacDonnell, and Wyndham of devolution of financial and limited parliamentary power to bodies sitting in Ireland was exactly the sort of measure which Asquith, Grey, and Haldane saw as the first 'step'. Supported by Redmond, if not by Dillon, as well as by many Free Trade Liberal Unionists, the Dunraven plan seemed

---

[1] Rosebery to the Liberal League, 10 June 1904, LLP 144.
[2] Perks to Rosebery, 22 Apr. 1904, RP, box 41.
[3] Haldane to Rosebery, 12 June 1904, RP, box 24.
[4] Haldane to *The Times*, 5 Jan. 1904; Perks in Grimsby, *The Times*, 25 Mar. 1904. Perks told Rosebery: 'It is certain that the Irish and the nonconformists will not—cannot—work together' (19 Mar. 1904, RP, box 41).

THE PROBLEM OF IRELAND 281

to allow Ireland to be treated in a bipartisan way.[1] As
Asquith commented,

an approach was being made nearer and nearer to a state of things
when, with the general consent of reasonable men in all parties of the
state, statesmanship would be able to take seriously in hand the task
of broadening the base and liberalising both the methods and the spirit
of Irish administration.[2]

It would be the function of the Liberals 'to go on with the
sympathetic policy where the Government dropped it'.[3] The
implications of the fact that the government had already
abandoned this bipartisan policy, by allowing their ex-
tremists to drive Wyndham from office, were not discussed.

While Asquith and Grey took this conciliatory line,
Rosebery returned again to the tactical position. He argued
that the Unionist proposals were quite sufficient in themselves, and that the government was 'not particularly subject
to any reproach of not being sufficiently attentive to the
wrongs of Ireland'. Any suggestion 'for establishing a
Parliament, however subordinate, in Dublin' must be subject
to a special general election.[4] Rosebery continued to draw
attention to the more extreme statements of the Irish leadership; Perks continued to encourage Rosebery in his hostility
to the Nationalist M.P.s.[5] By so doing they maintained the
impression that the Liberal League was an anti-Home Rule
organization. Lawson Walton found Rosebery's Irish speeches

worse than 'methods of barbarism'. I joined the Liberal League with
the main object of attaching Lord R. to the Liberal coach in order to
extricate us from the Dutch. Now we are well on the road he threatens
to plunge us into an Irish bog.[6]

Rosebery, however, had a point. Although the tactical position for the Liberals seemed clear enough, there was as yet
no lead from Campbell-Bannerman. Campbell-Bannerman
had observed to Gladstone in October 1904 that 'Ireland

[1] West Ridgeway to Asquith, 10 Feb. 1905, AP 10, f. 136.
[2] Asquith in Birmingham, *The Times*, 25 Feb. 1905.
[3] Grey in Northallerton, *The Times*, 16 Mar. 1905.
[4] Rosebery to the City Liberals, *The Times*, 10 Mar. 1905.
[5] Rosebery in Epsom, *The Times*, 20 Mar. 1905; Perks to Rosebery, 25 Mar.
1905, RP, box 41.
[6] Lawson Walton to Gladstone, 18 Mar. 1905, HGP 46062, f. 168.

would need careful handling', and he seems to have decided to avoid commitment to a specific plan until the
last possible moment.[1] During the debate on the Address
early in 1905, all the Liberals had supported the 'purely
negative' amendment of Redmond, which committed them
to no particular future policy.[2] Negotiations took place
between Morley, whose exact status in these conversations
is unclear, and the Irish leaders, but Campbell-Bannerman
remained uncommitted.[3] At the beginning of August,
Campbell-Bannerman played the card he had used with
effect during the South African disputes, and removed himself to the Continent, allowing the situation to come to a head
in his absence. He remained abroad until 12 November 1905,
thus missing the traditional autumn speech-making season.

The Asquith committee played down the Irish question
during this campaign. They seem to have felt that the step
by step policy had won the day by default. Asquith, referring
to the impossibility of the introduction of a Home Rule Bill
in the new parliament, wrote to Gladstone:

> Everybody knows (no one better than J. M. [Morley]) that this is
> the actual state of the case, and no one intends (least of all J. M.) to
> devote either the second or third or any session to forming or carrying
> a Bill which . . . will wreck the fortunes of the party for another 20
> years.[4]

Believing this, they avoided mention of Ireland in their
speeches.[5] But after his speech at Earlsferry in October
1905, Asquith was heckled on Ireland, and replying to a
heckler said:

> If by Home Rule is meant, as I presume it is, the introduction of
> a Bill for the establishment of a Legislative in Dublin . . . I am of
> opinion, speaking for myself, that it will not and cannot be any part
> of the policy of the next Liberal Government . . . step by step should
> be the aim and ideal of the Liberal policy.

[1] Bannerman to Gladstone, 10 Oct. 1904, HGP 45988, f. 124.
[2] 4 H, cxli. 623 (20 Feb. 1905); Asquith to Bannerman, 17 Feb. 1905, CBP
41210, f. 243.
[3] See Gwynn, op. cit., p. 108, and McCready, op. cit., pp. 339–41.
[4] Asquith to Gladstone, 22 Oct. 1905, HGP 45989, f. 131.
[5] The Times: Grey in London, 1 June 1905, in Manchester, 14 Oct. 1905;
Asquith in Earlsferry, 12 Oct. 1905, in Edinburgh, 23 Oct. 1905, in Kent, 8 Nov.
1905.

Heckled about taking office 'dependent on an Irish majority', Asquith blandly replied: 'That is a question I entirely decline to answer.'[1]

Morley responded to these impromptu remarks by advocating Home Rule, although he did not 'expect to see reform of the Irish Government the first measure of the new Parliament'.[2] Asquith made no public response to Morley, assuming that Morley's views were 'a mere splenetic outburst', though he warned Gladstone that Morley's views must not receive 'any countenance, open or ambiguous, from C. B. or any other person'.[3] Asquith was wrong in his assumption that step by step had already won the day. Campbell-Bannerman was still keeping his options open, and told Gladstone:

. . . that there would be time or opportunity for anything like a full blown H.R. Bill is utterly unlikely; but we do not know how circumstances may change, and I doubt the wisdom of precluding any approach to it being made.[4]

Rosebery, prompted by Perks, who thought Asquith's replies to the heckler 'too weak',[5] sensed something of this, and at Stourbridge declared that 'ambiguity and reticence only spell distrust and disaster.'[6] While accepting that MacDonnell's policy was right for a future Liberal government, Rosebery devoted the main emphasis of his remarks to a demand that 'those who are in favour of a statutory Parliament in Dublin' should clearly state that it was either impossible in the coming parliament, or should be placed first and treated as 'the main and supreme question' at the election.[7] Haldane thought this 'an extraordinary good lead', and Grey found the speech 'refreshing'.[8]

---

[1] Asquith in Earlsferry, *The Times*, 12 Oct. 1905; for a fuller version, see *The Scotsman*, 12 Oct. 1905.
[2] Morley in Forfar, *The Times*, 21 Oct. 1905.
[3] Asquith to Gladstone, 22 Oct. 1905, HGP 45989, f. 131; more quoted in McCready, op. cit., p. 342.
[4] Bannerman to Gladstone, 26 Oct. 1905, HGP 45988, f. 196.
[5] Perks to Rosebery, 21 Oct. 1905, RP, box 41.
[6] Rosebery in Stourbridge, *The Times*, 26 Oct. 1905.
[7] Ibid.; for more of the speech, see James, p. 453.
[8] Haldane to Rosebery, 26 Oct. 1905, RP, box 24; Grey to Rosebery, 26 Oct. 1905, RP, box 23.

Public exposure of the unresolved contradictions

When Campbell-Bannerman returned to Britain on 12 November 1905, Asquith saw him the next day and discussed a large number of topics with him.[1] At this and at a subsequent meeting Asquith 'got an assurance that CB agreed with his (A's) Irish declaration'.[2] Asquith passed on this information to Grey, who was staying with Haldane in London.[3]

Following these conversations, Campbell-Bannerman made his famous declaration at Stirling on 23 November. In this he virtually accepted the step by step procedure, though he did not mention it by name. But he did not say what the first step might be, he showed himself in sympathy with Nationalist aspirations, and he trusted 'that the opportunity of making a great advance on this question of Irish government will not be long delayed'.[4]

Rosebery responded to this at Bodmin. Understanding that Campbell-Bannerman 'had hoisted once more in its most pronounced form the flag of Irish Home Rule', Rosebery declared he could 'not serve under that banner'.[4] On 27 November Grey, after consultation with Haldane and prompting by telegraph from Asquith, announced that 'there had been a misunderstanding', and that he 'did not agree with the interpretation that he [Rosebery] had placed upon Sir Henry Campbell-Bannerman's speech'. Asquith subsequently endorsed Grey's view.[5] Campbell-Bannerman refused Rosebery's requests to elucidate the position, and, believing Rosebery to be 'off his head', declined to elaborate his original Stirling statement.[6] Thus were the senior members of the League seen openly in disarray.

---

[1] Jenkins, pp. 147–9.

[2] Grey to Rosebery, 29 Nov. 1905, RP, box 23.

[3] Ibid., and Haldane to Spender, 27 Nov. 1905, SP 46388, f. 160. The details of Bannerman's arrangements with the Irish are controversial, see Lyons, *John Dillon*, p. 281 n. 1.

[4] *Bannerman*, ii. 182–3.

[5] Haldane to Spender, 27 Nov. 1905, SP 46388, f. 160; Asquith to Grey, n.d., in Trevelyan, *Grey of Fallodon*, p. 94; Grey in Newcastle-under-Lyme, *The Times*, 28 Nov. 1905; Asquith in Wisbech, *The Times*, 29 Nov. 1905.

[6] Bannerman in Partick, *The Times*, 29 Nov. 1905, and Bannerman to Bryce, 26 Nov. 1905, BP.

The Bodmin fiasco indicated publicly the breakdown in consultation within the League leadership which had been developing since 1902. The failure of Asquith to inform Rosebery of Campbell-Bannerman's views on Ireland was only a symptom of this, for Asquith, Grey, and Haldane had already decided not to inform Rosebery of their plans to place Campbell-Bannerman in the Lords, or of their negotiations with the Court to achieve this end.[1]

But the Bodmin fiasco also highlighted the basic difference on Irish policy between Rosebery and Perks on the one hand, and the Haldane group on the other. Rosebery was quite right in his thinking about Campbell-Bannerman's speech. As he wrote to Spender, 'my main objection to the speech of CB is that he, the actual leader and proximate leader of the Liberal party associates himself with the aspirations and objects of the Irish party.'[2] Campbell-Bannerman certainly did so associate himself, and his opinions were quite acceptable to Redmond.[3] But so also did the Haldane group. As they had often pointed out, step by step was an argument about means, not ends. Grey felt that 'if CB could only occasionally cross a t and dot an i it would be better', but he substantially agreed with the Stirling speech.[4]

What was revealed at Bodmin was not merely a short-term lack of co-operation and communication, but a deep division in approach to Irish policy which had been inherent within the League since its inception. The step by step men saw their policy both as a solution to the political situation at Westminster, and as a solution to the problems of Irish government. Rosebery's aim was purely negative, and was to ensure that a Liberal government should never become committed to a Home Rule policy, in any form.

There was some justification in Rosebery's case. The step by step policy came to nothing. Within five years the Liberals were once more dependent on the Nationalists for their majority. They were again committed to a complete Home

[1] See above, p. 112.
[2] Rosebery to Spender, 30 Nov. 1905, SP 46387, f. 59.
[3] See Gwynn, op. cit., p. 115.
[4] Grey to Gladstone, 29 Nov. 1905, HGP 45992, f. 120.

Rule Bill, the 'final scheme' in one great Act which Haldane, Grey, and Asquith had so deplored, and which threatened to bring the nation to the brink of civil war. Moreover, the Haldane group did not squarely face the facts, first that the presence of Walter Long as Chief Secretary in 1905 marked the collapse of Unionist co-operation in a bipartisan policy, and secondly that the Nationalists had always made it plain that, while they would take what they could get from the Unionists, they would expect much more from the Liberals.[1] Like so many other Liberal Imperialist policies, the success of the step by step policy depended on 'the general consent of reasonable men in all parties of the State', that is, on a movement of opinion towards the centre. But in Ireland the reverse occurred. Polarization of opinion caused the Nationalists to reject the first step, the Irish Council Bill of 1907, thus saving the Lords a similar labour.[2] Though the step by step policy achieved its tactical objective of gaining time for the Liberals to attempt social legislation in the 1905–10 period, it did not, in the long run, modify the means by which the Liberals tackled the reform of Irish government.

[1] Redmond in 4 H, liii. 371 ff. (11 Feb. 1898).
[2] Lyons, *John Dillon*, pp. 290–8.

CONCLUSION

THE Liberal Imperialist movement before 1906 did not have the success for which its members hoped. Politically, the incompetence of the 'babies in intrigue', as Morley called them, was clear for all to see.[1] Attempts at organization were always too late and too slow. The senior Liberal Imperialists failed to link themselves organizationally with their prospective followers until many of those followers had committed themselves elsewhere. The Liberal League at a constituency level failed to make much impact, partly because it was non-existent in the areas in which a major Liberal recovery was vital—the big English boroughs. At a parliamentary level the League failed to act as an effective focus of Liberal Imperialist opinion because it was organized too late and because its leaders disagreed about priorities.

This failure to build up a substantial political following was important because it meant that the Liberal Imperialists were always putting forward their policies from a position of weakness. Since they consistently appeared as dissenters, rather than as 'the orthodox church', they were constantly open to the charge of heresy, and therefore, to avoid excommunication, had to temper their views to fit those of the majority.

The constant bungling of the Liberal Imperialists is partly to be explained in terms of the personalities involved —the erratic and petulant waywardness of Rosebery, the angularity of Grey, the public unattractiveness of Haldane and Perks, the lack of passionate commitment of Asquith. But four other factors contributed to their political failures.

First, there was the problem of dual allegiance. Perks, their most effective political organizer, was primarily a nonconformist who wished to use the Liberal Imperialist movement to gain a power base at Westminster for his style of nonconformity. Asquith's first loyalty was to the Liberal

[1] See above, p. 85.

party; he wished to use the Liberal Imperialist movement to prevent defections from the Liberal party and to enlarge that party's scope. As a result he frequently seemed to face two ways; indeed it was his intention that each group—the Liberal leadership and the Liberal Imperialists—should see him facing in its direction. That a schism was avoided was in large measure due to his skill and success in maintaining this pose.

Grey had little idea of the practical working of politics. He seemed to assume that nobility of manner was sufficient in itself. His inability to decide on clear political priorities meant that sometimes he spoke like a loyal Liberal, sometimes like the protagonist of some new centre party. But his remarks were never supported by sustained action. His presidency of the Imperial Liberal Council contributed nothing to the development of that body. Grey was undecided whether he wanted honourable independence or the shackles of office; in the end he conveniently persuaded himself that to refuse office would be dishonourable.

More than any other Liberal Imperialist, Haldane tried to develop a coherent body of Liberal Imperialism. Haldane's basic principle was that of an evolutionary approach to policy. This implied the idea of the clean slate, and of moderate, step-by-step development in domestic, Irish, constitutional, and imperial policy which would make liberalism a political creed founded on the concept of the organic state. Haldane was responsible for what originality there was in Liberal Imperialist ideas and policy. The idealist principles from which he developed his views were not, of course, his own, but as a combination of leading politician and thinker on the fringe of original thought, respected in his own right by philosophers, he was a quite exceptional figure in British politics.[1] But the Haldanian synthesis of man of thought and man of action did not quite come off, for he lacked the ability to project his ideas clearly and persuasively either to his colleagues or to the electorate, and he lacked that combination of charm and ruthlessness necessary in a fully successful politician.

[1] See J. M. E. M'Taggart's review of *The Pathway to Reality* in *Monthly Review*, 15, June 1904.

Rosebery certainly had charm, but he lacked ruthlessness, both in political behaviour and in the examination of his own ideas. Self-indulgence characterized Rosebery's thought and action. He moved uneasily between loyalty to the Liberal Imperialist movement and to the Liberal party. Rosebery seemed to hold two quite different sets of political ideas simultaneously. He had a view of British party politics which was unusual and which formed the basis of an ill-worked-out pragmatic view of the solutions to Britain's problems. At the same time, however, he expressed strictly traditional views when the occasion called for them—as in the Education Bill debates in 1902. Rosebery's failure to reconcile these two approaches and his consequent appearance as a curious mixture of Webb the Fabian and Perks the unreconstructed nonconformist, did much to rob the Liberal League of a clear identity.

As a result of this dual allegiance, it was never clear whether the League was trying to permeate or proscribe. Its members tried to hedge their bets; they hoped to use the League both as a haven in the event of a schism and as an instrument of permeation. But its appearance as the former invalidated its function as the latter.

The second factor, the unwillingness of the senior Liberal Imperialists to involve themselves in effective organizational activity, can be explained by their élitist views. With the partial exception of Rosebery, who had an instinctive flair for catching the public mood, the Liberal Imperialists had little contact with, or sympathy for, the rank-and-file Liberals of their day. Complex speeches on efficiency and the clean slate were delivered to agricultural labourers in their predominantly rural and usually Scottish constituencies, but these speeches were intended not for their hearers but for their readers in *The Times* and in the *Daily News*. Only Rosebery possessed, in part, the Gladstonian ability to persuade such audiences that the speeches were in some way relevant to their interests. Liberal Imperialists were unsuccessful in persuading local Liberal associations that imperialism was the best means to unify the party. Indeed, the continual squabbles about imperialism at Westminster had, for the most part, little sustained local impact. As

Herbert Samuel remarked, 'when the forces of progress are divided in the House of Commons it is usually on some question of Empire policy . . . in a constituency it is usually on the question of labour representation.'[1]

Liberal Imperialists were intellectual Whigs. They believed that by virtue of their intellects they were the natural rulers of their party and their country, and they assumed that their 'effortless superiority' would carry them and their views effortlessly to the top. They too readily assumed that their opinions would be accepted; hence their lack of political organization. They expected that they could control the Liberal vote through the agency of the national press and, locally, through the influence of men of intellect in the Liberal League branches. Not only had they little contact with the Liberal rank and file, they also had little contact with the business world and its methods. They liked to talk of a 'business' approach to politics, but it is typical that Perks, the only businessman in the League leadership, was able, despite his obvious intellectual inferiority, to guide the League in the direction that he, rather than the Fabian intellectuals, wanted.

A third explanation for their lack of political effectiveness as a group is that the Liberal Imperialists were careerists in a not dishonourable sense. They believed that they were naturally fitted for office, and that the nation would be well governed by them. Lady Horner, a close friend of the Asquith committee, thought that 'if Asquith were Prime Minister, Grey Foreign Secretary and Haldane Lord Chancellor, all would be well with the world.'[2] Asquith, Haldane, and Grey did not dispute this view. Believing it, they were bound to be careful not to separate themselves too far from the only organization which could, for the time being, provide them with political power—the Liberal party. As usual, Rosebery put it best and lived up to it least:

Life in itself is but a poor thing at best; it consists of only two certain parts, the beginning and the end . . . Between those two points lies the whole area of human choice and human opportunity. You may

[1] S. Webb, H. Samuel, et al., 'How to Attain Liberal Unity', New Liberal Review, Oct. 1902.
[2] Frances Lady Horner, Time Remembered (1933), p. 195.

embellish and consecrate it if you will, or you may let it lie stagnant and dead. But if you choose the better part I believe that nothing will give your life so high a complexion as to study to do something for your country.[1]

In the pursuit of such service ambition was a necessary stimulus, and it was nothing to be ashamed of. Ambition to reach the highest position in the service of the state was, as Rosebery remarked, an 'exalting virtue'.[2] But personal ambition, and the assumption that it would be rewarded, did not go well with close co-operation within the Liberal Imperialist movement, especially when that movement failed to live up to its early expectations. Behind the many protestations of friendship there lay, especially in the persons of Asquith, Haldane, Perks, and Fowler, the toughness and determination to succeed which had ensured success in a harsh and competitive society.

Finally, it may be said that the use by the Liberal Imperialists in the Commons of Milnerism in South Africa as the issue on which to force a crisis within the party was politically disastrous. The details of Milner's policy did not particularly interest them, and were of little relevance to their primary concern, their general strategy of party reform, both ideological and electoral. But much of what the Liberal Imperialists had to say on policy generally was ignored, distorted, or forgotten because of their excessive loyalty to their misconceived view of Milner's South African policy. Rosebery successfully showed that it was possible to sound 'patriotic' on the South African question without being a fully-fledged Milnerite.

Ferguson believed that although politically Liberal Imperialism had been a débâcle, this was more than outweighed by the validity of its policies.[3] How true was this assessment?

Liberal Imperialism as conceived by Liberal Imperialists had two main characteristics: pragmatism in the form of the clean slate, and the attempt to solve both policy and electoral problems by the concept of efficiency. Liberal Imperialists

---

[1] Rosebery, *Miscellanies, Literary and Historical* (1921), ii. 207 ('The Service of the State', 25 Oct. 1898).
[2] Ibid., ii. 260 ('Questions of Empire', 16 Nov. 1900).   [3] See above, p. 121.

were not as pragmatic and as business-like as they liked to think. Only on Home Rule was the slate cleaned with much success, and even here there was disagreement about the degree to which it had been cleaned. Liberal Imperialists found that the 'old watchwords' whose irrelevance they liked to proclaim were not as 'unbusiness-like' as they had supposed. This applied particularly to the central tenet of free trade. When the challenge of Chamberlain and tariff reform came in full force, Liberal Imperialists rallied to the Liberal colours genuinely, and, after thought, without intellectual perjury. That is to say, their pragmatism was to be applied only within what Haldane called a limited 'ambit' and on the assumption that a traditional Liberal framework of society was accepted by both parties.[1]

With their assumption that politics centred on the middle ground between the parties, and that there was a single policy on major questions which would be naturally apparent to 'reasonable men of all parties of the state',[2] Liberal Imperialists had misread the temper of their times. They were consistently taken aback by the fact that large groups of people—employers and trade unionists, nonconformists and anglicans, protectionists and free-traders, Ulstermen and catholics in Ireland—had genuine and profound differences about the nature of society and how it should be organized. Once in office, their policies were to be even more open to destruction from both sides. Much of the nation was unenthusiastic about their élitist pragmatism and declined to clean its slate for the benefit of Liberal Imperialist free play of judgement, and the principles of administrative convenience which lay behind it.

Liberal Imperialists thought that the criterion of efficiency could be used simultaneously to solve electoral and policy problems. The tariff reform campaign pushed efficiency into the background, and its effectiveness as an electoral slogan to win over the middle class to a responsible and patriotic Liberal party therefore cannot be measured. The patriotic aspect of the efficiency campaign probably had some effect. As Ensor has observed, the business classes were 'intensely

---

[1] Haldane in Dundee, *Dundee Advertiser*, 11 Oct. 1901.
[2] Asquith in Birmingham, *The Times*, 25 Feb. 1905.

patriotic',[1] and the Liberal Imperialists were therefore removing a reason why such classes would *not* vote Liberal.
Whether their patriotic stand actually encouraged many
businessmen to do so is uncertain.

The Liberal Imperialists hoped to persuade the middle
class to accept social reform as a patriotic duty, necessary for
the strengthening of the empire. They believed that effective
social reform was possible, while still maintaining 'the social
structure of the nation intact and unbroken'.[2] It was, however, highly doubtful whether the efficient society envisaged
by the collectivist wing of the Liberal League—a society
well fed, well housed, well educated, and well insured—
could in the circumstances revealed by Booth and Rowntree
be achieved without substantial social change.[3] Typical
middle-class and landed members of the Liberal League,
such as Perks and Sir Charles Tennant, realized this, and
the League was hampered by the unwillingness of its
wealthier members to support extensive social reform.

Rosebery came to appreciate this problem, and after 1905
declared with reference to Liberal land legislation that, if
faced by the 'formidable option between protection and
socialism . . . he would have no hesitation in preferring protection'.[4] The tendency of Liberal Imperialists to move
away from the centre, both to the 'right' and to the 'left',
is symbolized by the fact that after the First World War
Ferguson was Baldwin's Secretary of State for Scotland, and
Haldane was Ramsay MacDonald's Lord Chancellor.

As a criterion for policy making, efficiency, if carefully
defined, might, at least in principle, be a viable proposition;
but it was not viably employed by the Liberal Imperialists.
This comment has been made on the English Idealists, the
intellectual mentors of the efficiency men:

There is a valid and significant form of Idealism to be found in the
work of Bradley, Green, Bosanquet and Royce, but they failed to

---

[1] R. C. K. Ensor, 'Some Political and Economic Interactions in Late Victorian
England', *Transactions of the Royal Historical Society*, 4th series, xxxi (1949).
[2] Asquith in Leicester, *The Times*, 25 Oct. 1896.
[3] See Charles Booth, *Life and Labour of the People in London*, 1st ser.: *Poverty*
4 vols. (1902), *passim*, and B. S. Rowntree, *Poverty, a Study of Town Life* (1901),
passim.
[4] Rosebery to the Liberal League, *The Times*, 13 Mar. 1908.

develop it fully and consistently. They came nearest to doing so in their social philosophy. . . .[1]

The same is true of the Liberal Imperialists. Their programme of social reform was integrated, coherent, and based on a consistently held view of the nature of society and of the state. Its relevance and practicability could not be assessed until cabinet office was achieved. As it turned out, the political failure of the Liberal Imperialist movement meant that the attempted redress of nonconformist grievances took precedence after 1905.

But in imperial affairs efficiency was not successfully developed by the Liberal Imperialists. The problem was that though they talked often and at length about efficiency and the national interest, they had no clear conception of what they meant by these terms in the imperial context. Since they had not clearly defined what imperial efficiency really meant, they were at the mercy of men like Milner, who had a clear definition.[2]

The principle of continuity again assumed a general agreement on what was the right policy for the nation. But what if this agreement broke down, as it did between the Liberal Imperialists and Milner on South Africa, and between Grey and Rosebery on the Entente policy? It was all very well for Rosebery to say:

That was a great word 'Thorough', bequeathed to us by one of the most memorable of British statesmen: a great word, not as he used it, but a word in itself which should thrill through all mankind from the age of reason to the shadow of death.[3]

But if 'thorough' was not used as Strafford (and Milner) used it, what did it mean, and how was it to be employed?

Liberal Imperialists were ready to use concepts like efficiency rhetorically for party purposes, but they did not preserve the necessary distinction between the rhetoric of party and the reality of policy. They were unwilling to equip themselves with the knowledge to apply such concepts specifically, partly through intellectual laziness, and partly

[1] A. J. M. Milne, *The Social Philosophy of English Idealism* (1962), p. 314.
[2] See E. Stokes, 'Milnerism', *Historical Journal*, vol. 5, no. 1 (1962).
[3] Rosebery, *Miscellanies*, ii. 252 ('Questions of Empire').

because their belief in judgement as the essential factor in statesmanship conflicted with the expertise required for the working of efficiency.

All this is to judge the Liberal Imperialists by the exacting standards which they set the 'nation of amateurs' whose incompetence they so frequently condemned.[1] But it was not the custom of British statesmen to prepare themselves in detail for office, far less to attempt a group reconstruction of party doctrine and behaviour on the scale intended by the Liberal Imperialists. Compared with most of their Liberal colleagues, and compared with the intellectual disarray of the party as a whole, the Liberal Imperialists had a relatively consistent view of affairs, were well-informed and obviously able men, and were accepted as such by their party.

The Liberal Imperialist conception of the Liberal party as national and moderate was a necessary contribution to Liberal thinking if the party was to regain its predominant position. Their assumption that there were policies of the centre on which reasonable men could agree was an assumption which a democracy must make if it is to survive.

The survival of the Liberal party depended on its success in preventing the development of a class-oriented electorate. The Liberal Imperialists realized this, and it was this perception which conditioned their approach to ideas and to politics, and their use of imperialism in the domestic context was intended to be an antidote to the development of class antagonism. Although their strategy was defective in some aspects of its conception, and in almost all aspects of its execution, they had at least identified and attempted to solve, both ideologically and electorally, the central problem facing the Liberal party.

They had therefore tried to perform both a Radical and a Whiggish function. As Radicals they had developed ideas which in the context of the liberalism of the day, and particularly the liberalism of other front-bench Liberals, were advanced.[2] At the cross-roads of the two liberalisms,

---

[1] Ibid. ii. 252. Typical of Rosebery's slackness was his speech on Glasgow housing, 10 Mar. 1902, when he used statistics so inaccurate that they had to be withdrawn from the published version (LLP 3, p. 27).

[2] Asquith was described in *Dod's Parliamentary Companion* as an 'Advanced Radical' until 1904.

they had, from the top level of the party, clearly pointed the way from the old to the new. As Whigs they fulfilled Hartington's classic definition of being 'a connecting link between the advanced party and those classes which possessing property, power and influence are naturally averse to change'.[1]

Liberal Imperialists were, moreover, working in a confused political situation. Ostrogorski's view of the future of politics was almost a commonplace in *fin de siècle* Britain, especially amongst progressive politicians. It was certainly a view which both haunted and at times encouraged the Liberal Imperialists in the development of their Leagues and Councils: 'the crumbling of parties is the rule ... "down with party" and "up with League", that is the cry of the political evolution which is beginning to take place.'[2]

It was unclear whether the party system, and especially the Liberal party within that system, could survive. If the Liberal party was to regain its position as the predominant national party, and assuming that the strategies of politicians could have an effect on electoral behaviour, the Liberal Imperialist combination of patriotism and social welfare was the most viable course developed for the Liberal party leadership to steer between the Scylla of Labour and the Charybdis of Unionism.

[1] See D. Southgate, *The Passing of the Whigs* (1962), p. 417.
[2] M. Ostrogorski, *Democracy and the Organisation of Political Parties* (1902), ii. 687–90.

APPENDIX I

Brief biographies of prominent Liberal Imperialists

ASQUITH, HERBERT HENRY (1852–1928); Liberal M.P., E. Fife, 1886–1918, Paisley, 1920–4; Home Secretary, 1892–5; vice-president Liberal League, 1902–10; Chancellor of Exchequer, 1905–8; Prime Minister, 1908–16; Earl of Oxford and Asquith, 1925; married Margot Tennant, 1894.

BOULTON, A. C. FOSTER (1862–1949); Canadian soldier and lawyer; Liberal M.P., Hunts., 1906–10, Hants, 1923; co-founder English Speaking Union.

BRASSEY, THOMAS (1836–1918); Liberal M.P., Hastings, 1868–86; at Admiralty, 1880–5; founded *Brassey's Naval Annual*, 1886; baron, 1886; governed Victoria, 1895–1900; chairman, Imperial Liberal Council, 1900–1; Liberal League councillor.

BRASSEY, THOMAS A. (1863–1919); son of T. Brassey; contested as a Liberal, Epsom, 1892, Christchurch, 1895, 1900, Devonport, 1902; became a Unionist, 1903; civil commissioner Pretoria, 1900.

CAMPBELL, REGINALD J. (1867–1956); congregational minister, 1895; methodist minister City Temple, 1903; anglican priest, 1916; Liberal League councillor; author and pamphleteer.

COOK, EDWARD T. (1857–1919); edited *Pall Mall Gazette*, 1890–2, *Westminster Gazette*, 1892–6, *Daily News*, 1896–1901, Ruskin's *Works*, 1903–11; Kt., 1911; Liberal League councillor.

DOUGLAS, CHARLES M. (1865–1924); philosophy lecturer, Edinburgh university, ?1892–9; Liberal M.P., N.W. Lanarkshire, 1899–1906; contested S. Lanarkshire as Unionist, 1910; agriculturalist.

EMMOTT, ALFRED (1858–1926); cotton merchant; Liberal M.P., Oldham, 1899–1911; Commons committee chairman, 1906; Under-Secretary Colonies, 1911; Commissioner of Works, 1914; directed War Trade Dept.; baron, 1911; Liberal Leaguer.

FOWLER, HENRY HARTLEY (1830–1911); Wolverhampton solicitor, 1855, mayor, 1863; Liberal M.P., Wolverhampton, 1880–1908; Under-Secretary Home Office, 1884; financial secretary Treasury, 1886; President, Local Gvnt. Board, 1892–4; Indian Secretary, 1894–5; vice-president Liberal League, 1902–10; Chancellor, Duchy of Lancaster, 1905–8; Lord President, 1908–10; Viscount Wolverhampton, 1908.

FREEMAN-THOMAS, FREEMAN (1866–1941); joint secretary Liberal League, 1902–10; Liberal M.P., Hastings, 1900–6, Bodmin, 1906–10; Baron Willingdon, 1910; George V's tennis partner; governed Bombay, Madras, Canada, 1913–30; Viceroy of India, 1931–6; Marquess, 1936; Brassey's son-in-law.

FULLER, JOHN M. F. (1864–1915); A.D.C. Indian Viceroy, 1894–5; Liberal M.P., Wilts., 1900–11; junior whip, 1906; governed Victoria, 1911–14; Bt., 1910.

GIBSON-CARMICHAEL, THOMAS D. (1859–1926); 11th Bt., 1891; Liberal M.P., Midlothian, 1895–1900; chairman, Scot. Lib. Assoc., 1892–1903; Liberal League councillor; governed Victoria, 1908–11, Madras, 1911–12, Bengal, 1912–17; baron, 1912.

GLEN-COATS, THOMAS (1846–1922); merchant, landowner, and soldier; Bt., 1894; Liberal League councillor; Liberal M.P., Renfrewshire, 1906–10.

GREY, EDWARD (1862–1933); 3rd Bt., 1882; Liberal M.P., Berwick-on-Tweed, 1885–1916; Under-Secretary Foreign Office, 1892–5; president Imperial Liberal Council, 1901; vice-president Liberal League, 1902–10; chairman, N.E. Railway, 1904; Foreign Secretary, 1905–16; Viscount, 1916.

HALDANE, RICHARD BURDON (1856–1928); Liberal M.P., E. Lothian, 1885–1911; vice-president Liberal League, 1905–10; Secretary for War, 1905–12; Lord Chancellor, 1912–15, 1924; Viscount, 1911.

HAMILTON, EDWARD WALTER (1847–1908); private secretary to R. Lowe, 1872–3, to Gladstone, 1873–4, 1880–5; joined Treasury, 1885, assist. secretary, 1894, permanent financial secretary and joint permanent secretary, 1902–7; K.C.B., 1894.

HARMSWORTH, R. LEICESTER (1870–1937); Liberal M.P., Caithness, 1900–22; co-founder of *New Liberal Review*; Liberal League councillor; brother of Northcliffe; bibliomaniac; Bt., 1918.

HART, HEBER LEONIDAS (1865–1948); LL.D., London, 1893; Liberal candidate, S. Islington, 1895, Windsor, 1910; chairman Imperial Liberal Council committee, 1900, but never a Liberal Leaguer; K.C., 1913; chairman Eighty Club, 1916; member Mixed Arbitral Tribune.

KEARLEY, HUDSON E. (1856–1934); founded International Stores, 1880; Liberal M.P., Devonport, 1892–1910; Liberal League councillor; Parl. Secretary Board of Trade, 1905–9; chairman Port of London, 1909–25; Baron Devonport, 1910; food controller, 1916.

MCARTHUR, WILLIAM A. (1857–c. 1925); born in New S. Wales; colonial merchant and banker; Liberal M.P., Buckrose, 1886–7, St. Austell, 1887–1908; junior whip, 1892–1905.

MUNRO-FERGUSON, Ronald C. (1860–1934); Grenadier guards, 1879–84; Liberal M.P., Ross and Cromarty, 1884–5, Leith Burghs, 1886–1914; Rosebery's personal private secretary, 1886, 1892–4; Scot. Lib. whip, 1894–1900; governed Australia, 1914–20; Viscount Novar, 1920; Unionist Secretary of State for Scotland, 1922–4.

NORMAN, Henry (1858–1939); assist. editor *Daily News*, 1895–9; Liberal M.P., S. Wolverhampton, 1900–10, Blackburn, 1910–23; founded Liberal Imperialist *World's Work*, 1902; wrote on Far East; Liberal League councillor.

PAULTON, James M. (1857–1923); war correspondent in Sudan; assist. private secretary to Asquith, 1893–5; Liberal M.P., Bishop Auckland, 1885–1910; joint secretary Liberal League, 1902–10.

PERKS, Robert W. (1849–1934); solicitor, financier, and methodist; Liberal M.P., Louth, 1892–1910; founded nonconformist parl. committee, 1898; vice-president Imperial Lib. Council, 1900; treasurer Liberal League, 1902–10; Bt. 1908.

PRIMROSE, Archibald Philip (1847–1928); 5th Earl Rosebery, 1868; Under-Secretary Home Office, 1881–3; toured empire, 1883–4; Lord Privy Seal, 1885; Foreign Secretary, 1886, 1892–4; president Imperial Federation League, 1887; chairman L.C.C., 1889–90; Prime Minister, 1894–5; president Liberal League, 1902–9; his horses won Derby, 1894, 1895, 1905.

REID, Thomas Wemyss (1842–1905); worked on provincial papers and edited *Leeds Mercury*, 1870–87; founded and edited *Speaker*, 1890–7; Kt., 1894; Liberal League councillor; biographer.

TENNANT, Charles (1823–1906); chemical manufacturer and landowner; Liberal M.P., Glasgow, 1879–80, Peebles, 1880–6; Bt., 1885; Liberal League councillor; Tariff Commissioner, 1904; father of Margot Asquith.

THURSFIELD, James Richard (1840–1923); Fellow of Jesus, Oxford, 1864–81; historian; writer on naval affairs; *Times* leader-writer on naval topics from 1887; Kt., 1920.

WALTON, John Lawson (1852–1908); Q.C., 1890; Liberal M.P., S. Leeds, 1892–1908; Liberal League councillor; Attorney-General, 1905–8.

WALTON, Joseph (1849–1923); merchant and 'Old China Hand'; Liberal M.P., Barnsley, 1897–1923; Liberal Leaguer.

WEBB, Sidney J. (1859–1947); colonial office civil servant; Fabian; on L.C.C. 1892–1910; labour M.P., Seaham, 1922–9; president, board of trade, 1924; Baron Passfield, 1929; secretary for colonies, 1929–31; Liberal League councillor; married Beatrice Potter, 1892.

APPENDIX II

Winning and losing Liberal League members in the 1906 General Election, taken from Perks's Memorandum, 27 January 1906, RP, Box 107

(Names and initials corrected where necessary)

Liberal League members elected M.P.

Agar-Robartes, T. C. R.	Grey, Sir E.	Nicholls, G.
Annand, J.	Haldane, R. B.	Paulton, J. M.
Armitage, R.	Hardy, G. A.	Pearson, Sir W. D.
Asquith, H. H.	Harmsworth, C. B.	Perks, R. W.
Astbury, J. M.	Harmsworth, R. L.	Raphael, H. H.
Barker, J.	Haslam, J.	Renton, Major A. Leslie
Barran, R. H.	Hazel, A. E. W.	Rose, C. D.
Beauchamp, E.	Hooper, A. G.	Scarisbrick, T. T. L.
Beck, A. C. T.	Hyde, Clarendon G.	Stewart-Smith, D.
Benn, J. Williams	Idris, T. H. W.	Tennant, E. P.
Boulton, A. C. Foster	Isaacs, R. D.	Tennant, H. J.
Chance, F. W.	Jones, D. Brynmor	Walters, J. T.
Cory, C. J.	Kearley, H. E.	Walton, J. Lawson
Cowan, W. H.	Kincaid-Smith, Capt. M.	Waterlow, D. S.
Dalmeny, Lord	Marnham, F. J.	Watt, H. A.
Emmott, A.	Montagu, E. S.	Wedgwood, J. C.
Faber, G. H.	Morgan, G. H.	Whitbread, S. H.
Fowler, Sir H. H.	Morrell, Philip	Whitehead, R. E.
Fuller, J. M. F.	Munro-Ferguson, R. C.	
Glen-Coats, Sir T. G.	Napier, T. B.	Lynch, H. F. B. (considers himself a Leaguer [Perks's note])

Total, excluding Lynch = 58

Liberal League members who stood but were not elected

Andrews, J. O.	Harben, H. D.	Morison, H.
Aston, A. W.	Hutchinson, Dr. C. F.	Pearson, H. W.
Benson, G. R.	Hutton, A. H.	Ridgeway, Sir J. West
Benson, P. G. R.	Lambert, R. C.	Schuster, Felix O.
Douglas, C. M.	Lawrence, A. W.	Somerset, H. S.
Ellice, Capt. E. C.	Lennard, T. J.	White, J. M.
Fisher, W. J.	Lister, R. A.	Whyte, R.
Freeman-Thomas, F.	Mendl, S. F.	
Grant, A.	Money-Coutts, H. B.	

Total = 25

Grand Total = 84 (including Lynch)

For Gladstone's undated [? 1905] list of League candidates who were not already sitting as M.P.s, see HGP 46107, f. 39, printed in M. Craton and H. W. McCready, *The Great Liberal Revival 1903–6* (Hansard Society Pamphlet 1966). Gladstone's list includes the following who stood in 1906 but are not in Perks's memorandum above: A. P. Hedges, C. S. Henry, J. D. Rees, J. E. Sears (elected); C. W. B. Prescott (not elected).

Other rather arbitrary and unreliable lists of Liberal Leaguers by Herbert Gladstone are in HGP 46107, ff. 39–40.

APPENDIX III

Asquith's Draft Liberal League Manifesto

The manuscript has no title and no date [? March 1902]; it is marked
Confidential. The additions in brackets and the excisions were made later
by Rosebery (RP, box 106).

1. If Liberalism is to regain its old position in the confidence of the
people it must be Progressive (Practical) and National.

2. It is in this spirit that the Liberal League has been founded. It
takes its stand & starting point in the doctrine & policy put forward
by its President, Lord Rosebery, in his speech at Chesterfield.

3. Its object is not to create or organise a section, but to serve &
promote the interests of the party.

4. It aims at a vigorous prosecution of the war until a satisfactory
settlement may be obtained, which will secure the pacification of
South Africa: that settlement to be on liberal and magnanimous terms.

5. As regards both Imperial and domestic policy, it considers that the
position of the Liberal party demands concentration of aim, recon-
sideration of methods, and a fresh start.

6. It does not aspire to prescribe a programme, but it believes that
there is much both at home and abroad which can be done by Liberals
best, or by Liberals alone.

7. The League has especially in view the social and economic
problems, so long neglected or postponed, of education, temperance,
housing, poor law reform, land tenure, & local taxation.

Not less serious, and calling with equal urgency for the application
of liberal ideas and methods, are such questions as the further development of the Constitution required by the growth of the Empire, the
relations between the two Houses of Parliament, and the gradual
provision of better machinery for the distribution and management
of Imperial and local affairs.

While the League holds that in the sphere of administration and
particularly in the conduct of our foreign relations and in the organisation of Imperial defence, there should be (so far as possible) continuity
of policy, it sees the need in this department also of greater energy

and efficiency, & of a close correspondence between expenditure and result.

It is hoped that the League will be a centre of communication & common effort for ~~Liberals~~ (those) who share these views & desire to give them practical effect.

The officers etc. etc. etc.

BIBLIOGRAPHY

All printed matter is published in London unless otherwise indicated.

I. PRIVATE PAPERS

*Wholly or partly unfoliated; references are as complete as possible. The Rosebery Papers when foliated will have an index to facilitate cross-referencing from box to volume numbers.

In the British Museum:

Balfour Papers
Burns (John) Papers
Campbell-Bannerman Papers
Dilke Papers
Gladstone (Herbert) Papers
Gladstone (W. E.) Papers
*Hamilton (Edward) Papers
Ripon Papers
Shaw (G. B.) Papers
Spender (J. A.) Papers

In the Bodleian Library:

Acland (Sir Thomas Dyke) Papers
*Asquith Papers
*Bryce Papers
Creighton Papers
*Hammond Papers
*Milner Papers
Morley–Carnegie correspondence (microfilm)

In the National Library of Scotland:
Haldane Papers
*Rosebery Papers

In Birmingham University Library:
*Allard Papers
Chamberlain (Joseph) Papers

In Edinburgh University Library:
Minute Book of the Scottish Liberal Association

In the London School of Economics Library:
Passfield Papers

In the Library of Congress:
Carnegie (Andrew) Papers

In the Beaverbrook Library:
Lloyd George Papers
Strachey (J. St. Loe) Papers

In private possession:
*Buxton Papers, in the possession of Mrs. E. Clay.
*Ferguson Papers, in the possession of A. B. L. Munro-Ferguson.
*Harcourt Papers, in the possession of Lord Harcourt.
*Perks Papers, by courtesy of Keith Robbins and Sir Malcolm Perks.

Grey's papers, and some of Munro-Ferguson's papers, were used by G. M. Trevelyan, but have not been subsequently traced.

II. OFFICIAL PRINTED SOURCES

(a) *Parliamentary Papers*

1895	LXX	C. 7824	(Ripon's letter to Governors-General)
1895	XLIII	C. 7862	(Bryce Royal Commission on Secondary Education)
1896	XXXIII	C. 8262	(Royal Commission on Anglo-Irish Financial Relations)
1898	L	C. 8655	(Royal Commission on the West Indies)

1899	XXXV	C. 9379	(Final Report of the Peel Royal Commission on Liquor Licensing Laws)
1903	XL	Cd. 1491	(Report of the Committee on Naval Reserves, Chairman, Sir E. Grey)
1903	XL	Cd. 1789	(Elgin Royal Commission on the War in South Africa)

(*b*) *Hansard*

Hansard's Parliamentary Debates, 1885–1914; third, fourth, and fifth series.

III. UNOFFICIAL PRINTED DOCUMENTARY SOURCES
(Documents, Speeches, Letters, and Diaries)

Asquith, H. H., *Speeches, 1892–1908* (1908), reprinted from *The Times*.
—— *Occasional Addresses 1893–1916* (1918).
Brassey, T. A., *Problems of Empire: Papers and Addresses* (1904).
Brassey, Lord (ed. A. H. Loring), *Papers and Addresses Political and Miscellaneous 1861–1894* (1895).
—— *Papers and Addresses: Imperial Federation and Colonisation* (1938).
Brett, R. (ed. M. V. Brett), *Journals and Letters of Reginald Viscount Esher* (4 vols., 1934–8).
Bullock, A., and Shock, M. (eds.), *The Liberal Tradition from Fox to Keynes* (1956).
Campbell-Bannerman, Sir H. (ed. *The Times*), *Speeches by the Rt. Hon. Sir Henry Campbell-Bannerman . . . 1899–1908* (1908).
Craigmyle, Lord (i.e. T. Shaw), *Letters to Isabel* (1936).
Fitzroy, Sir Almeric, *Memoirs* (vol. i, n.d.).
Gooch, G. P., and Temperley, H. (eds.), *British Documents on the Origins of the War, 1898–1914* (11 vols., 1926–30).
Grey, Sir E. (ed. P. Knaplund), *Speeches on Foreign Affairs 1904–1914 by Sir Edward Grey* (1931).
Haldane, R. B., *Education and Empire* (1902) (collected speeches).
—— *Army Reform and other Addresses* (1907).
—— *Selected Addresses and Essays* (1928).
Milner, A. (ed. C. Headlam), *The Milner Papers* (2 vols., 1931–3).
Rice, C. Spring (ed. S. Gwynn), *The Letters and Friendships of Sir Cecil Spring Rice* (2 vols., 1929).
Rosebery, Lord (ed. C. Geake), *Appreciations and Addresses* (1899).
—— (ed. anon.), *Lord Rosebery's Speeches* (*1874–1896*) (1896).
—— (ed. John Buchan), *Miscellanies, Literary and Historical* (2 vols., 1921).
—— (ed. anon.), *The Foreign Policy of Lord Rosebery* (1901).

Webb, Beatrice (ed. B. Drake and M. I. Cole), *Our Partnership* (1948).

Webb, Beatrice, *My Apprenticeship* (1926).

West, Sir A. (ed. H. G. Hutchinson), *Private Diaries of the Rt. Hon. Sir Algernon West, G.C.B.* (1922).

IV. PRESS, PERIODICALS, AND PAMPHLETS

(*a*) Newspapers

> *Daily Chronicle*
> *Daily Mail*
> *Daily News*
> *Dundee Advertiser*
> *Glasgow Herald*
> *Pall Mall Gazette*
> *The Scotsman*
> *The Times*
> *Westminster Gazette*

(*b*) Periodicals

> *Commonwealth*
> *Contemporary Review*
> *Empire Review*
> *Fortnightly Review*
> *Free Church Year Book*
> *Imperial Federation Journal*
> *Independent Review*
> *Liberal Magazine*
> *Monthly Review*
> *National Review*
> *National Service Journal*
> *New Liberal Review*
> *Nineteenth Century and After*
> *North American Review*
> *Progressive Review*
> *Review of Reviews*
> *Royal United Service Institution Journal*
> *Speaker*
> *Spectator*
> *The Liberal*
> *World's Work*

(*c*) Liberal League publications

Between March 1902 and December 1905 the League published nearly 200 pamphlets, most of which are held in the London School of Economics. Many were reprints of speeches, but some contained original material; the most important of the latter are listed below, with attribution where possible.

(No number) *Liberal League Manifesto* (May 1902).

LLP 1 *National Policy, with a Preface by Lord Rosebery* (the Chesterfield speech) (1902).

LLP 3 *Lord Rosebery in Liverpool and Glasgow, with a Preface by Lord Rosebery* (1902).

LLP 10 *Liberalism and Labour* (1902) (long pamphlet ? by J. M. Paulton).

LLP 11 *Higher Education in Germany* (n.d. [1902]).

LLP 14 *To Whom do we Owe the Peace?* (1902).

LLP 18 *The Principles of the Liberal League* (n.d. [1902]).

LLP 19 *The Corn Tax and British Commercial Policy* (1902) (long pamphlet).

LLP 20 *Speeches Delivered at the First Liberal League Dinner* (1902) (contains an attendance list).

LLP 21 *The Urgent Need for a Definite Naval Policy* (1902) (long pamphlet ? by J. R. Thursfield).

LLP 29 *Unionist Muddle and Waste: the Tories and the Navy* (1902).

LLP 31 *The Liberal League: its Purpose and its Progress* (1902).

LLP 64 *Wanted! Efficiency, not Tariffs: the Lesson of the Tinplate Trade* (1903).

LLP 74 *An 'Improvised' Army* (1903).

LLP 75 *The War Scandals: the Ignorance of the Tory Government* (1903).

LLP 76 *Lord Rosebery and the War Office Scandals* (1903).

LLP 119 *How Goods Pay for Goods: the Economics of International Free Trade* (1904) (long pamphlet).

LLP 128 *A London Banker on Mr. Chamberlain's Plan* (1904) (long pamphlet by Edgar Speyer).

LLP 129 *The New Slavery: the Case against Chinese Labour for the Transvaal* (1904).

LLP 130 *A Ministry of Labour: Mr. Asquith's Views* (1904).

LLP 135 *A White Man's Land: Liberal Imperial Policy on Transvaal Labour* (1904).

LLP 140 *To Protect Trade Unions* (1904).

LLP 141 *Why You Cannot Afford the Present Government* (1904).

LLP 158 *We Want Efficiency—Not Tariffs* (1904).

LLP 159 *The Risks of Retaliation—a Reply to Mr. Balfour* (1904).

LLP 167 *The Alien Bogey* (1905).

LLP 168 *How to Meet Competition* (1905).

(*d*) Contemporary articles on Imperial affairs

Arnold-Foster, H. O., 'The Liberal Idea and the Colonies', *Nineteenth Century*, vol. 14 (Sept. 1883).

Bellairs, Lt. Carlyon, 'The Responsibility of the Rulers for the Disturbances in China', *North American Review* (Aug. 1900).

Brassey, T. A., 'Can We Hold our Own at Sea?' *Fortnightly Review*, vol. 70 (July 1898).

Brett, Reginald, 'The Far Eastern Question', *Contemporary Review*, vol. 67 (Mar. 1895).

Dilke, Sir Charles, 'The Commander in Chief', *Empire Review* (Apr. 1901).

Walton, J. Lawson, 'Imperialism', *Contemporary Review*, vol. 75 (Mar. 1899).

(*e*) Contemporary pamphlets on Imperial affairs

A detailed survey of the very many pamphlets published during the Boer War will be found in J. S. Galbraith, 'The Pamphlet Campaign on the Boer War', *Journal of Modern History*, no. 24 (June 1952). No attempt is made here to cover the same ground.

Buxton, S. C., *Chinese Labour: the Transvaal Ordinance Analysed together with the British Guiana Ordinance* (Liberal Publication Dept.) (1904).

Haldane, R. B., *The Executive Brain of the Empire* (1905).

Hobhouse, E., *Report on a Visit to the Camps* (1901).

[Shaw, G. B.] Anon., *Fabianism and the Empire* (1900).

Shee, G. F., *The Briton's First Duty* (1901).

Stead, W. T., *The History of the Mystery* (1897).

—— *Shall I Slay my Brother Boer?* (1900).

(*f*) Contemporary articles on British affairs

Anon., 'Alien Immigration', *New Liberal Review*, no. 26 (Feb. 1903).

Cook, E. T., 'Lord Rosebery and the Copperheads', *Contemporary Review*, vol. 81 (1902).

—— 'Lord Rosebery and the Liberal Party', *New Liberal Review*, no. 7 (Aug. 1901).

Crewe, Lord, 'Ireland and the Liberal Party', *New Liberal Review*, no. 5 (June 1901).

—— 'The Outlook for Ireland', *North American Review*, vol. 119 (Sept. 1895).

Dell, R. E., 'Cleaning the Slate', *Monthly Review*, vol. 7 (1902).

Dilke, Sir Charles, 'Trade Unions and the Law', *Independent Review*, vol. 3 (June 1904).

Douglas, C. M., 'The Liberal League', *Contemporary Review*, vol. 81 (1902).

Duffield, W. B., 'The Inevitable Basis of Liberal Reunion', *New Liberal Review*, no. 28 (May 1903).

Farquharson, R., 'The Compleat Member', *New Liberal Review*, no. 15 (Apr. 1902).

Ferguson, R. M., 'Forestry—a "Depressed Industry" ', *Independent Review*, vol. 2 (1904).

Ferguson, R. M., 'The Drift of Land Reform', *Contemporary Review*, vol. 64 (Oct. 1893).

[Garvin, J. L.] Anon., 'A Palmerston—with Nerves', *Fortnightly Review*, vol. 72 (July 1899).

[Garvin, J. L.] Anon., 'Educating the Liberals: Lord Rosebery and Home Rule', *Fortnightly Review*, vol. 71 (Feb. 1899).

Grey, Sir E., 'Mr. Chamberlain's Fiscal Policy', *Monthly Review*, vol. 13 (Oct. 1903).

—— 'The Autumn Campaign', *Independent Review*, vol. 2 (1904).

Haldane, R. B., 'Great Britain and Germany: a Study in Education', *Monthly Review*, vol. 6 (Nov. 1901).

—— 'Hegel', *Contemporary Review*, vol. 67 (1895).

—— 'The Cabinet and the Empire', *Proceedings of the Royal Colonial Institute*, vol. 34 (June 1903).

—— 'The Eight Hours Question', *Contemporary Review*, vol. 64 (Oct. 1893).

—— 'The Liberal Creed', *Contemporary Review*, vol. 54 (Oct. 1888).

—— 'The Liberal Party and its Prospects', *Contemporary Review*, vol. 53 (Jan. 1888).

—— 'Lord Salisbury and the House of Lords', *National Review*, vol. 24 (Jan. 1895).

—— 'The New Liberalism', *Progressive Review*, vol. 1 (Nov. 1896).

Hart, Heber L., 'The Imperial Liberal Council', *New Liberal Review*, no. 3 (Apr. 1901).

Hirst, F. W., 'An Ideal Budget', *Independent Review*, vol. 7 (Dec. 1905).

Hobson, J. A., 'The Re-Statement of Democracy', *Contemporary Review*, vol. 81 (Feb. 1902).

Macpherson, Hector, 'Scottish Liberalism, Past and Present', *Speaker*, vol. 27 (June 1903).

'M.P.', 'The Liberal League', *New Liberal Review*, no. 15 (Apr. 1902).

Salisbury, Lord, 'Lord Rosebery's Plan', *National Review*, vol. 24 (Dec. 1894).

Samuel, H., 'The Budget and the Future Revenue', *New Liberal Review*, no. 5 (June 1901).

Spender, J. A., 'The Party Situation', *Contemporary Review*, vol. 84 (Nov. 1903).

—— 'Why I am a Liberal', *New Liberal Review*, no. 22 (Nov. 1902).

Trevelyan, C. P., 'The Future and the House of Lords', *Independent Review*, vol. 4 (Nov. 1904).

Webb, S., 'Lord Rosebery's Escape from Houndsditch', *Nineteenth Century and After*, vol. 50 (1901).

Webb, S., Samuel, H., *et al.*, 'How to Attain Liberal Unity', *New Liberal Review*, no. 21 (Oct. 1902).

(*g*) Contemporary pamphlets on British affairs

Anon. (Introduction by H. H. Asquith), *Employers' Liability* (1897).

Grey, Sir E., *Rural Land* (Eighty Club Pamphlet, 1892).

Haldane, R. B., *Constructive Liberalism* (Eighty Club Pamphlet, 1904).

—— *National Efficiency* (Eighty Club Pamphlet, 1906).

—— *Unearned Increment* (Eighty Club Pamphlet, 1892).

Liberal Colonial Club (membership list, 1907).

Liberal View (collection of Eighty Club articles, 1904).

MacColl, Revd. M., *The Education Question and the Liberal Party* (1902).

National Liberal Federation Annual Reports (1887–1905).

A Ratepayer (Introduction by R. B. Haldane), *National Efficiency and the Drink Traffic* (1906).

White, Arnold, *For Efficiency* (n.d.).

White, Arnold, and Wilson, H. W., *When War Breaks Out* (1898).

The National Liberal Club Library has an excellent collection for this period of association reports and election addresses of all parties.

V. BOOKS PUBLISHED BEFORE 1906

(*a*) Imperial affairs

Anon., 28 Years in India: *The Failure of Lord Curzon: an Open Letter to Lord Rosebery* (1903).

Brailsford, H. B., *The Broom of the War God* (1898).

Bryce, J. A., *Impressions of South Africa* (3rd ed. 1900).

Clarke, G. S., and Thursfield, J. R., *The Navy and the Nation* (1897).

Cook, E. T., *Rights and Wrongs of the Transvaal War* (1901, and rev. ed. 1902).

Cramb, J. A., *Reflections on the Origins and Destinies of Imperial Britain* (1900).

Dilke, Sir Charles, *Problems of Greater Britain* (2 vols., 2nd ed. 1890).

Dilke, Sir Charles, and Wilkinson, Spenser, *Imperial Defence* (1891).

Fitzpatrick, J. P., *The Transvaal from Within. A Private Record of Public Affairs* (1899).

Goldman, S. C. (ed.), *The Empire and the Century* (1905) (education chapter by Haldane).

Hirst, F. W., *et al.*, *Liberalism and the Empire* (1900).

Hobson, J. A., *Imperialism. A Study* (1902, and rev. ed. 1905).

Mahan, A. T., *The Influence of Sea Power upon History* (n.d. [1890]).

Milner, A., *England in Egypt* (1892).

Norman, Henry, *The People and Politics of the Far East* (New York, 1895).

Walton, J., *China and the Present Crisis* (1900).

(*b*) British affairs

Acland, A. H. D., and Jones, B., *Working Men Cooperators: What they have Done and What they are Doing* (1884).

Acland, A. H. D., and Smith, H. L. (eds.), *Studies in Secondary Education* (1902).

Ashley, P. (Preface by Haldane), *Modern Tariff History* (1904).

Asquith, H. H., *An Election Guide: Rules for the Conduct and Management of Elections in England and Wales under the Corrupt Practices Act, 1883* (1885).

[Barker, J. Ellis] Anon., *Drifting* (1901).

Booth, Charles, *Life and Labour of the People in London*; 1st ser.: *Poverty* (4 vols., 1902).

—— *Pauperism, a Picture, and the Endowment of Old Age, an Argument* (1892).

Buxton, S. C., *A Handbook to Political Questions of the Day* (7th. ed., 1888).

—— *'Fair Trade': Its Impossibility* (1885).

—— *Finance and Politics: an Historical Study* (2 vols., 1888).

Chesterton, Cecil, *Gladstonian Ghosts* (n.d., ? 1904).

Clayden, P. W., *England under the Coalition* (1892).

Donisthorn, W., *Law in a Free State* (1895).

Douglas, C. M., *John Stuart Mill* (1895).

Ely, R. T., *Socialism, its Nature, Strength and Weaknesses* (1894) (contains a good bibliography).

Green, T. H., *Lectures on the Principles of Political Obligation* (1895).

Haldane, R. B., *The Pathway to Reality* (2 vols., 1904–5).

Hobhouse, L. T., *Democracy and Reaction* (1904).

—— (Preface by Haldane), *The Labour Movement* (1893).

Marston, R. B., *War, Famine and our Food Supply* (1897).

Masterman, C. F. G., *In Peril of Change* (1905).

Masterman, C. F. G., *et al.*, *The Heart of the Empire* (1901).

Money, L. G. Chiozza, *Riches and Poverty* (1905).

Morley, J., *On Compromise* (1874).

—— *The Life of William Ewart Gladstone* (3 vols., 1903).

Ostrogorski, M., *Democracy and the Organisation of Political Parties* (2 vols., English translation 1902).

Reid, A. (ed.), *The House of Lords Question* (1898).

Reid, A. (ed.), *The New Party Described by Some of its Members* (1894).

Rowntree, B. S., *Poverty, a Study of Town Life* (1901).

Samuel, Herbert (Preface by Asquith), *Liberalism. An Attempt to State the Principles and proposals of Contemporary Liberalism in England* (1902).

Spender, J. A. (Preface by A. H. D. Acland), *The State and Pensions in Old Age* (1892).

Stead, W. T., *Coming Men on Coming Questions* (1905).

Stead, W. T. (Preface by Rosebery), *Great Japan: a Study in National Efficiency* (n.d., ? 1905).

Webb, S., *London Education* (1904).
—— *The London Programme* (1891).
—— *Wanted: a Programme; an Appeal to the Liberal Party* (1888).
White, Arnold, *Efficiency and Empire* (1901).

VI. BIOGRAPHICAL MATERIAL ON
PRINCIPAL LIBERAL IMPERIALISTS

ASQUITH

Alderson, J. P., *Mr. Asquith* (1905).
Asquith, E. Margot, *The Autobiography of Margot Asquith* (2 vols., 1920).
Elias, Frank, *H. H. Asquith* (1909).
Jenkins, Roy, *Asquith* (1964).
McCallum, R. B., *Asquith* (1936).
Oxford and Asquith, Earl of, *Fifty Years of Parliament* (2 vols., 1926).
—— *Memories and Reflections, 1852–1927* (2 vols., 1928).
Spender, E. Harold, *Herbert Henry Asquith* (n.d., ? 1915).
Spender, J. A., and Asquith, Cyril, *Life of Herbert Henry Asquith, Lord Oxford and Asquith* (2 vols., 1932).

FOWLER

Fowler, E. H., *The Life of Henry Hartley Fowler, First Lord Wolverhampton, G.C.S.I.* (1912).

GREY

Anon., *Sir Edward Grey, K. G.* (n.d.—*c.* 1918).
Buxton, Lord, *Edward Grey, Bird Lover and Fisherman* (1933).
Grey of Fallodon, Viscount, *Twenty-Five Years 1892–1916* (2 vols., 1925).
Grey of Fallodon, Lord, *Some Thoughts on Public Life* (Earl Grey Memorial Lecture, 1923).
Murray, A. C., *Lord Grey of Fallodon* (1947).
'Politicus' [D. P. Playfair], *Viscount Grey of Fallodon* (1934).
Robbins, Keith, *Sir Edward Grey. A Biography of Lord Grey of Fallodon* (1971).
Trevelyan, G. M., *Grey of Fallodon* (1937).

HALDANE

Grey, Viscount, *Viscount Haldane of Cloan, the Man and his Work* (1928).
Haldane, E. S. (ed.), *Mary Elizabeth Haldane 1825–1925* (n.d., ? 1926).
Haldane, E. S., *From One Century to Another* (1937).
Haldane, Sir J. A. L., *The Haldanes of Gleneagles* (Edinburgh, 1929).
Haldane, L. K., *Friends and Kindred* (1961).
Haldane, Richard Burdon, *An Autobiography* (1929).

Heuston, R. F. V., *The Lives of the Lord Chancellors 1885–1940* (Oxford, 1964).

Koss, S. E., *Lord Haldane, Scapegoat for Liberalism* (1969).

Maurice, Sir F. B., *Haldane* (2 vols., 1937–9).

Morgan, J. H., *The Riddle of Lord Haldane* (*Quarterly Review* reprint, Apr. 1929).

Sommer, D., *Haldane of Cloan* (1960).

Wilson, C. H., *Haldane and the Machinery of Government* (1956).

PERKS

Crane, D., *The Life-story of Sir Robert W. Perks, Baronet, M.P.* (1909).

Perks, Sir Robert, *Notes for an Autobiography* (privately printed, 1936).

ROSEBERY

Coates, T. F. G., *Lord Rosebery, his Life and Speeches* (2 vols., 1900).

Crewe, Marquess of, *Lord Rosebery* (2 vols., 1931).

Hammerton, J. A., *Lord Rosebery, Imperialist* (1901).

James, Robert Rhodes, *Rosebery* (1963).

Raymond, E. T., *The Man of Promise: Lord Rosebery* (1923).

Renwick, James, *Life and Work of Lord Rosebery* (1909).

Stoddart, Jane T., *The Earl of Rosebery, K.G. An Illustrated Biography* (1900).

VII. SOME SELECTED SECONDARY WORKS

Adam, R., and Muggeridge, K., *Beatrice Webb* (1967).

Amery, L. S., *My Political Life*, vol. i (1953).

Askwith, Lord, *Lord James of Hereford* (1930).

Asquith, H. H., *The Genesis of the War* (1923).

Beachey, R. W., *The British West Indies Sugar Industry in the Late 19th Century* (Oxford, 1957).

Bealey, F. W., and Pelling, H., *Labour and Politics, 1900–1906* (1958).

Bedwell, C. E. A. (Preface by Rosebery), *The Legislation of the Empire* (4 vols., 1909).

Beloff, M., *Imperial Sunset*, vol. i: *Britain's Liberal Empire 1897–1921* (1969).

Brown, B. H., *The Tariff Reform Movement in Great Britain 1881–1895* (1943).

Butler, J., *The Liberal Party and the Jameson Raid* (Oxford, 1968).

—— *Boston University Papers in African History* (vol. i, Boston, 1964) (on Milner).

Cambridge History of the British Empire (vols. iii and vii, Cambridge, 1959–62).

Campbell, C. S., *Anglo-American Understanding 1898–1903* (Baltimore, 1957).

Churchill, R. S., *Winston S. Churchill* (vols. i and ii, with companion vols., 1966–7).

Clegg, H. A., Fox, A., and Thompson, A. F., *A History of British Trade Unions since 1889* (vol. i, Oxford, 1964).

Cole, M. I. (ed.), *The Webbs and their Work* (1949).

Corder, P., *The Life of Robert Spence Watson* (1914).

Craton, M., and McCready, H. W., *The Great Liberal Revival 1903–6* (Hansard Soc. pamphlet, 1966).

Dangerfield, G., *The Strange Death of Liberal England* (1936).

Dilks, D., *Curzon in India* (2 vols., 1969–70).

Edwards, M. L., *Methodism and England, 1850–1932* (1943).

Ellis, T. I., *Thomas Edward Ellis Cofiant* (1948).

Fraser, P., *Joseph Chamberlain, Radicalism and Empire, 1868–1914* (1966).

Gardiner, A. G., *The Life of Sir William Harcourt* (2 vols., 1923).

—— *Prophets, Priests and Kings* (1908).

Garvin, J. L., and Amery, J., *The Life of Joseph Chamberlain* (6 vols., 1933–69).

Gibbs, N. H., *The Origins of Imperial Defence* [inaugural lecture] (Oxford, 1955).

Gilbert, B. B., *The Evolution of National Insurance in Great Britain: the Origins of the Welfare State* (1966).

Gilbert, M. (ed.), *A Century of Conflict, 1850–1950, Essays for A. J. P. Taylor* (1966).

Gollin, A. M., *Proconsul in Politics* (1964).

Grenville, J. A. S., *Lord Salisbury and Foreign Policy: the Close of the Nineteenth Century* (1964).

Gwynn, D., *The Life of John Redmond* (1932).

Gwynn, S., and Tuckwell, G. M., *The Life of the Rt. Hon. Sir Charles W. Dilke* (2 vols., 1917).

Haldane, Viscount, *Before the War* (1920).

Halévy, E., *A History of the English People in the Nineteenth Century* (vol. v: *Imperialism and the Rise of Labour*, and vol. vi: *The Rule of Democracy*, 1961 ed.).

Hamer, D. A., *John Morley, Liberal Intellectual in Politics* (Oxford, 1968).

Hanes, D. G., *The First British Workmen's Compensation Act, 1897* (Yale, 1968).

Hart, Heber L., *Reminiscences and Reflections* (1939).

Hewins, W. A. S., *The Apologia of an Imperialist* (2 vols., 1929).

Hirst, F. W., *In the Golden Days* (1947).

Horner, Lady F. J., *Time Remembered* (1933).

Howard, C. H. D., *Splendid Isolation* (1967).

Hurst, M., *Joseph Chamberlain and Liberal Reunion, the Round Table Conference of 1887* (1967).

Hyam, R., *Elgin and Churchill at the Colonial Office 1905–1908* (1968).

Jones, Henry, *Liberalism and the House of Lords* (1912).

Keeton, G. W., *A Liberal Attorney-General, Lord Robson of Jesmond* (1949).

Kendle, J. E., *The Colonial and Imperial Conferences 1887–1911* (1967).

Keynes, J. M., *Indian Currency and Finance* (1913).

Kiewiet, C. W. de, *The Imperial Factor in South Africa* (Cambridge, 1937).

Kilbracken, Lord, *Reminiscences* (1931).

Koebner, R., and Schmidt, H. D., *Imperialism: the Story and Significance of a Political Word, 1840–1960* (Cambridge, 1964).

Langer, W. L., *The Diplomacy of Imperialism 1890–1902* (2nd ed., New York, 1960).

Le May, G. H. L., *British Supremacy in South Africa 1899–1907* (Oxford, 1965).

Lloyd George, D., *War Memoirs* (2nd ed., 2 vols., 1938).

Lockhart, J. G., and Wodehouse, C. M., *Rhodes* (1963).

Lowe, C. J., *The Reluctant Imperialists: British Foreign Policy 1878–1902* (2 vols., 1967).

Lyons, F. S. L., *John Dillon* (1968).

—— *The Irish Parliamentary Party 1890–1910* (1951).

Maccoby, S., *English Radicalism, 1886–1914* (1953).

McKenzie, R. T., and Silver, A., *Angels in Marble* (1968).

Mallet, Sir C., *Herbert Gladstone, a Memoir* (1932).

Marais, J. S., *The Fall of Kruger's Republic* (Oxford, 1961).

Marder, A. J., *The Anatomy of British Sea Power* (Connecticut, reprint of 1964).

Marder, A. J. (ed.), *Fear God and Dread Nought* (1st vol., 1952).

Mills, J. Saxon, *Sir Edward Cook, K.B.E.* (1921).

Milne, A. J. M., *The Social Philosophy of English Idealism* (1962).

Monger, G. W., *The End of Isolation, British Foreign Policy 1900–1907* (1963).

Morgan, K. O., *Wales in British Politics 1868–1922* (Cardiff, 1963).

Morley, J., *Recollections* (2 vols., 1917).

Muirhead, J. H., *Bernard Bosanquet and his Friends* (1935).

Nevinson, H. W., *Changes and Chances* (1923).

Nish, I. H., *The Anglo-Japanese Alliance, the Diplomacy of Two Island Empires 1894–1914* (1966).

Partridge, F., *T. A. B. A memoir of Thomas Allnutt, 2nd Earl Brassey* (1921).

Pease, A. E., *Elections and Recollections* (1932).

Pelcovits, N. A., *Old China Hands and the Foreign Office* (New York, 1948).

Pelling, H., *Popular Politics and Society in Late Victorian Britain* (1968).

—— *Social Geography of British Elections 1885–1910* (1967).

Petrie, Sir C., *Scenes of Edwardian Life* (1965).

Pope-Hennessy, J., *Lord Crewe 1858–1945, the Likeness of a Liberal* (1955).

Porter, B., *Critics of Empire, British Radical Attitudes to Colonialism in Africa 1895–1914* (1968).

Pound, R., and Harmsworth, G., *Northcliffe* (1959).

Pyrah, G. B., *Imperial Policy and South Africa 1902–10* (Oxford, 1955).

Robinson, R., and Gallagher, J. A., with Denny, A., *Africa and the Victorians, the Official Mind of Imperialism* (1961).

Rowland, P., *The Last Liberal Governments* (1st vol., 1968).

Sacks, B., *The Religious Issue in the State Schools of England and Wales 1902–1914* (Albuquerque, 1961).

Samuel, Viscount, *Memoirs* (1945).

Sanderson, G. N., *England, Europe and the Upper Nile 1882–1899* (Edinburgh, 1965).

Schreuder, D. M., *Gladstone and Kruger. Liberal Government and Colonial Home Rule 1880–85* (1969).

Schumpeter, J. A. (ed. Sweezy, P. M.), *Imperialism and Social Classes* (Oxford, 1951).

Semmel, B., *Imperialism and Social Reform* (1960).

Shephard, E. H., *Drawn from Life* (1961).

Southgate, D., *The Passing of the Whigs 1832–1886* (1962).

Spender, J. A., *The Life of the Rt. Hon. Sir Henry Campbell-Bannerman, G.C.B.* (2 vols., n.d. [1923]).

Stansky, P., *Ambitions and Strategies* (Oxford, 1964).

Steiner, Z., *The Foreign Office and Foreign Policy 1898–1914* (Cambridge, 1970).

Stokes, E., *The Political Ideals of English Imperialism* (inaugural lecture, 1960).

Taylor, A. J. P., *The Struggle for Mastery in Europe 1848–1918* (Oxford, 1954).

—— *The Trouble Makers. Dissent over Foreign Policy 1792–1939* (1964).

Thompson, L. M., *The Unification of South Africa 1902–1910* (Oxford, 1960).

Thornton, A. P., *The Imperial Idea and its Enemies* (1959).

Tyler, J. E., *The Struggle for Imperial Unity 1868–1895* (1938).

Wells, H. G., *The New Machiavelli* (2nd ed., 1911).

Wolf, L., *Life of the First Marquess of Ripon* (2 vols., 1921).

Woodward, E. L., *Great Britain and the German Navy* (Oxford, 1935).

VIII. LEARNED ARTICLES AND THESES

Butler, J., 'The Liberal Party and South Africa 1895–1902' (Oxford D.Phil. thesis, 1963).

Cumpston, M., 'Some Early Indian Nationalists and their Allies in the British Parliament 1851–1906', *English Historical Review*, lxxvi (1961).

Dunbabin, J. P. D., 'Parliamentary Elections in Great Britain 1868–1900', *English Historical Review*, lxxxi (1966).

Edwards, M. S., 'S. E. Keeble and Nonconformist Social Thinking, 1888–1939' (Bristol M.Litt. thesis, 1969).

Ensor, R. C. K., 'Some Political and Economic Interactions in Late Victorian England', *Transactions of the Royal Historical Society*, 4th ser., xxxi (1949).

Fox, K. O., 'Labour and Merthyr's Khaki Election of 1900', *Welsh History Review*, 2, no. 4 (1965).

Fraser, P., 'The Liberal Unionist Alliance: Chamberlain, Hartington and the Conservatives, 1886–1904', *English Historical Review*, lxxvii (1962).

Galbraith, John S., 'The Pamphlet Campaign on the Boer War', *Journal of Modern History*, no. 24 (June 1952).

Gilbert, B. B., 'The Grant of Responsible Government to the Transvaal: More Notes on a Myth', *Historical Journal*, x, no. 4 (1967).

Hamer, D. A., 'The Irish Question and Liberal Politics, 1886–1894', *Historical Journal*, xii, no. 3 (1969).

Harnetty, P., 'The Indian Cotton Duties Controversy, 1894–1896', *English Historical Review*, lxxvii (1962).

Hilborn, K. H. W., 'British Policy and Diplomacy in the Near East during the Liberal Administration, August 1892–June 1895' (Oxford D.Phil. thesis, 1960).

Hyam, R., 'Smuts and the Decision of the Liberal Government to grant Responsible Government to the Transvaal, January and February 1906', *Historical Journal*, viii, no. 3 (1965).

Kellas, J. G., 'The Liberal Party in Scotland, 1876–1895', *Scottish Historical Review*, xliv (1965).

King, A. S., 'Some Aspects of the History of the Liberal Party in Britain, 1906–1914' (Oxford D.Phil. thesis, 1962).

Koss, S. E., 'Morley in the Middle', *English Historical Review*, lxxxii (1967).

Low, A., 'British Public Opinion and the Uganda Question October–December 1892', *Uganda Journal*, xviii (Sept. 1954).

McCready, H. W., 'Home Rule and the Liberal Party 1899–1906', *Irish Historical Studies*, xiii, no. 52 (1963).

—— 'Sir Alfred Milner, the Liberal Party and the Boer War', *Canadian Journal of History*, ii, no. 1 (1967).

Miller, T. B., 'The Egyptian Question and British Foreign Policy, 1892–1894', *Journal of Modern History*, no. 32 (1960).

Morgan, K. O., 'Wales and the Boer War—a Reply', *Welsh History Review*, 4, no. 4 (1969).

Penson, L. M., 'The New Course in British Foreign Policy, 1892–1902', *Transactions of the Royal Historical Society*, 4th ser., xxv (1943).

Rempel, R. A., 'The Unionist Free Traders, 1903–1910' (Oxford D.Phil. thesis, 1967).

Shields, R. A. M., 'Imperial Policy and the Ripon Circular of 1895', *Canadian Historical Review*, xlvii, no. 2 (1966).

Stokes, E., 'Milnerism', *Historical Journal*, v, no. 1 (1962).

Sutherland, Mrs. G., 'Some Aspects of the Making of Policy in Elementary Education in England and Wales 1870–1895' (Oxford D.Phil. thesis, 1970).

Trainor, L., 'The Liberals and the Formation of Imperial Defence Policy, 1892–5', *Bulletin of the Institute of Historical Research*, xlii, no. 106 (1969).

Tyler, J. E., 'Campbell-Bannerman and the Liberal Imperialists (1906–8)', *History*, xxiii (1939).

Weston, C. C., 'The Liberal Leadership and the Lords' Veto, 1907–1910', *Historical Journal*, xi, no. 3 (1968).

INDEX

Names in **bold type** are the subject of Brief Biographies in Appendix I